Praise for *Big History and the Future of Humanity*

"Brilliant. It pushes the project of theorizing big history a lot further, in exactly the right way, alert to the dangers of over-theorizing or theorizing on too limited information. It will be a major contribution to the discipline."
David Christian, Macquarie University, author of Maps of Time: An Introduction to Big History

"This book has convinced me not only that Big History is interesting and exciting, but has established a genuine intellectual basis for integrating historical knowledge, and historical method, with those of the natural world. This is a framework in which, ideally, all history should be investigated, taught and discussed."
R.I. Moore, Emeritus Professor, Newcastle University

"The most exciting book that I've read in 30 years. A masterpiece!"
Barry Rodrigue, University of Southern Maine

"Narratives don't come much grander than the current scientific view of the history of the Universe . . . Spier is one of a small band of exponents of big history, the effort to put the whole story together in an academically rigorous way . . . Everyone should have access to this."
Times Higher Education Supplement

To:
William Hardy McNeill:
The historian I admire the most in the whole wide world.

We remain submerged in a vast evolutionary process that began with the Big Bang (probably) and is heading to an unknown future – a system in which matter and energy evolve, stars form and break apart, the solar system took form and will eventually collapse (but not before life does), and human societies emerged on planet Earth, beginning an evolution whose end is not in sight. (William H. McNeill, *The Global Condition* (1992), pp. xiv–xv.)

FRED SPIER

BIG
HISTORY
AND THE FUTURE OF
HUMANITY

WILEY-BLACKWELL

A John Wiley & Sons, Ltd., Publication

This paperback edition first published 2011
© 2011 Fred Spier
Edition history: Blackwell Publishing Ltd (hardback, 2010)

Blackwell Publishing was acquired by John Wiley & Sons in February 2007. Blackwell's publishing program has been merged with Wiley's global Scientific, Technical, and Medical business to form Wiley-Blackwell.

Registered Office
John Wiley & Sons Ltd, The Atrium, Southern Gate, Chichester, West Sussex, PO19 8SQ, United Kingdom

Editorial Offices
350 Main Street, Malden, MA 02148-5020, USA
9600 Garsington Road, Oxford, OX4 2DQ, UK
The Atrium, Southern Gate, Chichester, West Sussex, PO19 8SQ, UK

For details of our global editorial offices, for customer services, and for information about how to apply for permission to reuse the copyright material in this book please see our website at www.wiley.com/wiley-blackwell.

The right of Fred Spier to be identified as the author of this work has been asserted in accordance with the UK Copyright, Designs and Patents Act 1988.

Library of Congress Cataloging-in-Publication Data
Spier, Fred, 1952–
  Big history and the future of humanity / Fred Spier.
    p. cm.
  Includes bibliographical references and index.
  ISBN 978-1-4443-3421-0 (hardcover : alk. paper) ISBN 978-1-4443-3943-7 (paperback : alk. paper)   1. Civilization–Philosophy.   2. History–Philosophy.   3. World history–Philosophy.   4. Human evolution.   5. Human ecology.   6. Biocomplexity.   7. Complexity (Philosophy)   I. Title.
  CB19.S679 2010
  909–dc22

                                                                                    2009044655

A catalogue record for this book is available from the British Library.
This book is published in the following electronic formats: ePDFs [ISBN 978-1-4443-2350-4]; Wiley Online Library [ISBN 978-1-4443-2349-8]

Set in 10.5 on 13pt Minion by Toppan Best-set Premedia Limited
Printed in Malaysia by Ho Printing (M) Sdn Bhd

1   2011

CONTENTS

LIST OF FIGURES

PREFACE AND ACKNOWLEDGMENTS

The biggest philosophy, foundation-shaking impression was seeing the small-ness of the Earth. ... Even the pictures don't do it justice, because they always have this frame around them. But when you ... put your eyeball to the window of the spacecraft, you can see essentially half of the universe. ... That's a lot more black and a lot more universe than ever comes through a framed picture. ... It's not how small the Earth was, it's just how big every-thing else was. (Apollo 8 astronaut William Anders in Chaikin & Kohl (2009), p. 158.)

This book is about big history, the approach to history in which the human past is placed within the framework of cosmic history, from the beginning of the universe up until life on Earth today. This book offers a fresh theoretical approach to big history that, I hope, will provide a better understanding not only of the past but also of the major challenges humanity will be facing in the near future.

My search for a theory underlying big history has been motivated by a deep concern about what humans have been doing to our living conditions on planet Earth. My environmental preoccupation, in its turn, came as a direct result of the Apollo moon flights during the late 1960s and early 1970s. The mission that left the most enduring impression took place in December of 1968, when Apollo 8 went to the moon for the first time and orbited our celestial companion 10 times before returning to Earth. In the Netherlands, I watched their exciting black-and-white live transmissions from space, while snapping pictures with my photo camera mounted on a tripod in front of our television set. This was before the days of home video recorders or any other devices that could record television pictures. I felt that I was witnessing events of great importance, while I was not certain whether these images would be preserved or be available to me. I took pictures of the launch; of the first live broadcast from space, which included the first crude images of Earth; and of the moon's surface as seen from lunar orbit. On our family television set,

Earth from space looked like a white blob, the result of overexposure by the Apollo television camera. I was very curious to know what the astronauts were really seeing, what 'the good Earth' looked like from space, as Apollo 8 commander Frank Borman called our planet during the famous Christmas Eve broadcast from lunar orbit.[1]

I did not have to wait long. Soon my family received the 10 January 1969 issue of *Time Magazine*, which showed a selection of pictures taken by the astronauts. The opening picture of its 'lunar album' was the famous Earthrise photo, depicted on the cover of this book, with the caption: The Awesome Views From Apollo 8. While looking at this picture, I experienced a shock that I had never felt before and never have experienced since. Within a second, it changed my perspective of Earth beyond recognition. I tore the picture out carefully, stuck it onto the wall of my room and looked at it for years. I still have this picture and treasure it greatly.

None of my education had prepared me for this new look at Earth. At school, I had received a classical Dutch – perhaps West European – education, which included Latin and ancient Greek; modern languages such as English, French and German; mathematics, physics, chemistry, geography and history. Yet these portions of discrete knowledge were never related to one another or presented from one single perspective. This had left me totally unprepared for the extraordinary sight of our blue-and-white planet surrounded by dark space, rising above the forbidding gray lunar landscape. These pictures showed for the first time how different Earth was from its cosmic surroundings.[2] It also made people around the globe wonder what we were doing to our home in space. This led to an unprecedented upsurge of environmental awareness, including the establishment of the first Earth Day in 1970.

The most influential environmental publication at the time was a study commissioned in 1970 by an independent group of intellectuals who called themselves the Club of Rome, because they had started their meetings in this ancient city. Executed at the Massachusetts Institute of Technology under the leadership of Dennis Meadows and financed by the Volkswagen Foundation, the final report was titled *The Limits to Growth: A Report for the Club of Rome Project on the Predicament of Mankind*. It was published in many languages, including Dutch. Great attention was paid to five variables deemed important: population growth, food production, industrial production, the limited supplies of natural resources and the inevitable pollution. The resulting conclusion was that all of these factors in whatever combination would act as a break on human well-being in the near future. Especially in the Netherlands, this study received a great deal of attention and sold very well. According to Frits Böttcher, a Dutch member of the Club of Rome, this would have been the case because the Netherlands had the highest income per hectare in the world and, as a result, already was experiencing many of the discussed problems on a daily basis.[3]

While this was going on, none of the people I was surrounded by, including my teachers at secondary school and later at university, ever mentioned the profound change in perspective the pictures of Earth from space had produced, but preferred to stick to their established educational programs. Given this situation, I kept most of my thoughts and feelings to myself. Yet I began to feel what I would now describe as a most distressing disconnect. Not only was I increasingly worried about environmental problems, but I also wanted to know how humanity had gotten itself into this situation. This curiosity about human history was fueled by a paragraph in the Dutch introduction to *The Limits to Growth*, which stated that we would only be able to effectively change our current situation for the better if we understood how the current situation differed from those earlier periods of history that had shaped humans in a biological and cultural sense.[4] At that time, academic environmental history did not yet exist, nor was I aware of any world history accounts that could help me in this respect. As a result, I began a long intellectual search for a better understanding of human history, which reached its culmination when I became familiar with big history.

For me, big history has become a wonderful way of explaining how both my own person and everything around me have come into being.[5] In big history, any question can be addressed concerning how and why certain aspects of the present have become the way they are. Unlike any other academic discipline, big history integrates all the studies of the past into a novel and coherent perspective. In doing so, big history has provided me with a new and most satisfying connect. And judging by the large numbers of students who take big history courses every year on a voluntary basis, it may provide a similar connect for them also. Most of my students were born well after the Apollo space program had ended. For them, the moon flights are part of deep history. Since the end of the 1960s, however, many university courses, especially in the humanities, have not changed a great deal. As a result, many students may still be experiencing similar disconnects.

Inspired by the Earthrise photo, over the past 30 years I have striven to attain a detached overview of history with the aid of a theoretical point of view. While such an approach is extremely common within the natural sciences – natural scientists would not know how to do science in any other way – even today most historians and social scientists tend to focus on details at the expense of losing the overview. My approach to history has led to an account of human affairs on this planet that is, therefore, rather different from the more established historical narratives.

The theoretical approach to big history, which will be explained in chapter two, is based on the knowledge gained during my rather diverse academic career. I first completed a study of biochemistry, specializing in what was then called the 'genetic engineering' of plants. The promise of this type of research was that this would help boost world food production.[6] Yet I kept a nagging fear that this might not be sufficient to solve the problems mentioned in *The Limits to Growth* report. After having finished my study of biochemistry, I therefore decided not to pursue a career in this field, even though I was offered several PhD positions. Instead, I started to drift, in an attempt to find a solution to the question of how humans had gotten themselves into their current predicament.

For about one year, I worked on a Dutch ecological enterprise called Gaiapolis. This taught me a great deal both about the Dutch ecological movement and about life in general. I also began to travel overland through Europe, the Middle East and Africa, which helped me to become a little more familiar with life in poorer areas of the world. During a train ride in the Central Sudan in 1979, I met German cultural anthropologist Joachim Theis, whose balanced analyses of local Sudanese situations put me on the track of studying cultural anthropology. The first anthropological book that I read was Marvin Harris's general introductory textbook *Culture, People, Nature*, which I found fascinating. I was very fortunate to meet this intriguing anthropologist personally in 1988.

Thanks to the generous support of my parents, I studied cultural anthropology and social history in the Netherlands in the 1980s and early 1990s. During this period, I carried out a long-term study of religion and politics in Peru during its entire known history with emphasis on one single rural village, the parish of San Nicolás de Bari de Zurite, situated near the ancient Inca capital of Cusco. The central idea behind my research was to find out how a community of largely self-supporting peasants was dealing with nature, what its history had looked like and, most notably, how and to what extent this area had been influenced by the outside world. Because environmental studies did not yet exist in the Netherlands, I decided to focus on the local Andean religion, in the hope that a good many environmental ideas and practices would be expressed in it (which turned out to be the case).

During this period, the Dutch cultural anthropologist Mart Bax, who supervised my work in Peru, introduced me to the process-oriented approach to history that had been developed by German sociologist Norbert Elias, as well as to his own elaboration of this theory within the field of religion and politics. Later, I also received the equally critical support of Dutch sociologist Johan Goudsblom, who became my second PhD supervisor. One of the most important things I learned during that period was that most of the history of the Peruvian Andean village that I had been studying was inextricably linked to major processes in human history. I summarized my research in two books.[7] It is only now, though, after having developed the theoretical model explained in the present book, that I more fully understand how very rationally these Peruvian peasants were exploiting their surrounding natural environment.

After having finished my PhD project in 1992, virtually all interest in Latin America suddenly evaporated in the Netherlands as a result of the collapse of communism in Central and Eastern Europe. Instead of supporting research and developmental aid in countries that were a battleground in the Cold War, West-European governments suddenly began to fund efforts to integrate Central Europe into the European Union. This made it virtually impossible to continue any further research in Peru. Fortunately, at the same time Johan Goudsblom became acquainted with David Christian's pioneering big history course, thanks to a visit in 1992 to Macquarie University, in Sydney, Australia. In this course, lecturers ranging from astronomers to social scientists all told their part of the grand story. This initiative very much appealed to me also, because it would provide exactly the type of historical overview that I had been trying to find. In 1993, Goudsblom and I started preparing the first University of Amsterdam big history course, which was modeled on Christian's approach. Our first big history course was held in 1994 and has been running annually ever since.[8]

In November of 1992, I was very fortunate to meet the US world historian William H. McNeill in Amsterdam. Ever since that time, he has lent me his critical and most generous support. It was critical, not only because it helped me to sharpen my views, including the writing of this book (he challenged me several times to do better in his own, inimitable, most positive way), but also because I might otherwise not have survived the vagaries of academic life, after having set off into the big history direction, for which there was no safe haven within academia. I dedicate this book to him as a small token of my enormous gratitude for all he has done for me.

While I was structuring our first big history course in 1994, I realized that by doing so I was also structuring big history itself. This most exciting insight led to my book *The Structure of Big History* (1996) in which a general structure for all of history is proposed. A visit to the Santa Fe Institute in October of 1996, where I presented my new book, introduced me to complexity studies. Although during the subsequent years this subject began to loom ever larger, I was unable to use it for achieving a good synthesis with regard to big history. In 2000, US astrophysicist Eric Chaisson visited our course and gave a great lecture. He then introduced me to his ground-breaking views on energy and complexity by presenting me a copy of his manuscript in preparation with a request for commentary. This provided me food for thought for several years.

The breakthrough toward my current approach happened in February of 2003, while the annual Amsterdam big history course was running. After returning from a lecture, my American wife Gina – while preparing a delicious Italian dinner – asked me the simple question of why big history happened the way it did. Trying to be as clear and succinct as possible, I suddenly realized that this was a question no one had ever posed to me in such a way. I also saw that the answer might be both simple and elegant. This book offers my answer to Gina's question. The first summary of this approach was published in 2005 as an article by the English-language Russian journal *Social Evolution & History*, titled 'How Big History Works: Energy Flows and the Rise and Demise of Complexity.' This book is both an elaboration and a refinement of the arguments put forth in that article.

I am fully aware of the fact that our scientific knowledge keeps evolving. Even during my 15 years of teaching big history, major changes have taken place, such as the sudden emergence of dark energy in cosmology. As a result, the story of big history keeps changing, which will make many of the 'facts' presented in this book appear outdated somewhere in the future. Yet I hope that my novel theory of history will last longer. If that does not happen, I very much hope that this book will have stimulated attempts to replace it with a better approach.

In big history, it is clearly impossible to personally peruse all of the extant sources. In addition to reading as much as possible, my solution has been to submit my ideas to specialists in the various fields, ranging from astronomers to social scientists, many of whom have provided me with most valuable feedback. Although this has helped me to keep my knowledge about all of these different fields as up-to-date as possible, I cannot guarantee, of course, that the views presented in this book always represent the latest and best in science. I have also been deeply influenced in my thinking by many people before I started writing this book. Without them, this book would surely have been different, if it had existed at all. Furthermore, many scholars lent their critical support to this project. I am thus indebted to a great many people in a great many ways, some of whom are sadly no longer among us.

I mention them here in alphabetical order: Walter Alvarez, Mart Bax, Craig Benjamin, Charles Bishop, Maurice Blessing, Svetlana Borinskaya, Julián Cconucuyca F., Ernst Collenteur, Lennart Dek, Carsten Dominik, Randy van Duuren, Dennis Flynn, André Gunder Frank, Adriana Galijasević, Tom Gehrels, Mr. & Mrs. Louis Giandomenico, Arturo Giráldez, Leonid Grinin, Huib Henrichs, Ed van den Heuvel, Henry Hooghiemstra, Teije de Jong, Machiel Keestra, Bram Knegt, Marcel Koonen, L. W. Labordus, Alexander Malkov, Koen Martens, John R. McNeill, Akop Nazaretyan, Juan Victor Núñez del Prado, Don Ostrowski, Maarten Pieterson, Robert Pirsig, Nikolai Poddubny, Harry

Priem, Esther Quaedackers, Lucas Reijnders, Richard Saunders, GertJan Savonije, André Schram, Vaclav Smil, M. Estellie Smith, Graeme Snooks, Jan Spier, Paul Storm, Egbert Tellegen, Joachim Theis, Machiel van der Torre, Bart Tromp, Antonio Vélez, Erik Verbeeck, John de Vos, Jan Weerdenburg, Jos Werkhoven, Peter Westbroek and Ralph Wijers.

I am also indebted to all other lecturers not mentioned above, to a great many students as well as to others who contributed in ways that I may not exactly remember or may not even be aware of anymore.

I am especially grateful to David Christian for many wonderful and stimulating discussions; William McNeill, for his unfailing support and always wise criticism; Bob Moore, for his constructive criticism, his excellent corrections of English in all of the chapters and his critical support for getting this book published; Eric Chaisson, for pointing out crucial errors while making important suggestions; Karel van Dam and Gijs Kalsbeek, for carefully commenting on the manuscript; Frank Niele, for his sharp criticism, which substantially improved my treatment of energy; Barry Rodrigue, for his tireless efforts to weed out stylistic errors while providing most stimulating commentary and support; Jeanine Meerburg, for her unfailing support of this project (and of big history); my father and mother, for their loving support and interest; the Institute for Interdisciplinary Studies, for providing the opportunity to write this book; and last, but certainly not least, my wife, Gina, for her unceasing interest, stimulation and loving support, as well as our children Louis and Giulia, for their patience and curiosity. None of the persons mentioned above can, of course, be held responsible in any way for the views expressed in this book.

Fred Spier

I

INTRODUCTION TO
BIG HISTORY

Introduction

This book is about big history: the approach to history that places human history within the context of cosmic history, from the beginning of the universe up until life on Earth today. In a radical departure from established academic ways of looking at human history, in big history the past of our species is viewed from within the whole of natural history ever since the big bang. In doing so, big history offers the modern scientific story of how everything has become the way it is now. As a consequence, big history offers a fundamentally new understanding of the human past, which allows us to orient ourselves in time and space in a way no other form of academic history has done so far. Moreover, the big history approach helps us to create a novel theoretical framework, within which all scientific knowledge can be integrated in principle.

The term 'big history' was coined by historian David Christian.[1] In the 1980s, Christian developed a cross-disciplinary course at Macquarie University, in Sydney, Australia, in which academics ranging from astronomers to historians gave lectures about their portions of the all-embracing past. This course has become a model for other university courses, including the ones I have been teaching since 1994, first at the University of Amsterdam and later also at the Eindhoven University of Technology.

Although all the knowledge taught in big history courses is readily available in academia, only rarely is it presented in the form of one single historical account. This is mostly the result of the fact that over the past 200 years, universities have split up into increasing numbers of specializations and departments. Since the 1980s, however, academics ranging from historians to astrophysicists have been producing new grand historical syntheses, set forth in books and articles.

In the pages that follow, I seek to explain big history. Within the emerging field of big history scholarship, this book presents a novel account of our all-embracing past. Building most notably on the work by US astrophysicist Eric Chaisson, a historical theory of everything is proposed, in which human history is analyzed as part of this larger scheme. In chapter two this theoretical approach will be introduced, while in the subsequent chapters it will be applied to big history. In this first chapter, a selected number of themes are discussed that are vital for a better understanding of big history.

Studying the Past

To understand the view of history proposed in this book, it is important to first address the question of how the past can be studied. Harvard historian Donald Ostrowski succinctly formulated his answer as follows: 'We can't study the past precisely because it's over, gone.'[2] By saying so, Ostrowksi pointed to the undeniable fact that all we know about history can only be found in the present, because if this knowledge were not available here and now, how could we possibly know about it? This is just as much the case for the history of the universe as for the history of us people.[3] The idea that all historical knowledge resides in the present is not a new point of view among historians. Yet it is rarely stated very clearly.[4] As I hope to show, in big history, this issue is perhaps even more urgent than in traditional historical accounts.

Because all evidence of the past can only be found in the present, creating a story about the past inevitably implies interpreting this evidence in terms of processes with a certain history of its own. We do so, because we experience both the surrounding environment and our own persons to be such processes. As a result, all historical accounts are reconstructions of some sort, and thus likely to change over time. This also means that the study of history cannot offer absolute certainties, but only approximations, of a reality that once was. In other words, true historical accounts do not exist. This may sound as if there is endless leeway in the ways the past is viewed. In my opinion, that is not the case. Just as in any other field of science, the major test for historical reconstructions is whether, and to what extent, they accommodate the existing data in a concise and precise manner. Yet there can be no way around the fact that all historical reconstructions consist of a selected number of existing data placed within a context devised by the historian.

The idea that all our knowledge of the past resides in the present also means that we do not know anything about things that may once have happened but did not leave any traces in the present. We do not know anything either about events that actually did leave traces in the present that have not yet been uncovered or interpreted as such. All of this may well be the largest portion of what has happened in history, yet we will never know for sure. Surprisingly, perhaps, this rather problematic aspect of studying the past appears to have received very little attention among historians. Yet if the opposite situation existed, namely that we had at our disposal exhaustive information about everything that had ever happened, we would be totally drowned by the available data. Furthermore, as William McNeill has argued, the art of making a persuasive historical reconstruction consists to a considerable extent of what is left out.[5] As a result, all historical reconstructions are rather patchy maps.

To make a reasonably persuasive historical reconstruction, we need to do at least two things, namely (1) find out what has happened to the data since they were generated, including their discovery by humans, and (2) find out what these data tell us about the past. Inevitably, academic studies of history always involve these two types of reconstruction, although this is certainly not always shown explicitly. For big history, Bill Bryson's best-selling overview *A Short History of Nearly Everything* may serve as an illustration of mostly the first type of historical account, while David Christian's magnum opus *Maps of Time: An Introduction to Big History* offers an example of both types of historical reconstruction.[6]

Any scholarly account of the past is constructed by using logical reasoning, including some sort of theoretical framework, which may be either implicitly or explicitly formulated. Ideally, all the available data should fit this framework. In practice, however, that is rarely the case, which often gives rise to long discussions of how the past should be viewed. These general issues have been discussed by generations of historians and philosophers. It is not my intention to provide an overview of these issues here. Yet it may be helpful to consider that an important human characteristic that allows us to make reconstructions is our capacity for pattern recognition and map making. Humans are endowed with this capacity to a much greater extent than any other animal.[7] This capacity has allowed our species to become what it is today.

However uncertain historical reconstructions may be, the only firm statements we can actually make all deal with the past. Clearly, we do not have any data at our disposal of what the future will bring. As a result, we can only construct more or less likely scenarios of the future, based on observational data in the present. One might argue that it is possible to make firm statements about the present, but unfortunately, also the present is a rather fleeting category. Although the present is 'where the action is,' as soon as we talk about it, it has become part of the past. This is also the case for scientific experiments. Even while performing scientific measurements, those aspects of the present we are seeking to get a grip on are gone forever. What we do retain, however, if we do our work well, are the observational data, which may be more or less durable, depending on how well we did our job in recording them. As a result, every study of the present inevitably becomes a reconstruction of the past. That is why the study of history should be regarded as both the queen and king of the sciences.

The present is actually an even more problematic category. I sometimes point out to my students that, while looking at each other during our meetings, we are looking at images of each other's pasts. There is no way around this conclusion. Everything we perceive about one another is based on sensory data: within a student-teacher setting, this is mostly sound and light, but also smells. These data take time to reach us. Sound in air at sea level under so-called standard conditions travels at about 1,225 km per hour (761 miles per hour), while light in a vacuum moves at about 1,079,252,848 km per hour (about 670,616,629 miles per hour). Although, within an academic class setting, the resulting time lags are very small and therefore in practice virtually negligible, they do exist. As a result, we are always looking at images of the past, while the only present we can be sure of is to be found within ourselves.

Yet even that statement is problematic. One may wonder, for instance, where within us the present would be located. Is it situated in our brains, where supposedly the awareness of us and of the surrounding world resides? Surely, any sensory data that we pick up with, for instance, our eyes or our fingers must have taken time to reach our brains. And then, one may wonder, where exactly in our brains? My conclusion is, therefore, that all the commonly used views of a shared and known present are human constructions.

While considering direct human interactions, this may sound like nitpicking. Yet in big history, these problems soon become overwhelming. For what can we say about the present of larger settings, such as our current position within the universe? Because the universe is so large, it takes a long time for all the light to reach us. In general, the farther light has traveled before it reaches us, the longer it has existed. Astronomers therefore often say that, by capturing light from the sky, we are probing back in time.[8] This immediately means that, with the current state of knowledge, it is impossible to gain an overview of the universe in its present form, because most of the light that is being emitted now in the universe has not yet reached us.

The study of history inevitably implies using a time frame that allows us to order the events that we are studying according to when they happened. During the past centuries, historians have expended a great deal of efforts in constructing such a reliable chronological time frame, which has become the backbone of history. This historical time frame is centered on Earth, while the recurring events of Earth's orbit around the sun (years) and its rotation around its own axis (days and nights) provide stable markers that make it possible to subdivide the chronological time frame into days, weeks, months, years, decades, centuries and millennia. For studying the period of recent human history, about

10,000 years, these rotational movements have been sufficiently stable as not to cause any serious problems. Yet as soon as we start examining the history of Earth, which covers a period of about 4.6 billion years, we find that the rotation of Earth around its own axis has slowed down progressively, while we cannot be sure that its orbit around the sun has not changed either. In other words, while the years might have been different in the past, days and nights were significantly shorter also.

Because, in big history, we want to trace back events to the beginning of the universe, now thought to have happened about 13.7 billion years ago and thus long before Earth and the sun came into being, these issues become even more severe. Clearly, we cannot trace the remnants of early cosmic events in any other way than by observing them in the present from an Earthbound perspective. As a result, while making our reconstruction of big history, we inevitably use an Earthbound time frame that ends in the present. We simply do not have any other time frame at our disposal that can do the job. The time frame of our big history account is thus by necessity centered upon us. This does not mean, of course, that the evolution of the universe is Earth-centered. It only means that our account of it is centered on the present.

This point may need some further elaboration. With the exception of meteorites and other cosmic objects, all the data we receive from the rest of the universe consist of forms of electromagnetic radiation. Depending on the distance and our relative velocities, it takes a certain amount of time before this radiation reaches us. The radiation emitted by events that happened long ago and far away may reach us only now, while the radiation of other events that happened more recently and closer, may reach us at the same time. We do not know anything, however, about still other events that may have happened recently but far away, because that radiation has not yet reached us. In a similar way, we also do not know anything about events that happened a long time ago close to Earth, because that radiation has already passed us and will never return.

As a result, our ability to reconstruct the past of the universe with the aid of observed electromagnetic radiation is limited. For the past 10,000 years of human history, for instance, we cannot even tell how our own Milky Way has developed, because we are still waiting for most of the radiation to arrive. For what happened in the universe during the period of globalization (about 500 years), we only have data about the universe at a distance of, at most, 500 light years, which is a very small portion of our galaxy. In other words, the closer we come to the present, the less we know about the universe at large. And, as soon as we reach the present, we have only data at our disposal that deal with us – all the other data are about the past that is gone forever. This is why big history accounts are by necessity Earth- and human-centered.

One may argue that, because humans have been observing the sky for thousands of years, we possess data that actually make it possible to reconstruct longer stretches of cosmic history. The records of ancient star explosions, for instance, made by contemporary observers, coupled with modern observations, make it possible to reconstruct a sequence of events that happened after these cosmic fireworks went off. But that does not invalidate the general principle, namely that if we want to study empirical data from the universe that were generated close to the present, they must have been generated close to us. It may be fair to assume that the rest of the universe has developed in ways that are similar to our closer cosmic surroundings. If this were the case, our big history view would indeed be larger. Yet, with current detection techniques, such an assumption cannot be based on empirical data and could possibly be wrong as a result. If one wants to stick to a big history account that is based on empirical data, it is by necessity Earth-centered.

In sum, because the data that we use to reconstruct the past inevitably reside within the present, our analyses are always anthropocentric and geocentric to some extent. The art of making grand historical analyses of cosmic history consists, therefore, first of all in recognizing this, and then in dealing with the data accordingly. This is not easy. Yet it appears to be the only reasonable thing we can do.

The idea that our knowledge of the past resides within the present can be turned around by saying that, if we really want to know how everything we observe originated, we have to study big history. For instance, in chapter three we will see that the building blocks that are shaping our personal complexity today, as well as all the complexity surrounding us, can all be traced back to the emergence and evolution of the universe. This very basic insight offers a compelling reason of why big history would be important for all people who are interested in the origins of everything from a scientific point of view.

Most human societies have understood this intuitively. As David Christian has often emphasized, every known society has told stories about how they themselves and everything around them came into being. From an academic point of view, such narratives are now considered origin myths.[9] But this does not mean that these stories should be considered unimportant. To the contrary, they have often provided shared orientation, meaning, identities and goals. Up until today, most, if not all, humans have been exposed to such stories in one way or the other. We do not know, of course, whether all people have always fully believed them. Surely, it seems wise to suspect that skeptics would have existed in all human societies. Yet we may also suspect that in most, if not all, early human groups the majority shared most of these views, especially because quite often, the number of available competing world views would have been limited, if they existed at all.

During the emergence of early state societies between 6,000 and 5,000 years ago, the new state elites began to promote their favored origin stories, while competing versions were often marginalized. For a long time, most, if not all, of these mythical big histories were local or regional in nature. This reflected both the size of the societies who told these stories and the extent of their contacts with others. For instance, the Inca view of the past did not include the Aztecs in Mexico, let alone Europeans (although some of their stories were later construed as referring to white people). The center of the world was their own region. Their capital city of Cuzco, for instance, was considered to be the navel of the world.

When societies became larger and more interconnected, some of these origin stories spread far and wide, while others fared less well. Examples of successful origin stories include Genesis in the Bible, similar stories in the Koran and also Hindu historical narratives.[10] The globalization process, starting in the sixteenth century CE, has led both to the worldwide dissemination of these privileged origin stories and to the marginalization, if not total extinction, of most other such accounts.[11] It is only very recently that societies emerged in which modern scientific ideas have permeated the public sphere, while the mythical origin stories have mostly been relegated to the private sphere. In the meantime, the study of history had been virtually monopolized by universities, where it is defined as the history of literate people, resulting in the exclusion of all other accounts of the past. Why would modern academia define history in such a way?

A Very Short History of Academic History

The modern academic discipline of history emerged in the nineteenth century as part of the formation of nation states in Europe and the Americas. The first task of academic historians was to formulate a proud history of their own nation state (still known as 'patriotic history' in the Netherlands), which would provide a common identity to the inhabitants of these new social entities. In doing so, they followed in the footsteps of Roman historians of antiquity such as Titus Livius. The project of producing patriotic histories led to a great emphasis on the use of written documents. Over the course of time, historians also began to study other aspects of both their 'own' and other regions, while the study of national histories has become far more detached. Yet within academia, the study of human history as a whole has only rarely been practiced until today.[12] This remarkable situation may be linked to the fact that to do so would produce global identities, which are not directly associated with any presently viable state society.[13]

As a result of the emphasis on written sources, most historians begin their overviews of the past with the rise of literate societies. The attention is usually focused on those early states (often called 'civilizations') that are considered to be the precursors of their 'own' societies. The rest of human history is called 'prehistory' and is left to archaeologists.[14] Whereas this academic division of labor appeared to have been caused mainly by the emphasis on written sources, there may also be another aspect to it. US historian Dan Smail emphasized in 2005 that the time span modern historians cover, about 6,000 years, is very similar to the total duration of history as told in the Old Testament. The reader may recall that, according to the famous calculations made by English bishop James Ussher in 1654 CE, the biblical world would have been created in 4004 BCE. Would this similarity between the biblical time span and the period established historians usually cover be coincidental, Smail wondered, or would modern historians perhaps still be 'in the grip of sacred history'?[15]

In the eighteenth and early nineteenth centuries, as Smail argues, a good many popular human histories were written in Western Europe and North America that began with the biblical account. Subsequently, the recently acquired knowledge about the histories of people all around the world was integrated into this narrative. Some of these books became very popular and were printed in considerable numbers. Yet when nation states began to take shape – and with them the academic historical profession – these accounts were ignored within academia. No secular academic histories of humankind took their place, even though Leopold von Ranke, a major culture hero of academic historians, was very much in favor of writing human history, which he called both Weltgeschichte (world history) and Universalgeschichte (universal history).[16] Enlightenment historians, such as David Hume, Edward Gibbon, William Robertson and François-Marie Arouet de Voltaire, who became culture heroes for academic historians, distanced themselves from religious approaches and, perhaps as a result, largely abandoned the search for origins. While sometimes attacking the popular human histories, these authors produced histories of 'their' nations, of similar other nations as well as of 'their' cultures by tracing them back to antiquity.[17]

During the first half of the twentieth century, only a few dedicated and courageous academic historians, most notably Arnold Toynbee, kept the study of human history alive. Outside of academia, however, human histories remained popular, such as the books written by H. G. Wells. More likely than not, this interest was stimulated by the ongoing process of globalization. Even though, for instance, British historian Geoffrey Barraclough argued strongly in favor of new forms of 'universal, or general, history' as long ago as 1955, until today most academic historians have not yet embraced any such accounts of the human adventure on Earth.[18] In the middle of the twentieth century, however, some change began to take place. Following Toynbee's example, a few farsighted scholars took the lead, most notably US historians William H. McNeill and Leften S. Stavrianos, while English historian John Roberts wrote *History of the World*. All these authors realized that for a good understanding of recent history it was important to trace the past all the way back to the origin of Earth, if not further. More recently, historian Bob Moore at the University of Newcastle, one of Roberts's students, has been an English pioneer in human history. In the 1980s, the idea of human history (usually called 'world history' in the United States) began to globalize. A good example of this type of scholarship is *The Human Web* by father and son William H. and John R. McNeill, published in 2003.

Not only have academic historians paid relatively little attention to human history as a whole, but by defining history as the history of literate people, they have also ignored the past of almost everything else we can observe around us. As a result, the history of life has become the domain of biologists; geologists are taking care of the history of our planet; while astronomers and cosmologists have been reconstructing the history of the universe. During the past 50 years or so, only very few academics have tried to forge all these stories into one single coherent historical account explaining how we, as well as everything around us, have come to be the way we are now.

A Short History of Big History

Because an established academic discipline of big history does not yet exist, no one appears to have written a history of big history and, as a result, start a big history tradition. All the established academic disciplines, by contrast, have created their own histories and traditions. Not unlike the proud patriotic histories of nation states, the histories of academic disciplines typically revolve around their culture heroes, while they rarely mention the social and ecological circumstances within which these people operated. Their lesser heroes are usually only mentioned in specific textbooks, while the villains, or the less welcome aspects of the heroes, are usually kept out of the story as much as possible. This almost inevitably conveys the idea of 'progress' in science.

Keeping these caveats in mind, we will now take a look at the vestiges that could become a history of big history. As yet, I cannot claim to have a good overview that highlights all the major players, good or bad. My research has led to some unexpected findings, and it may well turn out to be that there were actually far more early scholars who produced big histories than those mentioned here. Like all other academic accounts, my history of big history is a snapshot in time and thus likely to change somewhere in the future.

The first big history pioneer – and thus our first culture hero – may well have been Alexander von Humboldt (1769–1859), a most intelligent and sensitive man of Prussian descent. During his lifetime, von Humboldt was about as famous as Albert Einstein is today. Most of his work was read all over the North Atlantic academic world. Usually known as the father of geography (where he was adopted as one of its culture heroes), von Humboldt was interested in everything ranging from peoples and their cultures to the cosmos as a whole. Late in life, von Humboldt began to write a multi-volume series called *Kosmos*, in which he intended to summarize all the existing knowledge about the history of nature, including human history as he understood it. He called his approach 'a cosmical history of the universe.'[19] The first volume was published in 1845 CE in German. These books were widely read and translated into many languages. Unfortunately, von Humboldt passed away before finishing his project. In the first volume, he summarized his program as follows:[20]

> Beginning with the depths of the space and the regions of remotest nebulae, we will gradually descend through the starry zone to which our solar system belongs, to our own terrestrial spheroid, circled by air and ocean, there to direct our attention to its form, temperature, and magnetic tension, and to consider the fullness of organic life unfolding itself upon its surface beneath the vivifying influence of light. ... By uniting, under one point of view, both the phenomena of our own globe and those presented in the regions of space, we embrace the limits of the science of the Cosmos, and convert the physical history of the globe into the physical history of the universe, the one term being modeled upon that of the other.

Alexander von Humboldt, as shown in Figure 1.1, did not operate within a university setting. He was able to do a considerable part of his research and writing thanks to an inheritance, which made him financially independent. Such independence is characteristic of many original thinkers, including Robert Chambers, Charles Darwin, Albert Einstein and James Lovelock.[21] Even though von Humboldt was never attached to a university, he was part and parcel of the emerging North Atlantic scientific tradition, to which he contributed a great deal.

Before von Humboldt was ready to write *Kosmos*, he had pursued what can be considered an exciting career by almost any standard. Trained as a mining inspector, von Humboldt at the end of the eighteenth century traveled through the Americas for five years together with his French companion Aimé Bonpland, experiencing the most amazing adventures while making an almost unbelievable range of scientific measurements. At 29 years of age onboard a sailing ship waiting to leave Spain for the New World, von Humboldt formulated his main goal in a letter dated 5 June 1799, as follows:

Figure 1.1: Alexander von Humboldt, painted by Friedrich Georg Weitsch in 1806. (Source: Staatliche Museen zu Berlin.)

I shall try to find out how the forces of nature interact upon one another and how the geographic environment influences plant and animal life. In other words: I must find out about the unity of nature.[22]

Although this sounds familiar to scientists today, to search for an explanation of the workings of nature without invoking any supernatural influence was still a revolutionary idea 200 years ago.

At the time, the only Europeans allowed to travel in the Spanish Americas were Spanish nationals. Even such people were subjected to a great many restrictions. This was part of the Spanish governmental efforts to keep control over their American colonies, which had become economically self-supporting. As a result, for most Europeans and North Americans, the Spanish-American colonies were almost a *terra incognita*. However, because a considerable part of the Spanish royal income was derived from mining activities in the Americas, and because the royal finances were in dire straits, any research that would help to discover more such wealth was seen as a welcome asset. This explains why Alexander von Humboldt received special royal permission to do his research, which he used for his own benefit. It also helps to explain why his voyage was followed with such great interest in Western Europe and on the eastern seaboard of the recently formed United States.[23] The contemporary globalization process allowed von Humboldt to travel the way he did and also become famous for it, at least within learned European and American circles. And it was also very helpful that, unlike today, quite a few leading politicians were good scientists.[24]

Alexander von Humboldt took great care to specify his academic sources. These included the outstanding scholars of his day, such as French mathematician and cosmologist Pierre Simon de Laplace and British naturalist Charles Lyell.[25] This allows us to understand the intellectual regime within which von Humboldt was operating. By the early nineteenth century, these enlightened scholars, mostly naturalists, were already convinced that the cosmos and Earth had existed far longer than the biblical account allowed, and that one could understand nature and humankind better by using science rather than by following religious traditions.

Most notably, French (German-born) scholar Paul-Henri Thiry Baron d'Holbach (1723–89) had been a leading force in promoting such ideas. After inheriting a fortune, he had become financially independent. A leading atheist thinker and a most active participant in the French Enlightenment, d'Holbach wrote and translated countless articles on a great variety of subjects for Diderot and d'Alembert's famous *Encyclopédie*. In his widely read and famous book *Système de la nature ou des loix du monde physique et du monde moral* published in 1770 in Amsterdam under the pseudonym of Jean Baptiste de Mirabaud, d'Holbach placed humans squarely within the rest of nature, including the universe, which he saw as solely ruled by matter, motion and energy (a rather modern point of view). The thrust of his argument was to deny any religious explanations of nature or divinely decreed moral rules for humans. Instead, d'Holbach argued that humans should be free to pursue happiness, which, if done properly, would automatically lead to harmonious societies. More likely than not, this revolutionary approach to human morality inspired Thomas Jefferson to include the famous phrase 'the pursuit of happiness' into the US Declaration of Independence of 1776.[26] Because d'Holbach did not attempt to

[handwritten margin note: In 19th century — happiness the pursuit of harmony not pleasure]

sketch a history of everything, he should not be considered an early big historian. Yet his approach of viewing humans as part of nature ruled by natural laws very much contributed to paving the way for big history.

By that time, a few enlightened European philosophers had also made considerable contributions to the understanding of nature and human societies without invoking supernatural influences. In his major book *Le Monde, ou, Traité de la lumière*, published posthumously in 1664, French philosopher René Descartes analyzed the workings of the heavens in terms of natural processes without any divine intervention. Elaborating these ideas in 1755, German philosopher Immanuel Kant anonymously published his ideas of the cosmos, including a theory of how the solar system emerged that is still accepted today, as well as the idea that nebulae were actually island universes far beyond our Milky Way. Like Descartes, Kant thought that all these things would have come into being as a result of natural forces. In Kant's view, however, divine action was still detectable in the ways in which the natural laws shape reality. This was apparently an attempt to hedge himself against accusations of being an atheist. In 1784, Kant promoted the idea of universal history – we would call it human history today – solely based on natural explanations, although with a teleological slant. According to the great philosopher, there was a purpose in nature for human history, namely 'the achievement of a universal civic society which administers law among men to produce perfect world citizens.'[27] Although Kant never wrote a comprehensive analysis from one single perspective, he should be considered another important forerunner of big history. Similarly, Georg Wilhelm Friedrich Hegel's *Enzyklopädie der philosophischen Wissenschaften im Grundrisse*, first published in 1817, may also be considered a precursor of big history. In this monumental work, Hegel strove to find a common philosophical basis for all of nature including humanity.[28]

The second big history pioneer known to me was Scottish publisher and author Robert Chambers (1802–71). Like Alexander von Humboldt, Chambers was familiar with most contemporary science, including, of course, the Scottish Enlightenment. He lived in an increasingly entrepreneurial society that was rapidly industrializing. As a result of the introduction of steam presses, the publishing business was becoming more profitable, which is how Chambers made his money. His book titled *Vestiges of the Natural History of Creation* was anonymously published in London by John Churchill in 1844. In contrast to von Humboldt's treatment of the history of the universe in *Kosmos*, which is mostly descriptive, Chambers' *Vestiges* offered a dynamic history of everything, beginning with the origin of the universe in the form of a fire mist, and ending with the history of humanity. This dynamic approach to all of history was perhaps Chambers' major contribution. In my view, this book consists of a great number of challenging hypotheses, some of which still look surprisingly modern. These include the ideas that the emergence of matter would have taken place in a fire mist and that civilizations emerged as a result of specific ecological and social constraints. But Chambers, of course, was a man of his time and had other ideas, such as a racial theory about the evolution of humans, which would have started at the lowest stage with black savages while Caucasian whites were to be found at the pinnacle of history.[29]

According to British historian James Secord, who wrote an illuminating study on *Vestiges* and its effects on contemporary society, Chambers was motivated to write this book, among other things, to promote a middle course between political radicalism inspired by the French revolution and evangelical Christianity.[30] It is not clear to what extent Chambers might have been influenced by von Humboldt's work. In England, both Chambers' *Vestiges* and von Humboldt's *Cosmos* appeared in print more or less at the same time, while von Humboldt had already been lecturing about these things for about 20 years. Whatever the case, *Vestiges* caused a huge stir in Victorian Britain and sold well accordingly. Following the works of Lyell and von Humboldt, *Vestiges* suggested a time span for the history of Earth and of life that was far longer than the biblical account allowed. *Vestiges* contributed, therefore, a great deal to preparing the ground for Charles Darwin's and Alfred Russel Wallace's later work on the evolution of life.[31] Only in 1884 was the identity of the author posthumously revealed.

During the second part of the nineteenth century, to my knowledge, no new big histories were published. The academic world was busy splitting up into clearly demarcated disciplines, while historians were oblivious to any attempts to place humans within a wider terrestrial or cosmic context, focused as they were on constructing patriotic histories and civilizational trajectories. As a result, there was no room for big history within academia. Yet there remained potential room for large-scale accounts within the walls of science. Nineteenth-century naturalists increasingly adopted historical approaches, while at the same time the biblical account was losing credibility within academia as a literal historical source. One may wonder, therefore, why no scholars appear to have been interested in producing big histories during this period. It may be that the strong feelings of nationalism resulting from the development of nation states discouraged any such attempts. But possibly, a few big histories were actually published during this period and only need to be rediscovered.

Whatever the case may turn out to be, in the twentieth century big history re-emerged. The first pioneer was English author H. G. Wells with his book *The Outline of History* (1920). Wells was motivated to write his all-embracing history because of the effects of the First World War, by many considered horrifying. Wells hoped that by doing so, he would help to foster a global identity, which would contribute to preventing further major wars.[32] Because most scholars still considered the universe to be stable and infinite, Wells concentrated his efforts on the history of Earth, life and mankind (as he called it).

It took until the 1970s before new versions of big history were produced. I do not know why it took so long. Possibly earlier twentieth-century big history texts do exist and only need to be found.[33] By the 1970s, the effects of the Apollo moon flights together with the ongoing globalization and industrialization again stimulated the idea of looking at things as a whole. The first modern big history account known to me is a large volume titled *The Columbia History of the World* (1972). This book was the result of a team effort of scholars from Columbia University and counts more than 1,000 pages, 45 of which were devoted to the period ranging from the emergence of the universe to the rise of agriculture.

It may be coincidence – although I think not – but very soon after the Apollo flights had taken place most of the current major scientific paradigms (in the sense of Thomas Kuhn) of the history of the universe, the solar system and Earth became accepted within mainstream science.[34] This coincided with the introduction of novel techniques to determine the ages of rocks with the aid of radioactive decay. Furthermore, new ways were discovered or refined to determine the age of other objects and events, such as the counting of tree rings, genetic dating and the detection of electromagnetic radiation that had originated in the early universe. All of this led to what David Christian calls a 'chronometric revolution.'[35] As a result, scientists were able to construct much more precise accounts of the history of life, Earth, the solar system and even the universe.

During the 1980s, a few innovative and insightful US scholars, such as geologist Preston Cloud at the University of Minnesota, astrophysicist G. Siegfried Kutter at Evergreen State College in Washington State and astronomers George Field and Eric Chaisson at Harvard University, used this new knowledge to achieve fresh grand syntheses. This included university courses and books dealing with a scientific-based history of everything, with emphasis on their own specializations. Being natural scientists, they paid only limited attention to human history. Subsequently, these large-scale accounts of history began to fuse into a new genre, increasingly known as 'big history' among historians in Australia, Western Europe and the United States, as 'cosmic evolution' among astronomers and astrophysicists and as 'universal history' in Russia.

Austrian philosopher Erich Jantsch was the first to develop a systematic model for big history in *The Self-organizing Universe* (1980), in which he summarized many important principles. Soon after its publication, however, Jantsch passed away, which may partially explain why his book did not become better known among academics. Remarkably, in Russia Jantsch's work served as a source of inspiration for a number of scholars, including psychologist Akop

Nazaretyan, to formulate their own approaches to universal history. Unfortunately, these scholars have published most of their work in Russian, which has not facilitated the globalization of their insights. Also in other countries, such as France, England, Colombia and Peru, widely interested and intellectually gifted scholars began to write big histories. Today, it may well be that such people can be found in almost every country on Earth.[36] And although William McNeill has never taught nor investigated big history himself, he has argued in favor of this approach, as well as actively supported it, from at least as early as 1991.[37]

By the end of the 1980s, among academic historians there were at least two pioneers who began to teach the big story: David Christian at Macquarie University, in Sydney, Australia, and US historian John Mears at Southern Methodist University in Dallas, Texas. While John Mears took up the gigantic task of designing a big history course that he taught all by himself, David Christian invented a course model in which specialists were involved. Astronomers taught about the history of the universe; geologists explained Earth history; biologists lectured on life and evolution; while archaeologists and historians took care of human history. This course model not only produced an amazing synergy among the teachers, but also served as an example for similar courses in Australia, the United States and the Netherlands.[38]

A Historical Theory of Everything?

My efforts at organizing big history courses led to the historical theory of everything that will be presented in the next chapter. This theory does not include a claim to be able to explain every detail of everything that has ever happened in history. Yet by thinking big, it is possible to discern general patterns that would remain obscured if one were to examine only smaller portions of our past. It may be that, at this point, the reader would not be interested in delving into a theoretical discussion without seeing some of the meat of history on its theoretical bones. If this were the case, it might be better to skip chapter two and continue with chapter three. As soon as the need emerges for theoretical clarification, the reader could then return to chapter two.

Whatever the reader may decide to do, it may be worthwhile to point out that my theoretical approach could already be discerned in the way I earlier explained the rise of big history in the early nineteenth century. It would, for instance, not have been possible to predict or explain everything that Alexander von Humboldt did. Yet we can have some hope to be able to explain the rise and demise of the social and ecological circumstances, with all their opportunities and limitations, within which individuals such as von Humboldt got the chance to do what they did. This involves, of course, a considerable amount of hindsight.

Natural scientists may argue that, in contrast to the study of human societies, they can predict with great precision the future of a great many phenomena, such as the Earth's orbit around the sun (which is not entirely regular). My response would be that this is only the case because these are rather simple regimes, in which patterns occur rather regularly. One wonders whether natural scientists would also be able to predict with similar precision a possible supernova event that might end the existence of our solar system over billions of years, or any possible future impacts on Earth by meteorites whose trajectories cannot be measured yet. It seems to me that in such cases natural scientists would rely on exactly the same approach as the one advocated here.

Hindsight is both a strength and a weakness. It is helpful, because it allows us to achieve an overview of processes of longer or shorter duration. Yet hindsight may also lead us into the trap of a circular argument by assuming that things happened in a certain way because the circumstances were right, while we define which circumstances were the right ones, because at such moments those particular things happened. In the following chapters, I will seek to avoid this trap while making use of the advantages hindsight has to offer. Whatever the case may be, the vantage point of hindsight is simply inevitable in any type of historical reconstruction. And let us not forget that hindsight is also part and parcel of our elusive present, and therefore likely to change over time.

2

GENERAL APPROACH

The object of this introductory notice is not, however, solely to draw attention to the importance and greatness of the physical history of the universe, for in the present day these are too well understood to be contested, but likewise to prove how, without detriment to the stability of special studies, we may be enabled to generalize our ideas by concentrating them in one common focus, and thus arrive at a point of view from which all the organisms and forces of nature may be seen as one living active whole, animated by one sole impulse. ... The physical history of the universe must not, therefore, be confounded with the Encyclopedias of the Natural Sciences, as they have hitherto been compiled, and whose title is as vague as their limits are ill defined. In the work before us, partial facts will be considered only in relation to the whole. (Alexander von Humboldt in *Cosmos* (1845), p. 55)

Introduction

Following the approach outlined above by the illustrious German scientist more than 150 years ago, in this chapter a general explanatory scheme for big history is proposed. Any claim to explain all of history must sound very audacious. So let me be clear about my aims and claims. First of all, explaining the past always implies striking a balance between chance and necessity. This point of view was expressed by the natural philosopher Democritus of ancient Greece (460–370 BCE), while French biochemist Jacques Monod said essentially the same more recently (with proper reference to Democritus).[1] My explanatory scheme is about necessity. It consists of general trends that not only make possible certain situations but also constrain them. Yet within these boundaries there is ample room for chance. Although I will not systematically focus on chance in this book, the reader should keep in mind that chance effects do influence the course of history.

Everything that cannot be explained sufficiently is usually seen as the result of chance. This approach relegates chance to a rather unsatisfactory residual category. However, one may wonder whether pure chance actually exists. Whereas physicists claim that statistical chance rules in nature, most notably in quantum mechanics, in my view pure chance does not exist in reality, because everything is influenced by everything else either directly or indirectly.[2] In other words, as soon as the first regularities emerged, that was the end of pure undiluted chance. Yet within these emerging regularities, a great deal of chance effects do occur, in the sense of events that are so chaotic they cannot be seen as a direct result of those regularities. From the viewpoint of big history, it may therefore be argued that the increase of complexity over time would have led to a corresponding decrease of pure chance events. If correct, this might be a major trend in big history.

Even though a great many events have taken place in big history in which chance has played a role, a large number of unmistakable regularities and trends can be discerned. Apparently, these chance effects have jointly produced structured patterns of many different kinds. For instance, the collisions of all the molecules within an ocean are to a considerable effect based on chance. Yet such an ocean exhibits clear patterns, including currents, waves and varying degrees of salinity. While acknowledging chance effects, it is my first aim to explain such larger emergent properties.

While most processes are extremely complicated in their details, their overall structures may sometimes be surprisingly simple, if considered with the aid of a top-down approach (as exemplified by the Earthrise picture). By starting at the beginning of history, the big bang, the analysis is by necessity top down. By subsequently focusing on our galaxy, then on our solar system and finally on our home planet, it is relatively easy to recognize general patterns that would have been very hard to distinguish had we followed a bottom-up approach, by starting with our own societies today and then widening the view. Such an approach would soon become overwhelming. Because the details are already very complicated, widening the view only leads to more complications, which would be way too hard for even scholarly minds to handle. Yet by starting the analysis at an elevated level, it is relatively easy to see general patterns that might escape one's attention if one were to follow the bottom-up approach.

This does not mean that I think bottom-up approaches are unimportant. Indeed, if one wants to paint a reasonably reliable picture of what developments looked like at a local or regional level, it is essential to immerse oneself into a great many details, as I discovered myself while doing research into religion and politics in the Peruvian Andean village of Zurite. But if one wants to understand how these events were embedded into larger processes, the combination with a top-down approach is indispensable.

Because my explanatory scheme deals with everything ranging from the smallest particles to the universe as a whole, it needs to be formulated in very general terms. It must consist of those general aspects of nature that galaxies, solar systems, human societies, bacteria, molecules and even the tiniest particles all share. As will be shown, this includes the terms 'matter', 'energy', 'entropy' (disorder) and 'complexity'.

Before we can explain history, we need to discern those major regularities that we seek to explain. This raises the profound question of whether such regularities can be detected at all. Whereas many traditional accounts of human history consist of major events that are placed within a chronological time frame, I am following the approach to history in which important processes play a major role. These include the agrarian revolution, state formation, globalization and industrialization. Within these larger processes, a great many smaller-scale processes can be distinguished, such as the establishment of the Catholic Church in colonial Peru (which I studied myself in more detail).

All the events that historians consider important must, of course, find their proper place within these larger processes. The industrial revolution, for instance, can be interpreted as a process that first began in England, while it has now spread all around the inhabitable world. Within such a general framework, one can fruitfully study the industrialization of specific countries such as South Korea. While many historians have not yet embraced the process approach, all natural scientific accounts of big history, ranging from cosmic evolution to Earth history, are phrased in such a way. As a result, the process approach to human history advocated here fits very well within this larger context.

If we want to explain big history, we must inventory the major processes that have taken place. In my book *The Structure of Big History* (1996), I explored this theme by proposing the term 'regime' as the general key concept for indicating all the processes that make up big history. With the aid of this concept, the most important regimes were discussed, including their interactions. I placed great emphasis on human history, because this was the only discipline still lacking a central paradigm in Thomas Kuhn's sense. This approach provided a general structure for big history that, at the time, felt like a major theoretical step forward. About six years later, it dawned on me that regimes would be very useful for not only structuring big history but also explaining it.

In October of 1996, I visited the Santa Fe Institute in New Mexico, which is dedicated to the study of what they call 'complex adaptive systems.' As the term suggests, these are forms of complexity able to adapt to the prevailing circumstances. During that visit, I began to wonder what regimes and complex adaptive systems had in common. It seemed to me that all complex adaptive systems are regimes of some sort. Yet because in big history many regimes are not adaptive, including stars, galaxies and black holes, complex adaptive systems should be regarded as a subset of all the regimes that have existed in the universe. As a result, in big history there are at least two types of regimes, complex adaptive systems and complex nonadaptive systems. Interestingly, the term 'regime' appeared to cover all forms of complexity that have ever existed.

I prefer the term 'regime,' rather than 'system,' because there are no forms of complexity that are completely stable over time. This is especially important within the social sciences, where the term 'system' often bears the connotation of a static entity.[3] Because we need to bridge the gap between 'the two sciences' in big history, we must make an effort to find terms that are acceptable to all sectors of academia. In my usage, the term 'regime' is a shorthand expression for conveying both the structure and the change of processes. Given the remarkable variety of regimes found in the modern scientific literature, ranging from celestial regimes to regimes of the tiniest particles, I have some hope that the term 'regime' may actually become more widely accepted as an analytical term.[4]

The shortest summary of big history is that it deals with the rise and demise of complexity at all scales. As a result, the search for an explanation boils down to answering the question of why all these different forms of complexity have emerged and flourished, sometimes to disintegrate again. Here I will argue that the energy flowing through matter within certain boundary conditions has caused both the rise and the demise of all forms of complexity. Right now, this may sound very abstract, and I can only hope that the elaboration below will bring this formulation alive. Before exploring this concept in any further detail, we will first examine the scientific meaning of the key terms 'matter,' 'energy' and 'complexity.'

Matter and Energy

It is surprisingly difficult to find a satisfactory answer to the simple question of what matter and energy are. Eric Chaisson, for instance, defines matter as 'anything that occupies space and has mass,' while he describes mass as 'a measure of the total amount of matter, or "stuff," contained within an object.'[5] In my opinion, this is a circular argument. Yet I have found no physics textbooks that provide any further clarity. Apparently, it is very difficult to define matter unambiguously. A similar problem appears while trying to define energy.[6] Why would that be?

In my opinion, this problem is first of all caused by the nature of defining things. Inevitably, any definition involves a short description of a concept in terms of other concepts that are considered to be unproblematic. In doing so, the often tacit assumption is made that there are unproblematic concepts. Yet as soon as we start probing these supposedly unproblematic concepts, we find that they are problematic also. The second problem is that if one wants to define concepts that are considered basic, or fundamental, such as matter and energy, there are no even more fundamental concepts available that can be used for these definitions. This explains why basic concepts can probably never be defined satisfactorily.

In the second place, like almost all scientific terms, matter and energy were first used as everyday concepts. When these concepts began to be employed as scientific terms, their meanings were narrowed, first by specific language and later by mathematical formulas. Although this approach has led to a great many deep insights, one may wonder whether there are limits to the application of terms derived from everyday human experience to either the smallest particles or the largest possible structures in the universe. This has led to, for instance, some confusion about questions such as the dual character of light as a wave and a particle (though without mass). It may well turn out to be that in the next century, scientists will design more detached terms that would make our current terms and theories look hopelessly old fashioned. Yet we live here and now, and we have to make do with the best possible scientific terms currently at our disposal.

The first scientific use of the term 'matter' can be traced back to at least c.400 BCE in ancient Greece, when Democritus of Abdera theorized that all the everyday stuff we could observe was composed of extremely tiny, and therefore invisible, *atomoi*, portions of matter that could not be split up any further. These ideas re-emerged during the rise of modern science in Europe.

The first emergence of the term 'energy' may be similarly ancient. Greek philosopher Aristotle would have coined the term *energeia* around 350 BCE, while arguing that 'every object's existence is maintained by *energeia* related to the object's function.'[7] A more modern scientific use of the term 'energy' appears to date back only to the early nineteenth century. This was the period of the industrial revolution, which was driven by steam engines. Because these machines were used by commercial enterprises to make money, there was a premium on any invention that could improve their efficiency. Over the course of time, this led to a new branch of science, now known as thermodynamics, in which terms like 'energy' and 'entropy' (disorder) began to figure prominently. During the same period, scientists also investigated both the domain of the very small particles and the largest discernable structures in the sky. A few outstanding scientists, such as Lord Kelvin and Ludwig Boltzmann, soon realized that the new thermodynamic concepts could be applied to the universe as a whole. Yet a fully fledged application of thermodynamics to living matter only emerged in the 1970s.

Let us now return to the question of how to define 'matter' and 'energy.' Given the fact that our scientific understanding of matter and energy has evolved from everyday concepts, and given the issues related to defining these things, I propose to tackle the definition of matter and energy in the following way. Here, 'matter' is defined as anything that we humans in principle can touch: an everyday concept that hopefully makes some sense. Touching also includes scientific measurements. For instance, we usually measure mass with the aid of other masses, often with a scale of some sort. Of course we are unable to touch any matter beyond our reach, including most of the matter that exists in the universe. The presence of matter far away from us is inferred by the light it has emitted or by its gravitational effects on forms of matter that do emit light.

In big history, light plays a major role. The light we observe with our eyes is, in fact, only a small portion of a whole range of wavelengths that scientists call 'electromagnetic radiation.' In this book, the shorthand term 'light' will often be used for indicating electromagnetic radiation. According to natural scientists, light can be described as waves with a particle-like character, in this case particles without mass (whatever that means). Because light supposedly has no mass, it would not be matter. Yet its effects on matter, for example on our eyes or another type of light detector, are clearly visible. We can only measure light through its interactions with matter and through our subsequent interactions with that matter. If there were no matter at all in the universe, it would be impossible to detect any light. Thanks to the effects of light on matter, we can infer the masses of structures far away, such as planets, stars and even entire galaxies. We do so by measuring the light that was emanated from such structures that hit detectors mounted within our telescopes. The resulting pictures are interpreted in terms of established scientific theory. In this way, scientists have estimated the masses of things far beyond our direct reach.

In our current scientific thinking, light is considered a form of energy. There are many other forms of energy, including kinetic energy and nuclear binding energy, all of which have in common that we can detect them as a result of their effects on matter. The effect of light on a detector is such a case, while a collision between two moving cars – two chunks of matter that in their violent encounter convert kinetic energy into a change of matter – presents another example of the same process. A closer examination of the effects of energy on matter has led scholars to the profound insight that it is energy – and energy alone – that can make matter change. It makes sense, therefore, to define 'energy' as anything that can change matter, either its structure or its movements, including making it more, or less, complex.

Complexity

As was mentioned, big history deals with the emergence and decline of complexity. In the beginning, there would not have been any complexity at all. The further the universe evolved, the more complex some portions of it could become, most notably galaxies. Yet after a rather stormy beginning, most of the universe became, in fact, rather empty and therefore not complex at all. Today, after almost 14 billion years of cosmic existence, the human species is arguably the most complex biological organism in the known universe.

Unfortunately, no generally accepted definition of 'complexity' appears to exist.[8] As a result, there is no established way of determining different levels of complexity. Yet it surely makes sense to call certain configurations of matter more complex than others. Who, for instance, would be willing to argue that a bacterium is more complex than a human being, or that a proton would be more complex than a uranium nucleus? It is often said that a system (I would prefer 'regime') is more complex when the whole is greater than the sum of its parts.[9] This idea was coined in the 1890s by two German founders of gestalt psychology, Christian von Ehrenfels and Max Wertheimer. In modern complexity studies, this difference is expressed in terms of emergent properties: characteristics of a certain level of complexity that cannot be derived from a lower level. Life, for instance, is such a characteristic, because it cannot be derived from the molecules that constitute a living entity. French founding father of sociology August Comte and, in his footsteps, German sociologist Norbert Elias characterized these properties in terms of relative autonomy: different levels of complexity that cannot be reduced to lower levels.[10]

Because no generally accepted definition of 'complexity' appears to exist, I decided to tackle this problem by making an inventory of its major characteristics. First of all, there is the number of available building blocks. As more building blocks become available, structures can become more intricate. The same is the case when the variety of the building blocks increases. Clearly, with a greater variety of building blocks, more complex structures can be built. The level of complexity can also increase when the connections and other interactions between and among the building blocks become both more numerous and more varied. On the whole it appears, therefore, that a regime is more complex when more and more varied connections and interactions take place among increasing numbers of more varied building blocks.

At different levels of complexity, different types of building blocks can be discerned. The basic building blocks of ordinary matter are protons, neutrons and electrons. These elementary particles can combine to form chemical elements, which are building blocks on a higher level of complexity. The chemical elements, in their turn, can combine to form molecules, which can be seen as building blocks on an even higher level of complexity. They may jointly form stars, planets and black holes, which are the building blocks of galaxies that, in their turn, may be the building blocks of galaxy clusters. Chemical elements may also combine to form molecules. At a higher level of complexity, a great many different molecules may jointly form cells, which may combine to form individuals that, in their turn, may be the building blocks of society. All these different levels of complexity should be considered relatively autonomous with regard to one another, which simply means that such a particular level of complexity exhibits emergent properties that cannot be sufficiently explained from the properties of a lower level of complexity.

There is another important aspect to complexity, namely sequence. Digital computer information, for instance, consists of only two elementary building blocks, namely ones and zeros. Yet by using enormous amounts of ones and zeros in specific sequences, humans have been able to generate a great deal of complexity. Apparently, the sequences in which these building blocks are organized can produce considerable levels of complexity, while only a slight change in sequence can wreck this complexity entirely. The sequence of building blocks, and thus information, mostly matters in life and culture. In life, the genetic information is organized in long strands of DNA molecules, in which the sequence of the building blocks is of overriding importance for determining what happens inside cells. In a similar way, sequence is also important for all cultural information and communication.

One may argue that lifeless nature can also exhibit certain sequences and can thus carry information. Sediments, for instance, may consist of a great many layers, each containing fossils of many different kinds, which are interpreted by scientists as clues to a more or less distant past. Yet there is an important difference between such things and genetic or cultural information. Sediments and fossils do not perform any functions for the regime as a whole – they are just there. The information stored in genetic molecules and in cultural depots, such as books and computer hard drives, by contrast, can always be interpreted as having some function for the individuals they belong to.

While comparing different forms of complexity, one has to take into account their complexity per unit mass (kilogram). Otherwise, a piece of rock weighing a few kilograms, just by its sheer size and consequently its large number of atomic building blocks, would have to be considered much more complex than a tiny microorganism. Yet as soon as we compare rocks and microorganisms per unit mass, then this little living thing suddenly appears much more complex, thanks to its greater variety of building blocks and connections.

The approach of defining complexity in terms of building blocks, connections and sequences should in principle allow us to determine to what extent the whole is greater than the sum of its parts. Yet this is very difficult in practice. For how would we rate the different aspects and which equations would we use? What would count for more: a greater variety of building blocks, more and more varied connections, or perhaps a longer and more varied sequence? Right now, I find it impossible to rate all these aspects in a way that would allow us to compute levels of complexity reliably. If possible at all, achieving such a goal even in terms of a first order approach could well constitute an entire research agenda. And even if we could achieve this, would this lead to a sufficiently precise characterization of the emergent properties of that particular level of complexity? As a result, for the time being, we have to rely on qualitative, rather subjective, statements of how to assess all the levels of complexity in the known universe. This may be unsatisfactory, yet to my knowledge this is the best available approach today.[11]

The terms 'order' and 'complexity' do not always mean the same thing. A crystal consisting of sodium chloride (ordinary salt), for instance, may be extremely regular and orderly, because it is made up of alternating positively charged sodium ions and negatively charged chloride ions that are located in a very orderly fashion. Yet such a crystal should not be considered extremely complex, because it has only a few building blocks that interact with one another in very simple ways. I prefer to reserve the term greater complexity for biological organisms, in which a great many molecules of different kinds interact in myriad ways. As a result, the opposite of disorder consists of two types of order: on the one hand a type of very regular order that is not by necessity very complex, and on the other hand a type of order that consists of a great many structured compounds that interact with each other.

Forms of greater complexity never suddenly emerge all by themselves out of nothing. Instead, they always develop from forms of lower complexity. Human societies, for instance, emerged out of groups of primates, which, in their turn, developed from earlier, less complex, life forms. This is just one example of a very general rule. Such a process usually takes large amounts of time. The destruction of great complexity, by contrast, can go very quickly, while it may revert to very low complexity without passing through a great many intermediate stages. This happens, for instance, when humans are cremated after having passed away.

On our home planet, we cannot create any new complexity without destroying existing forms. We simply do not have a new set of building blocks at our disposal that we can use for a new construction within free, empty space. Instead we are surrounded by existing forms of complexity that we reshape. As a result, while creating new forms of complexity, we are also continuously destroying old ones. And we should not forget that humans have also engaged in destroying forms of complexity without creating new ones.

Let us now take a crude qualitative look at the various levels of complexity that can be discerned in big history. According to many scholars, there are three major types of complexity: physical inanimate nature, life and culture. In terms of matter, lifeless nature is by far the largest portion of all the complexity known to exist in the universe. The following example may help to grasp the significance of its sheer size. Let us assume for the sake of simplicity that the whole Earth weighs about as much as an average American car, about 1,000 kg. The combined weight of all planetary life would then amount to no more than 17 mcg. This more or less equals the weight of a tiny paint chip falling off that car. Seen from this perspective, the total weight of our solar system would be equivalent to that of an average supertanker. Because the mass of our galaxy is not well known, it is hard to extend this comparison any further. But even if life were as abundant in our galaxy, or in the universe as a whole, as it is within our solar system, its relative total weight would not amount to more than a paint chip on a supertanker.

All of this cosmic inanimate matter shows varying degrees of complexity, ranging from single atoms to entire galaxies. It organizes itself entirely thanks to the fundamental laws of nature. Whereas the resulting structures can be exquisite, inanimate complexity does not make use of any information for its own sustenance. In other words, there are no information centers that determine what the physical lifeless world looks like. It does not make any sense, therefore, to wonder where the blueprint of our solar system is stored that would help to shape Earth or our solar system, because it does not exist.

The second level of complexity is life. As we just saw, life is a rather marginal phenomenon in terms of mass. Yet the complexity of life is far greater than anything attained by lifeless matter. In contrast to inanimate complexity, life maintains itself by continuously harvesting matter and energy with the aid of special mechanisms. As soon as living things stop doing so they die, while their matter disintegrates into lesser levels of complexity. To achieve these elevated levels of complexity, life organizes itself with the aid of hereditary information stored in DNA molecules. While trying to find out how life works, it does therefore make a great deal of sense to wonder where the information centers are located that help configure it, what this information looks like, how the control mechanisms work that help to translate this information into biological shapes and what the limitations of these mechanisms are in shaping organisms.

The third level of complexity consists of culture: information stored in nerve and brain cells or in human records of various kinds. The species that has developed this capacity the most is, of course, humankind. In terms of total body weight, our species currently makes up about 0.005 per cent of all planetary biomass. If all life combined were only a paint chip, all human beings today would jointly amount to no more than a tiny colony of bacteria sitting on that flake. Yet through their combined efforts humans have learned to control a considerable portion of the terrestrial biomass, today perhaps as much as between 25 and 40 per cent of it. In other words, thanks to its culture this tiny colony of microorganisms residing on a paint chip has gained control over a considerable portion of that flake. To understand how human societies operate, it is therefore not sufficient to only look at their DNA, their molecular mechanisms and the influences from the outside world. We also need to study the cultural information that humans have been using for shaping their own lives as well as considerable portions of the rest of nature.

In contrast to genes, the building blocks of cultural information cannot be defined unambiguously. It is, therefore, even more difficult to rigorously define cultural complexity. Cultural concepts not only are flexible and apt to change very quickly, but also need to be interpreted by people. While genetic information needs to be interpreted unambiguously in living cells by its cellular machinery to function properly, such a lack of ambiguity in interpretation is rare in human societies, if it ever occurs.[12] Nonetheless, cultural information has allowed many animals, including humans, to successfully wage the struggle for life.

The greatest complexity known to us, namely life, may well be a marginal phenomenon, in the sense both that it is exceedingly rare and that, in terms of matter concentration, it can be found on the margins of larger regimes. Life as we know it exists on the surface of a planet situated relatively close to the edge of its galaxy. Most of the planetary matter is below our feet – it is not surrounding us. In the solar system, most of its matter is concentrated in the sun and not beyond the Earth's orbit around the sun. A similar observation can be made for our position within the galaxy. Yet, as Eric Chaisson observed, this is not the case for the complexity within life. The greatest biological complexity, most notably DNA and brains, is found in well-protected areas and not on their edges. These types of greater complexity are there because they need to be protected against matter and energy flows from outside that are too big, which would lead to their destruction. Apparently, life has created a space suit to protect its greatest levels of complexity. In fact, terrestrial life may actually have succeeded in turning the entire biosphere into a space suit. This is, in my view, the essence of James Lovelock's Gaia hypothesis discussed in chapter five, which states that terrestrial life has evolved feedback mechanisms that condition the biosphere in ways that are advantageous for its continued existence.

During the history of the universe, all these forms of physical, biological and cultural complexity would have emerged all by themselves. In the scientific approach, the possible influence of supernatural forces bringing about complexity is not considered to be an acceptable explanation, because we have never observed such forces at work. The major question then becomes: how does the cosmos organize itself? This question becomes even more difficult when we realize that in our daily lives we usually observe the opposite, namely the breakdown of complexity into disorder. Children's rooms, for instance, never clean themselves up, while cities without a trash-collecting regime would soon choke in their own refuse. This tendency is known as the Second Law of Thermodynamics, which states that over the course of time, the level of disorder, or entropy, must rise. In other words, the history of the universe must also be the history of increasing disorder. Any local rise in complexity must, therefore, inevitably have been accompanied by a larger rise of disorder elsewhere. Given this situation, how could complexity have emerged all by itself?

Energy Flows and the Emergence of Complexity

To understand the rise and demise of complexity, it is important to make clear distinctions between the emergence of complexity, its continuity during a certain period of time and its eventual demise. According to the modern view, the emergence of any form of complexity requires an energy flow through matter. Only in this way is it possible for more complex structures to arise. The emergence of life, for instance, must have required a continuous energy flow. But also stars need an energy flow to come into being, while the same happened to planets and galaxies, as we will see in the coming chapters.

As soon as complexity has emerged, it depends on its nature whether energy is required to keep it going. Some forms of lifeless complexity are close to thermodynamic equilibrium, which means that in the prevailing circumstances very little spontaneous change occurs. Rocks swinging through empty space, for instance, do not need an energy flow to keep more or less the same shape for long periods of time, as long as they are not disturbed by outside events. The same is the case for galaxies and black holes. Yet even these relatively simple structures are never completely sealed off from what happens in the rest of the universe. As a consequence, they are undergoing change through energy from outside, such as cosmic radiation, collisions with other celestial bodies or the decay of their atoms over extremely long periods of time. And because they lack an energy flow that would counter these trends, such simple structures will eventually decay and thus lose whatever complexity they had in the very long run.[13]

More complex forms of lifeless nature, most notably stars and planets, are often not very close to thermodynamic equilibrium and can only exist because of an energy flow that allows them to retain their shape. Such objects are said to be in a dynamic steady state. To be sure, stars and planets are continuously changing, yet they may maintain their shapes more or less over long periods of time. Stars, for instance, can shine for as long as they release energy within their cores through the process of nuclear fusion, in which hydrogen is converted into helium. The current, much less dynamic, layered complexity of Earth, by contrast, which consists of its outer crust, mantle and core, emerged as a result of the energy flows acting during its emergence, which are now mostly gone. Today, the dynamic surface complexity of our home planet is determined by the heat released deep within it through processes of nuclear fission as well as by the energy from outside received from the sun.

As Russian-born Belgian scientist Ilya Prigogine argued, all life forms are far from thermodynamic equilibrium. In contrast to lifeless nature, all life forms must harvest matter and energy from outside on a continuous basis. Humans, for instance, have to keep eating, drinking and breathing on a continual basis to keep our complexity going. If we stopped doing so, our complexity would very soon begin to disintegrate. The energy that we ingest serves many purposes: keeping our metabolism going, making plans, moving around etc. During these processes, the ingested energy is transformed from high-quality to lower-quality energy. As a result, we constantly generate heat (a form of lower-quality energy) that we subsequently radiate out into the surrounding environment. This is one of the ways humans get rid of the inevitable disorder (entropy) that is produced to keep our complexity going. If we were unable to radiate this energy, we would soon suffocate in our own heat. Another major way of discarding entropy is to follow the call of nature by excreting wastes. These characteristics apply not only to humans but also to all other living beings.

To sum up, the complexity of humans, Earth and the sun all have in common the need for an energy flow through matter to keep going while producing entropy. Canadian energy expert Vaclav Smil formulated this in 1999 as follows:

> Energy is the only universal currency: one of its many forms must be transformed to another in order for stars to shine, planets to rotate, plants to grow, and civilizations to evolve. Recognitions of this universality was one of the great achievements of nineteenth-century science, but, surprisingly, this recognition has not led to comprehensive, systematic studies that view our world through the prism of energy.[14]

While flowing through matter, energy inevitably changes from a more to a less productive state. This can be caused by the absorption of some of this energy by the matter that is becoming more complex. Many molecules produced by life, for instance, can only be formed by adding energy. Yet as soon as these forms of greater complexity break down, this energy is released again, although always in a lower-quality form. The need for the absorption of certain amounts of energy to make possible the emergence of complexity is a very general principle. It should be seen as a refinement of the earlier-mentioned general approach consisting of energy flows through matter as an absolute requirement for the emergence of complexity.

By flowing through matter, energy always changes from a higher-quality to a lower-quality form. For instance, the energy stored in our food intake is clearly more valuable for keeping our complexity going than the leftover energy in the products we excrete. Apparently, some forms of energy are better able to produce or maintain complexity than others. In the science of thermodynamics, the ability of energy to change matter is expressed with the term 'free energy.' In this book, which offers a first crude look at this new general approach to big history, we will not systematically examine how energy changes while flowing through matter. Instead, we will mostly consider only the energy input. In a more refined analysis, it will, of course, also be important to investigate systematically how energy changes while flowing through matter.

Can we measure and calculate these energy flows through matter during all of history? In his ground-breaking book of 2001 *Cosmic Evolution: The Rise of Complexity in Nature*, Eric Chaisson sought to do so by defining the concept of 'free energy rate density,' indicated with the symbol Φ_m, as the amount of energy that flows through a certain amount of mass during a certain period of time. For human beings, for instance, it is the amount of energy we ingest during a certain period, let's say 24 hours, divided by our body weight. In principle, Chaisson's approach allows us to calculate these values for every form of complexity that has ever existed, ranging from the tiniest particles to galaxy clusters. This makes it possible to compare all forms of complexity systematically. Unfortunately, the term 'free energy rate density' is rather bulky, while it is equivalent to 'power density,' a term that is often used by physicists, as Chaisson noted in his book. Because in 2009 Chaisson began to use the term 'power density' instead of 'free energy rate density,' this will be our preferred term.[15]

Chaisson next showed that a clear correlation exists between the intuitively defined levels of complexity observed in the known universe and the calculated power densities. Surprisingly, perhaps, whereas humans may seem vanishingly small compared to most other aspects of big history, we have generated by far the largest power densities in the known universe.[16] In Table 2.1, Chaisson summarized some of his findings.[17]

For many people, these results are counterintuitive. One would expect, for instance, the power density of the sun to be much greater than the power density of our brains. Yet whereas the sun emits far more energy than the energy that is used by our brains, the power density of the brain is much larger, because the brain is so very small compared to the sun. In general, the power

Table 2.1: Some estimated power densities (reproduced with permission)

Generic Structure	Approximate Age (10^9 year)	Average Φ_m (10^{-4} watt/kg)
Galaxies (Milky Way)	12	0.5
Stars (Sun)	10	2
Planets (Earth)	5	75
Plants (biosphere)	3	900
Animals (human body)	10^{-2}	20,000
Brains (human cranium)	10^{-3}	150,000
Society (modern culture)	0	500,000

densities of life are considerably greater than those of lifeless matter. Apparently, these tiny living regimes generate much greater power densities than their lifeless counterparts.

For a good understanding of the numbers in this table, we need to consider Chaisson's calculations in more detail.[18] Let us start with the power density for galaxies. Many people may think that galaxies are simply collections of stars. If that were the case, the power density of a galaxy would simply be the average of all the power densities of its individual stars. Yet Chaisson's power density for galaxies (in fact our own galaxy) is considerably smaller. In addition to the fact that a considerable amount of matter in our galaxy consists of gas and dust, the power density for our galaxy is also lower because all the so-called dark matter is included in its total mass. Unfortunately, as will be explained in chapter three, we do not know whether dark matter actually exists. Furthermore, our galaxy is thought to harbor a rather heavy black hole in its center, consisting of extremely dense matter, which would exhibit very little complexity, if any. Because gas, dust, black holes and dark matter do not release any energy, while they may form a considerable portion of the galaxy's mass, they lower its power density, which is therefore smaller than the power density for stars. In fact, Chaisson's value for stars was calculated for our sun, which is an average star.

Whereas the energy flows emitted by stars keep them going, they did not create the overall structure of our galaxy: a large swirling cloud of stars with huge arms. The energy flows that once gave rise to this galactic structure are absent in Chaisson's calculations. The reason for this is that the structure of our galaxy emerged a long time ago, while today it does not need energy any more to keep going. But this can change. As soon as galaxies collide, a flow of kinetic energy is generated that reshapes them. Such a cosmic encounter is expected between our galaxy and its nearest neighbor, the Andromeda nebula, to take place between 2 and 5 billion years from now. Also within galaxies there is constant change, including contracting gas clouds and exploding stars, which releases energy that reshapes these galaxies. Seen in the long run, however, these energy flows and their effects are probably minute compared to the output of all the combined stars and, as a result, do not have to be taken into account for computing a first-order estimate of our galaxy's power density.

Chaisson's power density for galaxies characterizes a relatively stable galactic regime and not a regime in rapid formation or decline. This is actually the case for all of Chaisson's power densities – they all characterize dynamic steady-state regimes. In other words, the energy flows needed for the emergence of these regimes do not play a role in Chaisson's table of calculations for the present.

Let us now consider Chaisson's power density for planets. In fact, this value does not reflect the complexity of any known planet as a whole. It was calculated for only a thin slice of the outer shell of Earth by estimating the amount of solar energy reaching the terrestrial surface during a certain period of time, while using the weight of the atmosphere plus an oceanic layer of 30 m as the total mass. According to Chaisson, this is where most of our planet's complexity resides. Because the geothermal energy generated deep inside Earth is several thousand times smaller than the radiation energy received from the sun, Chaisson did not include geothermal energy in his calculation.

The next power density in Chaisson's table, the average power density for plants, is an average value that includes all living matter, while the value for animals was calculated for the energy used by the human body. This power density was arrived at by calculating the average food intake per body weight. Nonetheless in reality, as Chaisson pointed out, the power densities of vertebrate animals vary by almost a factor of 10.[19] This raises the issue of whether those vertebrate animals that exhibit the largest power densities, namely birds, should be considered the most complex. Chaisson's estimate for human society (modern culture) is based on the current energy use of 6 billion people with an average body weight of about 50 kg (adults and children).[20] In this case, most of the energy does not flow through human bodies. If it did, humanity would cease to exist instantaneously.

The power densities provided by Chaisson for human history exhibit some further problems. Dutch environmental scientist Lucas Reijnders has pointed out that, thanks to their fire use, early humans may have achieved very high power densities. They might have manipulated enormous energy flows by burning large tracts of land, which created desired forms of complexity, such as grasslands, while destroying other forms of complexity, usually woodlands. By stoking fires, they roasted food, while keeping themselves warm and safe from predators. In doing so, the amounts of energy used by recent Australian aboriginals were one to two orders of magnitude larger than those of the average US citizen in 1997.[21] This makes one wonder how large the power densities were that early humans were able to achieve in Australia and elsewhere, wherever nature could be set on fire on a large scale. If one wants to use the power density as a measure of complexity, as Chaisson suggests, Australian aboriginal society would have to be considered more complex than modern industrial societies. This seems unsatisfactory to me.[22]

Today, most of the energy employed by humans is not used for keeping their bodies going or burning the land but for the creation and destruction of what I will call 'forms of constructed complexity': all the material complexity created by humans. These include clothes, tools, housing, engines and machines and means of communication. With the aid of these things, humans have transformed both the surrounding natural environment and themselves. To be sure, not only humans but also many animals have produced a great many forms of complexity. Well-known examples include spider webs and beaver dams. Yet it seems fair to say that humans have developed this capacity to a far greater extent than any other species.

Complexity constructed by humans can be divided into two major categories. On the one hand there are things that do not need an energy flow for their intended functioning, while on the other hand there are things that do need such an energy flow. The first category, which could be called 'passive constructed complexity,' includes things such as clothes, housing and roads. This type of complexity is made by humans as well as by a great many other animals. The second type of complexity, things that do require continuous external energy sources for their intended functioning, will be called 'powered constructed complexity.' This category includes machines driven by energy from wind, water and fossil fuels. To my knowledge, only humans have constructed forms of complexity driven by external energy sources. In this sense, humans are unique in the known universe.

Many forms of powered constructed complexity exhibit much higher power densities than the power densities of human brains (about 15 watt/kg) or human societies (about 50 watt/kg). As Chaisson pointed out, jet engines achieve power densities between 2,000 watt/kg (Boeing 747) and 80,000 watt/kg (F-117 Nighthawk).[23] Relatively high power densities are characteristic not only of jet planes but also of a great many household appliances. While performing a few calculations at home, my son Louis and I found that even our humble vacuum cleaner exhibited a power density of about 180 watt/kg, thus outperforming our brains more than tenfold.[24] This does not imply that jet engines and vacuum cleaners should be considered more complex than human brains. Unlike forms of complexity that emerged spontaneously, forms of constructed complexity are not using this energy for the purpose of achieving greater complexity within themselves. Instead, they were designed to use considerable amounts of energy to perform certain tasks, such as moving heavy objects through the air or achieving a certain degree of order within our living space.

Although a great many complications emerge on closer inspection, Chaisson's analysis seems fair enough as a first-order approach. With it he provides what US physicist Murray Gell-Mann calls 'a crude look at the whole,' which in the natural sciences is considered perfectly legitimate.[25] Chaisson is well aware of this. As he formulated it:

A second caveat [the first caveat was the danger of anthropocentrism] concerns the level of detail in our computational analysis; to be honest, we have skirted some of the hardest details. In particular, as noted at the outset of our calculations, the values for Φ_m employ only bulk flow, that is, total energy available to a handful of representative systems. Accordingly, quantity, or intensity, of energy has been favored while largely neglecting measures of quality, or effectiveness of that energy. Clearly, a more thorough analysis would incorporate such factors as temperature, type, and variability of an emitting energy source, as well as the efficiency of a receiving system to use that free energy flowing through it. After all, input energy of certain wavelength can be more useful or damaging than others, depending on the system's status, its receptors, and its relation to the environment. Likewise, the efficiency of energy use can vary among systems and even within different parts of a given system; under biological conditions, for example, only some of the incoming energy is available for work, and technically only this fraction is the true free energy. That energy might benefit some parts of a system more than others is a necessary refinement of the larger opus to come. For this abridgment, our estimates suffice to display general trends; the next step is a more complete (perhaps we should say more "complex") study to examine how, and how well, open systems utilize their free energy flows to enhance complexity.

Even the absolute quantity of energy flowing through open systems needs to be more carefully considered in a detailed analysis. Not just any energy flow will do, as it might be too low or too high to help complexify a system. Very low energy flows mean the system will likely remain at or near equilibrium with the thermal sink, whereas very high flows will cause the system to approach equilibrium with what must effectively be a hot source – that is, damage the system to the point of destruction. ... Sustained order is a property of systems enjoying moderate, or "optimum," flow rates; it's a little like the difference between watering a plant and drowning it. In other words, a flame, a welding torch, and a bomb, among many other natural and human-made gadgets, have such large values of Φ_m as to be unhelpful.[26]

All of this should also remind us again of the fact that the data shown in Chaisson's table are about relatively stable matter regimes with relatively stable energy flows, and not about the emergence or decline of specific forms of complexity.

In his approach, Chaisson employed these numbers first of all as a way of measuring different levels of complexity. This was his way of tackling the issue of how to rigorously define and measure different levels of complexity. At the same time, Chaisson also used these numbers as an indication of the energy needed to achieve or maintain certain levels of complexity. This latter approach will be followed in this book. In the next chapters, I will explicitly not employ the concept of power density as the one and only yardstick for measuring different levels of complexity. It will only be used as an indication of the energy that is needed for complexity to emerge and continue to exist.

The Goldilocks Principle

As Eric Chaisson noted but did not elaborate, complexity can only emerge when the circumstances are right. This includes, in the first place, the availability of suitable building blocks and energy flows and, in the second place, a great many limiting conditions such as temperatures, pressures and radiation. Complexity cannot emerge, or is destroyed, when the circumstances are not right. The destruction of complexity is usually caused by energy flows or energy levels that have become either too high or too low for that particular type of complexity. For instance, if biological organisms such as ourselves found themselves without protection in temperatures that were continuously either below 10 degrees Celsius or above 40 degrees Celsius, they would cease to exist. Apparently, there is a certain bandwidth of temperature levels within which humans can live. Such bandwidths exist not only for all living species but also for rocks, planets and stars. In other words, all relatively stable matter regimes are characterized by certain conditions within which they can emerge and continue to exist. In reference to a popular Anglo-Saxon children's story, this will be called the Goldilocks Principle.

For those readers not familiar with the story of Goldilocks, she is a little girl who happened to wander into a house in a forest where one young bear lives with his parents. The bears are, however, not at home. Goldilocks, hungry and adventurous, first tries out the porridge bowls on the counter top. She finds that the porridge in the biggest bowl is too hot and the porridge in the middle-sized bowl is too cold, but the porridge in the little bowl is just right. Then she tries out the chairs: the biggest one is too hard, the middle-sized one is too soft and the little one is just right. And so it goes on until the bears come home and do not like what they see. As a result, Goldilocks flees.[27]

I am not the first to employ the term 'Goldilocks Principle.' Over the past 10 years, a few scientists have begun using this term for indicating the circumstances that limit the emergence and continued existence of various forms of complexity. To natural scientists, the Goldilocks Principle may be obvious, because they perform all their analyses from this point of view. Surprisingly, however, to my knowledge no one has yet elaborated this principle systematically for all of big history.[28]

The Goldilocks Principle points to the fact that the circumstances must be just right for complexity to exist. It is important to see that these circumstances are often not the same for the emergence of complexity and for its continued existence. For instance, Goldilocks circumstances favoring the emergence of the smallest particles only existed during the first few minutes of cosmic history, as we will see in the next chapter. Apparently these conditions were very restrictive. Yet during the billions of years that followed, Goldilocks circumstances have favored the continued existence of these tiny particles, of which everything else consists, from galaxies to human beings. In this book, a great many examples of this general principle will be discussed.

Goldilocks requirements do not exist by themselves, but they always depend on the type of complexity under consideration. Humans, for instance, cannot live below or above certain temperatures, while our direct needs also include sufficient air pressure, oxygen, food and water. The Goldilocks requirements for stars, by contrast, are very different. Stars need huge amounts of closely packed hydrogen surrounded by cold empty space. As a result of gravity, these enormous balls, consisting of mostly hydrogen and helium, create so much pressure in their interiors that nuclear fusion processes ignite, thereby converting hydrogen into heavier (and thus more complex) helium nuclei while releasing energy in the form of radiation. These stellar Goldilocks circumstances are very hard to reproduce on Earth, which explains why nuclear fusion has not yet become feasible as a way of generating electricity.[29] In sum, all Goldilocks circumstances are characterized by certain bandwidths. In the natural sciences, the upper and lower limits of these bandwidths are known as boundary conditions.

More than any other animal, humans have created a great many Goldilocks circumstances that help them to survive. They can have both a social and a material character. Material Goldilocks circumstances include clothes, housing, tools of many kinds and roads, while an example of social Goldilocks circumstances would be presented by traffic rules. The rules are meant to define human behavior in ways that allow members of our species to reach their destination relatively efficiently while at the same time seeking to preserve the complexity of all the participants involved. Those who fail to obey the traffic rules usually do so to reach their destination more quickly at the risk of compromising safety. In fact, all social rules can be interpreted

Figure 2.1: Goldilocks falling from a tree. Apparently, she has overstepped her boundaries. Soon, her complexity will be damaged as a result of the impact caused by gravitational energy. (Drawing by Giulia Spier, 4 years old.)

as Goldilocks circumstances that have been created by humans to preserve certain forms of complexity.

Goldilocks circumstances tend to vary both in space and in time. I will call such changes 'Goldilocks gradients.' This concept was first coined as an answer to the question of why the surface of our planet appears to be such a good place for the emergence of greater complexity. Why, indeed, do humans live on the outer edge of our home planet and not deep below its crust? My answer to that question is that the outer edge of our planet exhibits marked differences in the Goldilocks circumstances in space over relatively short distances, in other words: steep Goldilocks gradients. This allows life to capture large amounts of energy while discarding large amounts of entropy. This will be elaborated in the coming chapters. Suffice to say here that among biologists, steep Goldilocks gradients between different ecological zones are known as 'ecotomes' and have been studied intensively.[30]

A better understanding of complexity requires the concept not only of Gold-ilocks gradients in space but also of Goldilocks gradients over time. Whereas the range of planetary climate zones from the tropics to the arctic can be seen as a Goldilocks gradient in space, climate change happening within these zones can be interpreted as a Goldilocks gradient over time. Climate gradients over time may exhibit more or less regular patterns, such as those caused by regular changes of the Earth's orbit around the sun, the so-called Milanković cycles. This will be explained in more detail in chapter four. Suffice to say here that climate gradients over time have profoundly affected life on Earth for as long as we can detect.

In sum, to understand the rise and demise of any type of complexity, we must not only look at energy flows through matter but also systematically examine the prevailing Goldilocks circumstances. I think that the 'energy flows through matter' approach combined with the Goldilocks Principle may provide a first outline of a historical theory of everything, including human history. While this theory cannot, of course, explain everything that has happened, it does provide an explanation for general trends that have happened in big history.

Because a new, rather unbeaten, track is followed in this book, my effort should be seen as a first attempt at formulating a coherent theoretical frame-work for big history. This approach may actually constitute an entire interdis-ciplinary research agenda that, if pursued, would allow scientists ranging from astronomers to historians and anthropologists to collaborate in unprecedented ways while speaking the same scientific language. This may sound idealistic, yet in fact this process has already started.[31]

In the pages that follow, I will offer a simplified overview of big history. For obvious reasons, it is impossible to offer detailed discussions about everything that has ever happened in one book. This problem does not exclusively exist in big history. Any overview of any portion of history is bound to be a simpli-fication of reality, because no historian will ever know all of the details of his or her subject. Furthermore, choices have to be made all of the time about what to include and what to omit. I very much hope, though, that the general trends in my big history account do accommodate most, if not all of the details. This would constitute a major test for my theory. Unfortunately, within the scientific community disagreements exist about a great many aspects of history, while the established scientific theories, most notably perhaps in cosmology, are cur-rently insufficient to explain all of the observations. As a result, a great many choices had to be made concerning the question of which version of history would be presented here. Although I offer conflicting views of history in a number of cases, I found it impossible to outline all of the controversies that I encountered.

Notwithstanding all of these caveats, I hope to persuade the reader that my theoretical scheme does indeed offer the contours of a fresh, integrated approach for looking at images of the past in a way that reunites academic fields and disciplines that have grown apart, while providing general explanations of what we think the past looked like. Whereas we may never be able to explain everything that has happened, I hope to make clear that the opposite position, namely that we are unable to explain historical processes from a general point of view, is untenable. The challenge consists of finding a middle ground between the Scylla of no explanation at all where chance rules and the Charybdis of seeking to explain everything but not allowing for any chance.

My general approach deals with the emergence, continued existence and inevitable decline of complexity in all of its manifestations within big history. Its coherent framework spanning all of time and space helps to justify why it is important to understand human history within its cosmic context.

3

COSMIC EVOLUTION

The Emergence of Simple Forms
of Complexity

Introduction

The history of the universe as told by cosmologists is completely in line with the idea that, within certain Goldilocks boundaries, energy flows through matter determine the course of events to a considerable extent, while chance is responsible for the rest. This should not surprise us, because this is the way astronomers and cosmologists interpret their data. As a result, this chapter offers very little new knowledge for astronomers, if any. It is remarkable, though, that no one appears yet to have written a systematic account of cosmic history explicitly phrased in these terms. My rendering of this story is, therefore, a restatement of the current scientific version of cosmic events with special emphasis on energy flows through matter and Goldilocks circumstances.[1] As we will see below, this theoretical approach only begins to make sense during the period when stable matter emerged. Before that time, the energy and temperature levels were so high that stable matter could not yet exist.

At the supposed beginning of time and space, it may be appropriate to say a few things about chronology. In cosmic evolution, the age of the universe is stated in years, while its earliest period is expressed in seconds. A year is, of course, usually seen as the time it takes for Earth to orbit the sun. But how is a year actually determined? This is not as easy as it may seem. Although the Earth's orbit around the sun is relatively stable, it is never exactly the same from year to year.[2] Furthermore, the rotation around the Earth's axis is slowing down, which leads to longer days and nights as well as to fewer days and nights per year. All of this has caused problems with the development of increasingly accurate time measurements. As a consequence, time is no longer defined according to celestial movements but in terms of the number of oscillations of a very specific type exhibited by the chemical element caesium 133. One second is now defined as the time that it takes for 9,192,631,770 of these oscillations to take place.[3] Although no full agreement exists, the year is often defined as a period of 31,557,600 seconds. Within cosmic history, this construction of time is also used to characterize the period during which caesium 133 did not yet exist, let alone terrestrial years, and even to the period when stable matter had not yet emerged. In other words, it is applied to a period when nothing existed yet with the aid of which time could have been measured.

While the current view of how the cosmos came into being is often considered to be very spectacular, it lacks the emotions, glamour and excitement that are characteristic of a great many traditional origin stories. According to modern scientists, the early universe would have been lifeless and, in fact, rather simple.

The Big Bang: No Complexity

According to the current scientific view, at the very moment our universe emerged an enormous amount of undifferentiated energy and matter was packed infinitely close together. This was the most simple and basic regime imaginable, as matter and energy would have been alike and no complexity of any kind existed. From that extreme moment, the universe began to expand rapidly under the influence of an unknown force, which it has continued to do ever since. This primordial event has become known as the 'big bang,' a term coined by British astronomer Fred Hoyle during a BBC interview in March of 1949. Hoyle used this term in a slightly derisive manner, because he was skeptical about what he considered to be an unlikely scenario. Even though the idea of a big bang appears to have come straight out of a more traditional creation story, virtually the entire astronomic community has now embraced it as the most likely explanation of how our universe emerged. Why would modern scientists think so?

Three independent sets of observational data exist that are interpreted as evidence for the big bang scenario. The first and most important data-set consists of images of portions of the sky that are thought to show distant galaxies. Although there are numerous exceptions that are interpreted as local or regional variations, the general pattern is that the smaller and fainter these images are – and thus the farther this light would have traveled before reaching us – the more it exhibits a so-called red shift. The central point is that this light contains a pattern of radiation that was emitted by specific chemical elements; however, this pattern exhibits longer wavelengths than those that are observed on Earth under static conditions. This shift toward longer wavelengths (and thus toward red light) is interpreted as a Doppler effect in the sky. The Doppler effect results from the fact that the wavelength of light, or sound, emitted by a source moving away from us appears to become longer. Thus, the red shift of galactic light shows that, at the time this radiation was emitted, these galaxies were receding from us. And the faster those cosmic objects were moving away from us at the time the light was emitted, the larger the red shift is.

A good correlation has been found between the luminosities of these galactic images and their red shifts: smaller and weaker galactic images are also more red shifted. This is interpreted as strong evidence for the idea that all of these galaxies have been moving away not only from us but also from each another. And because astronomers use these galactic images to determine space in the universe, the conclusion appears inescapable that, for as long as we know, the entire universe has been expanding. If this were the case, then during earlier stages of cosmic history the universe must have been smaller. And because we do not observe any data showing that the cosmic expansion has ever stopped or perhaps even reversed, cosmologists feel compelled to accept the idea that at the very beginning of cosmic history, all matter and energy were packed together as closely as possible. At a certain instant, this so-called singularity would have exploded. This moment, the big bang, would have been the beginning of time and space as we know them today. By combining estimates of the distances that the light emitted by these galaxies would have traveled before reaching us with their red shifts, it is possible to estimate the cosmic rate of expansion and, as a consequence, the current age of the universe. According to the most recent estimates, the cosmos would now be about 13.7 billion years old.

The second data-set consists of what is known as the cosmic background radiation, which can be observed all across the sky. It is interpreted as evidence dating from the period when the universe was about 400,000 years old. At that time, the cosmos would have become neutral, because most of the electrically charged particles, positively charged protons and helium nuclei, as well as negatively charged electrons, combined to form neutral atoms. In doing so, they canceled out each other's charges. As a result, light could begin to travel through the early universe almost unimpeded, because it was no longer scattered by a great many charged particles. The temperature of the early universe during this transition was about $3,000\,K$ (kelvin). This produced a rather uniform radiation of the same temperature. As a result of the subsequent expansion of the universe, today the temperature of this radiation dropped to a few degrees kelvin. This corresponds very well with the observed temperature of about $2.7\,K$. Although this data-set does not directly point to a big bang event, it fits the proposed scenario well.

The third set of observational data consists of the measurements of the composition of matter in the universe. This led cosmologists to conclude that about 70 per cent of all luminous matter consists of hydrogen, while about 27 per cent comes in the form of helium. All the other chemical elements, including the ones we ourselves consist of, make up only a few per cent of all matter.

These percentages are in close agreement with the results of theoretical calculations of what would have happened in a very hot and extremely dense universe that was expanding rapidly. In other words, current theory predicts that the early universe should have produced the percentages of hydrogen and helium that are inferred from the observational data. Over the past decades, these data-sets have been mined and refined. This has led to the historical account of our universe outlined below, in which the 'observable' cosmos would have begun to exist about 13.7 billion years ago and has expanded ever since.[4]

Recent Issues Concerning the Big Bang Scenario

While the three major data-sets mentioned above have provided plausible evidence for the big bang scenario, two more recent observational data-sets have led to serious complications.

The first issue concerns the movements of the galaxies. If our current theory of gravity is correct, there must be a great deal more matter in these galaxies than we actually measure by the light we detect, because the stars in these galaxies and the galaxies themselves appear to move in ways that cannot be accounted for only by the gravity exerted by the luminous matter. This has led to the hypothesis of dark matter, which would actually make up most of the matter in the universe. Dark matter would only show because of its gravitational effects, and would otherwise not, or only very weakly, interact with the type of ordinary matter that we are familiar with. As a result, all the ordinary matter in the universe would, in fact, constitute only a small fraction of all matter. However, a long and intense quest has not yet produced convincing evidence of dark matter. As a consequence, a few scientists have begun to question the established theory of gravity. It may turn out to be that the need for dark matter could actually be eliminated by adapting this theory. Yet most physicists are reluctant to change it, because during the past centuries Newton's theory of gravity, as well as Einstein's relativistic interpretation of it, have been found to explain so many observations so well.[5]

The second set of observational data that has caused severe theoretical problems for cosmologists consists of light that is emitted by a particular type of enormous star explosions in other galaxies, the so-called Type 1a supernovae. These huge stellar bangs are thought to produce well-known amounts of light. Measuring the intensity of this light should therefore enable us to estimate how long it has traveled before reaching us, provided that dust along the way would not have changed its luminosity more than astronomers calculate right now. The surprising result is that by combining the red shifts of these explosions with their luminosities, it appears as if the universe began to expand faster from at least 5 billion years ago, and perhaps much earlier than that. This is contrary to what one would expect, namely that the combined gravitational forces exerted by all the matter would slow down the expansion. Although there is no certainty yet about the validity of the observational data, many cosmologists interpret them in terms of a new – and as yet unknown – force that began to kick in from at least 5 billion years ago. Because scientists do not know anything else about this force, it is called 'dark energy.'[6]

As a result of the possible existence of both dark matter and dark energy, the observable ordinary matter and known energy may jointly make up only a small fraction of all the matter and energy in the observable universe. Nonetheless, these familiar forms of matter and energy appear to have produced most of the complexity that we can currently observe. Our big history account will, therefore, mostly deal with ordinary matter and energy. To be sure, dark matter may have helped to shape galaxies, while dark energy may have pushed them farther away from each other. This may well have influenced big history, including human history. But other than that, it appears at present that ordinary matter and the known types of energy have been the major players in determining the rise and demise of complexity in the universe.

The Radiation Era: The Emergence of Complexity at the Smallest Scales

In the very beginning, the moment of the big bang, there was only undifferentiated matter and energy. But as soon as the universe began to expand and cool down, a first differentiation took place into electromagnetic radiation on the one hand and briefly existing forms of matter on the other hand. In this early period of cosmic history, electromagnetic radiation dominated. During this so-called Radiation Era, very strong radiation existed together with a great many short-lived matter particles, which emerged out of radiation only to quickly annihilate each other and turn into radiation again. The conversion from radiation into matter and vice versa could take place according to the famous formula $E = mc^2$, of which the letter E denotes the energy content of the radiation, the letter m stands for mass, while the letter c indicates the speed of light in a vacuum. This was the only period in cosmic history in which Goldilocks circumstances existed that allowed this conversion to happen on such a large scale. As a result of these extreme circumstances, the early universe was a fast-changing regime of very low and fleeting material complexity.[7]

The expansion of the universe led to a rapid decrease of both temperature and pressure over time. This produced Goldilocks circumstances for the first emergence of matter. The first four minutes, in particular, exhibited by far the greatest and fastest change ever to occur in big history, because during that short period of time all the basic characteristics of the universe emerged.[8] This included, first of all, the emergence of the three basic natural forces, the strong (nuclear) force, electromagnetism and gravity, as well as the natural constants associated with these forces.

The strong force exerts a very powerful influence over very small distances. It acts on the major building blocks of chemical nuclei, protons and neutrons, by making them attract each other. Electromagnetism, by contrast, is less strong, but works over larger distances. It pushes particles with the same charges apart, while particles with opposite charges attract each other. As a result, electromagnetism tends to average out these differences and produce neutral matter. In consequence, large concentrations of positively or negatively charged matter cannot accumulate. This very much limits the distance over which electromagnetism can exert influence.

In chemical nuclei, a balance exists between the strong force and electromagnetism. While electromagnetism tends to push positively charged protons apart, the strong force makes them attract each other. Neutrons do not have a charge and are, therefore, not influenced by electromagnetism. The more protons a nucleus contains, the more neutrons it needs to glue the nucleus together by the action of the strong force. This poses clear limits on the size chemical nuclei can attain. The chemical element with the smallest nucleus is hydrogen (1 proton), while uranium has the largest stable naturally occurring nucleus (92 protons and 146 neutrons).

Gravity is a much weaker force than the strong force or electromagnetism, while it works over large distances. Under its influence, all particles that have a mass attract each other. In contrast to electromagnetism, which tends to produce neutral configurations that limit its effect over large distances, gravity can produce large concentrations of matter, such as stars, planets, black holes and galaxies, that exercise strong effects over large distances.

As a result of all these effects, the strong force and electromagnetism shape small-scale and intermediate-scale complexity (everything up to the size of rocks a few kilometers in diameter), while gravity shapes everything with a much larger mass (planets, stars and galaxies). In all such larger structures, the other two forces keep acting on smaller scales.

In the early universe, in addition to the three major natural forces, all the elementary particles emerged during the first minutes of cosmic history. These particles subsequently became the building blocks of all further complexity that has existed in the universe. Because it is unclear when dark matter would have emerged, our account of the emergence of matter focuses on the formation of ordinary matter.

The first stable nuclear particles that emerged out of radiation were the so-called baryons, most notably protons and neutrons. These relatively heavy particles are the major building blocks of atomic nuclei. Between 10^{-35} and 10^{-4} seconds after the big bang, the universe had cooled down sufficiently to make this possible. Only during this extremely short period of time Goldilocks circumstances existed that favored the emergence of baryons. These conditions included a reduction of the density of the early universe, which would have dropped from $10^{75} kg/m^3$ to $10^{16} kg/m^3$, and a decrease of the temperature, which would have gone down from $10^{27} K$ to $10^{12} K$. Because during this period the Goldilocks circumstances for the reconversion of matter into energy rapidly waned, most baryons were frozen out and could no longer change back into energy.[9]

In this scenario there is one major complication. When matter emerges out of energy, it does so in two types: on the one hand as the ordinary matter of which all of us consist, and on the other hand as antimatter, which is the exact mirror image of matter in terms of electrical charge and magnetic properties, while its mass is the same. Ordinary protons, for instance, are positively charged while antiprotons have a negative charge, yet both have the same mass. Every time a matter and antimatter particle meet, they destroy, or annihilate, each other and are transformed back into radiation.

This raises the profound question of why, after their emergence, all the matter and antimatter that had formed did not annihilate each other and reconvert into energy. Had this happened, there would have been no matter left in the universe but only radiation. This issue has not yet been resolved satisfactorily. According to the view espoused by the majority of the astrophysical community, during the emergence of matter and antimatter a very slight excess of matter formed, namely about one extra particle of ordinary matter for every 10 billion pairs of matter and antimatter particles. While most matter and antimatter subsequently annihilated each other and changed back into energy, this tiny surplus of ordinary matter would have formed all the ordinary matter that now exists in the universe.

At about 10^{-4} seconds after the big bang, the circumstances became right for the freezing out of the much lighter leptons, most notably electrons as well as the very tiny neutrinos (little neutrons). In ordinary matter, electrons surround chemical nuclei and help make them neutral. Electrons are also involved in the formation of chemical bonds that interlink the nuclei of chemical elements. In doing so, they help to keep molecules together. As a result, electrons play a very important role in the emergence of greater complexity. While neutrinos play a role in some nuclear reactions, other than that they hardly ever interact with ordinary matter. In consequence, their role in the emergence of greater complexity is very limited.

The process of the freezing out of the leptons was very similar to that of the baryons and lasted about 100 seconds. During this period of time, the temperature dropped from 10^{12} to 10^9 K, while the density went down from 10^{16} kg/m^3 to 10^4 kg/m^3. A similar annihilation process between particles and antiparticles would have taken place, leaving only a small residue of ordinary leptons.

As a result, after about 100 seconds of cosmic history only ordinary matter would have survived, which was bathed in an ocean of electromagnetic radiation. The matter existed mostly of protons, neutrons, electrons and neutrinos. While protons and electrons had formed in equal numbers, protons outnumbered neutrons by a ratio of about 5 : 1. It is unknown whether dark matter also emerged at this time.

The subsequent period, between 100 and 1,000 seconds after the big bang, produced Goldilocks circumstances that favored the emergence of the first heavier chemical nuclei, most notably helium and also some deuterium and lithium. These nuclei formed out of protons and neutrons under the action of the strong force. This process is known as primordial nucleo-synthesis. During this period, the temperature decreased from 10^9 K to about 3×10^8 K. Again this is a story of matter and energy interacting under very specific Goldilocks circumstances. This process went especially fast during the first few minutes and consumed all the leftover free neutrons, which were absorbed into helium nuclei.

While during this period a considerable amount of helium and very limited amounts of heavier nuclei emerged, most protons remained free and unbound. And because protons are the nuclei of hydrogen, this element remained abundant in the universe. Today, it makes up about 70 per cent of all stable observable matter, while helium amounts to about 27 per cent. The reason of why no substantial amounts of heavier chemical elements emerged during this early phase of cosmic history is to be found in the high rate of cosmic expansion. This meant that the Goldilocks conditions of temperatures and pressures required to cook heavier chemical elements did not prevail for long. Had the early cosmos expanded at a much slower rate, almost all matter would have been converted into iron – the most stable chemical element. Such a situation would not have favored the emergence of life and culture. Apparently, the rate of cosmic expansion as it happened was just right for the rest of cosmic evolution to take place the way it did.

What can be said about disorder, or entropy, during the Radiation Era? Because the very strong radiation kept all the matter that had emerged in a state of great disorder, entropy was then at, or near, a maximum for the prevailing circumstances. If the entropy had remained maximized during the rest of cosmic history, nothing much would have happened. Yet over the course of time, the universe kept expanding, while it separated into areas with large matter concentrations, the galaxies, which were separated by the growing inter-galactic space. Through this process, an enormous area of empty space emerged that could store increasing amounts of entropy. Had this entropy dumping ground not emerged, no forms of greater complexity would ever have existed.[10]

In sum, the Radiation Era was the period of cosmic history during which most of the material complexity at the smallest scales emerged out of energy under rapidly changing Goldilocks circumstances. The Goldilocks gradients favoring the emergence of first baryons and then leptons were short-lived and very restrictive. However, the continued existence of these particles required very different Goldilocks circumstances, which would actually reign in most parts of the universe during most of the time that followed. As a result, most of these particles have continued to exist until today. The Goldilocks gradient favoring the forging of heavier chemical nuclei was also short-lived. Yet, as we shall see below, during the cosmic history that followed, similar, longer-lived Goldilocks circumstances emerged in stars. The major difference is that while during the early phase of universal history these Goldilocks circumstances reigned everywhere in the still largely homogeneous cosmos, during later periods they could only be found locally, namely in stars that were surrounded by mostly empty space.

Erich Jantsch called the emergence of the smallest particles 'micro-evolution.' By providing the basic building blocks of complexity, this rapidly changing evanescent regime set the stage for the possible emergence of all sub-sequent larger-scale complexity, which Jantsch jointly called 'macro-evolution.' Over the course of time, cosmic micro- and macro-evolution would influence each other in a process that Jantsch called (cosmic) 'co-evolution.'[11]

The Matter Era: The Emergence of Complexity at Atomic and Molecular Scales

The ever-continuing cosmic expansion led to a dilution of both matter and electromagnetic radiation. At the same time, it stretched the photons' wave-lengths, which became longer as a result. Because longer wavelengths contain less energy than shorter ones, the energy content of radiation within a certain amount of space dropped more rapidly than the energy content of matter in that same area.[12] At a certain point in time, therefore, the energy content of matter would inevitably become larger than the energy content of radiation within a certain volume. From this point onward, radiation was no longer dominant. This monumental change signaled the transition from the Radiation Era to the Matter Era. According to a recent estimate, this transition would have taken place about 50,000 years after the big bang at a temperature of about

16,000 K.[13] Ever since that time, matter has dominated the universe, while energy flows through matter have made possible the emergence of greater complexity. It would take considerable time, however, before Goldilocks circumstances emerged that allowed this to happen.

As a consequence of the unrelenting expansion, the temperature of the early universe kept dropping. After 1,000 years of cosmic history, the average temperature had gone down to about 60,000 K, while after 1 million years the temperature became as low as only 1,000 K. Here on Earth, atoms will all dissociate into their constituent nuclei and electrons at about 4,000 K, while they will all recombine at about 3,000 K and below. Apparently, somewhere between 1,000 and 1 million years after the big bang, the temperature of the early universe had dropped to a Goldilocks level that allowed the primordial nuclei, mostly positively charged hydrogen and helium nuclei, to combine with negatively charged electrons to form the first neutral atoms, and a little later also the first small neutral molecules. According to the latest estimates, this would have happened at around 400,000 years after the big bang. By that time, the cosmic temperature would have gone down to 3,000 K. This was the period when the force of electromagnetism became more important than the temperature of the universe in shaping matter. Because electromagnetism tends to produce neutral combinations of positively and negatively charged particles, overall the universe suddenly became neutral.

Earlier it was mentioned that radiation is far less affected by neutral particles than by charged ones. Thanks to the neutralization of the universe, radiation was not obstructed anymore and could begin to travel freely. In other words, the cosmos suddenly became transparent. The cosmic background radiation mentioned earlier dates back to this monumental change. To the delight of the astronomical community, the cosmic background radiation exhibits a so-called almost perfect black-body curve, which is interpreted as an almost perfect thermal equilibrium between matter and radiation at the time of its emergence.[14] This means that at around 400,000 years after the big bang the universe was still largely homogeneous and that great differences in the composition and density of matter and energy did not yet exist. The tiny differences that do show up in the cosmic background radiation are currently under investigation. They are interpreted as small fluctuations of matter and energy density in the early universe.

At this point in time, most stable matter consisted of hydrogen, about 70 per cent, while 27 per cent came in the form of helium. In contrast to hydrogen, helium is chemically inert, which means that it cannot form bonds with other atoms. Hydrogen atoms, however, can form single bonds with a great many other atoms. Yet virtually the only available atoms to do so at that time were other hydrogen atoms. Over the course of time, this produced increasing numbers of hydrogen molecules, each consisting of two mutually bonded hydrogen atoms. Also small quantities of other reactive light elements, most notably deuterium (heavy hydrogen) and lithium, had emerged. Yet this did not lead to a great many new chemical combinations, because these simple chemical elements are unable to form complicated molecules. As a result, the possibilities for greater molecular complexity in the early universe were very limited.

Galaxy Formation: The Emergence of Complexity at Larger Scales

Between 700 million and 2 billion years after the big bang, galaxies formed out of the primordial materials that had emerged before. It was only during this period that Goldilocks circumstances reigned favoring galaxy formation. Ever since that time, however, galaxies have continued to exist. Apparently, the Goldilocks circumstances for the continued existence of galaxies were far less restrictive than for their emergence.

All the galaxies emerged out of primordial matter, mostly hydrogen and helium. Under the influence of gravity, these matter particles joined to form larger structures. The emergence of galaxies can, therefore, be seen as the process in which matter began to clump together, thus producing relatively small areas with large matter concentrations interspersed with large areas with very little matter. This produced enormous matter gradients in space. The existing radiation, by contrast, could not clump together in similar ways, because there is no known force that can make photons join together.[15] As a result, cosmic radiation kept diluting during the subsequent expansion of the universe, while matter coagulated in galaxies. Had matter diluted in a similar way as cosmic radiation, no greater complexity would ever have emerged. The period of galaxy formation thus heralded a monumental change in the way matter and energy were distributed in the universe. Whereas until that time the cosmos had been mostly homogeneous, suddenly it became a very lumpy place. As a consequence of the ongoing cosmic expansion, the galaxies became separated by growing areas of mostly empty interstellar space.

Although the precise mechanism of galaxy formation is still one of the unresolved puzzles of cosmic evolution, the general process is thought to have proceeded along the following lines. After the universe had become neutral around 400,000 years after the big bang, the unrelenting cosmic expansion led to a further decrease of the temperature and radiation levels, while the matter density decreased also. This period is called the 'dark age' and stretched hundreds of millions of years. The universe was dark, because the original fireball from the big bang had dimmed, while no stars existed yet that could emit any

Figure 3.1: The variation in the cosmic background radiation provides evidence for the first emergence of greater complexity. (Source: NASA.)

light. At around 700 million years after the big bang, however, quite suddenly considerable numbers of galaxies began to form. Apparently, by that time Goldilocks circumstances had emerged favoring their formation. The big question is how galaxies could have emerged from the earlier, mostly homogeneous, universe.

Galaxies are thought to have formed from large, spontaneously occurring concentrations of matter. The major questions are, therefore, when and how such matter concentrations first emerged. The oldest observational data available about the universe consists of the cosmic background radiation, which dates back to around 400,000 years after the big bang. This radiation exhibits the pattern of an almost perfect black body, which is interpreted by the idea that at that time, most matter and radiation were dispersed very evenly. Yet extremely precise measurements have revealed tiny variations in the cosmic radiation across the sky. These variations, as shown in Figure 3.1, are interpreted as the first clumping of matter under the influence of gravity. Apparently, around 400,000 years after the big bang the matter concentrations that would become galaxies were already emerging.

These variations in matter density would have come as a result of chance effects, leading to a chance distribution of matter all across the universe. Over the course of time, large numbers of particles bumped into each other and subsequently stuck together. This led to locally increasing concentrations of matter, which began to exert a growing gravitational attraction on other particles. As part of this process, regions with larger matter concentrations emerged, separated by areas that were slowly but surely depleted of matter. As a result, both galaxies and intergalactic space emerged as part of the same process. The temperatures were no longer so high that these emerging matter regimes would have fallen apart immediately, while the matter density was still sufficiently large as to allow sufficient amounts of matter to stick together.

The big problem with this scenario is that the force of gravity is not sufficiently strong to make all this matter condense into galaxies under the prevailing circumstances. Here, dark matter may come to the rescue. According to a recent model, dark matter would already have begun to clump together well before the neutralization of the universe. This early coagulation of dark matter would have been possible, because it did not, or only very weakly, interact with ordinary matter and radiation other than through gravity. The early clumping of dark matter led to the emergence of ever larger structures, which subsequently attracted ordinary matter through its enormous gravity, which coalesced into galaxies as a result. However, it may also be that we do not yet sufficiently understand the gravitational force. Possibly, a reformulation of this theory may explain the emergence of galaxies satisfactorily without using the concept of dark matter.

Already during their emergence, large numbers of galaxies receded from one another, as witnessed from the Doppler red shifts we measure today. In a number of cases, however, gravity kept galaxies close together, while countless numbers of galaxies may actually have merged with each other. Yet over the course of time, such cosmic meetings would have decreased in frequency.

All galaxies are rotating. This is a necessary condition for galaxies to exist, because if they had not rotated, all matter would have fallen right into the middle of the galaxy a long time ago, thus forming one big dense chunk of matter. Galaxies rotate as a result of the fact that any large-scale random movements of matter from which they formed were greatly strengthened as a result of the contraction of matter into galaxies. This worked essentially in the same way as the trick that makes an ice dancer suddenly spin much faster by holding one's arms close to the body. A similar effect would later cause the rotations of the central star and the planets in emerging solar systems.

All galactic centers harbor amounts of matter that are so dense we cannot observe them directly, because their gravity is so strong that anything that falls into them, including light, cannot escape anymore. These are the famous black holes. They can be observed thanks to their strong gravitational effects. Apparently, the coalescing of matter within galaxies led to two very different processes. On the one hand, billions of stars emerged, while on the other hand, unknown numbers of black holes were formed. This depended on the amounts of matter that joined. If these coalescing masses were smaller than 200 times the mass of our sun, they formed stars, while if they were bigger, they produced black holes.[16] Within these ultra-dense regimes, no greater complexity is possible, because the enormous forces of gravity exerted by all the combined matter would crush any structures that might evolve. Nonetheless, black holes may well have played a crucial role in the rise of complexity in cosmic evolution by keeping galaxies together. They may thus have contributed to creating Goldilocks circumstances that favored the emergence of greater complexity elsewhere in the galaxy.

Although invisible, the so-called super massive black holes that are at the center of galaxies produced spectacular cosmic fireworks, most notably during early galactic history. At that time, the large amounts of matter flowing toward these super massive black holes became so energized they emitted very strong radiation, about 100 to 1,000 times the entire output of our galaxy. Today, this radiation is observed in the form of quasars (quasi-stellar objects) which, given their red shifts, mostly date back to many billions of years ago, while the most recent quasar events would have taken place about 2 billion years ago. These were, in Eric Chaisson's words, 'the last of a dying breed.'[17] The lack of more recent quasars is interpreted by the idea that after billions of years of cosmic history, most of the galactic gas near the central black holes had been absorbed by them. As soon as this process had come to an end, the quasars stopped shining.[18] All the matter that did not turn into black holes either coalesced into stars or remained volatile in the form of gas and dust clouds. As a result of all these processes, large differences of matter concentrations over space emerged within galaxies.

In sum, between 700 million and 2 billion years after the big bang, galaxies emerged under the influence of gravity out of spontaneously occurring irregularities. Only during this period did Goldilocks circumstances exist for galaxy formation. The emergence of galaxies led to a differentiation between areas where there was a great deal of matter (galaxies) and intergalactic space, which was increasingly empty. The unrelenting cosmic expansion accentuated these differences and made any further galaxy formation impossible after about 2 billion years of universal history. Ever since that time, however, Goldilocks circumstances have existed favoring the continued existence of galaxies.

The differentiation into areas with and without matter was extremely important for the rest of cosmic history, most notably because it created an enormous entropy trash can.[19] Because during the very early stage of cosmic history entropy would have been maximized for the prevailing circumstances, an entropy dumping ground was urgently needed for greater complexity to emerge. This was the case because the second law of thermodynamics dictates that the emergence of any local or regional order must be accompanied by the production of more disorder elsewhere. The continuing expansion of the universe, together with the clumping of matter into stars and galaxies, provided room for disorder both within galaxies and in intergalactic space. It created a gigantic and very cold entropy sink for the radiation produced in stars and planets. Without such an entropy sink, greater complexity could not have emerged, because it would have been suffocated by the heat it inevitably produced. In other words, the emergence of a cosmic entropy trash can was an absolute Goldilocks requirement for the rise of greater complexity.

Although the process of galaxy formation came to an end around 2 billion years after the big bang, the evolution of galaxies has been an ongoing process. While the universe kept expanding, some galaxies may have retained their original size (and perhaps to some extent also their shape), while others would have changed dramatically as a result of collisions with neighboring galaxies, or perhaps even with entire groups of galaxies. As a result of these events, the masses of the observed galaxies range from only a few million times the mass of our sun to several trillion solar masses, while their shapes vary from spiral to globular galaxies.[20] Although the Milky Way is usually thought to be an average spiral galaxy, a French team of astronomers led by François Hammer argued in 2007 that our galaxy may actually be rather special, because it would not have merged with another galaxy over its entire history. This cosmic tranquility may have offered better Goldilocks circumstances for life to evolve.[21]

In sum, as a consequence of galaxy formation and development, the universe became more differentiated. Over the course of time, the steep matter and energy gradients that had emerged in galaxies made possible new matter and energy flows and thus also new levels of greater complexity. The expanding intergalactic space, by contrast, became increasingly empty and thus less complex. Looking at this process in terms of growing complexity, it is astonishing how much large-scale complexity was formed during this early period of big history, and how varied it became, solely on the basis of the two simple chemical elements: hydrogen and helium.

The Emergence of Stars

During the emergence of galaxies, between 700 million and 2 billion years after the big bang, also the first stars emerged. Apparently, at that time Goldilocks circumstances existed that favored star formation. In contrast to galaxies, stars have been forming ever since that time. Apparently, the Goldilocks circumstances for star formation are far less restrictive than those that favored galaxy formation. Indeed, star formation will continue as long as galaxies contain sufficient quantities of hydrogen and helium, the primordial building blocks of stars. Because over the course of time these large clouds of light chemical elements have decreased, both the numbers and the size of stars that formed have gone down also.

In early galactic history, large numbers of gigantic stars emerged, because there was a great deal of closely packed primordial material available from which they could form. This period is called the time of 'star burst,' because suddenly, many large stars were shining brightly for a short period of time. As a result, during the first few billion years of cosmic history galaxies produced much more light than during the subsequent period. Because over the course of time the numbers of primordial building blocks declined, the chances of star formation have dropped. As a result, fewer stars – most notably far fewer large stars – are formed today.

Stars form out of clouds of hydrogen and helium that first contract, and then collapse, under the influence of gravity. Erich Jantsch summarized this process as follows:[22]

> According to the simple condensation model (Steinlin, 1977), the formation of stars is imagined in such a way that clouds of interstellar matter at a temperature between 10 and 100 degrees Kelvin condense into a multiplicity of protostellar clouds due to the effect of gravity. Stars are generally born in clusters, especially in the spectacular spherical clusters which measure 20 to 400 light years in diameter. Besides spherical clusters, there are also open clusters with 5 to 30 light years diameter. In the case of the sun, the protostellar cloud reached beyond the orbit of Pluto. When such a protostellar cloud reaches a minimum density of 10^{-13} grams per cubic centimetre, it collapses at the speed of free fall. During this very fast contraction – it is estimated that the sun contracted within a decade from a diameter corresponding to the orbit of Pluto to one corresponding to the orbit of Mercury – pressure and temperature increase enormously. Thereby, the conditions are being re-created which correspond to an early phase of the universe, but which are more favourable for the synthesis of heavier atomic nuclei. Macroscopic evolution acts as a booster for microscopic evolution, which had become stuck.

Hydrogen and helium clouds may collapse to form stars for different reasons. First of all, this may happen spontaneously as a result of random collisions that lead to ever larger concentrations of cloud material. As soon as such a cloud becomes sufficiently dense, and thus its gravity sufficiently strong, it will pull the material together and form a star. But also a trigger from outside, such as birth of large stars, may emit so much energy that the surrounding clouds of light chemical elements are compacted sufficiently to start a chain reaction of star formation.[23] In addition, major stellar explosions of stars that have reached the end of their lives may sweep together loose material sufficiently to make it condense by itself under the influence of gravity. In all these cases, it is an energy flow through matter that causes the emergence of stellar complexity.

As soon as an incipient star becomes sufficiently large and dense, Goldilocks circumstances emerge that favor nuclear fusion. The enormous pressure in stellar cores caused by gravity presses hydrogen nuclei very close to each other. At the same time, the gravitational energy released by the star's contraction raises the temperature in its core to levels that allow nuclear chain reactions to ignite, forging one helium nucleus out of four hydrogen nuclei. During this process, a tiny amount of matter is converted into energy, while the rearrangement of the elementary particles in the nuclei also releases energy. This nuclear fusion reaction comes as a result of the interplay between two natural forces, the strong force, which pulls heavy elementary particles (baryons) together, and the electromagnetic force, which pushes particles with the same charge away from each other. Because hydrogen nuclei (protons) are positively charged, it takes a great deal of pressure to overcome the electromagnetic force and push them together so closely that the strong force, which acts only over very small distances, can play a significant role.

Such a Goldilocks situation favoring nuclear fusion emerged deep within the newly forming stars, thanks to the fact that gravity compressed matter and heated it up sufficiently. The ensuing interaction between the elementary particles under influence of the strong force led to the formation of helium nuclei, which consist of two positively charged protons and two neutral neutrons. Neutrons can loosely be described as protons without a charge. During this process, neutrons formed out of protons by emitting their positive charge in the form of positrons (anti-electrons).

In this situation, the strong force, which pulls protons and neutrons together, dominates the electromagnetic force, thanks to the fact that neutrons are neutral. They are, therefore, not affected by electromagnetism, and thus help to glue the nucleus together. At the same time, the emitted positrons rapidly combine with electrons to annihilate each other and convert into energy. As a result, the fusion between hydrogen nuclei inside stars produces helium nuclei while releasing energy.[24] This energy is subsequently dissipated to the star's surface, and from there into space, mostly in the form of electromagnetic radiation. This is a slow process. Today, for instance, it may take between 10,000 and 170,000 years (the estimates vary) for energy released in our sun's core to reach its surface.

The Goldilocks circumstances in stellar cores favoring nuclear fusion are similar to the conditions that reigned during the Radiation Era. This leads to the profound insight that Goldilocks circumstances that were characteristic of early cosmic history still exist in stars today, including our sun. A major difference is that the early universe was more or less homogeneous, while stars and their surroundings are not. In other words, while these Goldilocks circumstances existed everywhere for a very short period of time during early cosmic history, they can only be found within stellar cores in the current universe, which take up only a minute portion of cosmic space. Another major difference is that while the infant cosmos changed so quickly that there was hardly any time for nuclear fusion to take place, all stars, even the shortest shiners, live a great deal longer. As a result, stars became the major forges for creating greater complexity at small scales, while the cosmic trash can of interstellar space allowed stars to get rid of their entropy and keep their complexity going.

Why did stars form the way they did instead of collapsing entirely to form neutron stars and black holes? First of all, a lower Goldilocks boundary exists below that such a collapse is unlikely to happen. All the combined matter of planets such as Earth does not exert enough gravity to overwhelm the repellent action of the electromagnetic force. If it did, we would not have existed. Yet one may wonder why stars, all of which are much larger than our home planet, would not collapse entirely under their own weight. Apparently, there is a force that prevents this from happening. This is the outward pressure of the radiation resulting from nuclear fusion within stellar cores, which provides the force that counteracts gravity. As a result of these two counterbalancing forces, stars turn into dynamic steady-state regimes and remain so for as long as there is enough nuclear fuel to burn. It is this energy flow through matter that preserves the complexity of stars and prevents them from collapsing into matter regimes of greater density and lower complexity.

In doing so, stars became the first self-regulating structures. This works as follows. Any gravitational contraction produces higher temperatures in the core, which speed up the nuclear fusion process. This releases more energy, which makes the star expand. The stellar enlargement, in its turn, cools down the star, which slows down the nuclear fusion process. This lowers the star's radiation output and makes it contract again. As a result of this negative feedback loop, stars are self-regulating, dynamic steady-state, regimes, which maintain their complexity for as long as they do not run out of nuclear fuel.[25]

After their initial formation, stars do not need to harness matter and energy from outside anymore for their continued existence, as long as gravity keeps up the pressure and the resulting nuclear fires keep burning. In contrast to living beings, which have to extract matter and energy continuously from their planetary environment to maintain their complexity, stars do not need to harvest matter and energy anymore from the rest of the universe to shine after they ignited.

Stellar sizes exhibit a Goldilocks range, namely from about 0.01 times the mass of our sun to a maximum of about 200 times its mass.[26] Smaller bodies of hydrogen and helium do not ignite because they lack sufficient gravitational pressure, while incipient stars are too large to collapse under their own weight into black holes. Large stars burn their nuclear fuel fast and consequently exist for relatively short periods of time. The biggest stars would only shine for about 12,500 years. As a result, all the early large stars are now long gone, while all nearby giant stars must have formed recently. Little stars, by contrast, burn their fuel very slowly. As a result, the smallest stars will exist for about 16,000 billion years. This means that today, all of them are still in their baby phase, regardless of when they emerged. The root cause underlying these differences in stellar longevity is that larger stars convert hydrogen into helium much faster than smaller stars. While large stars have a great deal more fuel to burn, they burn it even faster.

Because large stars burn their nuclear fuel faster than smaller stars, their power densities are larger. However, it is not clear to me whether larger stars should therefore be considered more complex. It may actually be argued that little stars need comparatively smaller energy flows for reaching a comparable level of complexity. This would mean that little stars are more energy efficient than larger stars.

In Eric Chaisson's view of cosmic evolution, a process of non-random elimination would have taken place over long periods of time, eliminating the large faster burning stars, simply because they existed for comparatively short periods of time.[27] This would automatically lead to the survival of the longer-living smaller stars. One may therefore wonder whether during cosmic evolution greater energy efficiency is a trait that has an important survival value. We will return to this subject later.

In cosmic evolution, Eric Chaisson prefers the term 'non-random elimination' to 'natural selection,' because we do not know of any agent that would do the selecting. The term 'non-random elimination' was introduced by US biologist Ernst Mayr.[28] Chaisson's view of cosmic evolution is more general than the mechanism of natural selection in biology that was proposed by Charles Darwin and Alfred Russel Wallace. In contrast to life, there are no families of stars consisting of succeeding generations that are competing with each other for limited resources. Furthermore, information does not accumulate in stars that would help them to adapt to the changing circumstances. In contrast to life, stars and galaxies are complex, but nonadaptive, entities.

Stars as Nuclear Forges

As was mentioned before, during the early phase of galaxy and star formation hardly any elements other than hydrogen and helium existed. By necessity, therefore, all the early stars almost exclusively consisted of these building blocks. If these stars had any planets, they must have been composed also exclusively of hydrogen and helium. Even today, most of the planetary material in our solar system is still locked up in this form, most notably in the giant planets Jupiter, Saturn, Uranus and Neptune. Not very surprisingly, these large planets do not exhibit any great complexity. However, there are also four smaller inner planets in our solar system, including Earth, which mostly consist of much heavier chemical elements such as carbon, oxygen, magnesium, silicon and iron. Where did these more complex chemical elements come from, and for how long have they been around? The answer to the first question is straightforward: this was the result of nucleo-synthesis – the forging of new elements within stars. It is, however, much more difficult to know for how long heavier chemical elements have existed in the universe.

The process of nucleo-synthesis works as follows. The forging of helium out of hydrogen in stellar cores inevitably leads to the depletion of its main fuel supply, hydrogen, and to the formation of helium. In stars that are sufficiently large, after most of the burnable hydrogen has been used up, the unrelenting impact of gravity causes the core to heat to temperatures higher than 10^8 K. These are Goldilocks circumstances that favor new nuclear fusion processes, in which helium is converted into heavier chemical elements. As soon as the helium is burned up, if the star is large enough, its further gravitational contraction will cause the temperature to rise again. This provides Goldilocks circumstances for the emergence of ever heavier chemical elements, all the way up to iron. As was noted earlier, iron is the most stable chemical element, and therefore the heaviest element that can be formed under average stellar conditions. All these situations exist for sizable periods of time, which means that there is sufficient time to form considerable amounts of these more complex atomic nuclei.

During their final phase, which may last as long as a few thousand years, very massive stars are able to synthesize even heavier chemical elements through the process of neutron capture. This produces elements such as copper, zinc, silver and gold. After this process has come to an end, there is no nuclear fuel left that can be burned, and the energy flow that counterbalances gravity wanes. The resulting rapid collapse of these very heavy stars releases so much energy that they subsequently explode in the form of enormous fireballs, the so-called supernovae. These explosions provide Goldilocks circumstances for the emergence of the heaviest stable chemical elements, all the way up to uranium. Because these Goldilocks circumstances last for only very short periods of time, very heavy chemical elements are rare.[29]

It is difficult to know for how long such processes have taken place. Because heavier elements are relatively scarce, they are hard to detect in very faint, and supposedly old, light. However, already during the early period of galaxy formation, many large stars formed that burned relatively quickly. More likely than not, these giant stars would have forged heavier chemical elements also. The enormous energy flows that were released as a result of their explosions may well have destroyed most, if not all, nearby complexity that might have emerged. Yet these mega-explosions also spread the newly created heavier chemical elements through the surrounding galactic space. These cooler circumstances provided Goldilocks circumstances that favored the emergence of simple molecules out of the chemical elements such as water, which consists of hydrogen and oxygen; silicates, which is made of silicon, oxygen and metals; and small organic molecules, including simple amino acids, that are the building blocks of proteins.

In doing so, nature's construction kit was enriched with an increasingly large assortment of chemical building blocks. This may have happened from as early as 10 billion years ago, if not earlier. As a result, Goldilocks conditions that favored the emergence of rocky planets, and perhaps also life, might already have emerged during that time.

4

OUR COSMIC NEIGHBORHOOD

The Emergence of Greater Complexity

Introduction

As we all know, in our cosmic neighborhood, the solar system, the circumstances have been just right for the existence of life on at least one favored planet, the good Earth. We do not know whether life and culture as we know them are unique, or whether they have also emerged elsewhere in the universe. This is mainly because these forms of greater complexity are small and therefore hard to detect from great distances. Whereas life and culture generate far larger power densities than stars, the energy flows themselves are extremely small compared to the gigantic output of stellar objects. As a result, the radiation produced by other possible life forms or cultures is extremely hard to detect even within our own galaxy. The accumulated effects of life, such as planetary atmospheres rich in oxygen,[1] as well as some collective effects of culture, most notably the electromagnetic radiation from radio, television and cell phones, may be easier to find. Yet seen on a galactic scale – not to mention the cosmic scale – these effects are also exceedingly small. As a consequence, it seems unlikely that we will be able to discover life and culture far beyond our cosmic neighborhood with the aid of the current detection techniques. At some point in the future, scientists may detect life on Mars or on moons orbiting Jupiter or perhaps even Saturn. Today, however, Earth is the only place in the universe known to harbor life.[2]

If there is life elsewhere in the universe, it may well have preceded life on Earth. The first heavier chemical elements needed for life probably emerged as early as 10 billion years ago. Given the enormous numbers of galaxies – perhaps 100 billion in the known universe, each harboring perhaps as many as 100 billion stars – the chances appear considerable that life and culture would have emerged in other places also, quite possibly much earlier than on our home planet. Moreover, seen on a cosmic scale we do not even know whether life is, in fact, the next step toward greater complexity. Perhaps other forms of greater complexity exist out there that we are currently unable to detect or even imagine.[3] As a result, while discussing the emergence of life and culture on Earth, our big history account by necessity becomes solar-system focused and Earth centered.[4]

Not very surprisingly, most natural scientists studying the solar system, Earth and life analyze their data in terms of energy flows through matter within certain Goldilocks boundaries, producing or destroying complexity. Yet to my knowledge no systematic accounts exist that describe the emergence of our cosmic neighborhood explicitly in these terms.[5]

The Galactic Habitable Zone

The location of our solar system within our galaxy favors the emergence of life on Earth. This area, called the 'galactic habitable zone,' would have emerged about 8 billion years ago. Before that time, there would have been too many supernovae events that extinguished life. Eight billion years ago is a full 3 billion years before our solar system came into being. This means that there may well have been a great many places within the galactic habitable zone where life evolved before it did so in our own cosmic neighborhood.

According to Australian astrophysicists Charles Lineweaver, Yeshe Fenner and Brad Gibson, the galactic habitable zone is characterized by 'four prerequisites for complex life: the presence of a host star, enough heavy elements to form terrestrial planets, sufficient time for biological evolution, and an environment free of life-extinguishing supernovae.'[6] On the basis of these criteria, this zone was identified as an annular region situated at a distance of between c.23,000 and c.30,000 light years from the galactic center. It is mostly composed of stars that emerged between 8 and 4 billion years ago, which means that about 75 per cent of these stars are older than our sun. Because the radius of our galaxy is about 50,000 light years, the galactic habitable zone is located about half way from the center of the Milky Way. Yet by far the most stars of our galaxy are situated closer to the galactic center. As a result, in terms of where the galactic matter is concentrated, the galactic habitable zone is actually rather close to the outer edge of the Milky Way. The authors reasoned as follows:

> Thus, there is a Goldilocks zone of metallicity [for astrophysicists, metals are all chemical elements heavier than helium]: With too little metallicity, Earth-mass planets are unable to form; with too much metallicity, giant planets destroy Earth-mass planets [because they tend to move inward toward the central star]. … Early intense star formation toward the inner galaxy provided the heavy elements necessary for life, but the supernovae frequency remained dangerously high there for several billion years. Poised between the crowded inner bulge and

the barren outer Galaxy, a habitable zone emerged about 8 Gy [billion years] ago (68% contour) that expanded with time as metallicity spread outward in the galaxy and the supernova rate decreased. ... We find that ~ 75% of the stars that could harbor complex life are older than the Sun and that their average age is ~ 1 Gy older than the Sun. ... Other factors that may play an important role ... include the frequency of grazing impacts with molecular clouds, the circularity of stellar orbits and their proximity to the corotation circle, and the effect of starbursts and an active Galactic nucleus in the early history of the most central regions of the Milky Way.[7]

Closer to the galactic center, there would have been more supernovae events than toward the outside. However damaging these supernovae events were to any life that might have formed, they also produced the heavier chemical elements that are essential for life. The further out toward the galactic edges, the fewer of these elements would have emerged, simply because there were fewer supernovae events. This explains why there is an outer Goldilocks boundary for life within our galaxy. Because over the course of time supernovae events decreased while the numbers of heavy chemical elements increased throughout the galaxy, the Goldilocks boundaries suitable for life expanded both toward the galactic center and toward its outer edge.

Our galaxy has a rather flat circular structure with arms that extend far into space. Clearly, the outer edges of the Milky Way are to be found near the ends of those arms. Yet if one were to go up or down from the galactic plane where we are situated (namely at about 20 light years from the galactic plane), one would find that we are living relatively close to an outer edge of the Milky Way also, probably no more than about 1,000 light years. This means that we are surrounded by far fewer stars that could go supernova and extinguish us than had we been living deep inside a globular, sphere-shaped galaxy. This makes one wonder whether flat galaxies are more suitable for life than their globular cousins.

Within the galactic habitable zone, the Goldilocks circumstances for the emergence of complex life include a few more constraints. First of all, if the central star of a solar system were too large, it would burn too fast. As a result, it would not last for a sufficiently long period of time needed for complex life to evolve on its planets. The central star should perhaps not be too little either, because it might not provide enough energy to keep life going. This would very much depend on the proximity of a life-bearing planet to its central star, as well as on the possibility that life might use other energy sources than those provided by its stellar companion. But if life needed stellar energy for its continued existence, it appears inevitable that the less electromagnetic radiation its central star produced, the closer to it these life forms would have to be situated.[8] Furthermore, most stars evolve as twins, as double stars. Obviously, planetary orbits around double stars would be rather unstable. As a consequence, the energy flows received from such stars would vary considerably. This might make it difficult for complex life to evolve, yet it is not thought to be impossible.[9] All things considered, however, the chances of finding complex life appear to be considerably better near single stars.

The Emergence of Our Cosmic Neighborhood

Already in 1755, philosopher Immanuel Kant thought that the sun and the planets emerged from a rotating dust cloud that, under the action of gravity, turned into a flattened ring. Most matter would have ended up in the middle and formed the sun, while the leftover matter coalesced into planets, moons, asteroids, comets and whatever else is circling the sun.[10] In other words, gravity provided the energy flow that shaped our current solar system from a cloud of loose, rotating matter.

This makes one wonder why there would have been such a rotating and contracting dust cloud in the first place. The most generally accepted theory is that at around 4.6 billion years ago, a supernova went off in this part of the galactic habitable zone. This stellar explosion would have produced the radioactive elements such as uranium that we observe on Earth today. At the same time, the shockwave associated with this super blast would have swept an otherwise loose dust cloud together and would thus have contributed to creating Goldilocks circumstances for solar system formation. In other words, a spectacular but short-lived energy flow through matter would have triggered the emergence of our solar system. For lack of data, I found it impossible to calculate a power density that would characterize this event.[11]

While most chemical elements joined to form our sun, a small portion of these elements coalesced into rings that were spaced out at more or less regular distances. These rings consisted of a mix of both lighter and heavier chemical elements. Over the course of time, the heavy elements accreted to form the planetary cores, while the lighter chemical elements covered them with a layer that was solid, fluid or gaseous, depending on the circumstances.

Close to the emerging sun, it became comparatively hot. As a result, the lighter chemical elements were pushed away to the outer part of the solar system, while the heavier chemical elements coalesced into emerging planetary bodies. After about 100 million years, this led to the emergence of the four rocky inner planets Mercury, Venus, Earth and Mars. More to the outside of the solar system, it remained much cooler, which allowed the lighter chemical elements also to be accreted into planets. This allowed the large gas giants

Jupiter, Saturn, Uranus and Neptune to emerge (which, like the rocky inner planets, also have a core consisting of heavier chemical elements).

After about 1 million years, the sun lit up with some sort of an explosion. This so-called T Tauri wind blew away its outer gas shell and also ripped the atmospheres off the emerging inner rocky planets. This gas and dust was blown out of the planetary zone, although some of it was partially picked by the outer gas planets, most notably Jupiter. All of this explains why the inner planets mostly consist of heavier chemical elements while the outer planets are largely composed of lighter materials.

Not all of these rings coalesced to form planets. The asteroid belt between Mars and Jupiter consists of what is thought to be a failed process of planet formation. It failed, because the enormous gravity exerted by Jupiter would have torn apart any incipient planet that emerged in that area. Beyond the large gassy planets, smaller bodies such as Pluto, now considered to be a dwarf planet, circle the sun. They are surrounded by large clouds of matter and dust that also never coalesced into larger bodies.

In fact, Pluto and similar other celestial bodies are now thought to belong to the closest of these clouds, the so-called Kuiper belt, which is situated between 30 to 50 astronomical units from the sun. The astronomical unit is the average distance between Earth and the sun, about 150 million km. Farther away, the more hypothetical Oort Cloud is thought to be located between 50,000 and 100,000 astronomical units from the sun. The farthest extension of the Oort Cloud would thus be at a distance of about 1.5 light years away from the sun, or perhaps even more. Because the nearest stars are located at about four light years from the sun, our solar system may actually be exchanging matter and energy with its closest neighbors on a regular basis, and thus, over long periods of time, perhaps even with other celestial bodies on a galactic scale.

Most of the planetary complexity emerged during the early phase of solar-system formation. The energy flow that made this happen was first of all the so-called accretion heat resulting from the gravitational contraction that planets experienced during their formation. This would have amounted to about 2×10^{32} joule. This is the amount of heat needed to heat up all the water currently on our planet to about 6 million degrees Celsius (about half as warm as the sun's core).[12] As each of the planets formed, the heavier material sank to the center, while the lighter material floated toward the surface. In this way, Earth's metallic core was formed, which consists mostly of iron and some nickel. It became surrounded by a mantle mostly composed of silicates, which is covered by a thin surface crust of even lighter materials. The separation into these different layers released the so-called differentiation heat. This was about 10^{31} joule, which was thus more than a factor of 10 smaller than the accretion heat.[13] Over billions of years, most, if not all of the accretion and differentiation heat was radiated out into the universe. Yet it may be that even today, some of this original heat still lingers within Earth.

While this heat was being dissipated, the heat released by the nuclear decay of radioactive elements in both the core and the mantle began to drive Earth's internal complexity. This heat results from an unstable balance within large nuclei such as uranium and thorium, which consist of a great many protons and neutrons. These tiny particles are held together by the strong force, while electromagnetism pushes them away from each other. In such large unstable nuclei, the electromagnetic force dominates the strong force over the course of time, which slowly but surely leads to the breaking up of these large nuclei into smaller ones. This nuclear decay is accompanied with the release of energy. This so-called radiogenic heat warms up the planet while it is dissipated toward its surface, and from there into space. The resulting energy gradient produces large convection cells in the upper mantle, which bring about the process of plate tectonics, which makes large pieces of crust move. In doing so, plate tectonics shapes Earth's surface. The nuclear heat, which has decreased over time as a result of the declining amounts of radioactive materials (which are not replenished either), is thought to drive most of Earth's internal complexity today.

After the formative phase of our solar system had come to an end, it may have undergone some major changes. For instance, giant planets, most notably Jupiter and Saturn, might have migrated inward as a result of friction with neighboring dust clouds. This would have slowed down their speed, thus reducing the size of its orbit. As a result, the current orbits of giant planets may not have been the areas where they originally evolved. This migration process would also have influenced the circumstances of the inner planets, including Earth.

During the first 600 million years of their existence, the inner planets, and perhaps some of the outer planets as well, experienced a so-called cosmic bombardment of leftover pieces from the original accretion of the solar system that were attracted by the planets' gravity. This was, in fact, the last phase of the accretion process. The data that make astronomers think such a cosmic bombardment took place are mostly derived from counting craters on our moon, Mars and Mercury, which were combined with estimates of their age. On Earth, by contrast, the combined processes of erosion and plate tectonics have erased most, if not all of these traces. Slowly but surely, the cosmic bombardment decreased in intensity. Yet even today, Earth is still being hit by space projectiles of various sizes on a daily basis, mainly rocks, dust and water, totaling about 40,000 tons per year. It is thought that the early impacts of countless aqueous comets provided most of the water that still exists on Earth.[14]

Our home planet is accompanied by a single moon that is unusually large, compared to moons circling other planets. This raises the question of its origin.

Because the moon rocks that were brought back by Apollo astronauts mostly consist of minerals that are thought to be very similar to mantle material from Earth, scientists think that a passing object the size of Mars hit Earth with a glancing blow. As a result of this collision, a considerable amount of mantle material was torn out of Earth and subsequently formed the moon, while most of the matter in this enormous cosmic cannon ball was absorbed by Earth. Current computer models show this to be feasible. This would present another example of matter and energy flows both destroying and creating forms of complexity.

In sum, at about 4.6 billion years ago, the sun, the planets and all the other still-existing celestial bodies of various kinds emerged through the process of accretion under the influence of gravity, which provided the energy that shaped our solar system. This would have taken about 100 million years to transpire. Ever since that time, Goldilocks circumstances favoring planet formation have not existed anymore within our solar system. Over the subsequent 900 million years, most other celestial bodies within the planetary zone were eliminated by falling into the already existing ones.

The complexity of both stars and planets during most of their existence is rather low, compared to life, while their basic shapes are very predictable. In the words of Philip and Phylis Morrison: 'Astronomy is thus the regime of the sphere; no such thing as a teacup the diameter of Jupiter is possible in our world.'[15] In other words, spheres and clusters of spheres rule in the physical universe as a result of gravity. Because most matter in the universe rotates, the resulting centrifugal force causes these spheres (or clusters of spheres) to flatten. This explains why the sky is dominated by more or less flattened spheres or by constellations of such spheres in various shapes. Only comparatively small objects such as asteroids can attain more complex forms.

While circling the sun, all the planets tug at each other and, as a result, produce nonlinear, and to some extent chaotic, processes. This issue was already recognized by Sir Isaac Newton and has occupied the minds of astronomers ever since.[16] Yet before supercomputers and modern chaos theory appeared, these perturbation calculations were too difficult to tackle mathematically. These chaotic movements of the planets have had important effects on Earth history, as we will see below.

The Solar System Habitable Zone

Within our solar system, a Goldilocks zone exists that favors life. Earlier, we saw that the galactic habitable zone was defined as an area sufficiently removed from the galactic center, so that life would not be destroyed by supernovae events, but not so far away that there would be insufficient numbers of heavy chemical elements, the essential building blocks of life. Similarly, for at least 50 years scientists have been researching habitable zones (HZ) around stars such as our sun. In 1993, astrophysicists Kasting, Whitmire and Reynolds expressed the Goldilocks requirements of this zone as follows:[17]

> Our basic premise is that we are dealing with Earthlike planets with $CO_2/H_2O/$
> N_2 atmospheres and that habitability requires the presence of liquid water on the
> planet's surface. The inner edge of the HZ is determined in our model by loss of
> water via photolysis and hydrogen escape [the breakdown of water under the
> influence of sunlight into its constituent chemical elements oxygen and hydro-
> gen; the hydrogen escapes into space because it is too light to be kept in the
> atmosphere by the planetary gravitational force]. The outer edge of the HZ is
> determined by the formation of CO_2 clouds, which cool a planet's surface by
> increasing its albedo [degree of whiteness] and lowering the convective lapse rate
> [slowdown of heat transfer by convection currents in the atmosphere]. Conserva-
> tive estimates for these distances in our own Solar System are 0.95 and 1.37 AU
> respectively [AU: astronomical unit = mean distance between Earth and the sun,
> approximately 150 million km or 8 lightminutes]; the actual width of the present
> HZ could be much greater. Between these two limits, climate stability is ensured
> by a feedback mechanism in which atmospheric CO_2 concentrations vary inversely
> with planetary surface temperatures. The width of the HZ is slightly greater for
> planets that are larger than Earth and for planets which have higher N_2 partial
> pressures. The HZ evolves outward in time because the Sun increases in luminos-
> ity as it ages. A conservative estimate for the width of the 4.6-Gyr [billion year]
> continuously habitable zone (CHZ) is 0.95 to 1.15 AU.

In short, while Mercury, close to the sun, would have been too hot, the area including possibly Venus, certainly Earth and probably also Mars would have constituted the Goldilocks theater that favored the emergence of life, as shown in Figure 4.1.

This very much depended on the size of the planets that found themselves within this zone. If, for instance, Venus had been smaller and Mars had been larger, both planets could have supported life more easily. Venus would have had a thinner atmosphere and as a result would have been cooler (now it is far too hot to support life). A larger planet Mars, by contrast, would have been able to hold on to a thicker atmosphere, which would have enhanced a possible greenhouse effect, thus keeping Mars warmer than it now is. Well outside this habitable zone, some of the moons circling Jupiter and Saturn may also have provided Goldilocks circumstances for simple life to thrive. Because we do not know anything about possible life on these moons, this issue will not be con-sidered here in any further detail.[18]

Figure 4.1: The solar system habitable zone, orbits of planets not drawn to scale. (Source: NASA.)

Major Characteristics of Earth

The complexity of a planet such as Earth is caused by at least four major factors: (1) its own gravity, which keeps the planet together; (2) the energy generated deep inside, mostly through the process of nuclear decay of heavy chemical elements such as uranium; (3) the external energy received in the form of radiation from its central star, which mostly influences its surface and (4) cosmic gravitational effects, including collisions, exerted by other celestial bodies, including its central star, other planets, its moon(s), meteorites, comets and dispersed matter such as dust and water.

Today, Earth is characterized by important Goldilocks circumstances that have been part of our planetary regime for most of its history. First of all, our home planet is more or less the right size. If Earth had been smaller, its weak gravity would not have been able to retain its atmosphere or liquid surface water, both vital for life. Had Earth been a great deal larger, its resulting gravity would have crushed most living things on land, while more likely than not, any birds that had emerged would not have been able to take off. As a result of its size, Earth's interior is still hot. Even after 4.6 billion years, radioactive chemical elements still exist in Earth's core and mantle that produce heat. This energy causes movements in Earth's mantle, which produces ceaseless change on its surface, including earthquakes, volcanism, moving continents, mountain formation and ocean floor spreading. As a result, over the course of time the process of plate tectonics has been recycling most of Earth's surface, including waste produced by life, by subducting ocean floors (where such trash has been accumulating) underneath continents, where this material is broken down.[19] In doing so, plate tectonics has been functioning as both a trash can and a recycling regime for a considerable portion of the material entropy produced by life.

In the second place, Earth has been orbiting the sun at more-or-less the right distance for more than 4 billion years. As a result, the incoming solar radiation has never been too weak to provide sufficient energy for life to flourish (in which case all Earth's surface water would have been frozen), nor so strong as to destroy life (for instance, by boiling off all Earth's water into space). In the third place, Earth is endowed with a large moon, which stabilizes the rotation of Earth's axis. Without our moon, the angle of Earth's axis would have changed erratically. These movements would have produced considerable changes in solar radiation across Earth's surface. Although more simple life forms would have been able to thrive in the oceans during such variations in solar radiation, more complex life might have had a harder time surviving these changes.[20]

The particular characteristics of our home planet produce a large variety of living conditions.[21] Like all planets, Earth is a sphere. As a result, those portions of its surface that face the sun (the tropics) receive most of the sunlight, while the poles receive the least. Thus it is not surprising that the poles are generally much colder than the equatorial regions. This temperature gradient between the tropics and the poles produces a continuous flow of matter and energy from the equatorial zone to the poles, mostly in the forms of warm air and ocean currents, while cold wind and water currents return to the warmer areas.

Today Earth rotates around its axis every 24 hours. As a result, all regions of our planet experience continuous fluctuations in solar radiation, most notably day and night, of course, but also during the day. During Earth history, this rotational velocity has been slowing down because both the sun and the moon have been ceaselessly tugging at Earth, causing the ocean tides. The tides cause friction, which slows down the Earth's rotation. At the beginning of Earth history, a day and night would have lasted only eight hours. The Earth's rotation gradually slowed down to the current 24 hours, thereby producing a long-term Goldilocks gradient affecting all the terrestrial circumstances. It would also have caused the moon to slowly but surely move away from Earth.[22]

The Earth's magnetism is caused by its rotating iron core. This magnetic field directs charged particles from space that might damage life toward the poles that, by coincidence perhaps, are the areas least likely to harbor life. As a result, most life is shielded from the deleterious effects caused by such particles. The history of the Earth's magnetic field is not well known.[23] It appears to have reversed its polarity very quickly at irregular times, with periods varying from a few hundred thousand years to as much as tens of millions of years. The last major change would have taken place about 780,000 years ago. Because over the past centuries the Earth's magnetic field has been decreasing, we may actually be approaching another such dramatic flip-over event. This may lead to the temporary disappearance of terrestrial magnetism, which would allow cosmic radiation to come down everywhere on Earth unhindered, where it may cause harmful mutations in living beings. It may well be that earlier magnetic reversals were accompanied by similar waves of genetic changes induced by cosmic radiation, which may well have influenced biological evolution as a whole.

Today, the Earth's axis makes an angle of about 66.6 degrees with respect to the plane within which our planet orbits the sun. This angle is thought to be a remnant of the violent collision that tore the moon out of Earth. As a result of this tilt, the amount of solar energy that reaches particular areas varies during the year, which produces the seasons. These changes are more pronounced on land than in the oceans. Because it takes more energy to heat up water than land, it takes longer for oceans to warm up or to cool down. As a result, ocean temperatures tend to fluctuate considerably less than land temperatures.

The Earth's orbit around the sun fluctuates because other planets, most notably the giant planet Jupiter, are tugging at our home planet. These gravitational effects produce three major orbital regimes. In the first place, the Earth's orbit is shifting from a more elliptical to a more circular form and back again over a period of about 100,000 years. This orbital regime is known as 'eccentricity.' The second one, the angle between the Earth's axis and the perpendicular to the plane of its orbit around the sun, varies periodically between 21.5 and 24.5 degrees. This regime is called 'axial tilt' – it is officially known as the 'obliquity of the ecliptic' – and has a period of about 41,000 years. It is mostly caused by the gravitational pull of both the sun and Jupiter, while the moon's gravity exercises a stabilizing effect. The third important astronomical regime is the precession of the Earth's axis, the slow change of the orientation of the axial tilt – which is spinning like a top – with a period of about 21,000 years. This effect is the result of both the sun's and the moon's gravity. These three orbital regimes are jointly called the 'Milanković cycles,' in honor of the Yugoslav mathematician who elaborated the idea that these astronomical regimes would be related to climate change on Earth, because they change the amount of sunlight that falls on specific areas.[24] It is not known for how long these patterns have existed. In addition to being directly related to the ice ages, all these orbital regimes produce a great number of other intricate energy effects, including changes in wind patterns, ocean currents, cloud cover and rainfall.

The Earth's ever-changing geography, the result of the joint effects of plate tectonics and erosion, provides another important regime of Goldilocks circumstances. This included not only the division between land and oceans but also its particular shape in three dimensions, ranging from deep sea trenches to the tallest mountains.

Early Inner Planetary History

In the beginning, all the inner planets, including Earth, were hot. This was the result of both the accretion heat that had not yet been dissipated into the universe and of high levels of radioactivity in their cores. The original atmospheres of the inner planets were blown away by the ignition flare of the sun after it began to shine. The subsequent release of gasses (usually called 'outgassing') from the interior of the planets may have created secondary atmospheres. However, it is now thought that aqueous comets raining down on the planets provided most of the water, and perhaps most of the other gasses as well. On Earth and Mars, and perhaps on Venus also, oceans would have formed as soon as the temperature had dropped sufficiently. In addition to Earth, this may also have created Goldilocks circumstances for life to emerge on Venus and Mars. The inner planet Mercury, by contrast, would always have been too small and too close to the sun – and therefore too hot – to have retained a secondary atmosphere, let alone liquid water. Consequently, scientists think that life never evolved on Mercury.

When the sun first lighted up, it would have shone about 25 per cent less ferociously than today. Over billions of years, the sun's output would gradually have increased to what it is now, thereby producing a gradient in time that affected the entire solar system. During the early period, the solar system habitable zone was therefore situated closer to the sun, perhaps even allowing the emergence of simple life on Venus. Over the course of time, however, the heat from inside Venus dropped while the radiation received from the sun increased. This would have caused Venus, about the same size as Earth but situated closer to the sun, to heat up, experience a runaway greenhouse effect and thus become much too hot for life.

The planet Mars, by contrast, is considerably smaller than Earth. Because it is situated farther away from the sun, Mars receives considerably less solar radiation than Earth. After its initial atmosphere had been blown away, Mars would also have acquired a secondary atmosphere. Yet Mars was not large enough to enable its gravity to retain its atmosphere very well. As a result, the red planet lost most of its air and its surface liquid water and became a rather cold place. This would have killed most life that might have emerged there. Even so, it is thought possible that Goldilocks circumstances still exist favoring the continued existence of simple life forms in certain areas on Mars.

Early Earth History

The earliest period of Earth history is called the 'Hadean Era.' It stretches from about 4.5 billion years ago until the appearance of the oldest known rocks, about 3.8 billion years ago. At the beginning, the accretion heat, cosmic bombardment and radiogenic heat jointly produced a molten Earth. Yet over millions of years, Earth began to cool down, as the accretion heat was dissipated into space, collisions became less frequent and the radiogenic heat began to decrease.

At around 4 billion years ago, a solid rocky crust was beginning to form. Because rock is a poor conductor of heat, the emerging crust began to insulate the inner earth from space. As a result, more heat was retained, which made the inner earth heat up. This led to a new dynamic steady state situation, in which our planet evolved ways to get rid of this heat, most notably by volcanism and, probably much later, also by plate tectonics. It is therefore not very surprising that volcanism was rampant during the Hadean. At that time, the Earth's day and night would have been about 12 hours long due to a faster rotation on its axis.

Initially, the entire crust would have been more or less similar in composition, while it was covered by an ocean. Only between 3 and 2 billion years ago, when Earth had cooled down further, did a clear separation take place between the lighter land masses and the heavier oceanic crust as a result of plate tectonics. The landmasses consist of lighter materials, because they float on top of their tectonic plates, while the heavier oceanic crust is constantly pushed underneath them. About 2 billion years ago, the process of plate tectonics as we know it today would have been in full swing. The constantly moving plates hit, slid alongside or moved away from each other, producing volcanism, earthquakes and an ever-changing geography. Tectonic plates move on average about as fast as the speed with which human finger nails grow. But there are considerable differences. While the Atlantic Ocean is currently widening only between 10 and 20 millimeters every year as a result of sea floor spreading, the East Pacific Rise in the South Pacific grows larger at more than 150 mm every year.[25]

According to the standard view, Earth's initial secondary atmosphere would have consisted mostly of carbon dioxide as well as some other gasses, including nitrogen, sulphur dioxide and water, while its pressure at sea level would have been enormous, about 150 times today's value.[26] The early atmosphere would not have contained any free oxygen. While Earth was cooling down and the sun was still faint, the copious amounts of carbon dioxide in the atmosphere would have caused a greenhouse effect. This would have kept the Earth's surface sufficiently warm, so that any surface water that existed remained liquid.

The long-term development of the conditions on Earth's surface may perhaps best be described by saying that a rather uniform beginning was followed by an ever more differentiated range of circumstances, thus producing a great many regions, all with their own particular characteristics. Interestingly, such a general description would characterize just as well universe history, life history and human history. Nonetheless, the circumstances of Earth have always remained within very specific boundaries. It never became so cold that the entire planet would freeze over forever, or so hot that all the water evaporated into space. Furthermore, no celestial impacts, including radiation from supernovae, shook our home planet to the extent that all life was destroyed. These specific Goldilocks circumstances on the face of Earth have allowed life to survive and thrive for billions of years.

Life Is Very Special

The origin of life is still a major known unknown in science, notwithstanding a great many scientific efforts to elucidate it. The biggest problem in seeking to model the emergence of life is the fact that, more likely than not, this process took millions of years. And that long period of time is very hard to simulate in a laboratory.

It has often been argued that the emergence of life would have been very unlikely, had it been based solely on chance encounters of atoms and molecules. The process leading to life must, therefore, have been the result of several highly constrained, or channeled, processes – most of which are as yet unknown. This includes the fact that certain chemical bonds are much more likely to form than others. In addition, Earth's geology may well have provided sufficient building blocks, energy flows and catalytic circumstances that led to life. But it could also be that large amounts of molecules that would eventually constitute life emerged elsewhere in our galaxy, while they rained down on our planet over many millions of years, thus providing a fair share of the needed building blocks.

Compared to galaxies, stars or planets, even the largest life forms are tiny. Yet, as we saw in chapter two, life generates far greater power densities than lifeless objects. While our sun's power density currently amounts to only about 2×10^{-4} watt/kg, modern plants, for instance, handle about 0.9 watt/kg, while animals do even better, about 2 watt/kg. Clearly, in contrast to stars, life is able to generate considerably higher power densities while at the same time maintaining very moderate Goldilocks circumstances.

The emergence of life represented, therefore, the emergence of an entirely new mechanism for achieving greater complexity. Unlike stars and galaxies, life forms do not thrive because they use energy that originates from supplies of matter and energy stored within themselves. By contrast, all living things need to continuously tap matter and energy flows from their surroundings to maintain themselves and, if possible, reproduce. This is not a new insight. Already in 1895, Austrian physicist Ludwig Boltzmann stated that all life is a struggle for free energy.[27] In addition, all the biochemical compounds produced by cells are fulfilling functions for the survival of the organism. Such a higher level of organization has never been observed in lifeless matter.

All of this is possible, first of all, thanks to the information stored in biomolecules. All life forms contain hereditary information, which controls their own reproduction as well as the energy-generating and energy-consuming processes, jointly known as 'metabolism.' All of this is taking place inside cells, which can be seen as the building blocks of life. All organisms consist of cells. Many life forms come in the form of single cells, while more complex organisms, such as us, consist of a great many cells that cluster together. Cells are little envelopes, within which all the important molecules are produced and maintained that are needed for survival and reproduction. These include the information-carrying molecules deoxyribonucleic acid (DNA) and ribonucleic acid (RNA). These molecules not only carry information but also translate it into other molecular structures, while regulating a great many cellular mechanisms.

To be sure, there are also viruses. Such organisms consist of information in the form of DNA or RNA molecules, which are coated with proteins. Because viruses lack any form of metabolism, they always have to rely on living cells for their reproduction. In fact, viruses hijack these cellular mechanisms for their own purposes. In doing so, viruses may have played a major role in evolution by inserting their genetic information into that of other organisms, while they also have been swapping and transferring genes across the boundaries of a great many species to an extent that is only now being elucidated.[28]

The question of how to define life has not yet been resolved satisfactorily. Today, a great many definitions of life exist, which will not be discussed here. However, by following the approach advocated in this book, it may be possible to define life in a way that resolves many, if not all, of these issues. I therefore propose to define life as follows:[29]

A regime that contains a hereditary program for defining and directing molecular mechanisms that actively extract matter and energy from the environment, with the aid of which matter and energy is converted into building blocks for its own maintenance and, if possible, reproduction.

Within cells, a great many bio-molecules are manufactured, the most important of which are proteins. These are made by using information coded in DNA or RNA. Proteins act in many different ways. Their most important function is catalyzing chemical reactions that would otherwise not take place. Such proteins are called 'enzymes.' These bio-molecules can speed up chemical reactions by lowering the energy barriers that prevent these reactions from happening at the moderate temperatures and pressures that are characteristic of life. In other words, the most important function of enzymes is to provide Goldilocks circumstances that allow these reactions to take place as well as to regulate them. This is essentially what enzymes also do, for instance, in modern detergents, namely break down organic molecules (stains) that are hard to remove with more traditional soaps. But enzymes can not only break down molecules but also synthesize them, while they can also regulate the speed of chemical reactions. Inside cells, long and complicated chains of chemical reactions take place with the aid of a great many different enzymes. In addition to the cell's own reproduction, these reactions include the extraction of matter and energy from outside, the use of matter and energy for manufacturing the molecules needed for survival, the secretion of waste materials and, in more complicated cell structures, the processing of information within neural networks.

In general terms, with the emergence of life both the number and the variety of building blocks increased. The same happened with the connections and interactions between and among the building blocks, while the sequences of the building blocks also became ever more important. As a result, it seems fair to say that with the onset of life, a new level of considerably greater complexity had emerged.

To exist and multiply, life must actively tap matter and energy flows from outside itself on a continuous basis. And because these resources are finite on the good Earth, in the longer run this inevitably means a competition for resources. This insight forms the basis of Charles Darwin and Alfred Russel Wallace's theory of biological evolution, which can be summarized as a competition for matter and energy flows within two types of specific Goldilocks circumstances. The first set of Goldilocks circumstances includes all the effects that species have on each other by helping each another, by just being there, by competing for resources, by preying on each another or by polluting the environment. The second set of Goldilocks circumstances is provided by the surrounding inanimate nature which, in its turn, is influenced by both life and lifeless nature. Over the course of time, this process has produced an increasingly complex and ever-changing regime of Goldilocks circumstances on the surface of Earth, within which those species survived which succeeded in harvesting sufficient matter and energy to exist and reproduce, while all the rest went extinct.

As Erich Jantsch emphasized, the emergence of biological information coded in molecules that are transferred over generations opened up the possibility of learning processes. In Jantsch's words:[30]

> A new dimension of openness is introduced since via information the cumulative experience of many generations may be handed on. Whereas a chemical dissipative structure [a structure using matter and energy flows to maintain itself] is merely capable of ontogeny, of the evolution of its own individuality, and its memory is limited to the experience accrued in the course of its existence, phylogeny (the history of an entire phylum) may now become effective. At first, the ancestral tree is no tree, but a single thin line. The experience of earlier generations as well as the fluctuations and evolution are transferred vertically, which here means along an axis of time. This time binding makes the development of higher complexity possible than seems attainable by the ontogeny of material systems.

In short, over the course of time, the learning process made possible by the information stored in bio-molecules favored the emergence of far greater complexity than the levels that had been attained previously by lifeless nature.

The Emergence of Life

It is thought that all life forms are descended from one single common ancestor. Whereas today a great many different species inhabit almost every nook and cranny of our planet, ranging from the tiniest viruses to the largest plants and animals, all these life forms use very similar basic biochemical processes.[31] This is interpreted as clear evidence in favor of a common origin of all these life forms.

We do not know where, when and how life first emerged. Claims that life dates back all the way to about 3.8 billion years ago have been challenged. But there is firm evidence that it is at least 3.4 billion years old. Given the fact that Earth formed about 4.6 billion years ago, there may, or may not, have been a long period of physical and chemical evolution leading to the rise of early life. In fact, we do not even know whether life first emerged on Earth or whether it was transported to our planet from elsewhere by whatever celestial object happened to dive into our atmosphere. If life did originate elsewhere in the universe, we do not know when, where or how this happened. Yet because early life appears to have been remarkably well adapted to the circumstances of the early Earth, it seems likely that life emerged spontaneously on our home planet.

If life emerged on Earth, we do not know whether this happened only once. And if life entered Earth from outside, we do not know whether such foreign invaders arrived only once either. Because all current life forms appear to share one common ancestor, the almost inevitable conclusion is that any competing life forms that either originated separately on Earth or arrived from space did not survive into the present. In other words, the circumstances on Earth were not good enough for such alternative life forms (if they ever existed) to survive in the long run.

The emergence of life on our planet would have been preceded by a long process of increasing inanimate complexity. This process is usually called 'chemical evolution.' Under the influence of matter and energy flows, such as sunlight, volcanic activity, lightning and perhaps radioactive decay, increasingly complex molecules would have formed. Also, such molecules may have arrived from outer space. At a certain point in time, a spontaneous process of self-organization would have kicked in, leading to the emergence of life.

The presence of sufficient liquid water must have been an absolute requirement for the emergence and continued existence of life, because the matter and energy flows needed for the sustenance of life could not have existed without it. Until today, the availability of liquid water has posed very strict Goldilocks boundaries for the survival of life and culture on our home planet. Moreover, sufficiently large bodies of liquid water, such as oceans, must have had a dampening effect on temperature fluctuations caused by fluctuating energy flows from outside, because they can absorb a great deal of heat without a concomitant large rise in temperature. Such a situation produces rather stable temperatures and pressures, which would have helped early life to survive. This is not a new insight at all. Already in 1871, Charles Darwin suggested that life might have emerged in a 'warm little pond' under very specific conditions.[32]

Another reason for thinking that life originated in the oceans is based on the fact that the overall salt concentration within living cells is very similar to that of the modern oceans (which would have been similar in the ancient oceans). If the salt concentration of the pioneer cells had been very different from the surrounding water during their emergence, the resulting energy differentials would have destroyed those early cells almost immediately. Over the course of time, such energy differentials did develop, especially after life moved out of the seas onto land. By that time, however, life had become much more robust and was able to evolve protective means, which safeguarded cells in this initially very hostile environment.

The current most likely scenario for the start of life is called 'RNA world.' It consists of the spontaneous formation of RNA molecules, which were able to both carry information and catalyze important reactions, including their own reproduction. Such assemblages of RNA molecules could have produced the first viable living cells. Among the evidence supporting this hypothesis is the fact that today RNA molecules are present in all life forms and in many different sizes, where they fulfill a great many different functions. Furthermore, one of its main building blocks, adenosine triphosphate (usually abbreviated as ATP), is used by all cells as their major energy carrier.[33]

The oceans may have provided the matter and energy flows that allowed life to get going, most notably through undersea volcanoes, of which there were many, thanks to the fact that the insulating crust had caused Earth to warm up. Even today, such black smokers can be found in many places in the oceans. They are called 'black smokers' because they emit dark fumes. According to Eric Chaisson, they provided more than sufficient energy to sustain early life, approximately 50×10^{-4} watt/kg. Modern black smokers, by contrast, generate power densities in the order of only 10^{-4} watt/kg, which is still sufficient to keep the modern life forms going that are feeding on them.[34] In his book of 2005 *Energy: Engine of Evolution*, Dutch scientist Frank Niele calls this first energy regime the 'thermophilic (heat-loving) regime.'[35]

US microbiologists Eugene Canaan and William Martin suggested in 2005 that early life may actually have formed within bubbly porous silicate structures of mildly hot black smokers. Within great numbers of comparatively protected little bubbles of this kind, which are about the same size as cells, RNA and other molecules may have begun to interact. The porous walls of these bubbly silicate structures may also have acted as catalysts, thus allowing the production of more complex molecules.[36] When such bubbles full of emergent life over-flowed, they might have secreted little bubbles into the oceans that were perhaps surrounded by a layer of proteins and lipids. Such a process may have contin-ued for many millions of years without generating life. Yet even if it happened successfully only once, such a tiny bubble could have become the first living cell. A major reason for suggesting this mechanism came from the observation that today, the three major taxa of evolution, namely archaebacteria, prokaryo-tes and eukaryotes, all share major molecular mechanisms, while both their cell membranes and their ways of copying DNA are different. The earliest life forms might therefore have emerged without DNA or without specific cell mem-branes, which would have evolved separately later.

The emergence of life implied the emergence of matter regimes that absorbed energy flows to reach levels of greater complexity. Over the course of time, this process must have changed from passive to active absorption. At a certain point in time, early life evolved a mechanism that allowed it to actively extract matter and energy from its environment, which is what all life forms do today. This was a major transition. Given the fact that maintaining greater complexity requires considerable amounts of matter and energy, and thus a considerable, and continuous, effort, one wonders why life did not give up and disappear as a result. The inescapable conclusion is that during its emergence, life must have evolved an in-built drive that was strong enough to keep itself alive. It is unknown to me what the biochemical mechanism for this drive would consist of.[37] It is not clear as yet whether, given the right starting conditions, the emergence of life was inevitable (like the emergence of galaxies, stars and planets), or whether it was the result of an unlikely chance effect.

Like the heaviest chemical elements that emerged during supernova explosions, which also absorbed energy during their formation, the more complicated molecules that living cells began to construct could not have emerged without absorbing energy, which is released again as soon as these molecules break down. As a result of life's ceaseless activities over billions of years, the spontaneous accumulation of such energy-rich bio-molecules in favored places has produced most, if not all, of the fossil fuels we are burning today.[38]

If life indeed emerged in the relatively well-protected environment of the oceanic black smokers, it must have been adapted to these circumstances from the very beginning. As a result, early life must have been extremely dependent on the geothermal energy released from deep within Earth. Yet over the course of time, life learned to extract energy from its environment in many ways, most importantly from the electromagnetic radiation emitted by our central star. The harvesting of sunlight liberated life from its bondage to the black smokers and allowed it to populate the oceans, the land and the atmosphere. How life pulled off this trick will be discussed in the next chapter.

5

LIFE ON EARTH

The Widening Range of Complexity

Life, Energy and Complexity

The history of life over the past 4 billion years can be summarized as biological evolution in continuous interaction with its planetary and cosmic environment. In the beginning, there were only simple life forms. Yet over the course of time, life differentiated into a wide spectrum of biological species. While great numbers of simple microorganisms continued to exist, more complex life forms also began to emerge. Although the history of life has been punctuated by five large extinction events that caused a temporary sharp decrease of life's complexity, the long-term trend has been toward a variety of organisms that ranged from very simple life forms to increasingly complex ones.[1]

In contrast to lifeless nature, the greater complexity of life involves the active harvesting of matter and energy. This active harvesting costs energy also. In consequence, striking a balance between the costs and benefits of complexity began to play a role as soon as life emerged. For lifeless forms of complexity, such as stars, planets and galaxies, such a balance does not play a role, because they do not harvest matter and energy actively. The emergence of more complex life forms, however, was strongly linked to such a cost-benefit balance, in which the costs of achieving greater complexity were not greater than the benefits of having it.

This process, in its turn, was driven to a considerable extent by competition within and among species, which helped define what was advantageous for survival and reproduction and what was not. For instance, the complex animals that emerged about 540 million years ago were sufficiently able to catch their prey and defend themselves, compared to their competitors. Apparently, the cost of their new complexity was sufficiently balanced by the benefit of having it.

Because of the overriding importance of obtaining sufficient matter and energy to preserve its complexity, the story of life first of all deals with the ways of obtaining these matter and energy flows as well as using them appropriately, while seeking not to become a matter and energy source for other organisms. This point of view is not new at all and has been investigated already for many decades. All of these analyses make implicit, and sometimes explicit, use of the idea that energy flows through matter within certain Goldilocks boundaries bring about various levels of greater complexity.[2]

In contrast to cosmic evolution, which has been slowing down after a very energetic start, biological evolution has been speeding up. Life may have emerged as long ago as 3.5 billion years BP (before present). It remained rather simple until 2 billion years BP, when the first complex cells formed. It took another 1.5 billion years before complex organisms began to proliferate, around 540 million years ago. Ever since that time, the number of biological genera appears to have grown rapidly.[3] A similar acceleration can be witnessed in human history, during which both population numbers and technological skills have increased exponentially.

The underlying reason of why both biological evolution and human history have been speeding up can be found in the fact that both have been driven by learning processes. These learning processes first of all concerned the harvesting of enough matter and energy as well as the preservation of one's own complexity. An important part of this learning process was a continuous re-evaluation of the cost-benefit balance of complexity under pressure from Darwin and Wallace's process of natural selection (or non-random elimination). This process operates by eliminating both the unfavorable genetic make-up of a species and its insufficient cultural skills. For what matters in biological evolution is simply whether a species is able to reproduce successfully, or not. In the latter case, it is eliminated, while in the first case it survives.

Life forms are therefore sometimes called 'complex adaptive systems.' This term was coined by Murray Gell-Mann and coworkers at the Santa Fe Institute, a US interdisciplinary research institute dedicated to the study of complexity.[4] In contrast to inanimate nature, all life forms tend to adapt to the outside world, while often also seeking to adapt the outside world to themselves. For life, the adaptation to changing circumstances first of all takes place through the process of non-random elimination.

As a result of these learning processes, both biological evolution and human history are characterized by positive feedback mechanisms. Biological evolution is based on genetic learning, which is 'hardwired' in specialized molecules, while cultural learning takes place within brain and nerve cells, mostly in the form of 'software.' In the long run, these learning processes have a self-reinforcing character, as long as they favor the harvesting of sufficient matter and energy needed for survival and reproduction and the preservation of one's own complexity. In consequence, both biological evolution and human history exhibit similar exponential trends.

As soon as biological information emerged, the possibility for biological disinformation opened up also. Today, we witness at least two types, both of which are related to matter and energy use. The first form consists of biological species that are using the cellular metabolism of other species for their own propagation. This is what viruses do. They inject their own genetic information into host cells. This foreign information uses the cellular metabolism for creating new copies of itself, thereby exhausting the cell's capacity to keep its own complexity going. The second option consists of trying to avoid the fate of becoming someone else's matter and energy source by changing one's outward appearance. Organisms either mimic the shape and colors of organisms that their predators do not particularly like or adopt camouflage tactics.

Greater complexity also entails a greater risk of decline. As a result, more complex life forms may not live very long. This may be the case for both individuals and entire species. Moreover, biological evolution as well as human history have caused incisive changes in the natural environment. All of this has stimulated the ever-continuing emergence of new species as well as the decline of others. In this way, biological evolution and its planetary environment have been interacting for as long as life has existed on Earth.[5]

To survive and thrive, all life forms need to extract matter and energy from their surroundings on a continuous basis. While many biological species feed on others, by necessity there are great numbers of organisms that extract their matter and energy from the nonliving environment. These species, mostly microorganisms and plants, provide all the matter and energy for the rest of life. In other words, all complex adaptive regimes (life) are ultimately powered by complex nonadaptive regimes (inanimate nature).

More complex organisms tend to generate larger power densities. In other words, biological evolution shows a trend toward the use of increasing matter and energy flows by a significant portion of life forms, which apparently became intricate enough to handle the larger matter and energy flows without being destroyed by them. This must mean that such organisms, including us, have created Goldilocks circumstances within themselves that allowed them to handle these greater matter and energy flows without being irreparably damaged by them.[6]

Whereas more complex organisms tend to generate larger power densities continuously, some microorganisms are able to generate very large energy flows through matter for short periods of time.[7] For instance, when cultivated in optimal conditions, the bacterium *Azotobacter* can reach power densities of up to 10,000 watt/kg (humans on average make do with only 2 watt/kg). In these circumstances, *Azotobacter* is trying to replicate itself as quickly as possible, perhaps every 20 minutes or so. In doing so, it is not only maintaining its own complexity but also duplicating itself as quickly as possible. Because of the limited resources available, such a phenomenally high energy metabolism can only be maintained for brief intervals. During most of their existence, such organisms have to make ends meet with the aid of a far more limited energy supply. Apparently, these microorganisms are geared to harvesting energy as fast as possible, while the getting is good.

Humans, by contrast, rely on a rather different survival strategy, which includes attempts to secure a steady food supply as well as the creation of food storage regimes, both inside their bodies and elsewhere in protected places. In this respect humans are, of course, not unique. Many other animals, including bees and squirrels, have developed similar storage regimes. In life-less nature, by contrast, such matter and energy storage regimes have never been observed. The storage of matter and energy for later use appears to be a novel strategy, which is exclusively employed by complex adaptive regimes. It may well be that as life became more complex, their storage regimes also became more complex. Such a trend is apparent in human history, too. These storage regimes can be interpreted as the creation of specific Gold-ilocks circumstances facilitating the stabilization of irregular matter and energy flows.

During biological evolution, there may have been a trend toward greater energy efficiency, which means achieving more complexity with the same resources. One would expect greater thermodynamic efficiency to evolve espe-cially in situations in which resources were becoming scarce. Some evidence exists in support of this hypothesis. Many bacteria, for instance, appear to have evolved toward greater thermodynamic efficiencies as a result of compe-tition. Yet although a great many studies have been performed on energy efficiency by specific life forms, no one appears yet to have written a system-atic analysis of energy efficiency during the history of life. The lack of such an overview is surprising, given the fact that the study of thermodynamics had evolved already in the nineteenth century. Clearly, here lies a challenge for further research.[8]

As a result of the possible trend toward greater energy efficiency, organisms may have found similar solutions. For instance, a study by Russian scientist Anastassia Makarieva and co-workers published in 2008 compared the average resting metabolic rates (power densities at rest) of about 3,000 different species. Interestingly, these rates varied only fourfold, despite the fact that their body weights differed about 20 orders of magnitude. The largest organism they studied was the elephant (1 watt/kg), while the smallest was a bacterium (4 watt/ kg). Because most organisms' metabolic rates were clustered between 1 and 10 watt/kg of mass, the authors suggest that there may be an optimum meta-bolic rate that lies within this range. Organisms that lie close to this value would be the fittest.[9] Remarkably, with their average power density of 2 watt/kg, humans would be right in the middle of this range (the middle being defined as where most organisms cluster).

Achieving greater efficiency usually has a price tag attached to it, namely the need for greater complexity. For instance, the current efforts to reduce automobile fuel consumption have led to the more complex design of hybrid vehicles. A similar situation emerged when microorganisms learned to use oxygen to more fully exploit the energy stored in bio-molecules. This required a more elaborate biochemical metabolism (and thus higher costs).[10] Apparently, the greater complexity needed to achieve greater energy efficiency also costs energy, and may thus put a limit on such efforts.

The level of complexity that can be reached very much depends on the type of energy that can be harvested. In this respect, US historian Joseph Tainter and coauthors make a distinction between two types of available energy, high-gain and low-gain energy. While emphasizing that these are, in fact, the ends of a continuum of available energy, high-gain energy is a concentrated energy resource that can be harvested relatively easily, while a low-gain energy resource is not very concentrated and thus requires more of an effort to be exploited. In other words, for high-gain energy the return on investment is relatively high, while the opposite is the case for low-gain energy.

The resulting general pattern is simple. As soon as living creatures gain access to concentrated high-gain energy resources, they can achieve levels of greater complexity. Yet such a situation usually does not last very long. After a while, most organisms have to return to exploiting less concentrated, low-gain energy, which costs more to harvest and, in its turn, constrains the level of complexity that can be achieved. According to these authors, this pattern can be found in both biological and human history.[11]

The emergence of more complex life forms was not a quick and easy process and, as a result, such changes occurred only occasionally. Like the emergence of life itself, which would have happened only rarely, if not once, the emergence of more complex life was an exceptional event. The bewildering variety of different complex species that have emerged during biological evolution appears to contradict this common heritage, yet all these seemingly very different organisms share only a few basic *baupläne*, general structural regimes, with the aid of which all species are constructed. This means that all these very different complex life forms are descended from a very small number of complex biological species (which, in their turn, share a last common ancestor).

Through mutual interactions, the evolving geological processes and the broadening range of living organisms jointly began to shape the surface of our planet and, in doing so, produced ever-changing and ever more intricate Goldilocks circumstances on the face of Earth. Biologists call such circumstances 'niches' when they are occupied by one single species, while the term 'biome' is used when these areas comprise larger regions within which many different organisms are making a living.

The first scientist who systematically defined Goldilocks circumstances for plants and animals was Alexander von Humboldt. His boundary conditions include areas that share the same average temperature, air pressure or other factors that allow specific species to thrive.[12] Although very few people are aware of von Humboldt's pioneering work today, many of the Goldilocks circumstances he defined are still in use. They form, for instance, the basis of all weather reports, while they are also widely employed in the current discussion about climate change.

Whereas all life forms are surrounded by an ever-changing natural world, inside their cells they have maintained relatively stable dynamic steady-state regimes. Apparently, all life forms have learned to maintain Goldilocks circumstances within their cells, which are remarkably similar all throughout living nature. While simple cells mostly have a spheroid shape, the cells of more complex organisms have differentiated into a great many forms. Because cells are relatively small, and because many of them live suspended in, or surrounded by, water, they are not shaped by gravity but rather by the electromagnetic force. The molecules that make up the outer layers of cells attract each other through their electrical charges and cause surface tension, which tends to produce the smallest possible surface. And because the smallest surface containing the largest possible body is a sphere, single cells tend to assume such forms. Because gravity does not play a major role in shaping cells, their interiors could become very complex. Yet as soon as cells began to agglomerate into larger complexes, they became increasingly affected by gravity. As a result, the largest plants and animals today are not found on land but in the oceans, where buoyancy counteracts gravity.

Throughout biological evolution, all organisms that have survived for a reasonable period of time have been seeking to improve their intake of matter and energy, or at least not let it deteriorate.[13] Such an attitude is helpful for surviving the lean times when food is scarce. It may well be that as a result of the process of non-random elimination, this attitude has to some extent become hardwired in the genes. Yet if a species harvested far too much matter and energy, it depleted its surrounding environment. This may have undermined its own existence, which may have led to its extinction. It may therefore be the case that over the course of time, most, if not all, species were selected to harvest a little more matter and energy than what they actually needed, but not too much. If so, this makes one wonder whether humans are similarly hardwired.

Planetary Energy Flows and Life

The history of the major energy flows on the surface of planet Earth over the past 4 billion years can be summarized as follows. Slowly but surely, the geothermal energy flow from within Earth decreased. This came as a result of the dissipation of the original accretion heat into the universe, while also the radiogenic heat released by nuclear decay declined. The solar energy from outside, by contrast, increased by about 25 per cent.

During the early period, geothermal heat would have reached the surface of Earth almost everywhere with similar intensity. This means that there would not have been any great differences between the equatorial regions and the poles. Yet while the inner Earth began to cool down, solar radiation became stronger. Because of the fact that our planet is a sphere, solar radiation is the strongest in the tropics, while it is the weakest near the poles. As a consequence of the decreasing heat flow from within and the increasing solar energy flow from outside, the temperature gradients on the surface of Earth became larger, which must have strengthened wind and water currents from the equator to the poles and back. The cooling down of Earth also led to a differentiation of the Earth's crust into areas that were geologically active as well as regions that were more stable.

The geothermal energy flows set in motion the process of plate tectonics: large sections of the Earth's crust that are continually moving as a result of mantle convection. Atmospheric scientists Thomas Graedel and Paul Crutzen summarized its history as follows:[14]

> Although the evidence is sketchy, it is currently believed that tectonics has proceeded in three stages. The first was in operation from about 3.8 to 2.6 Gyr BP [1 Gyr = 1 billion years], during which time the heat flow from radioactivity was several times greater than its present value. This higher heat flow produced a less dense, more buoyant lithosphere, with vigorous convection, little subduction, and many relatively small plates that collided frequently. In the second tectonic stage, occurring between about 2.6 and 1.3 Gyr BP, a gradual decrease in heat flow resulted in the development of a few larger plates, but with too little difference between the densities and buoyancies of oceanic and continental crust to provide substantial tectonic activity. Finally, during the most recent 1.3 Gyr, the decrease in buoyancies of the oceanic crust relative to continental crust resulted in a gradual transition to the processes of modern plate tectonics, with crust subduction and regeneration.

As a result of plate tectonics, the land area has steadily become larger over the course of time, while the oceans have decreased in size.[15] Yet even today,

Figure 5.1: Earth as seen by the astronauts of Apollo 17. The effects of geothermal and solar energy are clearly visible, including the shape of the continents and the location of deserts, which contribute to define the Goldilocks circumstances for life. (Source: NASA.)

the oceans form about 70 per cent of the Earth's surface, thus leaving only about 30 per cent for all the land masses. Seen from space, our planet looks therefore like a mostly wet globe, as shown in Figure 5.1. The growth of the continents over the aeons must have improved the Goldilocks circumstances for land-locked species.

The decreasing geothermal flow would have diminished both the numbers and the activity of black smokers, thereby reducing the survival chances of the oceanic life that depended on their matter and energy flows. At the same time, life began to use the increasing energy flows from outside. This shift in the energy extraction by life mirroring the changing energy balance on Earth's surface may have been coincidental. Whatever the case may turn out to be, it is remarkable that life appears to have been following the energy flows during its history.

Specific numbers characterizing these changes in energy flows are very hard to find, if they exist at all. As a result, I found it impossible to answer even very basic questions. One would like to know, for instance, what the rates of change have been over the past 4.5 billion years of both the Earth's interior heat emission and the solar energy reaching the Earth's surface. Were these linear processes, or did perhaps spurts and slow-downs occur from time to time? One would also like to know what the curve looks like for the power densities characterizing the Earth's surface, beginning with a value unknown to me and 'ending' with 60×10^{-4} watt/kg today. As a result, most of what follows here cannot yet be expressed in numbers.

The Gaia Hypothesis

When life began to develop on Earth, inanimate and biological nature increasingly influenced each another. The first pioneering studies of these interactions were performed in the early twentieth century by Russian scientist Vladimir Vernadsky. But only since the 1980s have biologists and geologists begun to explore this idea systematically. In science, this approach is now known as 'System Earth.'[16]

The impact of early life must have been rather limited. Yet as life developed, it became increasingly influential. This happened in a series of waves. The first wave took place perhaps as long as 2 billion years ago, when the first free oxygen appeared in the atmosphere that was produced by life. The second wave occurred around 540 million years ago, when complex life forms proliferated. The third wave happened from about 400 million years ago, when complex life moved onto land. Ever since that time, all geological processes on the surface of the entire Earth were affected by life. It would, for instance, have facilitated the erosion of rocks by 'eating' them, or by keeping loose soil together with the aid of microbial mats.[17] These are just a few examples of the influence life has exerted on the Earth's surface. Surprisingly, perhaps, life may even have influenced plate tectonics. Surface water, possibly kept on Earth by life, may have lubricated the moving plates, thus making plate tectonics possible. Our planet's deeper interior, by contrast, would have remained the exclusive domain of inanimate processes undisturbed by life.

In the 1980s, while considering some of these effects, British scientist James Lovelock made a radical suggestion, namely that life not only influenced the face of Earth but also created and maintained planetary Goldilocks circumstances that favored its own survival. Most notably, this included a temperature regulation regime that allowed liquid water, vital for life, to have existed on the Earth's surface for more than 3 billion years, notwithstanding the fact that the sun's energy output would have risen by 25 per cent during the same period. Lovelock called the idea of life creating and maintaining the conditions needed for its own survival the 'Gaia hypothesis.' Gaia is the name of the ancient Greek earth goddess.

To evaluate the hypothesis that life may have contributed to water remaining liquid, we first need to know how scientists explain the fact that there is still water on the Earth's surface after such a long period of cosmic exposure. First of all, the Earth's distance from the sun is just right. Had our planet been situated closer to our central star, all of its water would have evaporated into space long ago. Earth also has the right size, which means that its gravity is strong enough to retain surface water.

Water molecules circulate through the atmosphere as a result of evaporation. As water molecules rise high up in the atmosphere, they may split up into their constituent chemical elements, hydrogen and oxygen, under the influence of sunlight. Whereas the much heavier oxygen either remains in the atmosphere or is captured on the Earth's surface, the hydrogen tends to escape into space, because it is so light that Earth's gravity cannot retain it. As long as there was little or no free oxygen in the atmosphere that could capture hydrogen before it escaped into the cosmos, this process would have continued unhindered. However, after all the available materials on the Earth's surface, mostly iron, had combined with the free oxygen, it began to appear in the atmosphere in sizable quantities. As soon as this happened, the free oxygen would have captured most of the free hydrogen by forming water molecules again, thus slowing down the loss of hydrogen. Over the course of time, this process would have helped to retain water on Earth, while it also contributed to the emergence of oxygen in the atmosphere.

There is a second process, this time mediated by life, that produced an oxygen-rich atmosphere, and thus helped to capture hydrogen atoms before they escaped into space. With the aid of sunlight, certain life forms learned to split up carbon dioxide molecules and combine the resulting carbon atoms with water, thus forming a great variety of organic molecules, part of which became buried in the Earth's crust. The leftover oxygen was emitted as a waste product. Like the oxygen produced by the dissociation of water molecules under the influence of sunlight, the oxygen produced by life began to build up in the atmosphere after the materials on the Earth's surface had become saturated with it.

Both processes led to the emergence of free oxygen in the atmosphere. As yet it is not clear which process would have contributed more: the physical process of the splitting up of water by sunlight or the dissociation of carbon dioxide by life with the aid of sunlight and water. Nonetheless, all Earth scientists agree that starting from about 2 billion years ago, life has greatly contributed to producing an oxygen-rich atmosphere and, in doing so, has helped to retain water on the Earth's surface. In addition, comets raining down on Earth throughout its entire history may have added considerable amounts of water, thus replenishing water that was lost as a result of hydrogen escaping into space.

These mechanisms explain why there is still water on our home planet, but they do not explain why most of the water is liquid instead of frozen or gaseous. As Lovelock has pointed out, this question is urgent because over the past 4.5 billion years the solar radiation would have become about 25 per cent stronger. Yet during this period, with ups and downs the Earth's surface has actually exhibited a cooling trend. According to Lovelock's hypothesis, this was caused by the fact that life has changed the conditions on the Earth's surface in ways that brought about the cooling process, first of all by sharply reducing the earlier high levels of carbon dioxide in the atmosphere. This lowered the greenhouse effect that this gas causes, which led to the cooling of Earth during the period when the sun's energy output was increasing. In the second place, life may, for instance, have stimulated increased cloud cover and more rainfall, both leading to global cooling.[18]

The idea that life could produce Goldilocks circumstances of the Earth's surface for its own benefit may not seem very plausible, for how would all these different life forms have been able to jointly create such a planetary regime with the aid of Darwinian evolution, a process that supposedly acts on individuals? As I see it, the answer may be surprisingly simple. This might have happened as a result of the non-random elimination of all those species that had spoilt their own Goldilocks circumstances. In other words, those organisms that made their own niche unlivable would automatically have eliminated themselves. The same process would have favored the survival of all those organisms that improved their living conditions or at least kept them sufficiently favorable. The improvement of Goldilocks circumstances for one species might, of course, have led to the deterioration of such circumstances for other species. If such a situation negatively impacted the species that caused these changes, it would, of course, have been eliminated also. But if not, such a process would automatically have led to positive feedback mechanisms that created Goldilocks circumstances for all the surviving species.

There is some evidence for feedback mechanisms creating or maintaining Goldilocks circumstances that operate well beyond the range of specific species. In 2006, for instance, Russian scientists Anastassia Makarieva and Victor Gorshkov proposed the so-called biotic pump theory. The central idea is that natural forests evaporate a great deal of water, which subsequently condenses in the air above the forests and becomes thinner. This lower pressure 'sucks in' moist air from the ocean that produces the needed rain. In this way, forests contribute to creating or maintaining their own watery Goldilocks circumstances. In another example, Russian paleontologist Alexander Markow suggested in 2009 that a more diverse ecosystem is more likely to contain biological genera that live for longer periods of time. The greater biodiversity tends to stabilize such an ecosystem, which, as a result, offers better conditions for long-term survival. This works as long as no new organisms appear that suddenly reduce the biodiversity by eating it.

If Lovelock's Gaia hypothesis is correct, the development of Gaia must have been a dynamic process with many trials and errors, which will continue as long as there is life on this planet. It is therefore not surprising, as US biologist David Ramp has emphasized, that today more than 99 per cent of all species have gone extinct. This would have happened, because all those species did not survive the onslaught of the ever-changing circumstances.[19] To be sure, the five large mass extinctions also wiped out enormous amounts of species. Yet in the long run and with ups and downs, this process must have produced a population of organisms that did not undermine their own Goldilocks circumstances too much during short periods of time, while they perhaps even improved them. Such a population of good Goldilockians is, of course, never stable. Newcomers armed with powerful innovations may upset these balances time and again, thus producing new extinctions.

Seen in this way, a self-regulating Gaia would be the inevitable result of Darwinian evolution. The remarkable similarity between life creating Goldilocks conditions within its cells and Gaia doing a similar thing on a planetary scale may not be coincidental. It may turn out to be that all successful long-living species need to have a built-in tendency to create long-term Goldilocks circumstances for themselves. All of this makes one wonder what humanity is currently doing to Earth. Not very surprisingly, this is one of Lovelock's major concerns.[20] We will return to this issue at the end of our story.

While the gentle but persistent actions of life have profoundly changed geological processes on the Earth's surface, the powerful forces of geology have, of course, also deeply influenced both biological evolution and human history. For instance, the process of plate tectonics produced changes in ocean currents, which subsequently influenced the global climate. Mountain formation led to increasing geographic differences on land, thus facilitating a greater biodiversity, while it also altered wind and rain patterns, thereby creating a wide range of microclimates. The fault lines separating tectonic plates are often places where rare minerals can be found, which were brought to the surface through the process of plate tectonics. Almost needless to say, the uneven distribution of such resources, most notably gold and silver, has decisively influenced human history.

The Emergence of Energy Harvesting
from Outside

During the earliest phase of biological history, all organisms consisted of single cells that fed on whatever matter and energy flows happened to reach them. The modern representatives of such cells are known as 'prokaryotes,' cells without nuclei. At a certain point in evolution, however, some single cells began to cooperate by clinging together, thus forming larger structures. In this way, the famous stromatolites formed, which consist of large conglomerates of cells that live in shallow sea water. The fossilized remains of ancient stromatolites date back to about 3.4 billion years ago, while some of their close family members are still alive today in Shark Bay on the west coast of Australia. Apparently, the strategy of clinging together has allowed the stromatolites to live in areas with Goldilocks circumstances for billions of years. Until today, clinging together is a strategy pursued by many organisms, ranging from bacteria to humans, usually for defending themselves against other life forms.[21]

The microorganisms that jointly formed the ancient stromatolites were perhaps similar to the modern cyanobacteria that make up today's stromatolites. If so, these ancient microbes were able to capture sunlight and use it for constructing new forms of complexity. This process is known as 'photosynthesis.' This would mean that around 3.4 billion years ago, some organisms had freed themselves from their dependence on geothermal matter and energy from within Earth and had started harvesting solar energy from outside. Dutch scientist Frank Niele calls this new way of obtaining energy the 'phototrophic (light feeding) regime.'[22]

This was a major step in biological evolution. Because this new strategy came at the expense of creating new forms of complexity within themselves that were able to harvest sunlight, there must have been some advantages in doing so. First of all, the process of photosynthesis allowed stromatolites to position themselves on the interface between the atmosphere, the land and the ocean, thus harvesting the steepest available energy gradients. This freed them from their dependence on the black smokers, which, by that time, would have been diminishing both in numbers and in activity. At the same time, one may suspect that all the organisms that depended on black smokers would have multiplied, thus leading to an increasingly severe competition for matter and energy. As a result, there would have been a survival premium for any organism that evolved ways to exploit new matter and energy flows.

The innovation of harvesting energy flows in the form of photosynthesis led to what biologists call a 'speciation event,' which was followed by an adaptive radiation: the appearance of a range of new species that subsequently occupy new niches. This is a very general evolutionary mechanism that can, of course, only take place when the innovation helps the organism to harvest matter and energy in better ways and thus preserve its complexity. According to Dutch paleontologist John de Vos, this mechanism operates not only in biological evolution but also in human history.[23] Thanks to the innovation of photosynthesis, such microorganisms multiplied in numbers while differentiating into an increasing range of species.

As a result of the unceasing activities of these new life forms, increasing amounts of oxygen were dumped into the atmosphere. At the same time, the levels of free carbon dioxide in the atmosphere went down, because life began to convert this gas increasingly into organic substances as part of the same process of photosynthesis. For a long time, the atmospheric oxygen rapidly combined with soluble iron in the oceans to form insoluble iron compounds, many of which still exist in the form of large bands of iron oxides. These bands currently provide our major sources of iron. After most of the soluble iron had become bonded, there were no other chemicals left on the surface of Earth that could bind oxygen in large quantities. Since that time, about 2 billion years ago, sizable amounts of oxygen began to accumulate in the atmosphere or were dissolved in the oceans. In addition, the naturally occurring process of the dissociation of water high in the atmosphere under the influence of sunlight also contributed to the rise of free oxygen. Remarkably, during the same period, the process of plate tectonics began to create clearly demarcated landmasses and oceans for the first time in Earth's history. This may have been a coincidence.

Thanks to the energetic activities of the ancient cyanobacteria, a piggy bank of solar energy began to accumulate on Earth. The solar-powered metabolism of living organisms became namely so effective in creating biomass that it left substantial energy deposits in the Earth's crust in the form of the oldest petroleum reserves, which are known as 'Proterozoic oil deposits.' The Proterozoic is the geological period that stretched between 2.5 billion years and 550 million years ago. These oil fields, the oldest of which would date back to about 1.3 billion years ago, can be found in many places, including Canada, the Middle East, Russia and Australia.[24]

For many organisms, the rise of free oxygen in the atmosphere and the oceans was a disaster, because oxygen was a poison for them. Such life forms either went extinct or found refuge in places such as the deep seas or far underground, where the oxygen concentration was low enough for them to survive. For other organisms, however, this growing supply of free energy provided new Goldilocks circumstances. They began to use the oxygen for the internal combustion of organic substances. The improved efficiency of internal combustion with the aid of free oxygen is impressive. This so-called aerobic respiration releases about 16 times as much energy as combustion without oxygen (anaerobic respiration). As a result, the innovation of aerobic respiration provided these organisms with an enormous advantage. This led to a large adaptive radiation all across the Earth's surface. It was in this way that the process of photosynthesis began to power most of life. The price these organisms had to pay was a greater molecular complexity, which may have made them more vulnerable.

The rise of an oxygen-rich atmosphere favored the emergence of larger and more complex cells. About 2 billion years ago, the first cells emerged that began to specialize in certain functions, such as photosynthesis or energy metabolism, while they subsequently fused into larger cells. In this way, new and larger cells emerged, which consisted of a greater variety of more complex building blocks and connections, thus making possible greater overall complexity. This development can be described as the emergence of an intra-cellular division of labor.

These so-called eukaryotic cells (cells with a clear nucleus) began to contain a great deal more genetic information in their nucleus. Specific organelles called 'mitochondria' specialized in energy metabolism; while in some cells organelles called 'chloroplasts' devoted themselves to capturing sunlight and using it for manufacturing biochemical compounds. The chloroplasts would have been descended from cyanobacteria that fused with eukaryotic cells and subsequently lost their autonomous functions. A similar fusion would have taken place with the ancestors of mitochondria, which, in all likelihood, were single cells that specialized in aerobic respiration.

Like the older cyanobacteria, all the new eukaryotic cells that contained chloroplasts no longer depended on the matter and energy flows from inside Earth. They could instead capture solar radiation and use it for producing biomolecules. In doing so, these organisms became dependent on a different set of Goldilocks circumstances. They needed to stay close enough to the surface of the oceans to capture enough sunlight, but not so close that the sunlight would destroy them. The innovation of photosynthesis led to adaptive radiations of both prokaryotic and eukaryotic cells into a growing number of species that were able to use different wavelengths of sunlight under a number of different conditions.

At a certain point in time, eukaryotic cells learned to pool their genetic resources during reproduction. This was the beginning of sexual reproduction as we know it today. A major advantage of this reproductive mechanism is that it allows faster genetic change, which, in its turn, facilitates survival during periods of rapid environmental change, including shifting competition for resources by other living species. No one knows when the first forms of sexual reproduction emerged. This monumental event in biological history would have taken place more than 600 million years ago, well before the spurt toward greater complexity described in the next section.[25]

The Emergence of the Biological Food Web

Between 575 and 540 million years ago – a period of a mere 35 million years – life suddenly became more complex. A wide range of large multicellular organisms emerged that were endowed with an amazing variety of organs. This was the beginning of complex life as we know it today. All these organisms consisted of groups of eukaryotic cells that specialized in performing functions for the entire organism, such as mouths, digestive tracts, brains, eyes and legs or fins.[26]

Apparently, for such organisms the cost of maintaining greater complexity was rewarded by better chances for survival and reproduction. Seen in this light, the emergence of complexity was a survival strategy for some species, but not for all, in which the benefits of harvesting sufficient matter and energy as well as the construction of Goldilocks circumstances in the form of sufficient means of defense against others outweighed the expense of creating and maintaining all these new forms of complexity.

As soon as more complex organisms had emerged, there was usually no way back. Only rarely have life forms become less complex. And if that happened, such species did so within very special Goldilocks circumstances, such as dark caves, in which eyes, for instance, were less useful, and were lost as a result. But there are no cases known to me of complex organisms that spontaneously dissociated into their constituent cells, which subsequently lived and reproduced independently.

A situation of constrained development along a certain path with no way back is known as 'path dependency.' This phenomenon is not unique for complex life. To the contrary, the concept of path dependency can be applied all throughout big history. As we saw earlier, stars, planets and galaxies can be interpreted as cosmic structures that develop along certain lines, because they are constrained by external and internal circumstances, such as their mass, size and neighbors. One can even argue that the history of the universe as a whole is constrained by a path dependency that is defined by the specific values of the natural constants, which allow only certain types of complexity to emerge. Had the force of gravity been much stronger, for example, or electromagnetism much weaker, the cosmos would have looked very different.

Let us return to the emergence of complex life. Complex life forms cannot spontaneously fall apart anymore and continue to live as independent single cells, because by joining forces while forming a complex organism, all these cells became specialized and mutually dependent. The emergence of complex life can, therefore, be described as the emergence of an inter-cellular division of labor. Because prokaryotic cells have never been observed to form such complex organisms, the intra-cellular division of labor of eukaryotic cells must have been an absolute precondition for the emergence of the inter-cellular division of labor. The emergence of complex organisms became possible thanks to the emergence of free oxygen in the atmosphere and the water. This oxygen could be transported to cells that were not in direct contact with the outside world and would otherwise not have survived. In doing so, such cells could make use of the more efficient aerobic metabolism.

The fact that the genomes of eukaryotic cells are considerably larger than those of their prokaryotic cousins may well have played an important role in the development of multicellular life. The more DNA a cell contains, the more information it has at its disposal that can code for greater complexity. And the more complex cells become, the more information they need to keep themselves organized. Whereas in principle each eukaryotic cell contains the entire genetic program of its overall organism, complex life forms use only a limited part of this genetic information for constructing the specialized cells, while making sure that only those genes are activated that are needed for making that particular type of cell. In doing so, interlinked groups of eukaryotic cells could become ever more specialized, and thus ever more versatile.

There were two major spurts in biological evolution that led to greater multicellular complexity. The first spurt is known as the 'Ediacaran,' which is named after the Ediacara Hills of South Australia, where the oldest such fossils were found. The Ediacaran organisms all had soft bodies, while bones or shells were entirely lacking. This period lasted between 575 and 542 million years ago. The second spurt took place about 540 million years ago and consisted of the emergence of a range of complex organisms with bones and hard shells. This period is known as the 'Cambrian explosion of life forms,' because of the rapidity of its emergence. It is named after Wales (Cumbria), where these fossils were first discovered. The Cambrian fossils represent all the *baupläne*, structural designs, which exist in modern complex organisms, plus a number of designs that did not make it into the present. It is not clear how the Ediacaran and Cambrian species are related. It appears as if during the Cambrian explosion most of the larger Ediacaran species had already gone extinct, while some of the smaller Ediacaran organisms may have evolved into Cambrian species.[27]

The selective pressure that drove these two spurts consisted of the new opportunities it offered for improving the harvesting and use of matter and energy. As a consequence, both the Ediacaran and the Cambrian developments led to a widening range of new life forms with increasingly intricate shapes. Yet at the same time, a great many organisms, mostly prokaryotes, but also some eukaryotes, remained small and comparatively simple. Apparently, within their specific Goldilocks niches they were able to keep harvesting sufficient amounts of matter and energy. As a result of these developments, the tree of life differentiated into a widening range of simple and more complex organisms.

Seen from a big history perspective, here we witness a major difference between physical and biological regimes. Whereas all complex life forms exhibit a clear differentiation of form and function within themselves, physical regimes, such as stars, planets or galaxies, can undergo a differentiation of form but not of function. To say, for instance, that individual stars fulfill the function of keeping the entire galaxy together does not make any sense to me. Yet for complex life forms, it makes perfect sense to wonder which functions organs such as hands fulfill for keeping the entire organism going.

As part of these developments, the first plants and animals emerged. All the major differences between plants and animals are related to the ways in which they harvest matter and energy, which produced their specific path dependencies. Virtually all plants are autotrophic (self-feeding) organisms, because they are able to extract their needed energy from sunlight and the required matter from their inanimate environment. With a few exceptions, plants do not eat other organisms. Specific plant organs, usually leaves, are actively extracting solar energy. The leaves tend to position themselves in ways that are the most favorable for capturing the right amount of sunlight, while their photosynthetic mechanisms are continuously fine-tuned. Other plant organs dig into the soil or float around in water to extract the required matter, while the roots also provide structural stability. For many plants, especially landlocked species, a structure was needed for connecting the solar-energy-capturing organs and the matter-gathering organs. As a result of these basic requirements, almost all plants share very similar baupläne. Because plants do not need to move and catch prey, they lack intricate brains. They would find it hard to move anyway, because capturing solar energy usually requires large surfaces. And because solar radiation is an energy source that consists only of photons and not of matter, plants produce comparatively little material entropy. In doing so, modern plants became able to handle power densities of about 0.09 watt/kg.

Animals, by contrast, extract their energy and matter from other life forms, from either plants or other animals. In doing so, animals harvest concentrated forms of high-gain chemical energy stored in bio-molecules. They do so at the price of maintaining expensive brains, muscles and digestive tracts, which jointly produce considerable amounts of material entropy. Animals use the captured energy for themselves in a constructive way, while they became increasingly destructive for the unlucky species that were eaten. Because animals needed to find plants or catch other animals, they developed ways of purposefully moving around, including eyes, brains and legs or fins. They also needed weapons to defeat their prey, as well as suitable digestive tracts to extract the desired matter and energy. As a result, many animals needed ever better offensive and defensive strategies. Also plants began to defend themselves against predators, for instance by producing toxins. All of this signaled the beginning of a biological arms race, the end of which is not yet in sight. In addition to plants and animals, fungi, microorganisms and viruses emerged. Fungi live off dead plant and animal remains, while predatory microorganisms and viruses began to extract their matter and energy from other living organisms, plants, animals and other microorganisms.

All these developments can be summarized as the emergence of an increasingly complex food web, within which growing numbers of organisms became dependent on others for harvesting matter and energy flows. Whereas plants and microorganisms harvested their matter and energy from inanimate nature, the animals and microorganisms that preyed on them jointly created an ever more complex structure of eating and being eaten. As a result of this development, life learned to use the solar energy captured by plants and microorganisms ever more efficiently. The emergence of this complex food web entailed an entirely new and ever more varied regime of Goldilocks circumstances, within which an increasing variety of matter and energy flows were exploited.

Over the course of time, the food web became a food pyramid. At the bottom, there are a great many different plants and microorganisms, which are eaten by considerably smaller numbers of animals, which, in their turn, are eaten by relatively few predators. At each step, a great deal of high-quality energy is converted into low-quality energy, which represents an increase in entropy. Some of this high-quality energy is concentrated in the form of chemical compounds, such as fats and meat, that may not always contain more energy per weight, but are a great deal easier to digest than most of the carbohydrates produced by plants. Because such high-quality energy sources are scarce, higher up the food pyramid fewer animals can make a living. The tiny single-cell microorganisms that tap matter and energy flows from all a great many different organisms, by contrast, usually operate in large numbers.

As a result of their greater complexity, one would expect the power densities of animals to be higher than those of plants. And, sure enough, the power densities of modern animals are in the order of 2 watt/kg, while plants only reach 0.09 watt/kg on average. It would be interesting to investigate this subject in more detail in terms of a historical process. Although a great deal of work has been done on quantifying matter and energy flows as well as energy conversions within specific portions of the food web, a historical analysis of the food web in terms of energy flows during all of biological evolution appears to be still lacking.

By producing more complexity, life also generated more waste (entropy). Whereas low-level heat could be radiated out into the universe, the rest of life's material garbage in the form of excrements of various kinds as well as dead bodies, remained on Earth. The physical processes of chemical oxidation, sedimentation and plate tectonics all facilitated the recycling of a considerable portion of this waste. But most of it was taken care of by scavenging life forms, for whom the material entropy produced by other organisms could still be used as food. In doing so, life and Earth jointly created their own waste disposal regime. This regime must have been an absolute precondition for the continued existence of life on this planet, because without it, life would have choked in its own waste products a long time ago.

One may wonder whether life possibly emerged elsewhere in the universe, only to find itself being poisoned by its own waste. As I see it, the emergence of a biological waste-recycling regime is an integral part of the Gaia hypothesis, namely life creating and maintaining Goldilocks circumstances needed for its survival. Here, we see again a major difference between life and lifeless nature. Although the universe as a whole functions as a gigantic entropy trash can, galaxies, stars or lifeless planets have never evolved any garbage solutions of their own.

The Emergence of Multicellular Organisms

It appears as if the Ediacaran adaptive radiation event and the Cambrian explosion of life forms were both caused by sudden changes of Goldilocks circumstances. Only 5 million years before the Ediacaran era began, the Earth's surface emerged from a deep freeze that had lasted about 60 million years. This intensely cold period is known as 'Snowball Earth,' because during that time most of our planet's surface would have been frozen over. Although during Snowball Earth no life would have existed yet on land, the cold would have severely restricted even the opportunities for oceanic life. After the big thaw began for unknown reasons, an enormous niche would suddenly have opened up for the lucky survivors. This led to the innovation of the intercellular division of labor and its subsequent adaptive radiation.[28]

In fact, Snowball Earth would have consisted of at least two, and perhaps as many as four, waves of cold periods interspersed with warmer times. According to atmospheric scientists Thomas Graedel and Paul Crutzen:[29]

[T]he earliest verifiable glacial epoch (but not necessarily the earliest glacial epoch that occurred) is at about 2700–2300 Myr BP. [Myr = million years BP] The glaciation appears to have been extensive, although the supporting record is quite fragmentary. Its cause is uncertain; it may have been a consequence of rather low solar luminosity, of the presence of significant landmasses to reflect radiation, and of low concentrations of greenhouse gases, although these speculations are not supported by evidence.

Following the glaciation (at about the junction of the Archean and Proterozoic time periods), Earth was apparently warm and devoid of permanent snow or ice for 1000 Myr or so. The second known glaciation occurred at about 950 Myr BP, and two others followed at about 820–730 Myr BP and 640–580 Myr BP. The late Precambrian was a major period of mountain building on Earth, and the glaciations may have been related to tectonic motions and continental disruption.

It thus appears that between 3 and 2 billion years ago, when the landmasses began to form and free oxygen appeared in the atmosphere, the first cold period set in. This makes one wonder about the possible role of the atmospheric oxygen, and thus also of life, in cooling the planet. The rise of free oxygen as a result of photosynthesis must have gone hand in hand with a decrease of atmospheric carbon dioxide, which was converted into bio-molecules, thus lowering a possible greenhouse effect that these molecules caused. Furthermore, free oxygen may have combined with atmospheric methane (a very powerful greenhouse gas) to produce carbon dioxide (which is a far less powerful greenhouse gas) and water. This may also have lowered the surface temperatures. Moreover, the emerging ozone layer in the stratosphere that formed out of free oxygen in the atmosphere under the influence of sunlight began to protect life in shallow sea water. This allowed such organisms to live closer to the surface and thus harvest more sunlight, which, in its turn, would have led to the production of more oxygen. And last but perhaps not least, it cannot be excluded that the emergence of eukaryotic life might also have contributed to this climatic change, for instance by producing more oxygen.[30]

US scientist Alex Pavlov and colleagues suggested in 2005 that there may also have been a cosmic cause for Snowball Earth, namely interstellar hydrogen gas and dust floating around in the Milky Way in large quantities.[31] During the 230 million years that it takes for our solar system to complete a single orbit around the galactic center, Earth would have encountered eight of these clouds. The influx of such materials would have blocked as much sunlight as the outpourings from three volcanic eruptions a year, but it would have lasted a great deal longer. The overall effect would have been Snowball Earth.

Clearly, the last word has not yet been spoken about the question of why Earth turned into a snowball during this period. But equally clearly, all the authors look for answers in terms of energy flows and Goldilocks circumstances. The same is the case for the question of why Earth did not remain frozen. Some scientists suggest that a temporary increase of volcanism would have heated up the Earth's surface. Alternatively, the process of plate tectonics would have moved the continents to places that favored a warmer Earth. Whatever the case may have been, the end of Snowball Earth would have led to a sudden rise of oxygen in the oceans as a result of increasing biological activity, thereby providing abundant fuel for multicellular innovations. This would explain why both the Ediacaran and Cambrian adaptive radiations occurred.

For as far as we know, these processes were unique in biological evolution. After the Cambrian explosion of life forms had taken place, the circumstances never became Goldilockian anymore for new *baupläne* to emerge, because such new creatures would have been eaten immediately by the already established animals before they could have evolved any suitable defense mechanisms. Apparently, the Cambrian survivors enjoyed what can be called an 'unbeatable head start.' As we will see below, the emergence of an unbeatable head start is a more general phenomenon in both biological and human evolution. This mechanism may also explain why all known life forms appear to have been descended from one single ancestor.[32]

The Emergence of Brains and Consciousness

The emergence of animals with brains and consciousness was a monumental transition in big history, which eventually led to animals able to contemplate the history of everything. In general, brains opened up the possibility of creating images of the world, and of oneself, within a three-dimensional structure of intensely interconnected neuron cells. Brains also allow those species that have them to analyze situations, make plans, as well as reach decisions on the preferred course of action. Furthermore, by steering organs such as tails, fins or limbs, species equipped with brains are able to make bodies move intentionally and achieve results that are completely out of reach for organisms that do not possess such data-processing organs. And last but not least, with the aid of memory such species are able to learn from their experiences and try to do things in novel ways.

The emergence of brains and consciousness is still poorly understood, even though many studies have been devoted to this issue.[33] In 2005, however, Dutch biochemist Karel van Dam came up with a surprisingly simple model that may help to explain these things.[34] His model begins with the generally accepted idea that at a certain point in time, single cells emerged equipped with a sensor that was able to detect food or danger. These cells also sported one or more little tails, with the aid of which they could either swim away from, or move toward, the detected source, depending on whether they liked it. As soon as sensor and tail became interconnected, a novel mechanism was in place for the microorganisms that possessed such organs to undergo a specific process of non-random elimination, for there must have been a survival premium for organisms that were able to do such things better. Furthermore, such microorganisms were able to learn (defined as the modification of behavior based on experience) by storing information of past events and using it for determined action. US biologist Daniel Koshland Jr. formulated this in 1980 as follows:[35]

> Bacteria do not have a long-term memory because they have no need for a long memory span. The average bacterium lives for several hours. It has no occasion to remember the contents of yesterday's newspaper or the names of its children. Since it is stripped for survival in an incredibly competitive world, it carries no unnecessary genes. Its memory time, however, is clearly optimized by evolution. It is short, because it must remember only its recent past, and it is not too short because it needs accuracy to assess chemical gradients.

Now what would happen, van Dam wondered, if such microorganisms evolved two sensors that were both connected to one tail, especially if these two sensors gave off different signals about where to go? One would expect that a more elaborate connection would emerge between the sensors and the tail able to make decisions about what action to take. To do so effectively, an image would need to be created of the situation as perceived by the sensors, with the aid of which such decisions could be taken. As soon as that had happened, living things were able to form a more detached image of the surrounding world for the first time in biological history. It was more detached, because there would have been some time for reflection on what course of action to take between the incoming stimulus and the subsequent reaction. This image would have been the first form of consciousness. Ever since that time, any change in such an image-forming regime that improved the harvesting of matter and energy favored the long-term survival of that species.[36] This would have included the storing of data in a rudimentary memory bank, as well as better control over organs that made the organism move into the desired direction.

According to Karel van Dam, multicellular organisms may have developed along similar lines. A few cells that served as sensors would have become connected to other cells that were able to process information and send commands to a tail. As soon as such a situation was in place, multicellular complexes would have evolved brains, map making and consciousness, as well as controlled behavior – ultimately leading to organisms such as you and me. As long as such images and their effects on the organism's emerging behavior improved its survival and reproductive chances, there must have been a positive reward on achieving reasonably reality-congruent images of the outside world.

Over the course of time, living organisms evolved an ever-widening range of sensors, with the aid of which they learned to navigate almost every nook and cranny on the surface of Earth. Yet only human beings have been able to develop instruments that not only enhanced their own sensors but also unlocked portions of the electromagnetic spectrum, most notably infrared and ultraviolet radiation from the lowest to the highest frequencies, that had not been accessible before to any other species.

The Increase and Expansion of Biological Complexity

Ever since the Cambrian explosion of life forms, the rise and demise of countless complex species could be witnessed, all of which were surrounded by a great many simple organisms. Most, if not all of these organisms were interlinked within an intricate food web. Although during this period a great many smaller innovations emerged that were followed by adaptive radiations, only a few major innovations led to fundamentally new organisms. The story of biological evolution is therefore extremely complex in its details, yet rather simple from a general point of view.[37]

Biological evolution has proceeded with a great many ups and downs. Most notably, there have been five major extinction events, some of which wiped out up to 90 per cent of all species, only to make room for new ones. The reasons for these mass extinctions are not yet well understood. Current explanations range from internal causes, including the collapse of food chains, to external causes such as sudden strong volcanic activity, plate tectonics producing ever-changing shapes of continents and oceans, the impacts of meteorites and even the effects of nearby supernovae. Whatever may have caused the mass extinctions, over the course of time life has always bounced back into a similar regime consisting of a spectrum of organisms ranging from the very simple to the very complex, from microorganisms to plants and animals, while the overall trend has been toward more complex plants and animals.

After the Cambrian explosion of life forms took place, more complex organisms have never emerged anymore out of microorganisms. Apparently, ever since that time selective pressures have been operating that kept small organisms simple. For many already complex plants and animals, by contrast, increasing complexity has been a good survival strategy, even though it was more expensive to maintain it.[38]

Over the past 500 million years, the process of plate tectonics has been slowing down while volcanic activity gradually became less intense. The movements of the tectonic plates exhibited certain regularities. Driven by energy emanating from the Earth's interior, all of the landmasses have joined at least three times, thus forming one large supercontinent and one large ocean, only to subsequently break up again.[39] The oldest known supercontinent is called 'Rodinia.' It existed between approximately 1.1 billion and 750 million years ago. Between 600 and 540 million years ago, the supercontinent of Pannotia existed, which was followed by the most recent supercontinent of Pangea. This enormous landmass existed in continuous form between 250 and 170 million years ago.[40]

For landlocked organisms living on such moving panels, this had far-reaching consequences. During the eras in which all the continents had joined, they could move around freely and interbreed for as long as they belonged to the same species. Yet as soon as the supercontinent broke into pieces again, many of them found themselves increasingly isolated, which led to the emergence of new species and even new genera. The formation of one large landmass would have been unfavorable for marine species living in shallow sea water, because these areas had dramatically decreased in size during such a supercontinental period. The process of plate tectonics also exerted incisive effects on other aspects of the geography including the climate, all of which must have influenced biological evolution.

Over billions of years, the solar output increased. Yet the Earth's climate did not heat up accordingly, but appears to have fluctuated as a result of the combined effects of plate tectonics, the Milanković cycles and the effects of life. The orbit of our solar system around the galactic center may also have led to more or less regular cosmic influences on Earth's climate, while the occasional impacts of large celestial bodies on our home planet and the possible explosions of nearby supernovae might also have changed the surface of our home planet. Furthermore, as a result of tidal friction Earth's rotation slowed down, which led to longer days and nights. All the animals that had developed biological clocks that were fine-tuned to this planetary rhythm must have felt a pressure to adapt. Seen from a general point of view, time and again, the story of life is the story of energy flows through matter within specific Goldilocks circumstances leading to the emergence and decline of countless forms of complexity.

Conquest of the Land

Until about 400 million years ago, all complex organisms by necessity lived in the oceans, which protected them against the strong ultraviolet solar radiation. The growing amounts of free oxygen in the atmosphere led, however, to the emergence of an ozone layer in the stratosphere that began to protect life against ultraviolet radiation. It is unclear when the stratospheric ozone layer would have become sufficiently thick to protect any adventurous land invaders.

Around 400 million years ago, some plants had left the cradle of their protective oceanic surroundings and began to colonize the entire planet. They were soon followed by animals. More likely than not, however, these intrepid species had been preceded by a great many microorganisms for an unknown period of time. These tiny life forms may have left only a few traces in the geological record, if any.

This was not an easy transition. According to US biologists James Gould and William Keeton:[41]

> Most of the problems of living on land relate to the need for copious amounts of water. Water is much more important for plants than for other organisms. For example, plants depend on obtaining raw materials – light, carbon dioxide gas, fixed nitrogen, minerals, and so on – which are normally very dilute. As a result, plants have evolved an enormous surface-to-volume ratio, which maximizes the area available to gather light and nutrients.

As a result, plants evaporate enormous amounts of water that need to be replenished. Although very important, the availability of water was only one of the problems organisms had to contend with when they began to live on land. Most notably, they needed to protect themselves against the (still) harmful effects of sunlight while trying to find sufficient amounts of matter and energy to keep their complexity going. For similar reasons, animals found this transition difficult also. As a result, both land plants and animals had to evolve space suits that could guarantee Goldilocks circumstances not only for themselves but also for their tender progeny. While plants evolved hard seeds for this purpose, animals began to lay eggs with hard shells, which provided watery Goldilocks circumstances for the unborn on land. It was only much later that the innovation evolved of keeping embryos within one's own body, which made hard-shelled eggs superfluous.

Because these innovations were expensive in terms of matter and energy, there must have been a payoff too. First of all, the amount of solar radiation that can be captured on land is larger than in the oceans. As a result, the new landlubbers could harvest more energy than their aquatic cousins. In the second place, by going on land organisms could escape the presumably fierce competition in the water. As a result of these advantages, life spread almost all over the Earth's surface, limited only by lack of water and temperatures that were either too low or too high.

The emergence of an oxygen-rich atmosphere allowed fires to burn for the first time in Earth's history. But for as long as there was no life on land, there was nothing that could catch fire (some occasional dried-up lakes filled with dead biomass perhaps excepted). In other words, fires could only begin to burn after sufficient amounts of combustible biomass had accumulated in dry places. Over the subsequent 400 million years, fires have changed according to the circumstances. During the Carboniferous and the Permian periods (between 360 and 248 million years ago), the percentage of free oxygen in the atmosphere would have gone up to as high as 35 per cent, making possible giant life forms, and probably also giant fires. The oxygen content could not go up any further, because that would have led to spontaneous combustion. This negative feed-back loop led to a process of spontaneous self-regulation, which limited the percentage of free oxygen in the atmosphere. After that exuberant period had come to an end, the oxygen percentage would have stabilized at around 21 per cent for the past 150 million years.[42]

During the Devonian and Carboniferous (408–290 million years ago), a great deal of dead biomass accumulated. At that time, massive warm swamps existed in which forests grew. When the plants and trees died, they were buried in the acidic waters and were subsequently often covered with sediments. This produced the coal fields that would later fuel the industrial revolution. After the Carboniferous had come to an end, however, far fewer such large-scale accumulations of biomass took place. Usually, this decline is attributed to the far colder conditions caused by the emergence of the supercontinent Pangea, which created unfavorable conditions for the existence of large, warm forest swamps. Yet I wonder whether this change was perhaps also related to the emergence of animals in the subsequent Permian (290–248 million years ago) that could eat plants more effectively, because they had developed specialized digestive tracts.[43] Before that time, animals and microorganisms had only been able to digest plants that had already died. The enormous petroleum reserves of the Middle East, by contrast, were presumably formed around 150 million years ago from the bodies of marine organisms that thrived in warm shallow seas.[44]

Further Increasing Complexity

Although life kept evolving during the subsequent 300 million years, these developments can hardly be called spectacular compared to the Cambrian explosion of life forms. On the Earth's surface, the Goldilocks circumstances kept fluctuating, while perhaps exhibiting a long-term cooling trend. The general pattern of biological evolution, however, did not change. A widening range of species was punctuated over time by some larger, as well as a great many smaller, extinction events.

Yet within this general pattern, smaller innovations often led to adaptive radiations. For instance, the emergence of nectar-producing flowers made the sexual exchange of genes possible at a lower cost, because this did not depend anymore on producing large amounts of wind-born pollen, only a small amount of which would reach other plants. It depended instead on far smaller amounts of pollen that were selectively transported from plant to plant by specific insects, which profited from the nectar the plants offered in return. Apparently it was cheaper, and more effective, for plants to produce nectar than large amounts of pollen. Similarly, the emergence of fruits attracted animals, which, by eating them, helped to spread the seeds more efficiently via their digestive tracts. All these developments produced a great many interdependencies between flora and fauna. Such innovations leading to adaptive radiations took place all across Earth, thus producing an ever-changing population of life forms.

During this period, a good many plants and animals learned to create, or adapt to, local and regional Goldilocks circumstances in ways that favored their own survival. Some plants, for instance, occur in such great numbers that predators find it almost impossible to completely overwhelm them. Alexander von Humboldt, and in his wake Charles Darwin, called such species therefore 'social plants.'[45] The reader may recall that the strategy of hanging together to improve one's survival chances was earlier employed by the cyanobacteria while joining to form stromatolites. Some animals followed a similar strategy by forming large herds. This stimulated processes of natural selection in which the weakest, most vulnerable, individuals were nonrandomly eliminated. Large assemblies of plants, animals and microorganisms jointly created entire biomes such as savannas, forests, tundras and coral reefs, all characterized by specific Goldilocks circumstances. Plants also created Goldilocks circumstances for themselves, for instance by dropping leaves, thereby producing humus in the soil that favored their continued existence. Also many animals, including insects, learned to actively construct Goldilocks circumstances. A few familiar examples include birds building nests, rabbits digging holes and ants and bees constructing their complex dwellings.

During this process, the brains of some animals became larger and more complex. Because brains are very expensive energy-wise, there must have been an advantage to possess them, namely the ability to harvest matter and energy more effectively while avoiding becoming someone else's food. In other words, brainy animals would have become better at both finding food and defending themselves.

The types of food that animals eat determine their development to a considerable extent. Animals that consume plants have access to food that is often comparatively easy to find. Yet it is often relatively low in energy content and hard to digest. As a result, large browsers have to eat large amounts of such food. Finding these resources may not be very difficult, but such animals usually need to move around and follow the plants for an all-year-round exploitation. For their defense, they rely on numbers and on speed, as well as on weapons such as horns and hooves. This is a major reason why such animals live in herds. As a result, they needed brains that helped them perform all these tasks, including the development of a social order.

Predators, by contrast, eat high-quality food in terms of easily digestible matter and energy. This type of food may be difficult to catch. In consequence, predators needed high speed, strength, excellent body coordination and effective weapons such as sharp teeth. Because their food is hard to catch, large predators often prefer to operate alone or in small groups. They usually do not need any additional defensive weapons, because their weapons of attack also help them to ward off threats from other animals. All of this posed limits on the possibilities for predators to become social animals.

Around 200 million years ago, warm-blooded animals would have emerged that were able to maintain their own body temperature. In doing so, they could maintain the speed of their own biochemical reactions at a steady rate, also when the temperature of the environment varied. This came at the expense of a considerably higher energy consumption. Warm-bloodedness was especially important for animals with larger brains, because a complex nervous system requires a rather constant body temperature.[46] It is not certain when the characteristic of warm bloodedness emerged. Some biologists even think that a few dinosaurs, of whom there were a great many at the time, were already warm blooded, and that over the course of time both birds and mammals were descended from them.

Between 200 and 63 million years ago, the dinosaurs reigned supreme, after which the impact of an asteroid would have ended their dominance on the face of Earth by causing a 'nuclear winter.' Large volcanic eruptions that took place more or less simultaneously in India, which produced large outflows of lava now known as the 'Deccan traps,' may also have contributed to the dinosaurs' demise by causing a similar global effect. In fact, one may wonder whether the famous asteroid impact on the edge of what is now the peninsula of Yucatán may have made the Earth's mantle tremble so hard that it triggered volcanic eruptions on the other side of Earth. Whatever the case may have been, because the surviving early mammals were warm blooded, they may have been better able to survive the ensuing colder circumstances than cold-blooded animals.[47]

Thanks to these new Goldilocks circumstances, which mammals maintained within themselves, warm-blooded animals with relatively large brains subsequently spread to many parts of the world with widely varying circumstances. In doing so, some of these animals developed even larger brains. In the next two chapters we will see how one such species succeeded in placing itself on top of the food pyramid and came to dominate the world.

6

EARLY HUMAN HISTORY

The Emergence of the Greatest Known Complexity

Introduction

An account of human history written with the Earthrise view in mind offers a perspective on our common past that is different from the established narratives. Most academic histories start somewhere between 6,000 and 5,000 years ago, when the oldest known written records were produced. The preliterate period, called 'prehistory,' is considered to be the domain of archaeologists and palaeo-anthropologists. However, just like the long early phase of biological evolution, during which many important developments took place, the long early phase of human history, which began around 4 million years ago, also showed major developments, most notably the change from the genetic and behavioral make up of ape-like creatures into patterns that are characteristic of modern humans. This chapter will deal with these changes, while the past 10,000 years of human history will be considered in chapter seven.[1]

The history of our species has been profoundly influenced by the prevailing natural circumstances, which include the ever-changing configurations of the landmasses and the oceans; climatic change; the availability of fresh water; the habitats of specific plants, animals and microorganisms; the nature of the land, including soils, mineral resources, mountains or flat lands, rivers, the proximity of seas and oceans, earthquakes and volcanic eruptions and last, but probably not least, meteorite impacts and perhaps even supernovae events. All these characteristics, and perhaps a good many more, may exhibit more or less regular patterns. Whereas many of these aspects have not always been beneficial to human complexity, none of them has undermined it completely until today.

Over the course of time, humans have learned to create, manipulate and exploit a great many natural circumstances to their own benefit. In doing so, they have created ever more intricate regimes of Goldilocks circumstances, which have, so far, ensured human survival and reproduction. As a result, human history represents a fundamentally new phase in biological evolution. For during the entire history of life, no other organism has existed that has changed the face of Earth in such profound ways within such a short period of time. Humans have been able to do so thanks to their unprecedented ability to process, store and transmit enormous amounts of information. This process is known as 'culture.' Whereas many animals exhibit forms of cultural learning, only humans have used it to such a large extent for shaping both their own history and the surrounding natural environment. For this reason, humans may well be the most complex adaptive species to have emerged on our planet.

What Makes Humans Different

The biological basis for the human ability to create unprecedented amounts of complexity is to be found in the fact that we are the most brain-endowed animals that have inhabited this planet so far. It is probably no coincidence that animals possessing the characteristics of both plant-eaters and predators developed the biggest and most complex brains per body weight and came to dominate the world. The major difference between ourselves and our closest cousins, the chimpanzees, is the fact that in relation to body size, our brains are about three times as large as those of the great apes, while our brains also appear to be more intricate. The development of the human brain may have been stimulated by a great many unrelated geological and biological changes, yet the general evolutionary trend was toward a species with a larger and more complex brain.

Our brain consists of enormous numbers of cells that are interconnected in such intricate ways that scientists still do not know the details of how they work together. Far more than any other animal brain, human brains facilitate map-making and communication, as well as the coordination and adaptation of behavior. As a result, large and complex brains allow humans to become a great deal better at harvesting matter and energy, as well as at creating unprecedented forms of complexity, including changing the prevailing circumstances into forms that were perceived to be more favorable.[2]

The disadvantage of having a large brain is that it guzzles up a great deal of energy. On average, the power density of the human brain amounts to a whopping 15 watt/kg, while the overall power density of human bodies is only about 2 watt/kg.[3] As US neuro-scientists Pierre Magistretti, Luc Pellerin and Jean-Luc Martin formulated it:[4]

> Although the brain represents only 2% of the body weight, it receives 15% of the cardiac output, 20% of total body oxygen consumption, and 25% of total body glucose utilization. With a global blood flow of 57 ml/100 g min, the brain extracts approximately 50% of oxygen and 10% of glucose from the arterial blood.

This prodigious energy consumption must have had a significant advantage. If not, large brains would have been eliminated nonrandomly a long time ago. Yet, while their brains became larger, humans multiplied, notwithstanding the fact that our species never possessed major biological weapons such as horns, hooves or venom. Apparently, until today the amounts of matter and energy that humans have been able to harvest thanks to their larger and more complex brains have outweighed the increased consumption of resources by their brains.

The major strength of brains is that they run complex software that can in principle be adapted quickly, according to the circumstances. This makes brainy animals far more flexible and adaptive, and thus far more effective, than other organisms. In contrast to the dominant mechanism for adaptation in biological evolution, in which change comes as a result of genetic variation, humans do it by changing their image of the surrounding world – called culture – and by adjusting their behavior accordingly. In other words, thanks to culture humans do not have to wait for the emergence of spontaneous genetic change that may help the lucky individuals survive the changing circumstances, while all the others go extinct. Humans only need to change their behavior, not their genes.

To be effective, cultural software must be shared with other people, including the next generation. Any increasing effectiveness of brains must, therefore, have gone hand in hand with improvements in communication. A few years ago, David Christian introduced the term 'collective learning' for characterizing this process. In Christian's view, collective learning operates for humans similarly to the ways natural selection (non-random elimination) has functioned in biological history, while the speed of cultural learning depends critically on both the number of interconnected people and the number of connections.[5]

Collective learning is not a uniquely human characteristic. Many other animals, including monkeys and apes, exhibit forms of cultural learning. The quality of this learning is still being assessed by researchers. Long-term historical developments in collective learning among other animals are virtually unknown for lack of evidence.[6] Yet it appears as if humans have undergone much more complex cultural learning processes. This may be related to the fact that while a great many young animals tend to copy the behavior of adults, grown-up animals have never been observed to actively teach the next generation in other species. Apparently, among humans the transmission of collective knowledge to the next generation is achieved more effectively.

In biological evolution, the emergence of the genetic language stored in the genome opened up the possibility of genetic disinformation. Likewise in human history, the improving quality of symbolic languages made possible the emergence of ever more powerful forms of symbolic disinformation. This would have made trust in each another, or the lack of it, a major theme in human history, especially if it concerned important aspects of life such as the preservation of one's personal complexity, the harvesting of sufficient matter and energy and the creation or maintenance of Goldilocks circumstances.

Over the course of time, the processes of cultural learning must inevitably have led to a process I will call 'cultural forgetting.' Not every form of knowledge that was once shared among groups of people has reached the present day. To the contrary, over the aeons, an unfathomable amount of collective knowledge has been lost. Had this not been the case, it would have been easier to reconstruct human history, because we would have virtually endless amounts of details at our disposal. Our major problem would then have been not to become overwhelmed by the available data.

During most of early human history, culture was probably mostly stored in human brains. As long as humans could not write or produce other abstract material symbols with the aid of which knowledge could be summarized, stored and conveyed effectively, there were severe limits on the amount of information people could accumulate as well as on its reliability, while there would have been a high premium on keeping information as simple as possible. It is therefore not surprising that in maps, mental or otherwise, major characteristics are emphasized at the expense of the details. The better brains became at doing so, the more effective they would be.

As soon as people began to produce tools and, much later, art, some information was stored in external objects on how to make them and what they might mean. But such information was always ambiguous, because its interpretation very much depended on the presence of people able to explain how such tools were made and what they were used for. As a result, we are still guessing at what early tools were used for as well as what early art forms might have meant for the people who produced them, even when such drawings, often animals, are very recognizable.

It was only when people began to write, and even more so when printing was invented, that ideas no longer needed to be stored in brains, but could instead be recorded elsewhere relatively faithfully. This freed up storage space within brains, while it made exchanges of information a great deal easier. These developments led, therefore, to an explosion of collective learning, especially when people became more numerous and better interconnected. More recently, the technology of computer data storage and exchange have caused similar explosions in collective learning. All these evolutionary steps have allowed humans to become better at harvesting matter and energy, as well as at constructing complexity and Goldilocks circumstances. Furthermore, as a result of the improving ways of recording and storing information, the process of cultural forgetting has declined, although it has not disappeared.

Energy and Complexity

Over the course of time, humans have constructed unprecedented amounts of complexity, ranging from very simple tools to large computerized factories. In this sense, humans are not entirely unique. A great many animals also create forms of constructed complexity. Birds build nests, for instance, while beavers make dams, rabbits dig holes, bees construct hives, ants build nests and spiders weave webs. This type of behavior is known in biology as 'niche construction.'[7] Those species that engage in niche construction subsequently become adapted to those circumstances, especially if these conditions continue to exist over many generations. A major difference between the ways in which humans and other animals construct complexity is that animals only very rarely, if at all, use elaborate tools for making things. Humans learned to make and use tools thanks to the fact that their upright stride freed their hands which, in its turn, made possible an unprecedented coordination between their stereoscopic eyes, evolving brains and ever more dexterous hands.

Not only are humans unique in the sense that they began to use an ever-widening tool set, we are also the only species on this planet that has constructed forms of complexity that use external energy sources: most notably a great many machines, but also sailing vessels, for instance. This was a fundamental new development, for which there were no precedents in big history. This capacity may first have emerged between 1.5 and 0.5 million years ago, when humans began to control fire. From at least 50,000 years ago, some of the energy stored in air and water flows was used for navigation and, much later, also for powering the first machines. Around 10,000 years ago, humans learned to cultivate plants and tame animals and thus control these important matter and energy flows. Very soon, they also learned to use animal muscle power. About 250 years ago, fossil fuels began to be used on a large scale for powering machines of many different kinds, thereby creating the virtually unlimited amounts of constructed complexity that we are familiar with today.

For as long as humans and animals used only their own muscle power for constructing forms of complexity, the required energy flowed through their own bodies. Yet this energy was not used to create or maintain more body complexity. Instead, it was used for the construction of a great many types of external complexity. Seen from a general point of view, the production of external complexity can be seen as so many attempts at creating Goldilocks circumstances that favor the maintenance of one's personal complexity.

During human history, the direct energy used for maintaining bodily complexity may have fluctuated between 2 and 5 watt/kg. A more limited consumption on a structural basis would have led to the decline, if not demise of human body complexity, because 2 watt/kg is the minimum amount of energy needed to maintain our own complexity. A much larger intake than 5 watt/kg would have had a similar effect, because it would destroy our bodies also after a certain amount of time. The energy used for constructing, maintaining or destroying complexity, by contrast, has ranged from very little during early human history to the enormous amounts consumed today. For lack of reliable data, it is difficult, if not impossible, to estimate the power densities of complexity created by humans during their history. Even a crude attempt at determining such values would constitute an entire research program very much along the lines pioneered by von Humboldt.

During human history, the efficiency with which energy and other resources have been used may have exhibited certain trends. Using large amounts of energy does not necessarily lead to the creation or maintenance of a great deal of complexity. For instance, early steam engines, internal combustion engines and jet engines were not very efficient. Yet over the course of time, their efficiencies increased. It may be that, with large ups and downs, human history as a whole can be similarly characterized as a process of increasing energy efficiency. More likely than not, the efficiency of using natural resources became a major consideration as soon as they were perceived to be scarce.

Many scholars have interpreted culture in terms of collective efforts at solving problems of daily life.[8] All of these problems involve energy. US geologist M. King Hubbert, who gained worldwide fame for his controversial, yet correct, prediction in 1956 of peak oil production in the United States at around 1970, formulated this as follows:[9]

> Since energy is an essential ingredient in all terrestrial activity, organic and inorganic, it follows that the evolution of human culture must also be a history of man's increasing ability to control and manipulate energy.

Such an approach to human history may not be popular among historians and social scientists. Certainly, human behavior is far more complex and varied than just harnessing matter and energy. Yet it cannot be denied that like all other life forms, humans are unable to escape the consequences of the second law of thermodynamics. If we want to prevent our bodily complexity as well as all the complexity that we have created from descending into chaos, we must keep harvesting matter and energy flows on a regular basis. This is the bottom line of human history. I will therefore argue that during most, if not all, of human history, the quest for sufficient matter and energy to survive and reproduce within certain Goldilocks circumstances has been the overriding theme. Whatever other plans human beings may have sought to execute during their history, if these plans did not take into account their ceaseless struggle against entropy, they were doomed to fail.[10]

All human actions have inevitably produced waste, in other words, entropy. While the low-level radiation produced by human activity was easily radiated out into space, a legacy of material disorder began to accumulate on the surface of Earth over the course of human history. This may have started very modestly with, for instance, leftover rubbish resulting from the production of flint tools. Yet increasing human activities must have gone hand in hand with the growth of material entropy in the natural environment produced by human action.

The Emergence of Early Humans

Depending on what one would call early humans, it may be fair to say that human history began about 4 million years ago. During the first 2 million years, humans had to adapt themselves to the ever-changing environment to survive, while their abilities to adapt the landscape to their own benefit were limited. Yet from about 2 million years ago until the present day, humans have increasingly learned to harvest matter and energy more effectively, as well as to adapt ever greater portions of the surrounding natural environment to their own desires. In doing so, humans have often sought to change the prevailing circumstances into situations that resembled the Goldilocks circumstances within which they had first emerged. This general strategy has allowed our species to spread around the world and do all the things humans do today.

The first early humans emerged on the savannas of East Africa. This landscape was, and still is, characterized by a rather mild climate. All year round, the temperatures would have ranged between 20 and 30 degrees Celsius. This did not differ a great deal from the average human body temperature, yet it was low enough to allow the early humans to get rid of their excess heat. As a result, our earliest ancestors would not have needed protection against high or low temperatures in the form of body hair, which they may have lost as a result. Also the air pressure on the East African savannas is rather mild, on average about 900 hectopascal. As a result, there was enough oxygen in the air for a great many physical efforts, such as running over longer distances. British geographer I. G. Simmons characterized the living areas of early humans as follows:[11]

> On a large scale, they share all the characteristics of a savanna environment, with open as well as wooded vegetation and alternating wet and dry seasons. At more local scales it appears that most of the sites were at the interface between open and closed vegetation, whether along a lakeshore or a stream or a sinkhole; further, the sites were located amongst complex mosaics of environmental types, thus enhancing the variety of resources which were available.

In this situation, the ancient folk would have needed an average power density of about 2 watt/kg, because that was enough to keep their bodies going.[12]

According to the modern scientific view, our species owes its emergence to circumstances that were uniquely characteristic of East Africa, while they did not occur in any other place where great apes lived. During this period, for reasons not yet well understood, the African continent was becoming drier and colder. This climatological change had profound effects on the African flora and fauna. The tropical forests were retreating on both the eastern and western sides of Central Africa and were being replaced by savannas. As a result, the forest-dwelling species found themselves increasingly under pressure to adapt to a new life on grasslands interspersed with trees.

Among many larger species, including early humans, as well as antelopes and other herbivores, this led to the development of stiffer legs. While elastic legs are better for moving around in forests, stiffer legs are superior for living on grasslands, because they allow individuals to run faster and cover longer distances. During this period, many species that found themselves on the savannas developed stiffer legs and underwent adaptive radiations. Yet only among early humans did this lead to bipedalism: an upright way of walking. During the subsequent period of adaptive radiation, a whole range of early humans emerged.[13]

These developments were part of an even longer-term climate change. About 55 million years ago during the Eocene period, the climate and vegetation would have been warm all across Earth, despite vast differences in latitude and longitude. Subsequently, a long-term irregular cooling trend set in, causing both an increasing aridity and a thinning vegetation in Africa. This long-term climatic gradient over time was partially caused by plate tectonics. The African plate kept moving north, where it met the Eurasian plate. This collision shut down the connection between the Atlantic Ocean and the Indian Ocean, and caused a massive rearrangement of matter and energy flows all across the Earth's surface. Other geographic changes also took place, such as the collision of the Indian subcontinent with the rest of Asia, which led to the formation of the Himalayas. All these developments combined would have contributed to the long-term cooling and drying trend.[14]

As a result, the Goldilocks circumstances for life on the Earth's surface differentiated into a regime of increasingly diverse climatic zones. Warm and wet areas became increasingly restricted to the tropics, deserts shifted location, temperate zones emerged and even areas began to emerge that were covered by ice all-year round. These changing geographic circumstances led to increasing matter and energy flows from the tropics to the poles in the form of wind and water currents. These conditions also favored, for instance, the emergence of large grasslands, on which increasing numbers of large grazers and their predators made a living. This long-term ecological change in both space and time eventually produced the Goldilocks circumstances within which early humans emerged.

Plate tectonics may have played an additional role in driving early human evolution. During the period in which climate change led to a shift from woodlands to savannas, plate tectonics produced an East-West divide in Africa as a result of the splitting-up of its continental plate into two pieces. The resulting fault line linking the Nile, Rift and Zambezi valleys began to form an ecological barrier, separating East Africa from Central Africa. This development will eventually lead to the breakup of the African continent. Although a great many species could cross this 'barrier' and thus remained part of single gene pool, other organisms could not.

According to Dutch ethologist Adriaan Kortlandt, this ecological barrier prevented early hominids (or apes) on both sides of the great divide from interbreeding, because they could not swim and thus were unable to cross the rivers that emerged in these valleys. When the ecological circumstances began to vary on both sides of this ecological barrier, so did biological evolution, so that in the forests of Central Africa chimpanzees emerged, while on the savannas to the east of the Rift Valley early humans, the so-called Australopithecines, 'southern apes,' began to appear.[15]

These early humans would have walked upright, yet they did not possess larger brains. That would take another 2 million years. The Australopithecines would have fed themselves on whatever they could find, while seeking to avoid becoming a source of matter and energy for the large carnivores that were hunting on the savannas. As far as we know, these early humans did not produce any constructed complexity.

Although the geographic circumstances on the African savannas would have been rather mild, they were not stable. Seen over longer periods of time, they were punctuated by sudden climatic variations that came as a result of the changing configuration of the continents in combination with the Milanković cycles. As a result, the areas where the early humans lived were savannas during some periods, while they reverted back into woodlands during other epochs. This explains why early humans appear to have been adapted to both types of landscapes by developing an all-round gait with stretched, but flexible, legs. Even with stretched legs, it is possible to survive in forests as long as these legs did not become too stiff, or if the forests were not too dense to walk underneath the trees. During the forested periods, instead of swinging around tree branches like their cousins the emerging chimpanzees, the early humans would therefore have made a living on the forest floor.[16]

Improving Social Coordination

The upright stride made possible new forms of coordinated behavior. In his book *Keeping Together in Time* of 1995, William McNeill argues that before early humans could effectively speak with each other, the emerging capacity to move rhythmically together – today very visible in the forms of both dance and drill – may have been important for coordinating their behavior to an extent unknown among other primates. Because moving together in a rhythmical fashion stimulates strongly felt emotions of group identity, it would have allowed more effective social action on a larger scale than had ever been seen before, especially in warfare but also for great variety of other communal tasks. More likely than not, however, such coordinated rhythmic movements would not have produced any further evidence that survived the onslaught of time. It will, therefore, be difficult to assess the merits of this hypothesis, including the question of when this capacity would have emerged. Yet it remains striking, as McNeill observed, that for as far as we know, only humans appear to have acquired this behavior.

Early humans did not possess any natural weapons, such as large sharp teeth, antlers, strong hoofs or venom, to defend themselves against the dangers lurking on the savannas. Neither did they operate in large herds. One wonders, therefore, how early humans survived the threat of being eaten by large predators. To answer this question, Adriaan Kortlandt experimented *in situ* with a little machine driven by an electric motor that could swing a couple of thorny branches around itself. Underneath this machine, he placed a piece of meat, which attracted a few lions. As soon as they approached the meat, the machine would start to spin, which made it hard, if not impossible, to get closer to the meat without getting seriously hurt by the thorny branches. After one of the lions tried to do so anyway and got his nose injured, the lions gave up and retreated.[17] It is, of course, impossible to know whether early humans actually defended themselves in such ways. The research done by Kortlandt only shows that such a strategy might have been effective. However they did it, defending themselves against predators may have been one of the first ways in which our ancestors began to create Goldilocks circumstances that favored their survival. And, if they did so while moving together rhythmically, this type of behavior might have been even more effective.

Between 4 and 2 million years ago, early humans spread all over East Africa, wandering into areas that were ecologically different. It is unclear to what extent these early humans could communicate with each another with the aid of symbolic language. Although all of these early humans would have walked upright, their brains remained relatively small. One wonders, therefore, why after about 2 million years of roaming the East African landscape, some early humans began to develop larger brains.

Tool Making and Brain Growth

The growth of human brains may have been related to increasing tool use. Although humans are not the only animals who use tools, our species has developed this skill to a far greater extent than any other animal. The emergence of tool use was the result of an unprecedented coordination between stereoscopic eyes, brains and limbs, which had first emerged while our human ancestors were still a forest-dwelling species. The upright stride was also very helpful, because it allowed arms and hands to be used for a much wider range of purposes (although it became harder to swing around in trees). As a result, humans learned to perform ever more tasks with their hands, even while walking. Today, by contrast, great apes cannot do this; they have to sit still to execute such tasks. As a result of these developments, early humans slowly became more powerful with respect to other larger animals.[18]

While these early humans would still have relied mostly on gathering during this period, hunting appears to have gained in importance. Apparently, their increasing dexterity allowed early humans to move up the food pyramid. The importance of walking upright for tool use also explains why no other animal has undergone similar developments. For as far as we know, there have been no other brainy animals that began to walk upright while developing agile arms and hands.

Tool making became possible thanks to the improving coordination between stereoscopic eyes, brains, hands and legs. This coordination has allowed humans to accomplish unprecedented results. By throwing and catching things, they could achieve effects at ever greater distances. While humans may have begun by throwing sticks and stones, today they can steer spacecraft accurately across the solar system. The improving eye-brain-limb coordination allowed humans to row and sail boats, ride animals or carts pulled by animals and, much later, steer powered vehicles such as cars, ships, planes and rockets. With the aid of these talents, humans have also learned to manipulate ever smaller amounts of matter with growing precision, of which nano-technology and enormous particle accelerators are recent examples.

Over time, the human ability to change and shape ever larger amounts of matter also increased, more recently most notably in agriculture, mining and construction. Furthermore, the improving eye-brain-limb coordination has led to a great many forms of restrained behavior based on growing foresight and collective learning, in which the desire to achieve anticipated results or avoid unpleasant outcomes has played an increasing role. It must have been very profitable to learn that unpleasant actions, such as the harvesting of matter and energy, may actually yield pleasant results. This type of restrained behavior was a prerequisite for constructing all forms of external complexity as well as for doing things with it.

The oldest known utensils made by human hands are sharp objects made out of flint, which date back to about 2.5 million years ago. We cannot be sure, though, that these objects were the first tools made by humans. Flint tools have survived the onslaught of time because they are so durable. More perishable tools, perhaps made out of wood, will be very hard to find, if they still exist. Furthermore, we may not recognize the possible remnants of earlier tools, because they might be so primitive as to be virtually undistinguishable from naturally occurring materials.

Ancient flint tools are often interpreted as extensions of human teeth, which assisted these inventive humans to harvest matter and energy that were otherwise hard to access. This would have included the cutting of meat and marrow from bones. The sharp points may also have been helpful for defending human complexity. Tool making also improved thanks to the new possibilities offered by human hands, including the emergence of an opposable thumb, which allowed far greater dexterity. In sum, the emergence of tool use heralded the beginning of more effective ways of harvesting matter and energy as well as efforts to create new forms of complexity.

Through tool making, the process of non-random elimination would have stimulated the acquisition of larger brains, better eye-brain-hand coordination as well as the capacity for language and symbolic thought for as long as this facilitated survival and reproduction.[19] A sexual preference for such skills may also have stimulated the emergence of bigger and more versatile brains, especially if such individuals were able to harvest and provide more matter and energy. It may therefore not be coincidental that only 500,000 years after the earliest known tools had been made, a new human species emerged in East Africa called *Homo erectus* (upright man), with a far larger and presumably also more complex brain.

Climate change may also have played an important role in shaping human brains. Around 2.5 million years ago, the cooling and drying trend became stronger as the climatic fluctuations caused by the Milanković cycles deepened. This was the onset of the period of the ice ages, which was perhaps triggered by the joining of South and Central America at what is now the Isthmus of Panama and the concomitant rise of the Andean mountain range. This would have changed ocean currents as well as wind and rain patterns. According to Rick Potts, the emergence of tool making and brain growth would have been stimulated by these sudden climatic swings. In his words:[20]

Humanity evolved in a halting manner as environments became less predictable and more varied from place to place. Deterioration and change in habitats were hallmarks of nature well before our species emerged as a significant ecological factor. The two-legged toolmakers who survived were those able to cope with fitful alterations of their habitat.

The central principle of our evolutionary response is flexibility, the ability to adjust and diversify our behavior, physiology, and overall way of life. In the face of an erratic habitat, no better coping mechanism exists than the ability to modify one's surroundings. The ability to alter is, however, itself a product of nature, of the environments in which human ancestors lived, and the pace of change in these settings. In the end, we – the survivor – have acquired a ponderous capacity to alter our surroundings and, therefore, to mimic the very processes of environmental change that helped to create us.

The early humans would have reacted to these changing circumstances by seeking to improve their tool use to secure sufficient matter and energy flows. As Potts formulated it:[21]

It has occurred to many of us who are curious about the oldest stone tools that the hominids who processed their food partially *outside* of their bodies were the most liberated of all bipeds from the demands of any single type of environment. The new dental opportunities made possible by stone tools meant that the toolmaker could transcend the status code of any single habitat or slice of time. ... I believe that lithic toolmaking persisted as a useful strategy precisely because it enabled the hominids to switch from different resources when the old ones were gone. By chipping rocks, certain hominids discovered a new form of versatility. A heavy stone and a sharp-edged flake meant that a tremendous variety of items could be opened, cut, or crushed. Changes in food supply were handled by making implements capable of processing whatever kinds of food happened to be available. ... Stone flaking afforded a resilient means of obtaining needed resources in the full range of environments.

In sum, the deepening fluctuations of ecological circumstances stimulated early humans to adapt by seeking to change some of these circumstances to their favor with the aid of tools. Any success in doing so would have led to better tool making as well as to brainier humans through the process of non-random elimination. By acquiring increasingly refined and differentiated forms of behavior as a result of brain growth, these evolving humans were able to harvest sufficient matter and energy and, during the lean times, create more constructed complexity, while exercising a growing influence over the surrounding natural environment.

Although the full complexity of the human brain has not yet been unraveled, the physiological basis for their growth and increasing complexity may actually be fairly simple. It has long been noted that young chimpanzees resemble adult humans in terms of the size and shape of their heads as well as in the degree of adaptability of their behavior. Adult chimpanzees, by contrast, have comparatively smaller heads with a different shape, while they are far less able to learn and adapt. In 1918 as a result of such observations, Dutch anatomist Louis Bolk suggested that there may have been a process, which he called 'neoteny,' that puts a premium on conserving childlike features such as larger heads – and thus larger brains – into adulthood. As long as the advantages of adaptability, better learning capabilities and better communication outweigh the disadvantage of having to expend more energy and resources on raising children within a suitable Goldilocks environment, such a process would have taken place.[22]

It is thought that humans have undergone a process of neoteny, which led to the retention of youthful characteristics at a later age. This has allowed our species to learn things for longer periods of time. The price to pay was a growing vulnerability of small infants. While a great many newborn animals, such as horses and antelopes, are able to walk and join their herd very soon after birth, human babies are unable to move around for many months. As a result, humans have to expend considerable efforts on childcare, which must have been an especially important burden as long as they did not live in a single place for a long period of time.

Until very recently, the width of the female human pelvis placed a clear constraint on the head size that infant humans were able to attain and, as a result, the extent to which the process of neoteny could have proceeded. Any increase in width of the female pelvis would also have undergone a positive selection, of course, so one would expect this size to have increased also. Yet today, in wealthy countries, about 20 per cent, if not more, of all children are born with the aid of a caesarean section, which means that for such children this constraint has been eliminated. Under these changed Goldilocks circumstances, one would expect the process of neoteny to speed up again.

Brains and Intestines

The increase in human brain size went hand in hand with decreasing gut size, judged by the reduction in size of early human hips as well as by the fact that modern humans have far shorter intestines than chimpanzees (who have wide hips). At the same time, the overall power densities of humans and great apes are very similar, which means that they use similar amounts of energy per body weight, notwithstanding the fact that humans have bigger, energy-guzzling brains. How could that be?

British natural scientists Leslie Aiello and Peter Wheeler came up with an interesting answer.[23] They reasoned as follows: if larger brains are increasingly expensive in terms of energy usage, what did early humans do to provide this energy? Did they eat more of the same food to get the needed energy, or did they eat different, high-quality, foodstuffs? If they ate more of the same food, they would actually have needed even larger intestines.

Within this context, it is important to know that the power density of gut tissue is actually even larger than that of brains, because it takes a great deal of energy to digest food. According to Aiello and Wheeler, while the brain has a power density of 11.2 watt/kg, the gastrointestinal tract has an even higher value of 12.2 watt/kg.[24] What would be the evolutionary advantage of having a larger brain, if this only added extra costs in terms of additional guts that were needed to keep the brain going?

Yet, in fact, brain growth and gut reduction occurred together. Apparently, the increasing energy consumption of the brain was compensated for by the decreasing energy needs of smaller guts. This could mean only one thing: early humans were no longer able to eat large amounts of food with a relatively low energy content, such as grasses, for which they would have needed large and energy-expensive intestines. Apparently they began to subsist on more high-quality foods that were more easily digestible, such as animal proteins, seeds, nuts and berries. The harvesting of this high-quality food was perhaps the major advantage of having larger brains.[25]

The fact that our ape-like ancestors were unable to live exclusively on a diet of grasses is highly significant. For had our forefathers and -mothers been able to ruminate, they would have needed even larger intestines. As a consequence, they would have had even larger bellies, which would have made it difficult, if not impossible, to achieve an upright stride when the ecological circumstances changed, because their heavy bellies would have needed the support of four legs. This is, in fact, what happened to large grazers, such as horses and antelopes, who also successfully made the transition from woodland species to savanna dwellers during the same period. In other words, human beings developed the way they did at least partially thanks to the type of food our ancestors ate before they changed into early humans.

According to Aiello and Wheeler, there would have been at least two spurts in the process of brain growth and concomitant gut reduction. The first spurt would have taken place about 2 million years ago, when new tools and better gathering and hunting techniques would have allowed people to adopt a diet of high-quality food. During this period, the human teeth, jawbones and muscles controlling them also became smaller. This provides another indication that *Homo erectus* relied increasingly on higher-quality foodstuffs that were easier to chew and digest. As was noted earlier, their tools would have helped them by functioning as an external chewing and digesting apparatus. This innovation made humans more powerful, but also increasingly dependent on their new tool set. The second spurt in gut reduction coincided with the emerging human control over fire, when cooking replaced a considerable part of the digestive labor performed by the intestines. Cooking can also be seen as the externalization of the chewing and digesting apparatus. Fire control, like tool use, made humans extremely dependent on this newly acquired skill.

Fire Control

More than a century ago, Charles Darwin already recognized the importance of fire control for human history, even though fossils of early humans were then still completely unknown.[26] Today, scientists think that *Homo erectus* was the first human species who tamed fire, but it is unknown when they did so. The first concrete evidence dates back to about 790,000 years ago in what is now Israel. Yet fire control may actually have begun a great deal earlier, because the very first traces of such efforts would have disappeared long ago from the face of Earth. Circumstantial evidence of early fire control in Africa may date back to between 1.5 and 1 million years ago.[27]

Human history is intimately intertwined with fire control. As US scientist Stephen Pyne, one of the world's foremost experts on fire in history, formulated it:[28]

> We are fire creatures from an ice age. Our ancestors matured rapidly during the alternating climatic currents that sloshed through the Pleistocene. For more than two million years, the Earth swung between glacial and interglacial, pluvial and interpluvial, between cold and warm, wet and dry. Some places sank under ice and water, others dried and became windblown. Forests and grasslands ebbed back and forth over landscapes like vast tides. These are cycles that, at a faster tempo, favor fire. On the scale of the Pleistocene's long swell they favored a fire creature.

In addition, the long-term drying trend in Africa also would have favored fire control. The energy scientist Frank Niele, calls this stage of human history the 'pyrocultural energy regime.'[29]

Fire control allowed early humans to change a great many circumstances to their favor.[30] Burning the landscape stimulated the growth of certain plant and animal species, while diminishing the survival chances of others. In such ways, the early folk may have changed entire landscapes. Through cooking, roasting and smoking, humans gained access to an ever greater range of foodstuffs, and thus to new sources of matter and energy. While fire control did not allow humans to eat grass stalks, it did help them to digest the seeds of grasses such as wheat, rice and millet, as well as eat a great variety of beans. In doing so, humans turned abundantly available low-quality food resources into high-quality ones. This became especially important much later when humans began to practice agriculture. By becoming chefs of the paleolithic, early humans moved to the top of the food pyramid, while they also gathered considerable amounts of matter and energy from its lower sections.

In addition to culinary progress, fire control offered other advantages as well. Humans kept themselves warm at night by sitting close to campfires, while predators were kept at bay. Furthermore, the light provided by fires would have changed sleeping rhythms. The domestication of fire facilitated large game hunting, as well as the clearing of woods, to provide pasture for game animals. All of this signaled the speeding up of a major new long-term process, during which humans began to adapt the Goldilocks circumstances of the planetary environment to their own desires and designs.

As the hunted became hunters, a growing power difference between early humans and other large predators slowly but surely developed to the advantage of the fire wielders. During this period, only *Homo erectus* survived, while all the other early humans, who did not control fire, disappeared from the terrestrial stage. Dutch sociologist Johan Goudsblom has argued that fire control possibly allowed *Homo erectus* to prevail, either by enabling them to survive the changing ecological circumstances while other, less well-endowed, early humans were unable to do so, or by directly eliminating the other early humans.[31]

When humans began to use fire, they tapped a source of external energy for creating and destroying forms of complexity for the first time in history. As a result, we cannot use the concept of power density anymore, because the energy released by fire did not flow through human bodies. Moreover, it appears very difficult, if not impossible, to estimate how large the amounts of matter were through which this energy did flow. Because we do not know how often early humans set light to savannas or dry bush, or how large these areas were, it is impossible to estimate with any precision how much energy was released by a certain amount of biofuel as a result of early human action. It is possible, though, to estimate the amounts of energy that people used. As a consequence, from now on the term 'energy use per capita' will be used instead of power density.

Dutch environmental scientist Lucas Reijnders estimated that the amount of energy liberated by recent Australian aboriginals as a result of their profligate fire use were one or two orders of magnitude larger than those of the average US citizen in 1997.[32] It may well be that their ancient ancestors were able to release similar amounts of energy. If correct, our forefathers and -mothers may have handled enormous amounts of energy. It is unclear, however, how efficient this early fire use would have been. By burning the land, for instance, a great deal of energy might have been used for creating comparatively little greater complexity, while at the same time it would have destroyed considerable amounts of complexity. Yet such a judgment may depend on one's point of view. The early folk may, in fact, have seen it as the cheapest and most efficient solution to creating desired landscapes.

Fire control must have been a learning process. Because the early fires might easily have gotten out of hand while liberating copious amounts of energy, intended or unintended, such fires might well have destroyed a considerable amount of early human complexity. Perhaps a process of natural and cultural selection may have been operating that nonrandomly eliminated those fire users whose flames got out of hand too often. Yet as a result, the early folk would have learned to harness more energy and, in doing so, would have created more complexity. Furthermore, as Stephen Pyne has argued, growing human fire use would have led to the decrease of readily combustible materials, which would have led to smaller fires.[33]

In 2007, during one of our wonderful academic exchanges, David Christian posed the question of why the greatest known complexity (human societies) emerged on land and not in the oceans. As I see it, first of all, human arms and hands, which are needed to perform all these skills, can develop much more easily from paws or legs than from fins. In the second place, it may be much more difficult to find the right materials for making tools in the oceans than on land. And last but certainly not least, fire control, which has been essential for all the subsequent major energy innovations (most notably agriculture and industry), is not feasible underwater.

As a result, although quite a few intelligent animals live in the seven seas, the oceanic conditions were not Goldilockian for reaching levels of complexity similar to, or exceeding, the levels that humans achieved. In fact, the most intelligent sea creatures, such as dolphins and whales, were all descended from land animals and could successfully compete in aquatic conditions thanks to the intelligence they had gained during their earlier stay on land. While adapting admirably to the oceanic conditions, they were also limited by these circumstances. As a consequence, they could not create levels of constructed complexity similar to those that were invented by landlocked humans.

Migration

As far as we know, *Homo erectus* was the first human species to leave Africa and migrate over large portions of the Eurasian continent.[34] Apparently these early human adventurers were able to adapt to a great many different climatic zones with temperatures ranging between −40 degrees Celsius and +50 degrees Celsius, while harvesting sufficient matter and energy to survive and reproduce successfully for about 1.5 million years. This migration to areas characterized by an increasing variety of ecological circumstances was possible thanks to the increasing level of cultural adaptation *Homo erectus* had been able to achieve. This was the first time that an animal was able to colonize a considerable portion of the face of Earth with the aid of collective learning. In John de Vos's terms, this was the first instance of a cultural adaptive radiation. The major difference between a biological development leading to an adaptive radiation and a cultural innovation leading to a cultural adaptive radiation is that cultural innovations can readily be copied by others without any need for process of genetic exchange, which operates much slower for complex species.[35]

Given the lack of clear evidence (which would be very hard to find), we do not know whether these early world travelers possessed forms of fire control. More likely than not, they did, because this would have allowed them much greater access to matter and energy as well as an improved ability to change prevailing circumstances to their favor. Neither do we know with certainty whether these early migrants made clothes. There is indirect evidence suggesting that from 1.18 million years ago, people would have begun to wear clothes. This is based on the idea that the first clothes would have provided Goldilocks circumstances not only for humans but also for some of their parasites, most notably body lice. According to recent genetic studies, the oldest human body lice would have evolved about 1.18 million years ago.[36] This nicely coincides with the migration of *Homo erectus* into the colder parts of Eurasia, which would have stimulated a greater need for protective clothing.

By covering themselves with artificial skins, early humans would have made it more difficult to get rid of dirt sticking to their bodies. As a result, they might have felt a greater need to cleanse both themselves and their clothes. During human history, it is not at all clear what the standards of cleanliness have been, how often the cleansing actually took place and how effective it was. Yet slowly but surely, certain standards of cleanliness emerged, usually varying greatly both within and among societies, eventually leading to entire social rankings, including the Hindu caste system, which are based on the concept of cleanliness.[37] Such rankings can, in fact, be interpreted as religiously inspired cultural Goldilocks circumstances that were derived from earlier, also artificially created, Goldilocks circumstances.

Both US scientist James Trefil and British astronomer John Barrow have pointed out that modern humans may have been seeking to recreate East African Goldilocks circumstances in many places, as shown in Figure 6.1. While his plane was landing near Albuquerque, New Mexico, Trefil was surprised to see a large grass field in the middle of the desert. Apparently, humans were

Figure 6.1: A human effort to recreate the African savanna elsewhere on the planet, Amsterdam, Westerpark, winter 1995–6. (Photograph by the author.)

attempting to recreate the ecosystem in which their ancestors had evolved in a very different area at great costs.[38] Barrow noted that such landscapes usually sport single trees or small groups of trees, which would also reflect the savanna landscape. To appreciate this observation, we have to look no further than our own backyards, if we are fortunate enough to possess them. More likely than not, we will never know whether *Homo erectus* engaged in similar efforts. Yet it seems likely that any large-scale attempts at burning the landscape, especially wooded areas, would have produced such effects.[39]

Migrating out of Africa also meant moving down the disease gradient.[40] In tropical Africa, where solar radiation powers an extremely diverse ecosystem, a great many infectious diseases exist, some of which depend for their livelihood on at least two types of hosts: humans and other large animals on the one hand, and organisms such as insects, lice or snails that carry them to the big game while they themselves are not adversely affected, on the other hand. This has allowed such disease-causing microorganisms to remain virulent and very dangerous for humans. This situation may well have kept a check on human populations in Africa until very recently, the result being that other plants and animals enjoyed better Goldilocks circumstances. When *Homo erectus* moved to colder climates with less diverse ecosystems, many of these infectious diseases could not follow, because the other hosts they depended on were unable to accompany them. As a result, early human migrants would have left behind these tropical diseases and may have been healthier as a result.

British archaeologists Brian Fagan and Andrew Sherratt suggested that there may have been a large-scale ecological mechanism in operation that pushed people out of North Africa into Eurasia. They called this mechanism of changing Goldilocks circumstances the 'Sahara pump.'[41] During periods of large rainfall and vegetation growth in the Sahara, which produced abundant plant and animal life, people were sucked into the Sahara in search of matter and energy, only to be expelled again when drier times returned. According to Sherratt, 'This was a major engine of population dispersal, propelling hominids across the land-bridge of the Levant to seek their fortune in Eurasia.'[42]

While *Homo erectus* spread to many places in Eurasia, cultural change was still very slow by today's standards. Apparently, there was no strong positive feedback mechanism in place yet that could produce faster cultural change. It is not clear what the limiting factors were. Perhaps their brains and communicative capacities were still too small, while they lived in small bands that were rather isolated from one another. From about 500,000 years ago, cultural change appears to have speeded up a little, which points to a greater positive feedback. This may have been caused by improving brains and means of communication (emerging languages) or denser populations. In terms of complexity, that implied more building blocks as well as more, and more varied, connections between and among the building blocks.

Homo erectus appears to have been a landlocked species. Because these early humans could apparently neither swim over large distances nor navigate the seas, they only populated those areas in Eurasia that could be reached on foot, including islands that became connected to the continent during the ice ages, when the sea level had dropped sufficiently for land bridges to emerge.

The Rise of Modern Humans

It appears that around 200,000 years ago, modern humans, known as *Homo sapiens*, emerged, again presumably in Africa.[43] It is as yet unknown why. Thanks to genetic changes that still need to be elucidated, these modern humans possessed superior language and communication skills, while they were also technologically and artistically gifted. According to John de Vos, the major new development was the precision grip with the opposable thumb, which allowed humans unequaled technical precision.[44] Whatever the importance of the various aspects may be, all of these developments made modern humans potentially much more powerful. Over the course of time, this has allowed our species to harvest and handle enormous matter and energy flows as well as to construct an almost endless range of Goldilocks circumstances. The remarkable similarity of the genomes of our species and of our closest cousins, the chimpanzees, makes scientists think that the emergence of modern humans may have been caused by relatively minor genetic changes that produced large effects.

Around 100,000 years ago, the first members of *Homo sapiens* began to migrate out of Africa. On the land bridge between Africa and Eurasia, the remains of modern humans have been found in Skhul and Qafzeh, in what is now Israel, which date back to that period. By that time, the ability to speak in an elaborate symbolic language may have begun to emerge, which would have facilitated a much more efficient communication. Italian geneticist Luigi Luca Cavalli-Sforza thinks that this was a major factor stimulating the first migration out of Africa.[45] Yet this first wave of human migration into Eurasia may have been short-lived.

A second wave of migration out of Africa appears to have started between 80,000 and 60,000 years ago.[46] This period coincided with the general drying and cooling trend of the Earth's surface as a result of the last ice age. Genetic studies have led to the hypothesis that during this period, the population of early *Homo sapiens* also went through an 'evolutionary bottleneck,' in which its numbers would have been reduced to a mere 10,000 individuals. This population implosion might have been caused by the 'humongous' eruption of the volcano Toba on the island of Sumatra.[47] If correct, this would present another example of a change in ecological circumstances that profoundly influenced human history. This makes one wonder whether the Toba eruption and the general cooling of the climate jointly eliminated those early humans who were unable to survive those miserable conditions, for instance because they were not able to migrate successfully in adverse conditions, or survive otherwise, as a result of their more limited cultural skills.

The worldwide migration of modern humans was an unprecedented achievement, if one thinks of humans as animals, partially because of the range of environments in which humans learned to live, and partially because of the speed with which this process took place. In doing so, humans began to harness matter and energy in almost the entire inhabitable world, including high mountains, where the air pressure was no higher than 600 hectopascal. Such comparatively low air pressure makes it far more difficult to perform daily tasks as a result of the lower oxygen pressure, while it takes twice as long to cook foodstuffs due to the lower boiling temperature of water.

In contrast to *Homo erectus*, modern humans were able to navigate the seas. As early as 50,000 years ago, they reached Australia, while intrepid seafarers from Asia may also have been the first colonizers of the Americas. They might have achieved this either by crossing the Bering Strait or by island hopping, following the island chain that stretches all the way from Asia to the American Pacific west coast. Subsequently, the first explorers of the New World would have followed the coast all the way down to what is now southern Chile. Such a scenario explains, for instance, why some of the oldest evidence of human settlements in the Americas has been found in Southern Chile. For obvious reasons, it must have been a great deal easier to navigate the American Pacific coastline than to walk from Alaska all the way down to the Southern cone of South America. Apparently, by that time humans were able to harness water and wind energy for transporting themselves.[48] Because the sea level rose about 120 meters after the end of the last ice age, most of the evidence for early possible human settlements along the American Pacific coast would be underwater today. Furthermore, some people from Europe and Africa may have reached the Americas during this period by crossing the Atlantic Ocean.

During their expansion into the wider world, some intrepid modern humans must have met earlier humans who had settled and developed there long ago. The best known of these earlier humans were the Neanderthals, who lived in an area stretching from Western Europe to modern Iran, virtually exactly the same area that was later inhabited by so-called Caucasian white people. The Neanderthals would have descended from an earlier human species called *Homo heidelbergensis*, which was a further developed form of *Homo erectus*. The Neanderthals were remarkably sophisticated and are therefore considered to belong to a species known as 'archaic *Homo sapiens*.' The period during which modern *Homo sapiens* met the Neanderthals in Eurasia, between 40,000 and 30,000 years ago, was still part of the last ice age. The Neanderthals were well adapted to these rather frigid Goldilocks circumstances. There is still considerable discussion about the question to what extent *Homo sapiens* had superior biological characteristics as well as cultural skills than the Neanderthals.

At around 30,000 years ago, the Neanderthals went extinct and only *Homo sapiens* survived. The currently dominant academic opinion is that *Homo sapiens* replaced the Neanderthals thanks to their superior skills in a process we would now call 'genocide.' Yet it is considered possible that some modern humans mated with Neanderthals. If this indeed happened, it would mean that some specific Neanderthal genes might still survive in modern populations. The fact that the populations of Neanderthals and later Caucasians show such a remarkable overlap might point to such events. One also wonders about possible encounters elsewhere in Eurasia between *Homo sapiens* and earlier humans. For lack of sufficient research, such questions cannot yet be answered satisfactorily. Yet whatever may have happened during this period, only modern humans remained in most places starting from about after 30,000 years ago, while virtually all earlier humans had disappeared from the planetary stage.[49]

The migration of modern humans into unpopulated areas such as Australia and the Americas may have exhibited some general features. The first migrants would have had a relatively easy time, for as long as there were sufficient matter, energy and Goldilocks circumstances. Yet as soon as a region became settled, further migration into that area would have been more difficult, because the established residents probably did not always welcome newcomers. As a result, later migrants would have had a harder time, unless they possessed superior skills that helped them cross such human-created boundaries. This idea might explain why migration usually took place in waves and not in the form of a continuous stream. Yet such barriers would not have prevented the exchange of people, goods and ideas over shorter distances in the way of trade and exogamy. Over longer periods of time, such transactions would have resulted in the transfer of some of these aspects over longer distances.

It is not clear when the capacity for modern symbolic language evolved. Whereas most anthropologists think that this would have emerged about 40,000 years ago among anatomically modern humans, it cannot be excluded that this took place much earlier. Indeed, the Neanderthals may also have been able to speak in ways that would be recognizable as language today. Whatever the case may have been, the modern human capacity for language and symbolic thinking opened up an unprecedented potential for planning, for social coordination and for action, the limits of which have not yet been reached today. It also allowed for the retention of memories of past events to a far greater extent. In other words, better brains and improving symbolic language led to both more foresight and more hindsight. Over the course of time, symbolic language evolved into forms of writing, first in stone or on clay tablets, later on sheets made of paper or hides and much later in the form of printing and electronic data storage and communication. Every stage was more effective in terms of how many people could be reached, and was also cheaper as a result. The use of symbolic language was often more effective, and thus cheaper, than moving together rhythmically. Until today, however, language has not yet replaced dance and military drill entirely. Apparently there are still situations in which moving together rhythmically offers certain advantages.

Between 30,000 and 10,000 years ago, the human population density was still low in most places. According to British geographer I. G. Simmons, human populations varied from one person per 26 km^2 in fertile areas to one person per 250 km^2 in dry regions such as inner Australia.[50] Because early modern humans had to follow matter and energy flows, most of them would have lived nomadic lifestyles. Only in very resource-rich areas, such as sea shores close to ocean currents, which teemed with marine resources, were people able to settle permanently. Most of these places would now be submerged as a result of the sea-level rise that occurred after the last ice age ended.

The social organization of these nomadic gatherers and hunters appears to have been rather simple. In everyday life, they would have operated as part of family groups, often counting between 25 and 50 people. Such bands may have been part of larger groups, which encompassed perhaps as many as 500 people. Within such a larger social regime, exchanges of many kinds would have taken place at certain times. Depending on the situation, there would have been attempts to keep the population density low. According to Simmons: 'The breeding population of about 175 exercised, many interpreters think, strong population control, killing as many as 15–20 per cent of the children born alive.'[51] In other words, such people would have sought to strictly control the reproduction of their complexity in order not to overstep the boundaries of the prevailing Goldilocks circumstances.

The rise of modern humans may have led to some decrease of the surrounding ecological complexity. First of all, the burning of savannas and forests must have changed their biological composition, thus leading to decreasing numbers of less fortunate species, while at the same time other species may have profited. Because, over the course of the seasons, human fires were often set ablaze at more or less regular times, in contrast to spontaneous combustion, this produced a landscape that was characterized by a more regular low-intensity burning regime. This had an adverse effect on species that needed a good burn to reproduce, while it rewarded species that were better adapted to these more regulated circumstances.[52]

Modern humans may have exterminated some large animals, especially the ones that lived in areas that had never seen humans before, most notably in Australia and the Americas.[53] Yet it is not very clear whether climate change or diseases were also among the root causes of such extinctions. Whatever the case may have been, it remains striking that only a few thousand years after humans moved into these new territories, most of the large animals that lived there disappeared. If correct, this would represent an example of the decline of ecological complexity as a result of human action.

From time to time, sudden changes in the ecological circumstances, including droughts, storms, earthquakes, volcanic eruptions and celestial impacts, would have produced a decrease of human complexity on scales varying from the local to the continental.[54] The most recent large-scale disaster may have happened in North America. In 2007, a team of US researchers suggested that around 12,900 years ago, a comet exploded over North America into a number of giant fireballs, thus ending the so-called Clovis culture, while debris would have settled as far away as Europe. According to US oceanographer James Kennett, immense wildfires scorched North America in the aftermath, killing large populations of humans and mammals. 'The entire continent was on fire,' he says. According to other researchers, however, the climate cooled during that period, thus producing large amounts of dying combustible material, which gave rise to the wildfires. They see no need for a comet explosion.[55]

Early Religion

We do not know anything about the earliest ways in which humans interpreted the world surrounding them and their own position in it. Cave art as well as other artistic expressions, such as the famous 'Venus' statues, offer a few glimpses of what may well have been ancient religious representations, yet these are notoriously hard to interpret. As the skeptical US archaeologist Robert Wenke formulated it:[56]

> Paleolithic art has often been a "Rorschach test," in the sense that modern-day observers have tried to read into it the mind and spirit of primitive humans, but they have perhaps learned more about their own psyches than about the primitives.

Anthropological studies of recent gatherer and hunter societies may offer reasonable models of how our ancestors would have felt and thought about these things. Based on such reports, one suspects that ancient gatherers and hunters would have viewed the surrounding world as imbued with a great many spirits with whom they preferred to stay on friendly terms. In such societies, part-time religious specialists may have operated, the possible forerunners of modern 'shamans.' Such people, often both socially and psychologically very talented, are experts in dealing with the uncertainties of daily life that could not be resolved with ordinary means in terms of religious beliefs and practices.

In gatherer and hunter societies, these uncertainties would have included diseases and inevitable death, the lack of sufficient food or clothing as well as the dangers posed by both predators and other people. In my analysis of 8,000 years of religion and politics in Peru, I used the sociological term 'religious needs' for indicating those feelings of uncertainty that are generated by problems that cannot successfully be tackled with ordinary means and, as a consequence, stimulate a desire for religiously inspired ways of doing so.[57] To be sure, religious needs did not only occur among gatherers and hunters, but also have been an important characteristic of many, if not all human societies up to the present day. While some uncertainties have continued to exist, most notably the inevitable end to our own personal complexity, many other uncertainties have changed. As a result, most religious needs have varied during human history.

Because gatherer and hunter societies were small, most of their members would have shared their religious views, even though skeptics would also have existed in those early days. Yet in these supposedly tightly knit groups, most people would have exercised a considerable amount of pressure to conform, while orientation alternatives would hardly have existed, if at all. In my book on Peru, I summarized the efforts to force others to believe in religious ideas and engage in religious practices with the term 'religious constraints.' As I see it now, patterns of religious needs and constraints are intimately linked to the harvesting of matter and energy, to the prevailing Goldilocks circumstances, to the need for an explanation of how everything became the way it is and to the preservation of our own complexity, even though that might sometimes come at the price of the destruction of other forms of complexity, including other human beings and their possessions. Indeed, for as long as we can trace back religious world views, they have always dealt with the questions of how everything has emerged and how to preserve our well-being, as well as what happens after death.[58]

In sum, after 4 million years of early human history, it appears that around 10,000 years ago all the genetic aspects were in place that allowed humans to do all the things they are doing today. By that time, our ancestors had not yet produced any large amounts of long-lasting constructed complexity or any long-lasting waste. In the period that followed, however, all of this changed dramatically during a mere 600 human generations, when collective learning became the dominant factor in human affairs.

7

RECENT HUMAN HISTORY

*The Development of the Greatest
Known Complexity*

Introduction

In this chapter, we take an Earthrise view at the past 10,000 years of human history, when cultural change took over from genetic change as the dominant adaptive mechanism. During this period, our species developed from unknown numbers of small bands who made a living from gathering and hunting to today's societies, which range from communities of largely self-supporting farmers, still considerable in numbers, to service economies.[1]

Whereas during the past 10 millennia cultural change has become ever more important, human biological change has, of course, never come to a halt. In fact, cultural and biological changes have been influencing each other to an extent, which still needs to be elucidated. Keeping cattle and drinking cow milk, for instance, led to societies with genes that facilitated the digestion of these animal products. This genetic ability, in its turn, had a great many cultural effects, ranging from the emergence of farmer lifestyles in which such products became increasingly important to the recent growth of a worldwide dairy-based industry. Also the genetically determined differential resistance to infectious diseases discussed below has played a major role in shaping recent human history. These are just two examples of a very important aspect of our common past. Yet because we lack general overviews of genetic change during the past 10,000 years, most of the attention of this chapter will be focused on cultural change.[2]

In an Earthrise approach to human history, we look at the large-scale patterns of the major processes that have shaped our common past. In doing so, it is, of course, not feasible to discuss a great many details. In accounts of the history of the universe, it rarely worries people, if ever, that not all the known galaxies, stars, planets, comets, meteoroids and dust clouds are mentioned. In human history, by contrast, the audience usually expects detailed stories about particular events, most notably when dealing with the history of their 'own' societies. This is partly the result of feelings of identity that are stimulated by more traditional forms of history-writing, in which the history of one's own people – whatever that may mean – is given the central position.

While an Earthrise approach to human history may not foster any such feelings, it may stimulate another type of identity, namely the idea that all of us belong to one single, rather exceptional, animal species, which emerged on a rather exceptional planet somewhere in the universe; that our closest cousins are the primates; that we are, in fact, related to all life forms and that, seen from a cosmic perspective, our far cousins are the rocks, the water and even the stars. For if the current big history account provides a reasonably accurate overview of the past, everything would have descended from the 'fire mist' of tiny particles that emerged immediately after the big bang.

The approach of using energy flows through matter within certain Goldilocks circumstances to explain the rise and demise of complexity is equally applicable to recent human history. To my knowledge, however, only a limited number of scholars have used such an approach implicitly, while explicit analyses of this kind are unknown to me.[3] Nonetheless, it seems reasonable to assume that human cultural efforts have usually been aimed at changing both our behavior and the surrounding natural environment in ways that were perceived to be better. This would always have included the harvesting of sufficient amounts of matter and energy to keep one's complexity going as well as the creation of Goldilocks circumstances. In practice, quite often more matter and energy has been harvested than was actually needed to fulfill basic needs. In fact, as was argued in chapter five, all life forms, including human beings, may have become genetically predisposed to do so to survive the lean periods. Furthermore, the successful harvesting of matter and energy and the creation of Goldilocks circumstances by one particular group of people may have meant the opposite for other humans. As a result, human history acquired its own dynamics, which was not planned by anyone.[4]

If all of this sounds a little abstract, let us apply these principles to one example: the account of ancient warfare (supposedly) written by Roman general Gaius Julius Caesar, in which he explains how he conquered Gaul.[5] Here is a recent summary of that story:[6]

> Caesar's troops camped for the winter in various places in Belgium, but in the spring of 53 B.C.E., some of these camps were attacked by the local tribes and suffered serious losses. Caesar spent most of that year fighting these tribes, and effectively annihilated some of them, men, women and children. The next year an alliance of many Gallic tribes, under the leadership of Vercingetorix, rose against the Romans. They tried to starve out the Romans, burning many of their own towns and collected all their forces and supplies in a few heavily fortified strongholds. Caesar's forces took some of these towns, but failed to take others. In the end all the Roman forces were concentrated around the city of Alesia, but

failed to take it by storm. Caesar decided to starve the Gallic forces out, and after a prolonged siege Vercingetorix and the Gauls surrendered. It is estimated that one million persons died in the wars and another million was sold into slavery, draining Gaul of approximately one third of the entire population.

It is not difficult to translate this historical account into a struggle for domination consisting of efforts to change important prevailing circumstances in one's own favor, while seeking to destroy the other party's complexity either by outright killing or by destroying both its matter and energy flows and its Goldilocks circumstances. While the Roman armies were killing Gallic tribesmen and women on a massive scale, which led to a major loss of Gallic human complexity, the tribes of Gaul were willing to destroy a considerable portion of their own constructed complexity (their towns, which are human-made Goldilocks circumstances) as well as their amassed matter and energy supplies in order to deny these things to the Romans, in the hope that, by doing so, Roman complexity would collapse. The Gallic tribes decided, however, not to destroy all their constructed complexity or all their matter and energy supplies, because this might have led to the collapse of all their own complexity. This allowed the Romans to conquer sufficient amounts of these reserved supplies, and thus to maintain their own complexity and gain the upper hand. The Romans achieved final victory by surrounding the Gallic fighters in their major fortified complex construction (the town of Alesia) and by waiting until the Gallic matter and energy supplies had run out. This doomed Gallic independent complexity.

Let us now examine a few general human traits that made possible the spectacular events of the past 10,000 years. In addition to their precision grip, which allowed our species to construct unprecedented forms of complexity, all modern humans have possessed other specific, genetically conditioned attributes that other animals do not have. Most notably a more complex brain and larynx have allowed the human species to make better mental maps as well as to engage in more efficient forms of communication and social coordination. As John and William McNeill outlined in their book *The Human Web* (2003), this has allowed humans to increase their control over energy flows, which has enabled them to create and sustain ever greater and more intense webs of interdependence. William McNeill summarized this as follows:[7]

> What allowed humankind to expand its control of energy flows so greatly was a matter of communication and concerted action arising from agreed upon meanings. Insofar as these were created by words and gestures they consumed minute quantities of energy – yet like the proverbial butterfly's wing starting hurricanes – triggered comparatively enormous changes in energy flows across the face of the earth.

Yet although all modern humans supposedly possessed all these special genetic traits, a considerable amount of time elapsed after their first emergence about 200,000 years ago, before humans systematically began to extract more energy and weave larger and more complex webs. Apparently, their growing dexterity as well as their capacity for learning and communication did not immediately lead to major changes in the ways early *Homo sapiens* harvested its matter and energy. It appears likely, therefore, that the capacity for culture and communication was a most important precondition for all the major developments during the past 10,000 years, yet it cannot be considered to be its direct root cause.

The Agrarian Revolution

Around 10,000 years ago, humans began to profoundly transform their relationship with the natural world through the domestication of plants and animals. In doing so, humans greatly intensified their competition with other species concerning the capture of solar energy. For by domesticating desired plants and animals, as well as by excluding other species that were not considered productive, humans began to control the capture of solar energy that fell on areas where these useful plants and animals grew.

Undomesticated areas usually show a large biodiversity, within which all the species together succeed in capturing solar energy very efficiently as a result of their competition for this scarce resource. When humans began to practice agriculture and hold animals, they greatly simplified the ecology, because they sought to eliminate all those species that were considered harmful. As a result, in such domesticated areas, plants began to capture less solar energy that fell on them. From a human point of view, however, these areas yielded more useful energy.

The rise of agriculture can thus be summarized as human efforts that were aimed at concentrating useful bio-solar collectors (plants) and bio-energy converters (animals) within certain areas to improve the conversion of solar energy into forms of bio-energy that were helpful for maintaining or improving human complexity.[8] In doing so, humans created higher gain energy resources out of lower gain ones. Scientist Frank Niele calls this stage of human history the 'agro-cultural energy regime.'[9] It was this energy that drove the greater complexity of human agrarian societies. Apparently, the cost of harvesting this energy and maintaining the new complexity did not outweigh the benefits it entailed.

As a result of these efforts, the reproduction of a considerable portion of the global flora and fauna came under direct human control. For such species, it was no longer the process of natural non-random elimination, but rather human cultural selection that determined who would survive.[10] Through this process, the early agriculturists sought to secure for themselves a steady supply of matter and energy by extracting increasing amounts of solar energy stored in plants and animals from a certain amount of land.

The gain in useful matter and energy came at the expense of requiring more work. It is often assumed that the early gatherers and hunters had to expend less time and energy than agriculturists for procuring the needed matter and energy. In other words, for gatherers and hunters the energy return on investment was higher. These resources were, however, usually not very concentrated or varied greatly during the year. Unless such people lived in areas with very concentrated energy resources that could be stored all year round, such as near sea currents teaming with marine life, they had to live a nomadic lifestyle while they could not densely populate the land. As a result, they had to keep the complexity of their societies relatively low while seeking to limit population growth. Because the transition to agriculture and animal husbandry implied more work, the energy return on investment dropped. Yet the much larger concentrations of harvested matter and energy allowed far more people to live in a certain area. As a result, the conditions emerged for a rise of societal complexity.

Seen from a general point of view, the agrarian revolution can be interpreted as a process consisting of two types of complex adaptive regimes, humans on the one hand and plants and animals on the other hand, which mutually adapted to each other under human dominance, with the human aim to harvest increasing amounts of matter and energy from a specific area. As a result, domestication was favorable for both humans and the few plants and animals that came under human custody. British scientist Stephen Budiansky has even argued that from a domesticated animal point of view, it is actually not clear at all who tamed whom, because humans had to work hard to provide the animals with sufficient matter, energy and Goldilocks circumstances, while the animals had to do very little in return to prosper.[11] A similar argument can be made for plants. However, the fortunes of the domesticated plants and animals were strongly determined by human interests, and not vice versa. Whenever humans stopped taking care of them, their numbers rapidly dwindled.

The most important domesticated species were social plants and animals. These terms were already used by Alexander von Humboldt and Charles Darwin. The reader may recall that social plants, such as grasses, or animals, such as large grazers, all live in large numbers close together, which helps them not to be overwhelmed by predators. Social plants could therefore relatively easily be grown in sufficient quantities, while the sociality of animals facilitated humans to take over the role of the alpha male in domesticating herds.

Under human selective pressure, the domesticated plants and animals underwent genetic changes. Rather unsurprisingly, the edible portions of plants increased in size while their ability to reproduce independently declined. As a result, such plants could only survive thanks to human intervention. Apparently, humans selected for characteristics that otherwise either would have been nonrandomly eliminated or would have remained marginal. The first tamed animals, by contrast, were usually smaller than their wild cousins. The underlying reason for this would have been the overriding concern for the selection of animals that were tamer than their wild counterparts. Because virtually all domesticated animals were herd animals, it appears as if the early herders selected not so much the alpha males but rather their meeker followers, while they themselves took up the positions of the animal alpha males. The early domesticators may even have selected those animals that might not have survived the competition within their own social group, and thus had a problem harvesting sufficient amounts of matter and energy. The new Goldilocks circumstances provided by humans may have allowed such meeker animals better survival chances.

Whereas early modern humans had already moved to the apex of the existing food pyramid during their hunting stage while still gathering considerable amounts of matter and energy from its lower sections, the agricultural pioneers then began to restructure the entire food web to their own design. At the same time, at least partially unwittingly, they also began to change the rest of the biological food pyramid. Other less desired plants, animals and microorganisms, such as weeds, rodents, large predators and pests, tried to profit from the new Goldilocks circumstances formed by domesticated plants and animals. This led to shifts in the balances within the undomesticated food pyramid. As a result, humans had to expend tireless efforts in keeping those predatory organisms at bay, a process that has continued until today.

There has been an extensive academic discussion on the root causes of the agrarian revolution.[12] Yet even today, this process is not yet well understood. The agrarian revolution was preceded by a long incipient phase, during which people experimented with plants and animals in various ways. By burning the landscape at set times, for instance, hunters and gatherers would have favored plant and animal species such as wild cereals and large grazers that were later domesticated.[13] Traces of such efforts as well as of other early attempts at domestication may be very difficult to find. The incipient transition to agriculture and animal husbandry may well have been a very prolonged and gradual process that possibly took place all over the globe.[14]

It appears likely that global climate change played a major role in this process. The agrarian revolution took place as soon as the last ice age ended, which signaled the beginning of the current warm period known as the Holocene. This transition, which came as a result of the Milanković cycles, did not proceed smoothly but was characterized by some major temperature fluctuations. Around 13,500 years ago, the first warm period emerged. This was followed by a much colder period between 12,500 and 10,500 years ago, that is known as the 'Younger Dryas.' In 2009, a team of US scientists suggested that a large comet explosion above the North American continent around 12,900 years ago produced this global cooling (which is disputed by other researchers).[15]

Whatever the case may have been, only after these frigid conditions had finally come to an end did the Holocene begin. For a similar warm period we need to go back in time to the interglacial period about 125,000 years ago, when modern humans were still living only in Africa.[16] The emergence of the Holocene was, therefore, the first such large climate change experienced by modern humans all around the globe. In many places, the beginning of the Holocene favored different types of plants and animals than the ones that had existed before. Furthermore, in many of these places human population pressure had increased, which may have led to an intensification of their search for matter and energy. US archaeologist Bruce Smith summarized it as follows:[17]

> Climatic pressures and population growth appear to have contributed to the process, at a distance, by producing resource gradients and hardening cultural boundaries around rich resources. It wouldn't have been easy to simply move to a better location when times were hard; these societies would have needed a way of dealing with the possibilities of hard times right where they were. Within these zones, too, population growth or other factors might have heightened the ever-present fear of resource shortfall, even in times of abundance, pushing societies to increase the yield and reliability of some food resources, and pointing the way to domestication.

British archaeologist David Harris emphasized that to understand the transition to agriculture, we need to consider the seasonal variation of the food supply.[18] Whereas some periods of the year may have provided abundant food to gatherers and hunters, the leaner seasons would have implied scarcity. When growing population pressure and declining natural resources as a result of over-exploitation or climate change aggravated this situation, efforts to counter these problems may have led to the development of a regime of food storage. Growing population pressure and perhaps deteriorating climatic conditions would subsequently have pressured such people to devote more attention to the well-being of the plants and beasts they had come to depend on. As a result, they would slowly but surely have converted to agrarian life ways.

The agrarian revolution took place within a few thousand years in a number of regions on both sides of the Atlantic Ocean. These include the hilly areas of the Fertile Crescent, the similar hinterland of the Indus Valley, the rolling hills of East Asia, the elevated uplands of New Guinea (which have a subtropical climate), the highlands of Mexico and the Andean mountains (both of which have a subtropical, or even moderate, climate, depending on the altitude). All of these places had in common that they were hilly areas with subtropical climates. Apparently, such regions provided Goldilocks circumstances for the rise of agriculture. It is currently thought unlikely that the invention of agriculture emerged only once and subsequently spread across the globe, because these places would not yet have been sufficiently interlinked to make this possible at that time. It therefore appears as if the emergence of agriculture was a spontaneous process that took place independently in most, if not all, of these areas.

Agriculture emerged in a number of different ways. In Abu Hureyra, for instance, in what is now northern Syria, grain growing and animal domestication began as early as 13,000 years ago, during the transition to the first warm period, which ended in the much colder Younger Dryas. In the words of British climatologist William Burroughs:[19]

> The evidence indicates that hunter-gatherers at Abu Hureyra first started cultivating crops in response to a steep decline in wild plants that had served as staple foods for at least the preceding four centuries. The decline in these wild staples is attributable to a sudden onset of a drier, colder, more variable climate. Work by Gordon Hillman, of University College London, and his colleagues found that the wild seed varieties gathered as food gradually vanished, before the cultivated varieties appeared. Those wild seeds most dependent on water were the first to die out, then one by one by [sic] the hardier ones followed. So the hunter-gatherers turned to cultivating some of the foods they had previously collected from the wild. In an unstable environment, the first farmers started simply by transferring wild plants to more suitable habitats and cultivating them there. ... While the shifting pressures of the climatic changes around the Younger Dryas may have provided the initial impetus for the adoption of agriculture, in the long run the less variable climate of the Holocene was the vital factor for its survival.

Also in other places within the Fertile Crescent, people first settled close to rich wild plant and animal resources, and then began storing them for surviving through the lean periods. In other words, they settled near naturally occurring concentrations of matter and energy, which they began to harvest. Yet over time this would have led to population growth as well as to the degradation of their energy resources. This would have produced the need to expend more work in concentrating the needed resources, which led to the conversion to farming and animal husbandry. In the Andes, by contrast, gourds (perhaps for water storage) and peppers (perhaps as spices or medicines) appear to have been among the first domesticates, which does not point to any great need for food resources at that time. Yet during the centuries that followed, ancient Andeans and early Mexicans also developed rather similar agricultural regimes.

Such developments took place all around the globe. Notwithstanding all the emerging local and regional differences, plant cultivators and animal herders all around the globe began to resemble each other in general ways. Apparently, all of these people found themselves on a cultural path that was characterized by certain constraints that produced these similarities. This would have worked as follows. First of all, people began to depend on food-stuffs they had to take care of all year round. In doing so, they changed both the landscape and their own behavior. As a result of these activities, many wild species on which people had earlier depended for their livelihood became scarce or perhaps even disappeared, while the early cultivators blunted or lost their hunting and gathering skills. Thus, emerging farmers and herders had no choice but to continue along the path of agricultural complexity on which they had become dependent. This development was strikingly similar to the path dependency complex life forms found themselves in after they had emerged during the Cambrian explosion of life forms. Over the course of time, this path dependency led to an ever more refined agrarian regime, as well as to a decline of the gatherer-hunter regime.

It appears as if women cultivated the first plants while men domesticated animals. Although firm evidence is lacking, this would have been a logical extension of the traditional gender roles in gatherer-hunter societies, within which women would have gathered plants while men hunted animals. When the traction plow was introduced, men may have begun to take on the task of plowing, which might have been a largely female undertaking until that time. More in general, it seems as if men began to replace women in agriculture when the work became harder as a result of its intensification. If correct, this would mean that women were gradually being pushed into the developing domestic sphere during this period, while a male-dominated public domain would have begun to emerge.

The Developing Agrarian Regime

Over the course of time, a large variety of local and regional agrarian regimes developed, ranging from shifting cultivation in tropical forests to intensive cattle-raising on the Eurasian and African savannas. In general terms, this was a cultural adaptive radiation, which came as a result of a major cultural innovation. Not only were new species regularly introduced into the agrarian regime, but also novel skills were continuously added to the technical repertoire in the form of new tools, such as plows and millstones, as well as ways of making sure the land remained fertile, such as irrigation.

People also learned to exploit animals in more varied ways. Instead of keeping them only as a meat resource, humans learned to extract other resources from their beasts on a more permanent basis, such as milk and wool. In addition, the invention of the animal-drawn plow (the use of animal power for plant production), which emerged perhaps as long ago as 6,500 years, made agriculture a great deal more efficient.[20] Such a development could, of course, only take place in areas where there were suitable draft animals, sufficient amounts of animal fodder and sufficiently flat areas where these new plows could be used profitably. In the Americas, such beasts were absent. As a result, these developments took off in the New World only after Spaniards introduced the traction plow, together with the needed draft animals, usually oxen. Yet on the hilly slopes of the Andes, where even today traction plows cannot go, ancient foot plows operated by humans are still used to till the land.

The new farmers became tied to the land they worked, because they had become dependent on the crops they were taking care of. As a result, they began to live in more permanent settlements, where they also stored the harvest as well as the needed utensils, such as axes and millstones. In other words, the more concentrated and more localized matter and energy resources led to the emergence of a great many new types of localized constructed complexity and human-created Goldilocks circumstances. Because agricultural families became productive units, as they still are today in traditional farming societies, this may also have led to the growing importance of nuclear families within a larger family network. Pastoralists, by contrast, usually had to remain mobile, because they needed to follow their herds, which needed fresh pasture from time to time. Within such societies, there may have been a lesser emphasis on nuclear families. Furthermore, most, if not all, farming societies evolved cyclical calendars, in which specific times were determined for sowing, weeding and harvesting. Over the course of time, this led to new types of time awareness and social coordination.

The rise of agriculture and animal husbandry required the emergence or elaboration of storage regimes, which were meant to supplement an otherwise irregular food supply. These foodstuffs needed to be protected not only against the elements but also against human and animal greed. This led to the creation of human-made Goldilocks circumstances that were designed to protect them, in the form of constructed complexity, such as storage places, as well as through specific social regulations. After such storage regimes had emerged, humans became extremely dependent on them.

US ecological historian Alfred Crosby and US physiologist Jared Diamond, among others, have pointed out that Eurasia was the largest leftover portion of the supercontinent Pangea, after it had broken up into a number of pieces about 170 million years ago. It is therefore not surprising that the largest range of plants, and especially animals, was available for domestication in this part of the world. In addition, the east-west orientation of Eurasia produced similar ecological areas over large distances. This made the cultivation of certain species over large distances possible, thus greatly facilitating their dispersion.

In Africa and the Americas, by contrast, there were far fewer available animals that could be domesticated, while the dominant north-south axis of these continents made the spread of domesticates much more difficult. By going either north or south in the Americas, the natural circumstances often changed very quickly, which made it hard, if not impossible, for such plants and animals to prosper. In this respect, the Andean highlands offer an exception, because by going up or down similar circumstances could be found over larger distances. It is therefore not surprising that the Inca empire developed along the Andean north-south axis. Yet this was an exception, and compared to Eurasia, where the same crops could be cultivated in the temperate zone all the way from eastern China to western Europe, this was still a small area. As a result of this geographical advantage, Eurasians came to enjoy an unbeatable head start in agriculture and animal husbandry which, over the course of time, greatly contributed to more rapid social and technical development in that part of the world.[21]

About 1,500 years ago, the domestication of new terrestrial species appears to have come to an end. According to British scientist Neil Roberts, the last major species were domesticated around 3,500 years BP in the Old World (the camel in the Middle East, garlic in Central Asia and pearl millet in Africa). In the Americas, the domestication process ended about 1,500 years ago with the domestication of tobacco.[22] To my knowledge, the only exceptions are the rabbit (Middle Ages in Europe) and the sugar beet, which was domesticated in western Europe about 200 years ago under Napoleon, as an attempt to replace cane sugar, which had become scarce as a result of the British naval blockade. It may be that more recently unknown numbers of other minor species have also been domesticated.

To my knowledge, it is hardly ever recognized in the literature, if at all, that most of the domestication came to an end so long ago. It may be that by that time all the major terrestrial species that could be domesticated had already been tamed. But perhaps it was no longer worthwhile to domesticate new species, because it usually takes a long time and many generations to enhance those characteristics that are valued by humans.

The domestication of water-dwelling species, by contrast, may have begun much later, while it has not yet come to an end. Although in some areas fish have been kept in artificial ponds, such as rice paddies, for unknown periods of time, we witness a great many new attempts at domesticating fish today. The current over-exploitation of the wild marine resources as a result of intensive fishing has gone hand in hand with, for instance, the rise of salmon farms along many coasts where their wild cousins used to swim.

The end of the introduction of novel land species within the agrarian fold did not imply, of course, that agrarian developments as a whole came to a halt. To the contrary, the refinement of the tamed flora and fauna, as well as of agricultural technology, including the creation of Goldilocks circumstances such as rice paddies, irrigated terraces, floating fields and polders, has been an ever-ongoing process. Today, genetic modification plays a major role in changing those plants and animals on which humans depend for their livelihood.

As soon as the original domestication had taken off, people began to move crops and animals to other places that provided Goldilocks circumstances. This was the beginning of the globalization of domesticated plants and animals. Today, most domesticates have been transported to wherever they can be grown, while many types of agrarian produce are now shipped globally. In the early phase of agriculture, because of a lack of suitable means of transport, the large-scale movement of produce over larger distances was not feasible. The spread of cultivated plants and animals around the world was usually followed by the often unplanned expansion of their predators, such as insects, microorganisms and mice.

Social Effects of the Agrarian Revolution

The transformation into an agrarian regime led to incisive social change. First of all, children became a great deal more productive. In gatherer-hunter societies, children were often a burden, but they could contribute considerably to the household economy already at a young age in agricultural societies, by helping to sow, weed, harvest and tend animals. This change removed the constraint on population growth and actually put a premium on having more offspring, especially if the children were to provide care for their elderly parents. As a result, human population numbers began to increase rapidly. It has been estimated that the total human population would have amounted to between 1 and 10 million people around 10,000 years ago, while between 5 and 20 million people would have inhabited our planet some 5,000 years later.[23]

In the terms of US anthropologist Eric Wolf, while production remained kin-ordered, many other aspects of the social regime changed almost beyond recognition.[24] Most importantly, perhaps, the early cultivators became strongly tied to the land they worked. As a consequence, they became more tightly bound to each other. Their villages became 'social cages,' in which people lived in larger numbers and closer together than ever before.[25] While such agrarian societies appear to have remained relatively egalitarian for a long period of time, they became more hierarchical slowly but surely, thus leading to a type of society known in cultural anthropology as 'chiefdoms,' in which powerful men could impose themselves on increasingly larger groups.

There are a few striking parallels between the rise of complex animals and the emergence of agricultural societies. The increasing interdependence of cells within multicellular organisms, as well as their emerging inter-cellular division of labor, was paralleled by growing human interdependencies and an emerging social division of labor. The increased harnessing of matter and energy made both complex life and agricultural societies not only more productive and constructive but also more destructive. The other parallel is that during this phase of human history, cultural evolution speeded up, while the life span of human cultural regimes decreased.

As part of the emerging division of labor, farmers and herders often became dependent on each other, because the nomadic pastoralists needed the carbohydrates produced by agriculturists, while the farmers usually wanted some of the cattle protein, as well as other products such as wool, that were controlled by the herders. Although the new sedentary agriculturists had become much more powerful with respect to gatherers and hunters, they also became more vulnerable to attack, because they were tied to their land and their increasing possessions. The nomadic pastoralists, by contrast, depended on a food supply that could move. Nomads could attack, rob and flee almost with impunity especially after horses had been tamed. It is therefore not surprising that nomadic pastoralists often sought to obtain agricultural products by plunder, which was comparatively easy, given their mobility. In reaction, over the course of time agriculturists learned to protect themselves. As a result, a more or less stable balance of exchange emerged.

The emerging social agrarian regime may well have stimulated an intensification of the exploitation of the land. Bruce Smith explained this as follows:[26]

A newly sedentary people living in larger settlements would need new forms of social integration and interaction and new rules for the ownership and control of land and its resources. These changes may have encouraged the production of a greater harvest surplus, if such a surplus could have been used to establish and maintain contracts in a variety of ways: they could have been lent out to relatives or neighbors in times of need, offered up for community celebrations, or paid out as a dowry or brideprice when a marriage formed a new alliance between families. There are, then, a variety of social forces, other than competitive feasting, that could have encouraged family groups to invest more of their time manipulating seed plants in an effort to increase harvest yields and storable surplus.

Although the production of an agrarian surplus became possible, this did not lead to a noticeable accumulation of human-made complexity or to a rapidly growing social complexity for thousands of years. If current traditional agrarian societies provide a reasonably good example of what may have happened in the past, the produced surplus was mostly, if not entirely, consumed in competitive feasting and other social obligations, which would have had a strong economic leveling effect within such societies.[27] Such exchanges bring about a network of social obligations, which are helpful in surviving leaner times. As a result of this situation, no substantial surplus would have accumulated, which very much limited the emergence of more elaborate forms of social or technical complexity characteristic of 'civilized' societies. It may even be that such people preferred to keep the complexity of their societies as low as possible. This tendency may well be a fundamental human characteristic, which would have evolved simply because generating more complexity requires more energy. Indeed, one may wonder why people would create more complexity at the price of harder work for as long as they were relatively happy with the lives they led.[28]

In sum, after a revolutionary beginning the stage had been set for a type of farmer life that exhibited a remarkable continuity from about 8,000 years ago until very recently. It was only in the twentieth century that farmer regimes began to be transformed into industrial agrarian modes of production. Yet even today, in less industrialized regions, many aspects of agrarian regimes as they evolved thousands of years ago can still be seen.

The Emergence of Agrarian Religions

The transition to an agrarian regime required the acquisition of new forms of social conduct. The early farmers could, for instance, no longer consume all the available food, as gatherers and hunters used to do. Eating the seeds or exhausting the food supply well before the next harvest would have spelled disaster. Furthermore, they had to adapt their work rhythm to the agricultural cycle, which included sowing, weeding and harvesting. This led to the invention of ways to determine the appropriate time for doing so, which was often regimented in the form of cyclical calendars based on the movements of celestial bodies such as the sun, the moon as well as prominent stellar constellations such as the Pleiades. It may well be that by doing so, early agrarian societies began to define the first concepts of time.[29]

Attaining success in animal husbandry also required new forms of self-discipline. The emerging nomadic pastoralists had to learn how to manage their growing herds as well as not to slaughter their animals at will. As a consequence, they too needed to develop novel forms of foresight and discipline. Such standards of conduct were not inborn. They had to be learned. During the same period, the early agriculturalists began to abandon the standards of conduct characteristic of gatherer-hunter regimes.

As German sociologist Norbert Elias emphasized, the learning of certain forms of self-discipline goes hand in hand with the exercise of external constraint by other people. As an example, Elias suggested that the agrarian behavior was instilled by emergent agrarian leaders with the aid of religious beliefs and practices. In doing so, they may have provided binding solutions to these problems. This hypothesis would explain why in early agrarian societies a leadership emerged consisting of priest-chiefs that was stronger than ever before. Presumably, these leaders would have descended from the earlier shamans.[30]

Not all early agriculturists might have needed priestly predictions or their coercing behavior. Intelligent and sensitive stone-age farmers could have predicted the turn of the seasons by observing many aspects of nature, including recurring events in the sky such as the trajectory of the sun and of major constellations, the flowering of certain plants, the occurrence and behavior of specific animals and the onset or disappearance of rains, as many of them still do today. Based on such observations, such talented farmers might have been able to adopt the needed conduct all by themselves without any priestly intervention.

However, as Norbert Elias and Johan Goudsblom have argued, attaining success in agriculture and animal husbandry required the cooperation of a considerable number of people, including those who were perhaps not so very talented, as well as those who may have been early free riders. Any effective solution to these issues for the entire group would have been beneficial to all participants. This explains why early agricultural societies with priest-chiefs would have been more successful than those without this type of leadership. If most, if not all, early priest-chiefs were men, this would have contributed greatly to the emergence of a male-dominated public domain.[31]

More likely than not, agrarian religious vocabulary was expressed in terms of 'supernatural nature.'[32] This would have included spirits inhabiting Earth, most notably an Earth mother; mountain gods; winds of different kinds; thunder and lightning and the sun, moon, planets and celestial constellations. Like gatherers and hunters, early agriculturists probably tended to view nature as imbued with supernatural powers. This came as a result of their strong dependency on the surrounding natural environment as well as its precarious nature. Such naturalistic religions can still be witnessed today among largely self-supporting farmers and herders. With the aid of such religious representations and practices, modern farmers still seek to tackle problems of daily life that they cannot resolve by ordinary means. Although we may never be able to prove this conclusively, it seems reasonable to suspect that these religions emerged during the transition to an agrarian regime.[33] A major difference was that agricultural religions became much more institutionalized than gatherer-hunter religions.

Increasing Agricultural Complexity and Declining Untamed Complexity

A major effect of the agrarian revolution was population growth. The early farmers and herders rapidly multiplied in numbers and began to live closer together than people had done ever before. In other words, agrarian societies became more complex.[34] The growing population pressure led to the expansion of the agrarian regime into a great many areas that were occupied by gatherers and hunters. This expansion was feasible because farmers and herders had become more powerful than gatherers and hunters. It may also be that in many instances, gatherers and hunters adopted the new agrarian skills.[35] As a result of these developments, the human web became more complex and more tightly interconnected, which allowed for a faster exchange of ideas and objects over longer distances, which, in turn, very much contributed to an acceleration of the collective learning process. At the same time, the gathering and hunting skills must have declined among agriculturists, which can be interpreted as a process of cultural forgetting.

As was noted before, the early farmers needed to construct new forms of complexity. This included housing, storage places, pottery and agricultural tools, all of which had shapes that had not existed before in the known universe. In other words, with the rise of agriculture the 'age of the teacup' had definitely begun. Possessions became much more important, including prestige goods, such as jewelry and monumental graves, which contributed to distinguishing people from each other. To be sure, beautifully elaborated flint tools may already have served such a purpose for gatherers and hunters. Yet in contrast to agriculturists, such people could usually accumulate only very limited amounts of material possessions. Constructing all of these new forms of complexity required novel skills, as well as a more varied tool kit. As a result, a division of labor emerged in the form of part-time specialists who became experts at producing such things. Yet it appears that these emerging skilled workers first of all made a living through agriculture. Even today, such a situation can still be observed in largely self-supporting agricultural communities.[36]

As a result of their increasing production of complexity, early farmers also began to generate growing amounts of entropy. While most nomadic gatherers and hunters would have moved elsewhere when things became too disorganized and dirty, this was no longer an option for early farmers.[37] It is not well known how the ancient farmers tackled these problems, but the remarkably early production of fermented drinks (probably for everyday use) may have been a solution for the problem of how to deal with water supplies contaminated by the entropy generated by large concentrations of humans and animals as a result of their bodily functions.

As a consequence, many early farmers may have been under the influence of such intoxicants for the greater part of their lives. Today, this type of alcohol consumption among farmers can be observed all around the world, but it may well date back to the period when large human and animal concentrations began to pollute the water supply. Because most people were farmers during the past 10,000 years, it may well be that most humans lived under the influence of alcohol on a daily basis. The keepers of large animal herds living on the steppes, by contrast, usually did not invest a great deal in dwellings or tools, because they had to follow the livestock and the pasturage. Thanks to their nomadic lifestyle, herders did not have to worry too much about the production of entropy. They could simply go somewhere else when things became too dirty and cluttered.

The rise of complexity in agricultural societies went hand in hand with the simplification of ecosystems under human control. This was the result of human efforts to concentrate and harvest the solar energy captured by domesticated plants and animals. Although agrarian land is much less productive than undomesticated ecosystems in terms of solar energy captured by life, it is much more productive seen from a human perspective, because more plants and animals can be kept on it, which can be consumed.[38] Also keeping large herds of domesticated animals on steppes, while less useful wild species were increasingly marginalized, was an effort aimed at making these grasslands productive for humans by simplifying their ecology. Humans could not digest the grass because of their comparatively small intestines, but they could eat the meat and drink the milk produced by the animals they kept, while using their hides, wool and bones for constructing many things, ranging from weapons to clothing and tents.

The emergence of agriculture inevitably led to a decrease of the matter and energy flows harvested by a great many wild plants and animals. As a result, they were increasingly pushed back to places where farmers and herders could not, or would not, go.[39] This has led to the current situation in which many domesticated species thrive in larger numbers than ever before, while many larger wild plants and animals only survive because humans protect them against other humans, either in nature reserves or in zoos. Yet not all wild species suffered as a result of agriculture. Grain cultivation, for instance, supported growing numbers of mice which, in their turn, may have been pursued by increasing numbers of birds of prey. The need to protect the harvest against rodents led, among other things, to the introduction of cats into the agrarian regime.

The large concentrations of newly domesticated plant and animal species created Goldilocks circumstances for the microorganisms that fed on them. As a result, plant and animal diseases became more frequent. Because of the considerable genetic and physiological differences between humans and the domesticated flora, plant pests were usually unable to make the jump to human beings. Yet many animal diseases could do so successfully. In consequence, the growing contacts between humans and domesticated animals facilitated an increasing transmission of infectious diseases from animals to humans which, in turn, stimulated efforts to cure both humans and animals from the new sicknesses. This led to the emergence of both human and animal medicine.[40]

Although agriculture became the dominant way to extract solar energy from nature, its Goldilocks circumstances have been geographically more limited than those in which gatherers and hunters operated. Most notably, a suitable temperature range and water supply have been critical for determining agricultural success. Even today, agriculture has not yet spread as far and wide across the landmasses of the globe as gathering and hunting had done. Furthermore, the seas and the oceans are still places where gathering and hunting has prevailed until the present day.

It is not possible to calculate power densities that characterize the novel forms of complexity constructed by agriculturists for lack of suitable data. Any attempts to do so would, in fact, constitute an entirely novel research agenda. The only scholar who, to my knowledge, tried to estimate the energy use per capita during human history was US geologist and energy expert Earl Ferguson Cook. He put these figures forward in an article published in 1971 about the flow of energy in an industrial society. Interestingly, his rather basic and preliminary estimates appear to be the only general data available about energy use in human history. Other often-quoted authors, such as I. G. Simmons and John Bennett, based their analyses of the energy use in human history almost entirely on Cook's data.[41]

According to Cook, gatherer-hunters may have consumed 120 watt per capita as food and a further 80 watt per capita for 'home and commerce' as a result of the use of fire for heat and cooking. Early agriculturists would have eaten about 160 watt per capita and have used a further 320 watt per capita for 'home, commerce, agriculture and industry.' This increase mostly came as a result of the addition of animal muscle power. 'Advanced' farmers and herders would have consumed 240 watt per capita as food, about 480 watt per capita for 'home and commerce,' about 280 watt per capita for 'agriculture and industry' and about 40 watt per capita for 'transportation.' All these numbers are tentative estimates and should be viewed with due caution.

Although agrarian societies became far better at harvesting matter and energy than gatherers and hunters, not all early farmers were better off. More likely than not, the 'average' farmers often had a problem meeting their energy needs. The total amount of calories consumed by farmers may actually have gone up, but they needed to eat a great deal more because of the much harder manual labor they had to perform. As a result, the total amount of available food may often have been insufficient. In addition, compared to gatherers and hunters, farmers may have had a more limited access to nutritious wild food resources such as fruit and berries, which provided important vitamins.

Early State Formation

Between 6,000 and 5,000 years ago, the first states evolved. This happened most notably in Egypt, Mesopotamia and along the Pacific coast of South America. Somewhat later states emerged also in the Indus Valley (about 4,500 years ago), China (about 4,000 years ago) and Central America (about 3,500 years ago). State formation happened thanks to the fact that in principle the new agrarian life ways could generate sufficient amounts of matter and energy to make it possible. However, the first states did not emerge immediately after agricultural societies came into being. To the contrary, for thousands of years the global landscape remained dotted with small, relatively autonomous, agrarian villages that were not subjected to external control. Apparently, agriculture was an important precondition for state formation, but it was not its direct root cause.

From a sociological point of view, states can be defined as societies ruled by elites that control two indispensable monopolies. According to German sociologist Max Weber, the main state monopoly consists of the legitimized use of physical force in the enforcement of its order. The second state monopoly is, according to Norbert Elias, the right to levy taxes. As soon as either one of these monopolies breaks down, the state collapses. These monopolies did not appear overnight, of course, but emerged as part of a long-term process.[42]

The emergence of these two monopolies resulted from the fact that humans began to systematically tap other humans as matter and energy sources, and, in doing so, created Goldilocks circumstances for themselves. By competing for these resources, humans created new forms of complexity, namely states, that were characterized by ever more intricate interdependency networks. This development led to a new type of path dependency, because the people who profited from these new resources found it hard, if not impossible, to live outside states anymore. Apparently, the costs of achieving and maintaining state complexity must not have outweighed its benefits, at least for those who exercised enough social power.

In traditional history accounts, the emergence of states is often described as the 'rise of civilizations.' Yet for a long time, the people who actually enjoyed these cultural achievements remained a small minority, usually no more than about 10 per cent. In all states, until the industrial revolution, its other 90 per cent of inhabitants were farmers, who kept harvesting matter and energy from the surrounding natural environment. Although farmers provided the energy that kept the states going, they reaped relatively few benefits. State elites may have protected them against others, but this came at the price of heavy taxation.

In some respect, early states may have resembled forms of biological symbiosis, in which there is a certain mutual benefit for all of the organisms involved. Yet quite often, the balance of exchange among humans within state societies has been rather unequal. Over time, those who exploited farmers often took the view that it was best, as a matter of policy, to keep them on the margin of subsistence, and not allow them to retain any surplus. Furthermore, the occasional poor harvests, wars, pests and diseases, as well as outright plunder, would all have contributed to making farmer life miserable in state societies.[43] Because they had become tied to the land, farmers could usually not escape this situation.

In big history, simple general processes of energy extraction keep reoccurring in different forms. Like the emergence of the social division of labor during the rise of agriculture resembled the emergence of the workings of complex cells, the process of early state formation very much resembled the changes in the biological regime after predators began to emerge. At that time, the biological food pyramid began to consist of a great many plants and microorganisms that harvested solar energy and, to some extent, also geothermal energy, while they provided sustenance to a privileged minority that fed on them. Similarly, while farmers kept extracting solar energy, a small fraction of people began to divert their resources, directly or indirectly, for their own use, although it was not always clear what they gave the farmers in return. In doing so, a social food pyramid emerged, in which a small fraction of people collected the resources (food, labor and forms of constructed complexity) that had been produced by great numbers of other people.

The transition from relatively autonomous farmer societies to early states did not happen overnight. Over the course of time, as population pressure grew and resources were exploited more intensively, chiefdoms emerged, in which local strongmen were able to lead larger coalitions, perhaps especially in times of war, but also during large social gatherings. If recent chiefdoms provide a good model for what happened during this ancient transition, local leaders would have thrown large feasts, during which considerable amounts of produce were brought to a central place, where these big men ostentatiously redistributed them among their followers. As the power of local chiefs grew, they might have been able to keep a growing portion of this matter and energy for themselves. In such a way, the monopoly on taxation might have emerged. To keep control over their newly generated surplus and the people who generated it, the strongmen might have organized armed gangs, which might have offered protection in exchange for a certain amount of matter and energy. This would have signaled the emergence of the monopoly on the legitimized use of physical force. The increasing energy flow, the result of surplus production, made possible a rise in societal complexity.

The need to learn how to successfully store produce and seeds until the next season may also have contributed to the process of state formation, especially if local leaders assigned central storage places that fell under their protection. From time to time, these big men might have been tempted to keep some of this matter and energy to themselves. If they possessed sufficient power to turn such desires into practice, this would also have contributed to the emergence of the monopolies on taxation and the use of physical force.

For all of this to happen, the circumstances would have had to be 'just right.' It is therefore remarkable, as US archaeologist Robert Carneiro pointed out in 1970, that all early states emerged in areas that shared specific Goldilocks circumstances, namely fertile river valleys surrounded by almost inhabitable areas, often deserts. In Carneiro's terms, such areas were 'ecologically circumscribed.' In these fertile river valleys, the harvesting of matter and energy was comparatively easy, while in the surrounding deserts only limited opportunities existed to make a living. As a result, the people who lived in such valleys were even more constrained than other farmers, hemmed in as they were by large deserts. Over the course of time, this ecological situation allowed stronger people to dominate their weaker fellows.[44]

There were more ecological changes that contributed to early state formation. The sea level rise of about 120 meters that occurred after the last ice age had ended drove people upstream, most notably in Mesopotamia, but perhaps to a lesser extent also in the Nile Valley as well as in valleys along the Pacific coast of South America.[45] Furthermore, the first states emerged during a period of relatively high global temperatures, the so-called Holocene optimum, which may have stepped up the ecological circumscription. Moreover, in the northern hemisphere the fertile river valleys began to receive less rain during this period as a result of climate change caused by the Milanković cycles. This would also have contributed to the ecological circumscription as well as to in-migration, and thus to the emergence of early states. The increasing need for irrigation to step up agricultural production would have provided further opportunities for central control, because control over water on a larger scale can only be effectively achieved by an overarching organization that is able to negotiate, or suppress, local and regional rivalries.

All early states emerged near subtropical mountains where agriculture had been pioneered millennia before. Apparently, proximity to early centers of domestication was an important precondition for early state formation. Yet these hilly regions themselves hardly ever, if at all, became nuclei for these states. In fact, many of these areas have escaped effective central control until today, because both armies and bureaucrats find it hard to operate in such ecological conditions, while they are well suited for guerilla warfare.

In Eurasia, state formation began earlier and proceeded to a far greater extent than in the New World. This was the result of the unbeatable head start in agriculture that the Old World had enjoyed, thanks to its richness in adaptable flora and fauna. Moreover, on the great Eurasian plains, the comparatively easier exchanges of many types of things over long distances, as well as the greater scope for armies to operate, contributed to maintaining this lead.

Seen from a detached point of view, the interactions between emerging states and their neighbors can be interpreted as complex adaptive regimes in continuous interaction, ranging from attempts at complete destruction of neighbors to an almost complete submission to them. Whereas a great many states have collapsed over the course of time, these social entities have never completely disappeared. To the contrary, despite ups and downs, the process of 'statification' has proceeded to the point that, today, there are hardly any stateless areas left, at least on land. Apparently states are rather robust social regimes.

The forced surplus production of early states created a new energy flow, which made possible greater societal and material complexity. In early states, large amounts of this new matter and energy were invested in creating novel forms of architecture. This includes ziggurats in Mesopotamia, the Egyptian pyramids as well as the great many temple mounds in Peru called *huacas*. The emergence of European megalithic structures including Stonehenge would also be part of these developments, although these structures were presumably built by chiefdoms rather than by early states. Religion and the architecture of power were both prominent features of early state societies.

It may well be that in addition to serving agrarian needs, the emerging state religions often turned into attempts at fostering social cohesion among the inhabitants and at legitimizing the rulers' position.[46] As a result, a differentiation of religious needs and constraints took place between the local and state levels. The urgent needs for emerging rulers, namely how to stay in power and keep the emerging state together, translated into forms of religious constraint for the less powerful members of these societies. Most, if not all early state religions were phrased in the idiom of supernatural nature, in which the rulers were often depicted as descendants of the sun and the moon. As part of this process, early state religions became the dominant forms of public worship, while the older farmer religions remained important at the local level, because they kept serving locally felt needs. This differentiation into state religions and popular religions would have gone hand in hand with a growing differentiation of social life into a public, male-dominated sphere and a private sphere in which both sexes played a role.

The Emergence of Big States

The innovation of state formation led to a major cultural adaptive radiation. Within a mere 1,000 years after early states had emerged in ecologically circumscribed river valleys, states began to form also in other areas where, apparently, the combination of population growth and prevailing ecology provided Goldilocks circumstances for this to happen. With many ups and downs, the long-term trend was toward an expansion of state societies all around the globe at the expense of independent agriculturalists, as well as gatherers and hunters, most of whom slowly but surely became marginalized or even disappeared. To be sure, for a long time large tribal societies with sufficient destructive power – the Mongols offer perhaps the best example – could still overpower agrarian states. Yet to stay in power, such invaders could not maintain both their tribal behavior and their dominance over agrarian states for long. If the conquerors wished to consolidate their power, they had to adopt the lifestyle of the more complex societies they had conquered.

Big states became larger and more complex than any other human entity that had existed before. A few well-known examples from the Old World include the Roman empire, the Chinese empires and, largest of them all, the Mongol empire. In the New World, the Maya and Aztec states in what is now Mexico, as well as the Chimú state along the South American Pacific coast and the Huari and Inca states in the Peruvian Andes serve as examples. The emergence of big states facilitated a greater exchange of ideas, people and objects over increasing distances. This included a growing long-distance trade in both prestige items, such as gem stones and silk, and consumer goods, such as grain and wine, especially when these things could be transported by ships. As a result of the growing number of such interactions, the human web in Afro-Eurasia became increasingly complex. A similar process took place in the Americas, although at a lesser pace, while in Oceania no states emerged at all. Yet the human web became more complex also in that part of the world, thanks to the daring sea voyages its people undertook all across the Pacific Ocean, which led to the colonization of most islands. On Pacific islands such as the Hawaiian archipelago, chiefdoms had emerged by the time European explorers arrived. Apparently, the vast ocean surrounding the Hawaiian islands offered sufficient ecological circumscription for this to happen.

During the period between 4,000 and 500 years ago, people all around the globe became better at adapting themselves to the surrounding environment, as well as at adapting the environment to their own desires. Yet the vagaries of nature still exerted a major influence over human action, as US archaeologist Brian Fagan emphasized, including a severe drought that led to the decline of the Mayan states in Yucatán.[47] An interesting example of global climate change influencing societies in many places was suggested by Dutch climatologist Bas van Geel, leading a team of Dutch and Russian researchers. The decline of solar activity around 850 BCE and the ensuing wetter ecological conditions led, for instance, to a steep decline of living conditions in northwest Holland, as well as to the concomitant expansion of the Asian horse-riding Scythians, thanks to the fact that the wetter conditions on the Eurasian steppes provided more food for their animals. These examples offer just a few glimpses of what is a general, but still relatively unexplored, theme in human history, namely the effects of changing ecological circumstances on the levels of complexity human societies could attain.[48]

In state societies, a great many technologies were invented or improved, such as metal working, the production of textiles and pottery, architecture, shipping and warfare. Yet no major ecological transformation took place in the harvesting of matter and energy. As a result, all traditional states were powered by renewable solar energy captured by the farmers. Perhaps the most revolutionary inventions were the new military and social skills that the rulers needed for controlling the populace, as well as for defense and offense with regard to outsiders. This necessitated new forms of social organization, such as armies and a bureaucratic apparatus.

As part of the process of empire building, better means of communication were invented, such as long-distance roads and canals that were used by armies, relay messengers, tax collectors and bureaucrats, as well as a great many other ways of transmitting information over large distances with the aid of sound and visual signals, including fire, smoke and drumming. The new communication lines were also employed by traders, lone wanderers, missionaries and merchants.[49] Also, the roads, rivers and seas connecting states became more frequently used. All of this led to an ever-quickening pace of the exchange of produce and information and thus to a reinforcement of the positive feedback loop in the process of collective learning, while collective forgetting slowed down.

The Emergence of Moral Religions

In the Old World, state centers soon developed into growing cities. In Meso-potamia, for instance, the first urban areas emerged between 5,000 and 4,000 years ago (depending on what one would call a city). Very soon, sizable numbers of people began to live in cities and make a living by either producing forms of complexity or trading them. For such people, who constituted the emerging secondary sector, their dependence on other people for securing matter and energy had become important, while their productive relations with the surrounding natural environment began to disappear. One may suspect that many such urbanites conducted their transactions mostly within their larger family networks, as many of them still do today. Yet as cities grew and increasing numbers of people did not know each other personally anymore, a need for moral guidelines emerged, which prescribed how to deal with other people.

By that time, state elites had begun to formulate ways of desired behavior in the form of laws, while they were attempting to forge overarching state identi-ties with the aid of state religions or by using state bureaucracies. English-American social scientist Benedict Anderson has called the results of such efforts 'imagined communities,' because these people did not know each other anymore yet felt some kind of shared identity.[50] In most traditional states, the overarching identities were expressed in terms of religion and symbolic kinship, with gods, kings and queens often portrayed as the 'fathers and mothers' of their people.

Nonetheless, for many urbanites a great deal of uncertainty would have remained with regard to the question of how to deal with strangers, of whom there were many. These feelings of uncertainty led to new religious needs, and thus to new religions, in which moral guidelines became important, especially concerning the question of how to deal with strangers. Such tendencies could also be observed within the growing armies. As a result, new moral religions emerged, in which the desired conduct was defined in the form of teachings by divinely inspired men (usually no women, a result of the male dominance of the public sphere). In these new religions, the prominence of the issue of how to deal with the natural environment declined steeply. It is in this way that the emergence of Christianity, Islam, to some extent Hinduism (which remained a mixture between a moral religion and an early state religion) and Buddhism can be explained, while the Chinese moral teachings of Confucius represent similar developments without specific supernatural overtones.

As soon as sizable numbers of urbanites had converted to such a religion, it became advantageous for state elites to ally themselves with such a moral reli-gious regime. In this process, the moral religions themselves became religions of state, tending to a monopolistic pursuit of public veneration and celebration, if not of private devotion. As a result, the patterns of religious needs and constraints shifted again. Many rulers, for instance, began using the new moral state religions for legitimizing their power. The new state priests were usually willing to do so in exchange for a certain amount of matter and energy.

The transition to state religions led to novel definitions of religious orthodoxy, which first of all served the needs felt by the ruling elite. However, these new religious views were often not in tune with the religious needs experienced at local levels, especially among the farmers. As a consequence, major differences emerged between urban moral state religions and local farmer religions who, as a result of their direct productive relations with the surrounding natural environment, kept experiencing religious needs expressed in the idiom of 'supernatural nature,' such as a sun god and a moon goddess, mother earth and mountain gods. This often led to tensions between the religious representatives of moral state religions and the farmers, a situation that has continued to exist until today in many areas, such as Andean Peru. As part of this process, a great many religious compromises have been struck, the nature of which very much depended on the prevailing balance of power and interdependency between urban and rural areas.[51]

In the Americas, cities emerged far later than in Eurasia. As a result, moral religions had not emerged before the European invasion took place in the New World. All American state religions from before the European conquest were therefore phrased in terms of 'supernatural nature.' In these religions, codes of conduct concerning how to deal with others had evolved, of course, including the legitimization of state power, but these rules were always legitimized by referring to 'supernatural nature' and not by the teachings of supernatural human beings. In contrast to the new moral religions in the Old World, these rules were not intended for all people regardless of the society they lived in.

Energy and Complexity in State Societies

Although all states were different, over the course of time they began to exhibit similar characteristics, even though they were often almost, if not entirely, unconnected. Apparently, the internal dynamics of matter and energy flows and Goldilocks circumstances produced a regime of needs and constraints that caused these similarities. All states became stratified societies, which included a middle class specializing in the production and trade of increasing amounts of constructed complexity, as well as an upper class of rulers and priests, who monopolized the control over important means of violence and taxation, while they used religion to legitimize their privileged positions.

To maintain their positions, all state elites were supported by armies and bureaucratic organizations. The latter became specialists in gathering, ordering, storing and transmitting information with the aid of mnemonic devices, ranging from clay tablets to woolen cords with knots. Until that time, most cultural information had been stored in individual brains. The innovation of externally recorded information facilitated the control over far larger numbers of people and far greater amounts of matter, energy and constructed complexity than before, while it also opened up new opportunities for large-scale disinformation. Because control over information flows became essential for the powerful strata to retain the type of complexity they desired, enormous efforts were expended to keep control over them. This included attempts at limiting these information flows to privileged, often tightly controlled, professional groups, the use of secret codes as well as public displays of a great many types of propaganda. Yet in the long run, the global dissemination of the art of writing among increasing numbers of people was inevitable, which led to major changes in social complexity.

As John and William McNeill have argued, over the course of human history the skill to store and transmit information over ever larger distances and in ever increasing volumes has gone up enormously while the costs decreased. This trend may have started with the invention of writing, which was followed, much later, by the innovation of printing and, more recently, by electronic data technology. As a result, the human ability to learn from other people, as well as manipulate people, matter and energy, has increased immensely also. A similar trend took place with the transportation of goods. This began with merchandise carried by humans, followed by boats, pack animals, carts, ever larger sailing ships, steam trains and steam boats, cars and trucks and, most recently, planes and container ships. Every new invention opened up fresh opportunities for transporting goods over ever larger distances, while the costs of doing so went down. Both trends have enabled humans to construct ever larger amounts of complexity.[52] Because greater complexity always has a cost attached to it, people did such things only when they thought the profits would outweigh the investment.

As a result of the increasing division of labor and the growing social inequality, the flows of matter and energy within large states became increasingly complex. Let us first examine the top of the food pyramid. This consisted of the two most powerful elites: rulers and priests. Such people were, first of all, concerned about how to preserve the state and their religion, as well as their own positions. Consequently, they strove to control vital matter and energy flows and make sure that they themselves received a good share of them. In all state societies, the elites have invariably looked down on farmers. As a result, tilling the land and manual labor in general became low-prestige occupations.

Status hierarchies became increasingly expressed by ideas of cleanliness and dirt, including the ways in which people could avoid getting dirty hands. This happened most explicitly in India but also elsewhere. To this day, working the land is viewed by most others as a low-status occupation.

The bottom of the food pyramid was formed by large numbers of farmers, often including slaves. While these people were concentrating virtually all of the matter and energy that kept the state going, they usually found themselves caught between the actions of micro-parasites on the one hand and of macro-parasites (tax collectors) on the other hand, as William McNeill observed, while rodents, birds and insects prayed on their harvest.[53] Furthermore, warfare and conquest, such as the subjugation of Gaul by Julius Caesar, often wreaked havoc on the farmers. More often than not, a passing army left a hungry and dying farmer population in its wake after having plundered the land to such an extent that the soldiers could not return by the same route for lack of sufficient supplies. It is therefore not surprising that the farmers became susceptible to religious ideas that claimed to alleviate human suffering in another life in this or another world.

The emerging secondary sector of society lived mostly, but not exclusively, in or near urban settings. It consisted of specialists in the manufacturing of complexity, ranging from pottery to grand architecture. These often unsung heroes, who included a great many inventors, technicians, crafts people, builders and architects, engineers and scientists, were dealing with problems of daily life that could actually be solved. In his book *The Ancient Engineers*, US science author Lyon Sprague De Camp summarized their importance as follows:[54]

An engineer is merely a man who, by taking thought, tries to solve human problems involving matter and energy. Since the Mesopotamians tamed their first animal and planted their first seed, engineers have solved a multitude of such problems. In so doing, they have created the teeming, complex, gadget-filled world of today.

Civilization, as we know it today, owes its existence to the engineers. These are the men who, down the long centuries, have learned to exploit the properties of matter and the sources of power for the benefit of mankind. By an organized, rational effort to use the material world around them, engineers devised the myriad comforts and conveniences that mark the difference between our lives and those of our forefathers thousands of years ago. The story of civilization is, in a sense, the story of engineering – that long and arduous struggle to make the forces of nature work for man's good.

This rather positive assessment (engineers have also developed a good many destructive capabilities, many of which De Camp mentioned) underlines the importance of the emerging specialist sector. Their occupations were probably often profitable yet, with some exceptions, usually deemed less prestigious than those of rulers and priests.[55]

In the urban state centers, these developments led to increasing cultural complexity. The first large buildings were constructed, mostly huge artificial hills with a pyramidal shape. To build them, human efforts and animal muscle power, if available, were used to defy gravity and produce the first 'architecture of power.' Ever since that time, humans have continued to build this type of architecture. Although the more recent constructions have become much more intricate, for a long time they did not become a great deal taller. Only during the industrial period did it become possible again to construct taller buildings. The largest gains in height were actually made during the period of early state formation and not in recent times. Between 6,000 and 5,000 years ago, the height of buildings grew from at most 10 meters to about 137 meters (the Cheops pyramid in Egypt), an increase of more than a factor of 10. Over the course of time, the shape of buildings began to vary, ranging from temples and palaces to living quarters for the poor, while quite often their internal and external complexity became greater also. The shapes of smaller artificial objects such as teacups, far less constrained by gravity than large buildings, came to exhibit an ever-increasing variation over the course of time. Seen from a general point of view, the history of constructed complexity in all its manifestations can also be interpreted as a long series of innovations leading to ever so many adaptive radiations.

In 2003, Joseph Tainter and his coauthors suggested that large states may have known a specific life cycle based on the ways they procured their energy. The conquest of new areas was usually financed by plundering the available concentrated resources. For a short period of time, this produced a great amount of cultural complexity. Yet after the initial phase was over and conquest was no longer a feasible option for logistical or geographical reasons, state elites came to depend on taxes generated by agriculture, both in-kind taxes and money taxes. This was a low-gain energy resource. The resulting tax pressure often led to the degradation of these resources. As a consequence, greater efforts had to be expended in keeping the taxes flowing, which further degraded the tax base. This vicious cycle eventually led to the collapse of large states. This mechanism may well explain the long-term dynamism of most, if not all, agrarian states to a considerable extent.

In urban settings, a great deal of entropy was produced. Until very recently, judged by modern North Atlantic standards, cities were very dirty places. In his book *The City in History*, US historian Lewis Mumford formulated this as follows:[56]

For thousands of years city dwellers put up with defective, often quite vile, sanitary arrangements, wallowing in rubbish and filth they certainly had the power to remove.

US garbologists William Rathje and Cullen Murphy provided a graphic description of how early urbanites would have dealt with the entropy they produced:[57]

The archaeologist C.W. Blegen, who dug into Bronze Age Troy during the 1950s, found that the floors of its buildings had periodically become so littered with animal bones and small artifacts that "even the least squeamish household felt that something had to be done." This was normally accomplished, Blegen discovered "not by sweeping out the offensive accumulation, but by bringing in a good supply of fresh clean clay and spreading it out thickly to cover the noxious deposit. In many a house, as demonstrated by the clearly marked stratification, this process was repeated time after time until the level of the floor rose so high that it was necessary to raise the roof and rebuild the doorway." Eventually, of course, buildings had to be demolished altogether, the old mud-brick walls knocked in to serve as the foundations of new mud-brick buildings. Over time the ancient cities of the Middle East rose high above the surrounding plains on massive mounds, called tells, which contained the ascending remains of centuries, even millennia, of prior occupation.

In 1973, US civil engineer Charles Gunnerson calculated that if modern New Yorkers living on Manhattan were to spread their garbage evenly over their island instead of dumping it elsewhere, its rate of accumulation per century would be exactly the same as that of ancient Troy.[58] Nonetheless, as this example indicates, garbage regimes emerged that came to deal with dirt in more effective ways. This included sewage systems and the recycling of human and animal excrements in the form of fertilizer. Although working on the entropy side of life may sometimes have been profitable, until the present day it has rarely, if ever, been a prestigious occupation.

Comparatively dirty urban settings provided excellent Goldilocks circumstances for many infectious diseases. As a result, life expectancies remained low for a long time. As a consequence, cities depended on the influx of people from the surrounding countryside for maintaining their population numbers for most of their history.[59] Because many urban areas became better connected, epidemics began to rage over increasing distances, often inflicting untold suffering. Yet over the course of time, the survivors gradually became more resistant to these diseases through the process of non-random elimination of the weaker members of society. As part of the same process, many of the disease-causing microorganisms slowly but surely became less virulent and changed into children's diseases. In the New World, by contrast, there were hardly any domesticated animals and comparatively few cities, as well as fewer, and less intensive, exchange networks. As a result, the ancient Americans did not develop immunity against such infectious diseases, so when Eurasia and the Americas finally became interlinked, a great many Native Americans succumbed to the actions of Eurasian microorganisms.

Over the course of time, people became better at exploiting water and wind energy with the aid of water and wind mills. As De Camp formulated it:[60]

> When men learned to use the power of water and wind, it became possible to concentrate much more power in less space than had been the case before and thus easily to perform tasks that had been difficult or impossible.

At the same time, mariners learned how to use the energy in the prevailing patterns of wind and water circulation for traveling ever longer distances across seas and oceans.

In some areas, including Britain and China, coal mining became important, while in Central Asia natural oil was exploited for various purposes. Dutch scientist Frank Niele sees this development as the beginning of what he calls the 'carbo-cultural energy regime.'[61] Yet until the industrial revolution, most of the ways in which people extracted matter and energy from the environment and used it for productive purposes changed, in fact, very little.

While large and small states waxed and waned, inventions were made that provided a power advantage to those who possessed them.[62] Nonetheless, it proved impossible to monopolize such skills for long, with the result that the power differences would level out again. This competition provided the driving force that caused humans to create ever new forms of complexity. The invention of guns provides an excellent example of this process. When state armies equipped with guns of different sizes became sufficiently effective, all other states needed to either adopt this new technology or face defeat. Gun technology was, of course, based on the principle of concentrating energy for destructive purposes.

The First Wave of Globalization

A little more than 500 years ago, a new stage in human history began, namely the first wave of globalization, which was triggered by Christopher Columbus's transatlantic voyages. This first wave of globalization happened after Europeans had learned how to exploit the energy stored in winds and ocean currents to transport themselves and their cargo out into the oceans far beyond the familiar seashores. Much of their technical and intellectual knowledge had been borrowed from the Arab world and elsewhere in Asia, but had been developed further during sea voyages in the rougher West-European climate.

In doing so, Europeans began to sail the Seven Seas on ships armed with heavy guns looking for profit wherever it could be found. In a period of about 100 years, the European expansion led to the conquest of the large Spanish and Portuguese American colonies; to the establishment of worldwide oceanic trade routes, including European-dominated trading posts and production centers along many African and Asian coasts; as well as to the colonization of the eastern seaboard of North America mostly by northern Europeans. For the first time in human history, people began circling the globe within their own lifetime. Apparently, the expected profits exceeded the costs invested in creating and maintaining global complexity.

All of this led to the reunification of the three major world areas into one single human web, within which western Europe suddenly found itself no longer on the margin of the large Eurasian continent but right in the middle of the exploding transatlantic networks of exchange.[63] The effects of this process were greatly reinforced by the fact that, around the same time, the printing press with movable type had been introduced to western Europe, which led to a revolution in data storage and communication among its emerging middle classes. This innovation produced a positive feedback loop in the process of collective learning, which accelerated as a result, while the process of cultural forgetting slowed down again.[64]

A major immediate trigger for European expansion can be found in the Turkish expansion during the fifteenth century that led, among other things, to the conquest of Constantinople in 1453 CE, as well as to the resulting Ottoman dominance of the overland trade between Europe and Asia. This made such produce much more expensive in western Europe and stimulated attempts to find overseas trade routes that led to the unexpected result of the European discovery of the Americas. Yet had this not happened, intensive contacts across the Atlantic would have been established fairly soon anyway, given that Basque sailors, for instance, had already been fishing off Newfoundland from perhaps as early as 1430 CE, while European sailors were also discovering other major Atlantic wind and water currents that were useful for reaching distant destinations.

The Iberian conquest of the Americas represented the establishment of a traditional empire, but this time across an ocean (which had never happened before). While the Spanish and Portuguese were busy establishing their American colonies at great cost during the sixteenth century, Habsburg Spain also tried to hold on to its European possessions. In northwestern Europe, the emerging middle classes, mostly traders and craftsmen, made good use of this situation of imperial overstretch to escape from the control of their traditional rulers.

Thus, a new stage in human history began. New states emerged that were to a considerable extent, or even exclusively, ruled by mercantile and proto-industrial elites. This happened first in the Seven United Provinces of the Netherlands, then in Great Britain, followed by the United States and subse-quently by a growing number of states elsewhere in Europe and the Americas. In all these states, the emerging middle classes sought to create and maintain social and material Goldilocks circumstances that favored their own well-being, including the legal protection of private property, trading practices and finan-cial transactions.[65] This was the emergence of capitalism as we know it today.

Ever since that time, this process has gained momentum all around the world. Merchants became the protagonists of the early globalization process. In contrast to traditional elites and farmers, they were not tied to the land. They could only increase their matter and energy flows through trade. In doing so, they began to transport many types of agrarian produce and all sorts of pro-duced complexity with high added value all around the globe, often at great profit and within remarkably short periods of time, usually only a few years.

By 1580 CE, a European-dominated global trade network had been estab-lished by both peaceful and military means. This led to a global division of labor that, in its turn, stimulated a worldwide intensification of the extraction of matter and energy, their elaboration and exchange, as well as the reshaping of a great many local and regional Goldilocks circumstances. The transportation from one continent to the other of people (often in the form of slaves), plants and animals began a Columbian exchange that altered the ecologies of entire continents.[66] As a result, global cultural complexity began to rise again, while many forms of local and regional complexity were overwhelmed by the new global players, either succumbing or becoming marginalized.

In their global exploits, the Europeans received a helping hand from Eura-sian infectious diseases. They prevailed in the Americas thanks to the uneven balance of immunity against infectious diseases between the Old World and the New World, as it had developed over 10,000 years. While Eurasian microbes wreaked havoc among Amerindians, Europeans did not suffer similarly from Mexican or Peruvian micro-parasites. Of course, in many cases Europeans also possessed superior military technology. Yet until the nineteenth century, this superiority mattered very little along the black African coast, where the tropical diseases prevented the Europeans from establishing themselves further inland before the advent of modern hygiene and medicine. And, even then, West and Central Africa were still considered to be a 'white man's grave.' The great empires of South and Southeast Asia could only be conquered effectively when technical superiority resulting from the first wave of globalization and later also from industrialization tilted the balance of power decisively in favor of Europeans. In those parts of the world, Europeans and locals were more or less on equal footing in terms of immunity to diseases.

It has long been argued that the social structure of western Europe greatly stimulated this process.[67] Split up as it was in a great many states and fiefdoms that found themselves in an almost continuous state of war, there was no central authority that could impose order or make decisions concerning how to employ Europe's resources in a coordinated fashion. For instance, while the Turks were laying siege to Vienna, there was no overarching European ruler who could decide to use a joint pool of European resources to relieve that city. To the contrary, while Central Europeans were holding off the Ottomans the inhabitants of the Iberian Peninsula were busy conquering the Americas.

The internal European competition required increasing amounts of matter and energy, which stimulated efforts to find them elsewhere. In the words of Allen, Tainter and Hoekstra:[68]

> For societies powered by solar energy and using that energy so heavily within the limits of their own technology, the main way to increase wealth was to control more of the earth's surface where solar energy falls. It became necessary to secure the produce of foreign lands to subsidize European competition. New forms of energy, and nonlocal resources, were channeled into a very small part of the world. This concentration of global resources allowed European conflict to reach heights of complexity and costliness that could never have been sustained with only European resources.

The intense European competition led to a great many inventions that were rapidly communicated, thanks to the speeding up of the collective learning process. This made European societies much more powerful. An important aspect of this process was, as Alfred Crosby outlined, the increasing 'quantification of reality.'[69] This meant that, at that time, Europeans began to capture ever more aspects of the world in numbers perhaps more than anywhere else, ranging from measuring time and space to bookkeeping all the way to painting and music. This made European control over matter and energy a great deal more efficient. Almost needless to say, the increasing quantification of reality contributed to paving the way for the scientific revolution, which, in its turn, would pave the way for the industrial revolution.

In China, by contrast, central rule kept merchants under rather tight control. To be sure, in the early fifteenth century several very large seafaring expeditions were sent out under the leadership of Admiral Zheng He, which visited eastern Africa. According to disputed claims, his fleet may even have reached the Americas. However, these efforts were discontinued by court order, probably because it was deemed wise to expend their resources on keeping the Mongols out of the northern territories rather than on traveling to countries far away at great expense without a clear return on investment.[70]

Like the emergence of states, the first phase of globalization was a social regime transformation. Of course, there were a great many technical improvements, most notably transoceanic shipping, which, among other things, greatly facilitated the moving of people and produce around the world. Yet unlike the agrarian revolution or the later industrial revolution, the first wave of globalization did not lead to a major technological breakthrough in the ways societies harvested matter and energy, for all societies remained powered by renewable solar energy. The great innovation consisted of the interlinking of all the existing modes of production into one single global trade network, which was dominated by a relatively small number of players.

Amsterdam may well have been one of the first globalizing cities, if not the first. During its 'Golden Age,' people and produce from many places passed through this city. A prominent mapmaking industry had emerged here, producing world maps, atlases and globes, while the largest room of the Town Hall, later the Royal Palace on Dam Square, sported a marble floor with both an Earth map and a sky map (these maps still exist, although renovated). In other words, the proud locals made sure they could literally walk on top of both the world and the sky. In addition, a considerable number of allegoric ways of depicting the Earth (which I call 'Earth icons') were produced in this city during that period as a way of expressing that seventeenth century Amsterdammers were global players, not unlike the images many firms and mass media have been using over the past 15 years. For example, a popular Earth icon at the time was the virgin of Amsterdam holding Earth in her hand while overseeing mariners bringing in wealth from all around the world. Although at that time the word 'globalization' did not yet exist (it was presumably coined in the twentieth century), the proud Amsterdam burghers used the image of globalization in many such ways. One wonders whether in other major cities, first of all London and Paris, this also happened during that period.

As part of the first wave of globalization, the modern scientific method emerged. This development was closely linked to the technical advances that were being made in, for instance, oceanic navigation, mapmaking and gun technology. This included the invention of the telescope and the microscope, which allowed humans to see things they could not see with the naked eye. Over the course of time, humans learned to explore the entire range of the electromagnetic spectrum with the aid of countless new types of artificial sensors. This development, which is unique in biological history, has led to a great many new insights. As a result, our knowledge of the natural world rapidly increased, which produced, for instance, the first reasonably accurate representation of our solar system, a classification of living nature that is still in use today, a much better anatomy of human beings as well as more detached ideas about the very small particles everything consists of. In other words, during this period the foundations were laid for big history in its modern form. Rapidly increasing scientific and technological knowledge led to a far greater control over many aspects of nature, at least in the short term.[71]

Between 1776 and 1825 CE, most European colonies in the Americas freed themselves from Old World royal control. This became possible when the colonists were no longer dependent on forms of constructed complexity from Europe, notwithstanding a great many efforts by their European rulers to keep them so. The first independent state in the Americas was the United States. This new state was controlled by the wealthier members of society, most notably the landed establishment and the middle classes.

Subsequently, the French Revolution, which had found great inspiration in these developments on the other side of the Atlantic Ocean, set the tone for societal shifts all over Europe and the Americas. This led to the independence of the Spanish and Portuguese American colonies, which had become possible because the French occupation of the Iberian Peninsula during the Napoleonic wars weakened Spanish and Portuguese control over their American colonies to the extent that the emerging Central and South American middle classes could free themselves from their colonial masters. Many of these new states, however, soon found themselves in the grip of the local feudal landholding elites. As a result, even today, many Latin American lower and middle classes are still struggling to escape from the grip of the traditional ruling elites, while from an Amerindian point of view, European rule has never ended. Similar developments took place in other areas, most notably in Australia, New Zealand and Oceania.

Industrialization: The Second Wave of Globalization

The rise of industrialization in the late eighteenth and early nineteenth centuries implied a fundamentally new way of producing complexity, namely with the aid of machines driven by fossil fuels that consisted of solar energy stored in bio-molecules that had accumulated in the Earth's crust over millions of years. Until that time, these high-gain energy resources had not been considered useful for manufacture. To be sure, for a long time coal and oil had served as energy sources for burning fires and were used for making utensils out of metal and glass, yet they were not employed as a replacement for human or animal muscle power. The same was the case for peat, which had fueled

Holland's Golden Age during the seventeenth century. In this respect, Alexander von Humboldt's description of natural petroleum wells as a mere curiosity around 1800 CE in what is now Venezuela is enlightening. Little did he suspect that 200 years later these energy flows would provide most of that country's wealth as well as considerable political leverage.[72] During the industrial revolution, humans not only learned to use these very concentrated forms of energy for productive purposes, but also invented ways of condensing them even more by producing cokes from coal, gasoline from natural oil and electricity from both.

The industrial revolution thus gave rise to a novel way in which humans harvested energy to keep their complexity going. Apparently, the benefits of creating and maintaining industrial complexity outweighed the costs, at least in the short term. Until that time, all societies had almost entirely been powered by renewable solar energy through either agriculture or gathering and hunting. Yet by the early 1800s, the use of fossil fuels added enormous quantities of nonrenewable energy to the human repertoire, which were used for both constructive and destructive purposes. This allowed our species to at least temporarily produce and power an expanding range of ever more intricate types of constructed complexity, as long as the profits outweighed the costs. This development led to profound changes in social complexity. It caused incisive change in the form and shape of the human food pyramid, while the already existing trends of human-induced change in the food pyramid of life were greatly reinforced.

The industrialization of society greatly strengthened the general trends that had emerged during the first wave of globalization and, as a result, caused a second wave. Up until the end of the eighteenth century, virtually all production processes had been driven either by human and animal muscle power or by wind and water energy, all of which were locally or regionally available. Industrial production first emerged in areas that were well endowed with the needed new resources, mostly coal, iron and water, but its rapid diffusion soon stimulated a worldwide search for natural resources of many kinds. These resources were transported to factories, which subsequently turned out an increasing variety of products in unprecedented quantities at relatively low prices. In consequence, the selling of manufactured goods soon attained global dimensions, not least because the means of transport were revolutionized in the form of steam trains and steamships. The world population became ever more interdependent, as increasing numbers of regions became providers of natural resources for industry, as well as markets for its products. Industrialization made armies ever more destructive.

The rapidly growing and intensifying means of long-distance communication (first the telegraph and later the telephone, followed by radio, television and, more recently, the Internet) would not have been possible without an economy increasingly based on inorganic fuels. The same can be said for the recording of images through photography and film, as well as sound with audio recordings. All of this greatly contributed to global collective learning and entertainment, ranging from astronomy to popular culture.

Industrialization emerged first in Great Britain where, apparently, Goldilocks circumstances favored this innovation. Already by the end of the Middle Ages, the English began to mine coal, stimulated by the loss of forests, which had been a major source of fuel. They were also digging up other natural resources, such as iron and tin. In many of these mines, the high water table made it difficult, if not impossible, to reach deeper levels. As a solution to this problem, British engineer Thomas Newcomen improved the design of an already existing 'fire engine' (which was a primitive steam engine). In doing so, he invented the first steam engine that was able to pump out water and make mines accessible at lower depths. The central idea was to use two abundant resources, water and coal, for getting rid of ground water and to gain access to deep coal and other minerals. By later standards the Newcomen engines were rather inefficient.

In the 1770s, while seeking to mend a model Newcomen engine, Scottish engineer James Watt introduced a number of critical improvements, which made steam engines much more efficient. This allowed them to be used for a wider range of productive activities, first of all spinning and weaving. After having patented his inventions, James Watt and English entrepreneur Matthew Boulton set up a joint enterprise to manufacture and sell these new steam engines. The use of this new power source lowered the costs of constructing complexity enormously. This soon led to the emergence of a new type of entrepreneurs, industrialists who began to make a great deal of money by producing and selling an ever-expanding range of complexity produced with the aid of machines driven by fossil fuels.[73]

However important Watt's technological breakthrough was, the industrialization of society could not have taken place without a long history of specific political, economic, socio-cultural, technical and scientific developments, including the rise of a mercantile and proto-industrial entrepreneurial class, which had secured Goldilocks conditions for their businesses in the form of legal protection. In Great Britain, this included a temporary monopoly on inventions in the form of patents, which allowed inventors to make a profit from their ingenuity.[74]

The control over these new industrial production processes allowed the middle classes to become the most wealthy and powerful stratum of society. This was characterized by Karl Marx as the bourgeoisie taking over the state. Within only 100 years, this decisive societal change led to the emergence of modern democracies. First, the increasingly powerful middle classes claimed voting rights for themselves. Later, the emerging urban working classes succeeded in organizing themselves to the extent that they also gained access to the democratic process. After elections began to legitimize state rule, state religions were no longer needed to do so. This led to a substantial weakening of the bond between church and state. At the same time, many strata of society began to adhere to forms of worship that were more attuned to their living conditions and the corresponding religious needs.

As part of the transition from an agrarian to an industrial society, the farmers' custom of daily alcoholic drinks became stigmatized, not least because it became dangerous to operate machines under the influence of alcohol. This led to the ideal of a regime of soberness, at least during the day. These anti-alcohol campaigns were, of course, also directed against the heavy drinking by industrial laborers after having received their weekly pay. Given the rather dire and boring circumstances in which many of them had to work, it was not unusual to seek such a form of temporary escape. At the same time, new drinks not contaminated by microorganisms had become available in the form of tea and coffee, which are both stimulants. They were usually consumed with milk and sugar, which made them more nutritious. This made it possible to discontinue the daily consumption of home-brewed beers, which had served for a long time both as a safe drink and as a supply of energy. While in the late 1800s, bottled mineral water had already become available as a safe drink, treated tap water and soft drinks were added to this repertoire in the nineteenth and twentieth centuries. These were all industrial solutions to the problem of how to combat contamination (entropy) in the water supply.

Italian demographer Massimo Livi-Bacci has argued that making steam engines more efficient went hand in hand with the increasing efficiency of human reproduction. As he put it:[75]

> During the past two centuries, Western populations have undergone a similar process. Previously, slow growth was accompanied by considerable demographic waste. Women had to bear a half dozen children simply in order to achieve replacement in the following generation. Between a third and half of those born perished before reaching reproductive age and procreating. From a demographic point of view, old regime societies were inefficient: in order to maintain a low level of growth, a great deal of fuel (births) was needed and a huge amount of energy was wasted (deaths). The old demographic regime was characterized not only by inefficiency but also by disorder. The probability that the natural chronological hierarchy would be inverted – that a child would die before its parent or grandparent – was considerable. High levels of mortality and frequent catastrophes rendered precarious any long-term plans based on individual survival.

In short, the growing efficiency and predictability of industrial production was paralleled in people's personal lives.

Like the domestication of plants and animals, industrialization is an ongoing process that led to enormous power differences both within and among societies. While national cultural complexity rose once again in early industrializing societies, cultural change was also inevitable in the rest of the world as a result of industrialization. By the nineteenth century, the global human web had intensified to the extent that knowledge of major inventions was transmitted rapidly. In contrast to the rise of agriculture and the emergence of early states, which took place in seven world areas, industrialization was invented only once. Moreover, the industrialization of society produced another rapid wave of globalization, which made it impossible for societies elsewhere in the world to independently invent industrial production based on fossil fuels.

It did not take long before entrepreneurs and governments of many emerging nation-states, both in Europe and beyond, followed the British example by setting up modern industries. This was the beginning of the spread of industrialization across the face of Earth, a process that has not yet been completed. Like the transition to agriculture, the industrial revolution can be seen as a series of major innovations that led to cultural adaptive radiations. At the same time, this period witnessed the decline of older forms of complexity, most notably local forms of production.

All the countries that successfully industrialized became wealthy to an extent that was unparalleled in human history – first the elites, of course, and then sizable portions of the general populace later. Apparently, the industrial elites found it impossible to keep the new matter, energy and complexity to themselves. This was partly the result of the fact that increasing numbers of poor people began to live in cities, where those people posed a direct threat to the ruling classes through strikes, riots and threats of revolution. Cities underwent spectacular growth after the industrialization of agriculture and transportation had ensured that large urban populations could be sufficiently fed and public health improvements enabled them to replace their populations or even grow by themselves. All of this led to unprecedented waves of rural-urban migration that were fueled by the hope of finding sufficient matter, energy and Goldilocks circumstances. As a result, gigantic metropolitan areas emerged, which housed many millions of people.

Because the needed natural resources were often concentrated in relatively small areas, an 'oligopolization' process began, in which a few major players and businesses controlled them. Even today, a relatively small number of energy companies and mining businesses retains control over considerable portions of such resources. As a result, these businesses became enormously profitable. A similar process took place in the fabrication and trade of an unprecedented wave of novel types of complexity, which many people in wealthier countries now take for granted. British industrial textile production, for instance, almost entirely wiped out the Indian production of cotton clothes. Yet it proved more difficult to dominate the production and trade of constructed complexity than to control the access to natural resources, which led to the current situation wherein such businesses range from small family-based enterprises to large multinational companies.

During this second wave of globalization, the knowledge of science and technology increased rapidly. As part of this development, business enterprises opened scientific laboratories for product research and development. Governments also began to stimulate the production and dissemination of science, for instance, by funding universities and by including science in the curricula of the emerging national schools. This led to the 'scientifization' of society, as a result of which increasing numbers of people became dependent on modern science and technology. Yet even today, even in very wealthy countries, there are very few individuals who have an all-round view of science. This is first of all a result of the fact that the rapidly increasing scientific knowledge led to the differentiation of science into a great many disciplines. This so-called reductionist program received the most financial support, because of its often spectacular short-term results, while hardly any funding was made available for scientists who, like Alexander von Humboldt, opted for a more holistic approach.

As part of the growing competition among the first industrializing countries in Europe and the United States, governments installed nationwide obligatory schools to create a skilled workforce and foster feelings of solidarity by teaching of national history and geography. This led to the formation of nation-states in the second half of the nineteenth century, in which people acquired the identity of 'their' nation in addition to local and regional identities. This process was not entirely new, but it happened far more intensively than ever before, thanks to the new means of communications, such as trains and steam printing, and later cars, radio and television.

The industrialization of society produced tremendous power differences worldwide, especially between industrializing countries and other areas, but also within the industrializing areas themselves. The intense competition among the industrializing nations led to the further colonization of large parts of the world, often as a direct or indirect result of the quest for natural resources or out of a need for markets for industrial products. After most of the conquerable world had been subjugated, the industrialized nations battled it out among themselves in two 'world wars.' After the end of World War II, two major power blocks emerged, both of which competed for world supremacy during the Cold War. This global rivalry stimulated the development of many types of industrial skills as well as the construction of a great many novel forms of complexity.

This led to unprecedented levels of economic well-being, especially within North Atlantic societies. Industrialization led to more equal relations between the sexes, because it hardly made a difference in terms of physical strength whether it was a man or a woman who pushed buttons on machines or drove cars. The invention of far more efficient ways of controlling human sexual reproduction greatly contributed to strengthening this trend. All of this allowed women to enter the public domain.

This was the first time in human history that entire populations of nation-states became affluent, not only adults but also younger people. This new flow of energy among teenagers led to the emergence of a youth culture with its own music, movies, clothes, food and means of transport. As a result of all these new forms of complexity, the so-called generation gap emerged: a large division in cultural taste and habits between adults and their children. When these youngsters became parents in their turn, they did not perceive such a gap anymore, because they had become used to these differences (which continued to change, of course).

As a result of growing global exchange networks, industrial skills could not be contained for long within the countries that had first industrialized. A great deal of copying took place, which led to the global dissemination of industrial skills. Major innovations in transportation technology, most notably freight trucks and container ships, allowed the cheap movement of very large quantities of constructed complexity all across the globe. As a result, a great many products are produced wherever the costs are the lowest today. This led to a global spread of industry as well as to the concomitant de-industrialization of many of the originally industrialized areas in North Atlantic societies.

These developments have produced an unprecedented global division of labor, and thus a growing global complexity, at the expense of local and regional complexity. Notwithstanding the loss of most of their industrial capacity, the first industrialized nations have succeeded in remaining rather powerful until today, not least because they have been able to keep control over their production processes elsewhere. Because poor industrial laborers often live far away from the headquarters of large international firms today, their business leaders face comparatively few threats from their workforce. And as long as there are large numbers of poor people elsewhere able to do such jobs for little reward, the mere suggestion of moving production to other places is often sufficiently effective to keep the labor force subservient. This situation allows international entrepreneurs to remain very wealthy.

In Asia, such developments happened in places such as South Korea, Singapore, Hong Kong, Taiwan, Malaysia, the Philippines, Indonesia and China. Yet newcomers are increasingly challenging them, most notably in areas where production costs are lower and the needed skills are available. At the same time, industrialization has produced more wealth in the newly industrializing countries, which has stimulated democratization. The recent wave of economic globalization has led to a growing unease among some members of affluent nations about the unequal living conditions worldwide. Such protests are often summarized with the term 'anti-globalization.'

Informatization: The Third Wave of Globalization

All these developments are being greatly enhanced by the current revolution in information technology. The past 60 years have witnessed the emergence of the capacity to manipulate unprecedented amounts of electronic data with the aid of computers mostly linked by telephone wires or satellite connections. Apparently, the costs of these new forms of complexity did not outweigh their benefits.

This development began in the eighteenth century, after the first transatlantic telegraph cable had been completed in 1866. Around the same time a transcontinental telegraph connection was established in the United States. This was the beginning of a rapid expansion. Already in 1903, large parts of the world had become connected through intercontinental cables. Although by today's standards their data transmission capacity was very low, the emergence of a global electronic network was a revolutionary development at the time, which suddenly made more and faster communication possible. These networks kept expanding during the twentieth century. Especially the invention of the telephone helped to improve worldwide communication, while global data transfer technology kept developing also, most notably through glass fiber optics and with the aid of communication satellites.

The next greatest improvement in communication came as a result of the emergence of computers, which are, in essence, forms of constructed complexity that manipulate data. This allows computers to control external processes. While machines driven by fossil fuels replaced human and animal muscle power, computers began to take over functions performed by the human brain. The first computers of the 1940s and 1950s were very bulky. They functioned with the aid of a great many vacuum tubes, which broke down very often, while the connections were made by manually plugging in electric wires. By today's standards, they used a great deal of matter and energy for producing comparatively little complexity. The newer forms of data technology, by contrast, run on fast and small digital computers. This technology was a direct spin-off from the US Apollo moon project during the 1960s.[76]

When digital computers became linked to the global electronic network in the 1980s, a new communication revolution was unleashed. The Internet is, in fact, the electronic equivalent of the shipping container, because both are transporting forms of constructed complexity worldwide at low cost. Thanks to the information revolution, we are now witnessing a new explosion of externally elaborated and stored information, as well as its use for both information and disinformation. As a consequence, the process of collective learning is speeding up again, while collective forgetting is slowing down.[77]

Today, anybody with a computer connection can exchange information with others around the world by messaging or by putting it online. This has produced incisive change in the ways people are informed about almost everything. As a result, the balances of power and interdependency are changing rapidly. Politicians and medical doctors, for instance, have to adapt to a far more knowledgeable clientele. These are just two examples of global social change caused by new energy flows that alter societal complexity.

The emergence of modern data technology led to the growth of a great many service industries in the countries that had industrialized first. Until now, this new head start has allowed these countries to remain competitive while maintaining relatively high standards of living. Yet during the past 20 years, these skills have also been moving across the globe to wherever they could be exploited profitably, mostly because global data transfer became fast, cheap and reliable.

All of these developments can be summarized as the third wave of globalization. It was only during this period that the word 'globalization' was actually coined. Today, enormous numbers of people communicate all around the globe. This has produced the most complex cultural global web that has existed so far. Although this development has produced a considerable cultural convergence, there is still a great diversity in living conditions, skills and world views around the world.

As a result of the globalization of capitalism, unprecedented amounts of money are rapidly moving around the world electronically to places where profits are expected to be the largest. This has allowed the banking industry, which controls these movements, to become very wealthy and influential. Furthermore, the countries that first industrialized support currencies that have, so far, been relatively stable and reliable. Over the past decades, most notably the US dollar and, more recently, the Euro have been used by governments and individuals elsewhere both for savings and for conducting a great many transactions. This situation has contributed significantly to the current wealth in North Atlantic countries, and will last as long as other countries are willing to buy dollars and euros (which cost virtually nothing to make) in exchange for natural resources, industrial products and services.

In many affluent democracies, the former bond between state and church has broken down, though it has not yet completely disappeared. This formal dissolution between state and church has led to the privatization of religion. As a result, many such religions are now becoming more attuned to locally or regionally felt religious needs, while the exercise of religiously imposed constraint on behavior has dropped considerably. In many other parts of the world, however, the bond between state and church has not yet been dissolved to a similar extent, even though some of these countries have become extremely wealthy as a result of the natural resources that they are selling to the rest of the world. This is a direct consequence of the increasing production and consumption of constructed complexity worldwide, which stimulates a growing global competition over natural resources.

Notwithstanding all these developments, even today there are very large numbers of poor people living in less industrialized countries that still operate on an agrarian base. Because they are informed through the news media about better living conditions elsewhere, and because unprecedented transport facilities exist, this has led to vastly increased levels of worldwide migration. Most of these poor migrants are seeking to go to wherever the harvesting of matter and energy is perceived to be the best. These developments are not new, yet they happen now on a scale that is larger than ever before.

All of the above developments stimulate new feelings of uncertainty among both the rich and the poor. Such feelings are often expressed in new forms of religious fervor, including Islamic fundamentalism, US tele-evangelism and North Atlantic forms of Buddhism. As a result, over the past decades a global religious marketplace has opened up that is catering to a great many different religious needs. This has allowed a great many smaller religions to go global for as long as they cater to needs experienced elsewhere. Even the traditional Andean rural religion, for instance, has recently been recast into a vocabulary that addresses modern urban needs and has been globalizing as a result. This is just one example of a global religious phenomenon today.[78]

In 1961, in reaction to Soviet pioneering space flights, US president John F. Kennedy initiated the Apollo moon project as a way of restoring global confidence in American technological supremacy. For the first time in history, this allowed a living species from Earth to travel to our closest celestial companion and return safely to Earth, as shown in Figure 7.1. Unanticipated by most, the Apollo project produced the new look at Earth in the form of photos, such as the Earthrise picture, which greatly stimulated the idea of a fragile 'Spaceship Earth.' These photos provided a strong impetus to both the fledgling environmental movement and the newly emerging holistic scientific approaches, such as big bang cosmology, plate tectonics and Lovelock's Gaia theory, all of which made possible our current synthesis of big history.[79]

Figure 7.1: The amazing expansion of human control over matter and energy during the twentieth century: the Apollo 8 astronauts during the roll-out of the Saturn V rocket that would propel them into lunar orbit and back, fall 1968. (Source: NASA.)

Energy, Complexity and Goldilocks Circumstances

Today, there is a wide range of energy use per capita (per person) around the world. The International Energy Agency provides numbers for energy consumption in most countries, which are stated in tonnes of oil equivalent per capita (toe per capita). From their report *Key World Energy Statistics 2007*, a few selected data are presented in Table 7.1.[80]

Table 7.1: Energy consumption worldwide in 2007

	Energy Use in Watt per Capita
World	2,400
Bangladesh	230
Netherlands	6,650
United States	10,500
Qatar	25,900

Table 7.2: Energy consumption in human history

	Energy Use in Watt per Capita
Hunting man	200
Primitive agricultural man	480
Advanced agricultural man	1,040
Industrial man	3,080
Technological man	9,200

(Cook (1971), p. 136)

In Table 7.2, Earl Cook's tentative data about energy use in human history are summarized (the terms in this table were employed by Cook).

In both tables, the numbers for industrial societies are reasonably similar. Clearly, with the term 'technological man,' Cook meant the inhabitants of the United States. Interestingly, in 1971 the United States consumed only slightly less energy per capita than it does today, even though it lost a major portion of its energy-hungry industrial production since then. The agreement between the other figures is a little more problematic. This is probably the result of difficulties in estimating the energy use of ancient societies or in countries such as Bangladesh, where many people do not have good access to fossil fuels, while other forms of energy use may have escaped attention. Clearly, most of these numbers are tentative and provide, at best, a rough indication of the order of magnitude of energy use.

If these numbers are reasonably correct (and remember: these figures do not include the use of fire by gatherer-hunters and farmers), there has been a rise in energy use per capita from 80 watt per capita handled by early humans before they controlled fire to about 2,400 watt per capita for contemporary human society as a whole, while countries such as the United States consume about 10,000 watt per capita. This means that the energy use per capita would have multiplied by about 30 times during human history. Yet the total energy flows

Table 7.3: A few selected power densities

	Power Density in watt/kg
Stars	0.0002
Plants	0.09
Human body	2
Human brain	15
Traditional Dutch windmill	0.15
Modern German windmill	2
Vacuum cleaner	180
Jet engine Boeing 747	2,000
Space shuttle engine	2,120,000

handled by humans have risen considerably more, because the human population as a whole has risen from a few thousand people to more than 6 billion people today. This represents an increase by a factor of 1 million. The total amount of energy harvested by humans during their history must, therefore, have increased by a factor of about 30 million.

As was explained in chapter two, forms of constructed complexity powered by fossil fuels have achieved power densities surpassing anything else in the known universe. In Table 7.3, some of these numbers are summarized.[81]

These numbers provide some insight into the power humans have been able to unleash from nature for their own purposes with the aid of fossil fuels. Of course, these numbers should be interpreted as a rough estimate. Any attempt at calculating more systematic and refined numbers could only come as the result of an intensive interdisciplinary research program.

Until today, the Goldilocks circumstances have been more restrictive for industrial production than for agriculture and animal husbandry. Industrial societies emerged in temperate zones with temperatures usually ranging between −20 degrees Celsius and +35 degrees Celsius. The air pressure is usually close to 1,000 hectopascal (sea level), while there has always been an abundant year-round water supply. Industrial production has moved to places where the temperatures are often considerably higher, but the other conditions have not changed a great deal. Even today, for instance, there are very few industries in high mountainous areas or in regions lacking sufficient water. Apparently, the spread of industrial production across the globe has been even more limited than the spread of agriculture and animal husbandry, which, in its turn, was more limited than gathering and hunting. So, at the risk of stating the obvious, in contrast to gathering-hunting and the domestication of plants and animals, industrial production has not yet taken off in seas or oceans.

At the same time, industrialization has allowed humans to live in an ever-widening range of geographical conditions, thanks to the fact that our species has become more skilled in creating Goldilocks environments for itself. Most notably during the twentieth century, people began to create an ever-expanding range of microclimates. Not only were increasing numbers of buildings heated during the cold seasons, so were greenhouses for cultivating plants. The next step was the creation of cold microclimates during the hot seasons. This included refrigerated storage areas, railroad cars, freight trucks and ships, which made possible the large-scale production and transportation of meat and other perishable foodstuffs. Houses, offices, cars, factories and shopping malls were then cooled for comfort during the warm seasons. Cooled or heated microclimates for leisure activities were the next step, which included artificial ice rinks, skiing slopes and tropical swimming pools (not very surprising, because we are still tropical animals). The exploration of space led to the development of microclimates in the form of spaceships and spacesuits, while deep sea adventures necessitated the development of submarines and diving suits. Never before has a species created such an enormous diversity of Goldilocks circumstances.[82]

Industrialization has made it possible to feed entire populations with unprecedented amounts and varieties of foodstuffs. Especially in societies in which the service sector has become dominant, most people perform less manual labor than ever before. As a result of both developments, such people are becoming heavier on average than ever before. It is not yet clear what the upper limits of matter and energy are that people are able to digest every day, but in affluent societies sizable numbers of humans appear to be making a determined attempt to reach them. In other parts of the world, by contrast, great numbers of people are still struggling with the opposite problem, namely how to procure sufficient matter and energy on a daily basis to keep their complexity going.

Industrialized societies have become more powerful, yet also more vulnerable. Disruptions of the intricate electronic systems, for instance, with the aid of which societies are run today might cause havoc. Such disasters could come as a result of cosmic events. In a report issued in 2008, the US space agency, NASA, outlined that a major solar flare such as the one that happened in 1859, might destroy electricity grids on a global scale. This would cause extensive damage that would take months to repair. Almost needless to say, this would lead to a disastrous societal disruption.[83] Yet even more seriously, today, all industrial societies very much depend on the dwindling reserves of natural resources, most notably fossil fuels. The large-scale use of fossil fuels has made possible hitherto unimaginable levels of global cultural complexity at the cost of the decline of older forms of local and regional complexity. People, matter, energy and information circle the globe in unprecedented ways today. As part of this process, both the social and ecological Goldilocks circumstances created by humans have multiplied, while most of the life forms not directly controlled by humans for productive purposes are rapidly declining in numbers.

All of this has resulted in increasing amounts of material entropy on the surface of Earth in the form of waste products. Even though humans are producing an enhanced greenhouse effect as a result, most of the generated heat can still be radiated out into the cosmic entropy trash can. Virtually all of the other material remains of human action, however, will by necessity stay on this planet. For most of its history, humanity has relied on nature's biological waste disposal regime to get rid of its trash. Especially since the industrial revolution, however, a great many materials have been made that cannot easily be recycled by terrestrial biology. Today, this includes as many as 75,000 artificial chemicals, often with unknown effects on human, animal and plant health.[84] One wonders, therefore, whether humans will be able to invent an efficient trash recycling regime and, if not, what the consequences will be. Formulated in terms of Lovelock's Gaia theory, one wonders whether Gaia will eliminate (nonrandomly) the human species because it may be undermining its own Goldilocks circumstances.

In the 1930s and 1940s, scientists in different parts of the world began to explore nuclear processes, because they suspected that new and hitherto unimaginably large energy sources could be tapped. The first nuclear bombs, and later more peaceful forms of nuclear energy, demonstrated that they were right. However, the energy that can be liberated by nuclear fission comes from a rather limited piggy bank of uranium on Earth. This uranium would have originated from the supernova event that shaped our solar system and would thus date back to the origin of our cosmic neighborhood. The energy resulting from hydrogen fusion, by contrast, is stored in a similar, although much larger, piggy bank of hydrogen and deuterium (heavy hydrogen), which originated right after the big bang. Today, the greatest problem with controlled nuclear fusion is the problem of how to construct Goldilocks circumstances that can contain this process while allowing the continuous harvesting of sufficient energy. If scientists and engineers can find ways of doing so successfully, there may be a great deal of energy available in the future. Until today, however, a considerable portion of the energy liberated by nuclear fission, and especially by nuclear fusion, has been used destructively.

While human societies have exhibited a tendency toward greater complexity, the biosphere as a whole has shown a trend toward greater simplification as a result of human action. As a result, a relatively small number of species favored by humans has multiplied beyond anything they had achieved before, while most other species, especially those endowed with large bodies, have been declining as a result of either the destruction of their complexity or the habitat reduction and annihilation. In consequence, biological evolution may be undergoing today its sixth major mass extinction since the Cambrian explosion of life forms.[85]

As with biological evolution, human development appears to be driven by the competition for matter and energy. With each major ecological and social transformation, differences in matter and energy use developed as a result of the fact that the pioneers enjoyed a head start. Yet as skills spread, such differences have tended to even out. These developments began with tool use, followed by fire control, the agrarian revolution, state formation, globalization, the industrial revolution and the information revolution.

It is hard to make firm statements about a possible increase of efficiency in human use of matter and energy use. A greater efficiency would imply that more complexity could be produced with the same amount of energy or perhaps even with less energy. Judging by recent technological examples, such as windmills, steam engines, gasoline engines and computers, there has been a drive toward greater efficiency for as long as it was perceived to result in a competitive advantage. In very recent times, some people have begun conserving matter and energy out of environmental concern. It may well be that in the long run, human history has been characterized by a process of increasing efficiency.

Clearly, we are currently living in unprecedented times. Never before in Earth history has one single species determined its own ecological and social Goldilocks circumstances to such a large extent while using unprecedented amounts of matter and energy for constructing an almost endless range of complexity. It is no surprise, therefore, that many people are wondering what will happen in the near future both to humanity and to Earth.

8

FACING THE FUTURE

Introduction

If the rise and demise of complexity came as a result of energy flows through matter within certain Goldilocks boundaries during the entire past, it would be reasonable to expect that this will also be the case in the future. My scenarios of what might happen will therefore be based on this approach. However, before embarking on this trip I want to discuss a few general aspects of the art of forecasting the future.

First of all, we do not have any data about the future. From an empirical scientific point of view, it is impossible to say anything about what lies ahead of us. At the same time, all human efforts are by necessity future oriented, because all our actions are guided by an anticipation of expected results. So, despite the unreliability of such forecast, almost everybody is interested in what the future may bring.

Because futurology is a science without data, the best possible scientific image of the future we can project consists of plausible scenarios. This involves choices about which developments are most likely to happen. In doing so, a thorough knowledge of the past is indispensable. In the past, the future was never completely disconnected from what had happened before, so major trends that are visible today are more likely than not to continue in the future. For example, we may predict with a reasonable chance of success that the sun will rise tomorrow.

While making our scenarios for the future, we have to take into account that there are no completely stable trends. In fact, various types of change can be discerned. Some changes have a more or less cyclical nature, because they are often tied to cosmic cycles. The rhythms of day and night, as well as of the changing seasons, provide very basic examples of cyclical change (although there is always some change in the cycles themselves, too). In addition, there are forms of noncyclical change. Just now, for instance, it may be wise to prepare ourselves for the coming exhaustion of fossil fuels and the effects of climate change caused by human action. On the basis of such scientific insights, we may be able to construct an estimated time line for such processes.

In addition to known trends, a category of trends exists that can be described as 'known unknowns.' These include, for instance, the possible emergence of new infectious diseases, earthquakes and volcanic eruptions, violent solar flares and meteorite strikes, or perhaps even a nearby supernova explosion. The possible exploitation of nuclear fusion as an important energy source also falls within this category. Such developments can be described as nonlinear processes, in which small events today may cause large effects somewhere in the future. We know that these things may happen, yet we do not know when or how they will take place, if at all, or what their effects would be.

Lastly, there is a category of 'unknown unknowns,' namely events of which even the possibility is completely unknown and which are, therefore, totally unexpected. Such events may, however, exert a large influence somewhere in the future. The industrial revolution provides an example of such a development. Even during the seventeenth century, very few people, if any, predicted that within a few hundred years, societies would function with the aid of machines driven by fossil fuels. Similarly, humans may invent ways of tapping energy that are totally unknown to us now. Because such developments are totally unknowable, we cannot include them in our scenarios for the future, but we should keep their possibility in mind while making our forecasts of the future.

Furthermore, human action in reaction to scenarios for the future may cause feedback loops, which would change the projected outcome. For instance, will humans be able to install a regime that limits the projected emission levels of carbon dioxide to what are considered safe levels? Will humans be able to harvest sufficient new energy before fossil fuels run out? Such trends are very difficult to forecast. It is also possible that unforeseen human action may change events, or that unforeseen problems appear as a result of human intervention. All of this adds to the difficulties of forecasting the future of humanity in any detail.

In all scenarios for the future, one major point stands out. Humans are mostly interested in those facets of the future about which they feel uncertain. Whereas nobody is going to pay any money for the prediction that the sun will rise tomorrow, most societies are willing to remunerate specialists who can tell them what tomorrow's weather will be like, because this type of information can be of great importance for the plans that humans make for future action. While weather forecasts have become a great deal more precise over the past decades, there are still many areas of life in which the future appears uncertain, such as the current state of the global economy, which stimulates attempts to produce forecasts of many different types.

During most, if not all of human history, specialists have operated who claimed privileged access to knowledge about the future, which they were willing to share at a certain price. Well-known examples include oracles such as the one at Delphi in ancient Greece. Similar oracular regimes have operated in many societies at many different levels all around the world. In industrialized societies, the public oracles and court future-tellers have been replaced by scientific institutions that perform similar functions. Even today, in societies all around the world specialists are operating who claim to possess specialized knowledge about the future, based on science or otherwise, for the sharing of which they charge a certain price.

Let us now return to our own forecasts of the future. As we have seen before, some major long-term trends can be distinguished in big history. To form an image of the long-term trends that we should expect, we will first consider the longest term future, namely the fate of the entire universe.

A Very Short Overview of the Long Future of the Universe

In their book titled *The Five Ages of the Universe: Inside the Physics of Eternity*, US physicists Fred Adams and Greg Laughlin provide an illuminating overview of the future of the universe. Their analysis is based on the assumption that the universe will continue to expand as a result of dark energy, while there is not enough mass to pull the cosmos back into a big crunch. In addition, they assume that in the very long run the elementary particles, protons, neutrons and electrons, will not be stable, but that they will decay into forms of low-level energy.

Because the universe will continue to exist for a very long time to come, we need very large numbers to describe its future. To keep these large numbers manageable, Adams and Laughlin introduced the concept of a cosmological decade as 10^x years, in which x indicates the number of the specific cosmological decade. This is an exponential scale, which means that the numbers rapidly become bigger: every subsequent cosmological decade is 10 times longer than the preceding one. While the first cosmological decade was only 10 years long, the second cosmological decade lasted already 100 years. The 11th cosmological decade will last a full 100 billion years. That is the cosmological decade we live in today, after about 13.7 billion years of cosmic evolution.

According to Adams and Laughlin, we now live in the second era, which they called the 'Stelliferous Era.' This period will last until the 14th cosmological decade, when star formation will cease as a result of the exhaustion of hydrogen clouds in galaxies. Because stars are needed to power the type of complexity we are familiar with, this means that life as we know it will be possible only until that period of time. This leads to the inevitable conclusion that our existence is intimately linked with a rather youthful and buoyant universe. Long before the 14th cosmological decade, however, about 5 billion years from now, our sun will have spent its fuel and will cease to burn. This will spell the end of most, if not all, greater complexity within our solar system. And between 2 and 5 billion years from now, our galaxy will meet its nearest neighbor, the Andromeda galaxy, which may lead to a merger between the two.

After the 14th cosmological decade, the 'Degenerate Era' will begin, which will be followed by the 'Black Hole Era' in the 35th cosmological decade, and finally by the 'Dark Era' in the 131st cosmological decade. As these names indicate, during these periods the conditions for the emergence of greater complexity become less and less favorable, because the universe is running out of energy. This means that the universe will then go through a process of simplification. During the universe's further existence, circumstances that favor complexity as we know it will not exist anymore, because the cosmos will have run out of energy almost entirely. Around the 1,000th cosmological decade, a very long time from now, all of the matter in the universe will have disappeared as a result of the expected decay of all the elementary particles, protons, neutrons and electrons. From that time on, the entire cosmos will consist of nothing but low-level energy. This will spell the end of cosmic complexity.

If this scenario for the future is correct, the current complexity in the universe is an early, transient, but inevitable, phase of a long trajectory, which began with the emergence of matter and energy very soon after the big bang, while it will end with the final decay of matter (and thus the largest possible disorder, or entropy). Although the emergence of our current complexity came as a result of a great many random effects, it was also part of a highly structured process. While forming galaxies, stars, planets and smaller celestial bodies over the past 13.7 billion years, matter and energy were locked into a path dependency toward greater complexity that was strongly determined by the natural forces.

Over time, stars and planets will run out of energy and will thus lose their greater complexity, while in the very long run they are expected to evaporate entirely. Apparently, a sufficient supply of matter and energy exists only in the youthful universe that we live in, which, in combination with the balances between natural forces, produces Goldilocks circumstances that inevitably lead to the emergence of these types of greater complexity.

The Future of Earth and Life

If our solar system is not destroyed by a nearby supernova explosion, or by the merger with the Andromeda galaxy, its future will be closely linked to the fate of the sun. The remaining lifetime of our central star is approximately 5 billion years. During this period, the sun will heat up and shine ever brighter, so that the Earth's surface will have been boiled dry about 3 billion years from now. Long before that time, life on our planet will have ceased to exist as a result of the increasing solar radiation. During the last stage of its lifetime, the sun will swell in size to such an extent that it may reach the current orbit of Mercury, while its intense radiation may melt the Earth's surface. Although our planet would have become entirely uninhabitable by that time, life may continue to exist on moons that are circling the outer planets.[1]

This means that life on Earth may have less than 2 billion years left, about four times as long as the period that elapsed between the Cambrian explosion of life forms and today. During this time, solar energy from outside will continue to increase, while the nuclear energy from inside Earth will keep diminishing, thus leading to the inevitable slowing down of the process of plate tectonics. Because this important link in the planet's recycling regime would cease to function, the waste caused by life might begin to pile up to an unforeseeable extent and with unforeseeable consequences. It is not clear, however, when plate tectonics will come to a halt.

Because both matter and energy will be abundantly available for a great many millions of years to come, it seems fair to assume that life has a bright future on this planet, even though humanity is currently causing a major extinction event. Yet seen from a long-term perspective, human stewardship of Earth will probably not last more than another few million years, perhaps much less, before our species goes extinct. A few million years is about the average life span of a complex species such as ours.[2] It may be that, as a result of our unique abilities, humans will survive longer than that. As will be discussed, this would involve reaching a much better ecological balance in using natural resources. Nonetheless, seen on a longer time span humans will probably disappear from the face of Earth, after which biological evolution will probably produce countless new life forms, some of which we may not even be able to imagine, while countless other life forms will become extinct.

The Future of Humanity

Because I expect most people will feel the most anxiety about the future of our own species, the rest of the chapter is devoted to this subject. It will not come as a surprise that the fate of humankind appears to be intimately linked to the availability of matter and energy. This is not new. Many authors emphasized this point of view during the 1970s. Yet in the decades that followed, their stark messages were first disputed and then almost forgotten. Fortunately, during the years that I have been writing this book, a great upsurge in interest in energy studies has taken place. More likely than not, this came at least partially as a result of the steep rise of the energy price in 2008, as well as of a growing realization that we will soon be running out of nonrenewable energy. Examples of this renewed interest include a *National Geographic* special issue titled 'Energy for Tomorrow,' published in the spring of 2009, and English scientist David MacKay's wonderful book *Sustainable Energy – without the hot air* of 2008. As a result, many of the following suggestions about the future of humanity may soon be common knowledge.

Let us first return to some of the energy insights formulated in the 1970s and early 1980s. These views came as a direct result of both the Earthrise view and the so-called (first) energy crisis, which was caused by the Arab refusal to deliver sufficient oil to North Atlantic countries after the Yom Kippur War of 1973, because of their support to Israel. During that period, many people began to realize that humans were rapidly consuming a very limited supply of solar energy stored in bio-molecules.[3] In 1971, for instance, US energy specialist M. King Hubbert, of peak oil fame, summarized the situation as follows:[4]

> It is difficult for people living now, who have become accustomed to the steady exponential growth in the consumption of energy from fossil fuels, to realize how transitory the fossil-fuel epoch will eventually prove to be when it is viewed over a longer span of human history. The situation can better be seen in the perspective of some 10,000 years, half before the present and half afterward. On such a scale, the complete cycle of the exploitation of the world's fossil fuels will be seen to encompass perhaps 1,300 years, with the principle segment of the cycle (defined as the period during which all but the first 10 percent and the last 10 percent of the fuels are extracted and burned) covering only about 300 years.

In the same year, US scientist Howard T. Odum formulated his view of the importance of energy for generating complexity succinctly:[5]

> Most people think that man has progressed into the modern industrial era because his knowledge and ingenuity have no limits – a dangerous partial truth. All progress is due to special power subsidies, and progress evaporates whenever and wherever they are removed. Knowledge and ingenuity are the means for applying power subsidies when they are available, and the development and retention of knowledge are also dependent on power delivery.

Already during the early 1970s, it was clearly understood not only that an anticipated lack of fossil energy would cause problems, but also that we might be running out of other scarce resources while producing ever greater amounts of pollution. In other words, the question was whether we would have sufficient matter and energy to produce the desired complexity without drowning in the resulting entropy.

The first study known to me that sought to model this situation on a global scale was published in 1972 titled *The Limits to Growth: A Report for the Club of Rome Project on the Predicament of Mankind*. This book, which has been extremely influential in setting the tone in the public discussion, came as a result of a comprehensive study performed at the Massachusetts Institute of Technology by an interdisciplinary team of researchers led by US systems management scientist Dennis Meadows. His group made one of the first computer models, if not the first, of Earth as one single system in which matter, energy and entropy played a major role.

Their model consisted of five major variables: population, resources (including energy), food production per capita, industrial production per capita and pollution. These variables were linked with what were considered plausible feedback loops. The outcome of the so-called standard model was that while critical resources dwindled, around 2020 both food and industrial production would peak and then decrease as a result of both the exhaustion of natural resources and the growing pollution. The slowdown of industrial production would subsequently lead to a decrease of pollution. The world population would peak around 2070 and then collapse as a result of a lack of many kinds of resources.[6]

This was not a happy message in an age when 'progress' was a major catch phrase. The researchers subsequently introduced a number of additional assumptions, such as a stabilization of the population in 1975, or unlimited resources, and subsequently ran their model on the computer. In every case, a collapse occurred. Finally, they looked for other ways to stabilize the world system and came up with mostly negative results. Their findings led to a number of poignant conclusions and recommendations that should help us to strive for a more sustainable world. The researchers were very careful in stating their conclusions, because they were very much aware of the fact that the real world was a great deal more complex than their model, including the fact that many aspects of it could not be accurately measured or even expressed in numbers.

The Limits to Growth stimulated a great deal of further research into a new field that soon became known as 'environmental studies.' Almost needless to say, the well-known United Nations report *Our Common Future* (1987), authored by the World Commission on Environment and Development, was a direct consequence of this growing environmental awareness.[7] In this so-called Brundtland report, named after the chairperson of the commission that produced it, the now famous definition of 'sustainable development' was given as 'development that meets the needs of the present without compromising the ability of future generations to meet their own needs.' This definition is a little vague, given the fact that no one can know with any degree of certainty what future generations will need to meet their needs. Yet if they will need resources that are similar to the ones we are using today, this definition presents a major challenge to humanity.

Interestingly, also NASA had been greatly affected by these developments. In 1975, for instance, in his foreword to the official publication summarizing the Apollo expeditions to the moon, NASA administrator James Fletcher wrote:[8]

> Husbanding the planet's finite resources, developing its energy supplies, feeding its billions, protecting its environment, and shackling its weapons are some of these problems. If the zest, drive, and dedication that made Apollo a success can be brought to bear, that may be the most priceless legacy of Apollo.

Let us return to *The Limits to Growth*. While it was criticized many times from many different angles during the years that followed, its general message is still correct, even though, seen from a short-term perspective, the suggested time span for the exhaustion of scarce resources might have been a little pessimistic. According to a study by Australian scientist Graham Turner published in 2008, the actual developments over the past 30 years have, in fact, closely followed the forecast of the standard model in *The Limits to Growth*.[9] This does not mean, of course, that their subsequent projections will become reality. Yet given the fact that their rather crude computer model has been so successful in forecasting the past 30 years, it would be wise to take its longer-term scenario very seriously.

The Availability of Matter and Energy

From a thermodynamic point of view, scarce resources are scarce because there are few places on Earth where we can find them concentrated to the extent that they are useful to humans. Yet in many other places, such materials exist in a much more diluted form. If we had unlimited amounts of cheap energy at our disposal, we would be able to concentrate them sufficiently. In such a situation, no resources would be scarce, as long as we could get rid of the entropy generated by these efforts.[10] It follows that the availability of energy and of other resources is very tightly interlinked. For example, if we were able to distill ocean water cheaply and transport it at low cost to areas where it is needed, fresh water would not be a scarce resource anywhere.

The more people live on our planet, the more resources will be needed. Seen from this point of view, it is paramount to keep human population numbers in check. If the world population were to keep growing out of control, there would be no hope that we could ever achieve an ecologically balanced lifestyle without going through a deep socio-economic crash.[11] Fortunately, global population growth appears to be leveling off more or less spontaneously. This seems to be linked to increasing urbanization. In cities, children are expensive because they do not contribute economically for a long period of time. Most, if not all, cities have usually grown as a result of migration from the countryside, where children contribute to the economy already at an early age. Furthermore, cities were also often disease pools, which kept urban populations in check. Recently, the fact that more urban women have joined the public workforce has also contributed to the trend, while the introduction of generalized retirement pension regimes has led to a decrease of the direct dependency on one's own children as providers for old age (by whatever means), and thus to a lesser need to reproduce.[12]

As a result, the most critical question appears to be how much energy is available in the near future for constructing sufficient amounts of complexity, while keeping entropy down to desirable levels. Current estimates are not encouraging. Based on those of the International Energy Agency, as well as a seminal article by David Strahan published in 2008 in the British science magazine *New Scientist*, the proven energy reserves may be as shown in Table 8.1.[13]

These are, of course, rough estimates, which very much depend on critical variables, such as population growth, the use of resources worldwide and unexpected discoveries. Yet even if these estimates are doubled, there is still reason for grave concern. For obviously, as many people now realize, humanity's dependence on fossil fuels will not last for long. In fact, it may well be that the end game has already begun. If scientists are able to construct workable nuclear fusion reactors or any other similar energy source, this may greatly alleviate our future energy needs. But right now, the prospects for doing so are not favorable. Given this situation, humankind may have no choice but to return to a lifestyle based on renewable energy. In other words, the large energy subsidy delivered by solar energy stored in bio-molecules will soon collapse,

Table 8.1: Estimated duration of nonrenewable energy sources

Energy Source	Expected Time Before Exhaustion
Oil (including shale)	Max. 100 years
Coal	Max. 100 years
Natural gas (including methane clathrates)	Max. 200 years
Uranium	Several decades

which will lead to incisive changes in social and technological complexity, which are hard to forecast at present.[14]

Thanks to the fact that there has been a temporary subsidy of fossilized solar energy, which gave rise to the industrial revolution, a great many technologies have been developed that will make it easier to harvest forms of renewable energy, and thus return to a lifestyle that is directly powered by the sun, as well as (to a much lesser extent) by geothermal energy and by tidal energy resulting from the pull of gravity within the sun-Earth-moon regime.

As Tainter and coauthors have argued, all of these renewable energy resources are less concentrated than fossil fuels, which means that humans will have to expend more effort on harvesting them. Compared to fossil fuels, the current cost of producing these new types of complexity for harvesting renewable energy often does not outweigh its benefits, at least in the short term. In consequence, as long as fossil fuels remain affordable, it will be difficult to make the transition to renewable energy sources within the current economic regime, in which competitiveness is rewarded.

Today, we have access to three major renewable energy resources, namely solar energy and, to a much lesser extent, geothermal and tidal energy. Because the amount of solar energy that reaches Earth is many times larger than geothermal heat, it seems obvious that this is our major option (including wind and water power, both of which result from solar energy). Nevertheless, geothermal heat and tidal energy may be very useful sources of energy in favored places.

Given this situation, it seems wise to opt for a mix of different energy strategies. First of all, energy could be harvested locally and regionally, preferably as close as possible to where it will be used. This minimizes transport losses and expenses, and thus makes the best use of the available energy. But it may not be sufficient. Renewable energy is notoriously fluctuating, as it depends on variable resources, such as solar radiation, wind and water. Furthermore, in many places, especially cities, the energy use is many times higher than the amounts of energy that can possibly be harvested there. If we want to preserve the complexity of cities, locally generated energy will, therefore, often need to be supplemented by energy generated elsewhere.

In contrast to oil and coal reserves, solar energy is not very concentrated. As a result, the current return on investment for harvesting solar energy is considerably lower than for fossil fuels. It seems wise, therefore, to develop solar energy first in places where the largest energy gradient can be expected, namely in areas where there is sufficient sunshine and little or no vegetation – in other words, deserts. In an article in the science magazine *New Scientist* published in 2007, it was pointed out that about $10,000\,km^2$ of photovoltaic cells in Texas or New Mexico could supply all of the electricity needs of the United States, while 300,000 km² of solar cells in the Sahara desert could generate all of the world's energy needs, currently estimated to be about 15 terawatt. If these numbers are correct, it may indeed be possible to generate sufficient energy for keeping our complexity going, especially because there are many more places on our planet where solar energy can be captured and converted into electricity.[15]

If this is indeed going to happen, a number of practical issues can be foreseen. First, these solar energy plants will need to be produced as quickly and cheaply as possible, while we still have fossil energy resources left to do so. Furthermore, these enormous solar harvesting parks will have to be maintained: for example dust from dust storms, which are very common in deserts, will have to be removed. And not least, these thinly populated places now belong to people who are often very poor. A reassessment of their economic value may turn such people into new, and wealthy, solar sheiks, with the difference that while oil wealth is temporary, solar wealth would be much more sustainable. One may wonder what price these privileged owners would charge for solar power, as well as what they would do with the continuous influx of money they earn from it. Would other societies be willing to pay such a price, or might this perhaps lead to new wars and even new forms of colonization?

In addition to the social issues, a great many technical problems would need to be resolved. Because the harvesting of solar power varies as a result of the changes in incoming radiation, while demand also varies as a result of social needs, these two fluctuating regimes will need to be reconciled with the aid of an energy buffering regime. This could take many different forms, including the production of oxygen and hydrogen out of water, which can be rejoined in fuel cells to form water again, while releasing energy. Another option would be to produce artificial lakes, where surplus energy is used to pump up the water level, which can be released again when needed by powering water turbines. All of the engines and machines that are now running on fossil fuels would need to be converted to electricity. In other words, a great many new forms of constructed complexity will have to be designed and produced. As a result, the future for engineers appears to be exceptionally good.

The energy stored in oceans may also offer interesting options. This would include not only tidal energy but also, and probably much more importantly, the energy that can be harvested in the tropics and sub-tropical zones by exploiting the differences in temperature between warm surface water and much colder deep water. This might provide 'limitless energy.' Although this may sound a little optimistic, this process is being taken seriously by big business and may offer a good option. One of the advantages would be that this type of renewable energy would not fluctuate very much.[16]

The airline industry would have the biggest problem with the expected scarcity of fossil fuels, because the Goldilocks circumstances for airplanes require a light fuel that packs energy as densely as possible without being too difficult to handle. Jet fuel is perfect for this purpose, but hydrogen or electricity would not work nearly as well. Experiments are planned to produce jet fuel from algae in warm oceans, for instance near Hawaii, but given the amount of jet fuel used today, it seems fair to expect that the scarcity of fuels will lead to a sharp decrease of the complexity of airline schedules.

More in general, more expensive energy will inevitably mean a reduction in those forms of complexity that require a great deal of energy to make or maintain, first of all the industrial production of food and consumer items, as well as many forms of transportation, most notably airplanes and automobiles, but also trains and ships. If this assessment is correct, in wealthy countries, people will have to make do with fewer material means and will move over shorter distances. A similar trend may well take place also in less wealthy countries. The current electronic global complexity is probably less expensive to maintain and may thus suffer less reduction as a result.[17]

Exhaustion of Critical Resources and Growing Entropy

In addition to the transition to a renewable energy regime and the stabilization of the global population, humanity may soon face a host of other well-known problems, which can be summarized as the exhaustion of critical resources and the growth of entropy. This includes the exhaustion of the scarce resources needed, for instance, to produce and maintain solar panels; a lack of sufficient fresh water; soil erosion and the expected exhaustion of phosphate supplies as fertilizer, which is essential for agriculture.

While soil erosion and the growing scarcity of fresh water are widely recognized as serious problems, the coming depletion of phosphate reserves is not. Nonetheless, this may well be a much more serious issue, because the currently known phosphate supplies will last at most for 100 years. While phosphates are mined in a number of countries, Morocco and the Western Sahara hold about half of the known world reserves. The discovery of these deposits has allowed modern agriculture to achieve unprecedented production levels. Because the chemical element phosphor is essential for keeping together the backbones of DNA and RNA, while it plays a critical role in virtually all biochemical reactions in which energy transfers are involved, it cannot be substituted by anything else. Currently, after mineral phosphate is used in large quantities as a fertilizer, most of it ends up in the oceans in a very diluted form, from where it is very hard to concentrate to the extent that it can be used again. If we want to avoid the collapse of industrial agriculture as we know it – and thus a stark decline of this most important source of solar energy – new ways must be found to make sure that phosphate loss to the oceans is minimized.[18]

The current burning of large amounts of fossil fuels is leading to an increase of greenhouse gases in the atmosphere and the oceans, which will lead to an enhanced greenhouse effect causing climate change and an associated sea level rise. While some countries, such as Canada and the Russian Federation, may actually benefit from a warmer climate, because it would make their agriculture more productive, other regions may suffer, especially low-lying areas on the border of seas and oceans that are threatened by inundation. Great numbers of people live in such places, many of which may have to move inland if the sea level were to rise substantially. This development will also lead to the growth of an industry that offers solutions to these problems, ranging from dike construction to cooling appliances. The increase of carbon dioxide in the oceans is making them more acidic, which, if unchecked, will lead to large changes in its ecology that may be difficult to predict.

Furthermore, we are facing the well-known threat of the current enormous loss of biodiversity caused by human action, often referred to as the sixth major extinction event since the Cambrian period. For as long as humans will continue to claim more energy and resources from a finite planetary surface, this trend will continue, perhaps to the great detriment of future generations. Moreover, in commercial agriculture we are becoming dependent on a very limited number of plants and animals, which could easily be wiped out by new pests, thus potentially causing much harm and destruction to human societies. It may be wise to diversify our crops, as traditional farmers still do, which may lead to lower yields but will offer greater protection against such disasters. It may well be that we can learn a great deal from traditional farming practices by studying them carefully.

In addition to all of these problems, we are facing the issue of growing entropy, mostly caused by materials we dump on the surface of our home planet. In addition to growing trash dumps, this includes the dispersal on land, in the oceans, in the atmosphere and even in Earth's orbit, of trash of many kinds, as well as of a great many chemicals often with unknown consequences, which may be deleterious to human, animal and plant health. This also includes the growing carbon dioxide levels in the atmosphere that are thought to be causing human-induced climate change.

All of these issues are interrelated, because they all result from the efforts of humans to produce a large amount of complexity for themselves, often at the expense of the matter and energy available for other biological species. Although the short-term achievements have often been spectacular, unintended long-term effects may actually undermine the continued production of many of these forms of constructed complexity. In all of these issues, the available energy is of critical importance. This, and only this, will determine whether humanity will be able to shape sufficient amounts of constructed complexity and sustain Goldilocks circumstances to help it survive on this planet.

One wonders what the road toward a renewable energy regime will look like. If humanity is to survive on this planet, this transition is going to take place. Its details are hard to forecast, yet one thing seems clear: as in the past, the expected incisive changes in the ways humans harvest energy and use it for both constructive and destructive purposes will lead to equally incisive changes in the form and shape of both the human food pyramid and the general biological food pyramid.

Will Humans Migrate to Other Planets?

In contrast to more optimistic forecasters, I suspect that most, if not all, members of our species will keep living on planet Earth, for it seems unlikely to me that humans will be able to engage in long-distance space travel beyond our own solar system.[19] First of all, the distances are enormous. Even our closest stellar neighbor, Alpha Centauri, is about four light years away. If we assume – and this is a big if – that our intrepid space travelers would be able to reach the velocity of 1 per cent of the speed of light (which is a few orders of magnitude larger than what we are now able to achieve), it would take more than 400 years to reach this star and its companion (they form a pair of binary stars), taking into account the time needed for acceleration and deceleration. And what if these stars do not have a planet that has Goldilocks circumstances for life and humankind? Where would our adventurous space travelers go, if they still commanded sufficient resources that allowed them to make such a decision?

In addition to the energy needed for reaching their destination, the costs (in terms of matter, energy and artificial Goldilocks circumstances) of maintaining their own complexity, as well as of their offspring would be prohibitive, while our intrepid astronauts would find few, if any resources along the way to replenish their supplies. And as soon as our cosmic voyagers left the inner solar system, they would no longer have an energy source to power their complexity, for at a greater distance from the sun, its rays would be too weak to provide sufficient energy. Yet space travelers would need food, clothing and medical care, as well as a trash disposal regime (including how to deal with deceased space travelers). To minimize weight, there would thus be a great emphasis on recycling, which would involve the use of even more energy. As a result, such a space ship would have to look like a little Earth, with the difference that there would be no sun or geothermal heat to power it.

Moreover, as Francis Cucinotta of NASA's Johnson Space Center pointed out in 2009, the damage caused by cosmic radiation to human bodies today makes it dangerous to travel even through our nearest cosmic neighborhood. This includes longer-duration missions to the moon, as well as the shortest trip to Mars and back, which would require about 18 months. 'Right now there's no design solution to stay within safety limits for such a Mars mission,' Cucinotta said. 'Putting enough radiation shielding around a spacecraft would make it far too heavy to launch, so we need to find better lightweight shielding materials, and we probably need to develop medical techniques to counteract damage to cells caused by cosmic rays.'[20] If cosmic radiation is already a major problem so close to home for such a short period of time, it may well make long-distance space travel difficult, if not impossible, even when all the other requirements mentioned above could be met. All things considered, it seems to me that even if a few members of our species were willing to take these risks, the sheer expense of such an undertaking will ensure that most of us, as well as most of our progeny, would by necessity have to remain on our home planet. In other words, currently there are no Goldilocks circumstances for long-distance space travel.

Final Words

To me and many others, the most fundamental question concerning our human future is whether the inhabitants of planet Earth will be able to cooperate in achieving the goal of reaching a more or less sustainable future in reasonable harmony, or whether the current large division between more and less wealthy people, as well as the unequal distribution of power within and among societies, will play havoc with such intentions. Given that, within a renewable energy regime, resources would probably be more limited than they are in wealthy societies today, the main question is whether all humans would be able to live within reasonable Goldilocks boundaries. In addition, one wonders whether all of the planetary surface needed for energy and food production would leave any room for areas for wild species to live and prosper.

In this context, it may be worthwhile to recall the idea expressed in chapter five that humans may be genetically hardwired to harvest more matter and energy than is needed for survival and reproduction.[21] If that were indeed the case, would humans be genetically inclined to keep overstepping the Goldilocks boundaries of their existence on Earth? If so, might we be able to tame this biological instinct with the aid of culture? What social circumstances would favor such types of behavior? Furthermore, it is not very clear what sustainability actually means, because it very much depends on what people want to preserve. While there is no consensus about these issues today, it is even less clear what future generations would want to preserve. Yet if humanity is to survive on the good Earth with any comfort, this may well be the most fundamental issue that all of us, including my children, will have to come to terms with.

In biology, the process of non-random elimination operates over only one generation. As long as a species succeeds in successfully reproducing itself, it will not be nonrandomly eliminated. Today, we are facing the situation in which for most people on our planet this type of reproduction is more or less guaranteed, even though the circumstances that their children face vary enormously. Our problem is that we have to prepare for a situation that will become urgent over more than one generation. Would we be able to generate such a long-term cultural vision among sufficiently large numbers of people in a situation where there is usually a premium on short-term results, both in the economy and in politics? In other words, would we be able to tame both our biological instincts and social arrangements with the aid of culture?

More immediately, the theoretical framework advanced in this book may be capable of contributing to a reunion of the natural and social sciences. In his famous Rede Lecture at the University of Cambridge in 1959, Charles Percy Snow drew attention to the large separation between what he called 'The Two Cultures': science and humanities. He elaborated his point of view in a book titled *The Two Cultures and the Scientific Revolution*, which was published the same year. On p. 16, he wrote the following:

A good many times I have been present at gatherings of people who, by the standards of the traditional culture, are thought highly educated and who have with considerable gusto been expressing their incredulity at the illiteracy of scientists. Once or twice I have been provoked and have asked the company how many of them could describe the Second Law of Thermodynamics. The response was cold: it was also negative. Yet I was asking something which is about the scientific equivalent of: *Have you read a work of Shakespeare's?*

As we have seen, the second law of thermodynamics plays a major role in the theoretical approach advocated here. I find it appealing that the application of this law, and of the approach to which it contributes, to both human and natural history may help to bridge the gap between the two cultures.

Whatever happens, I hope that I have made it clear that the principle of tracing energy flows through matter within certain Goldilocks boundaries, leading to the rise and demise of complexity at all levels, not only greatly simplifies our view of the big past, but also helps to clarify the major issues that humanity will have to face in the near future.

Appendix

A SHORT TIME LINE OF BIG HISTORY

ABB: After Big Bang
BP: Before Present (In BP, the present is usually defined as 1950 CE)
CE: Common Era = AD (Anno Domini)
X years ago: x years before 2010 (date of publication of this book).

13.7 billion years BP	The big bang
First 4 minutes ABB	Emergence of elementary particles, protons, neutrons, electrons and neutrinos
4–15 minutes ABB	Nucleo-synthesis of deuterium, helium, lithium and beryllium
50,000 years ABB	Transition from the Radiation Era into the Matter Era
400,000 years ABB	Neutralization of the universe and the emergence of the cosmic background radiation
700 million to 2 billion years ABB	Emergence of galaxies and stars
9.1 billion years ABB =	
4.6 billion years BP	Emergence of our solar system
4.6–4.5 billion years BP	Emergence of the inner planets
4.5–3.9 billion years BP	Hadean Era, including the cosmic bombardment
3.8–3.5 billion years BP	Emergence of life
3.4 billion years BP	Oldest stromatolites and the emergence of photosynthesis
2.0 billion years BP	Emergence of free oxygen in the atmosphere and of eukaryotic cells
540 million years BP	Cambrian explosion of complex life forms
400 million years BP	Life moves onto land

200 million years BP	Emergence of warm-blooded animals
63 million years BP	Asteroid impact supposedly ends the reign of the dinosaurs and makes room for mammals
4 million years BP	Emergence of bipedal Australopitheces
2 million years BP	Emergence of *Homo erectus*
200,000 years BP	Emergence of *Homo sapiens*
10,000 years BP	Emergence of agriculture
6,000 years BP	Emergence of the first states
500 years ago	First wave of globalization
250 years ago	Second wave of globalization (Industrialization)
60 years ago	Third wave of globalization (Informatization)

NOTES

Notes for Preface and Acknowledgments

1. During the Apollo program, I watched all of the live television broadcasts together with my father, who sadly passed away in 2002. In the last week of December of 2006, I was very fortunate to visit the Kennedy Space Center with my son Louis, who is extremely interested in rockets and manned space flights. I thoroughly enjoyed sharing the experience with him of seeing all those historic Apollo sites and displays that I only knew through television, pictures and movies. This trip changed my early emotional perception from the one formed by a Dutch kid growing up in the 1960s and early 1970s as the Apollo program taking place in an almost mythical area that was out of personal reach to the one formed by an adult as events that happened in a place that could be visited.

   This experience reinforced once again my strong feeling that to be able to describe or summarize situations better, nothing surpasses direct personal experience. As a big history scholar, I, therefore, wonder how my assessments would have changed had I had a more direct personal involvement in these investigations. This seems to be just as much the case for astronomical, geological and biological observations, as for more traditional historical research and anthropological fieldwork. As a result, I feel a constant urge to go and visit places as well as to check versions of events myself, which is, of course, totally unattainable while dealing with big history.

   Over the past 40 years, I have done so much reading that I may well have over-looked referencing certain accounts that provided important information. Apart from the hopefully systematic treatment of my theoretical approach, I only claim some originality for points of view when they are specifically mentioned as such. All the other information has come from other sources. And even when I claim original-ity, this only means that I think I invented it myself. It may well be that others preceded me, and I invite all readers to point out to me whenever this might have been the case.

2. A great many references exist to the enormous social impact of the Earthrise photo. See MacLeish (1968); Goldberg (1991), pp. 52–7; Allen, Tainter & Hoekstra (2003), pp. 1–2; '50 years in space: My favourite photo,' p. 40 and Poole (2008). Over the years, I investigated intriguing aspects of this most famous photo, including the

question of who actually took it (Bill Anders) as well as what had happened during this short but intensive episode of the Apollo 8 moon flight; see Spier (2002). In May of 2009, during my second visit to the Kennedy Space Center, I found that the main logo on its space shop merchandise celebrating 'Apollo 40 years' depicted an Earthrise scene and not an astronaut on the lunar surface, even though President Kennedy's main objective had been to put a man on the moon and return him safely to Earth. Apparently, in retrospect the new view of Earth has been the most important result for NASA.

3. Böttcher in Meadows (1972), p. 7.
4. Böttcher, King, Okita et al. in Meadows (1972), p. 15. Interestingly, in the US edition of 1972, such an introduction is lacking.
5. Spanish philosopher José Antonio Ortega y Gasset (1883–1955) called this type of understanding: 'Yo soy yo y mis circunstancias' (I am me and my circumstances). In other words, big history provides me with a better understanding of myself and my circumstances.
6. My only entry in the biochemical literature is Ledeboer, Kroll, Dons et al. (1976).
7. Most of the results of my Peru research can be found in Spier (1994 & 1995).
8. More on the history of the University of Amsterdam big history course can be found in Spier (2005b).

Notes for Chapter One

1. David Christian holds three nationalities: British, American and Australian.
2. Donald Ostrowksi's posting on the H-World Discussion Group on 15 April 2005, as part of the discussion on 'Why is studying history important?' See www.h-net. org/~world/. See also Ostrowski (1989 & 2003). In a letter to the science magazine *New Scientist*, 16 June 2007, Thomas Shipp put forward almost exactly the same argument.
3. I have often wondered whether it would be possible to find distant mirrors in the sky, which would reflect light emitted from Earth a long time ago. If such mirrors existed, they would in principle allow us to view images of our own past (in our present, of course). In 2007, Ivan Semeniuk reported that astronomers are now using the reflections of supernova explosions on dust clouds in galaxies for tracing them, the direct light of which passed Earth hundreds of years ago.
4. For scholarly references to the idea that all of our knowledge of the past resides in the present, see Walsh (1951), p. 18; Bloch (1984), p. 23ff. and p. 48ff.; Collingwood (1993), pp. 251–2 and p. 364 (Bob Moore kindly supplied these references). See also Barraclough (1955), p. 23 and Wesseling (1995), p. 20. For Ostrowski's elaborations, see Hurwitz & Ostrowski (1983) and Ostrowski (1989). For discussions of major problems in reconstructing history, see Barraclough (1955), Bloch (1984), Carr (1968), Kitson Clark (1967), Collingwood (1993), Huizinga (1995), McNeill (1986b), Slicher van Bath (1978), Tosh (1992), Walsh (1951) and Wesseling (1995). Marc Bloch formulated his solution to these problems as follows (1984, p. 71):

'Every historical book worthy of the name ought to include a chapter, or if one prefers, a series of paragraphs inserted at turning points in the development, which might almost be entitled: "How can I know what I am about to say?" I am persuaded that even the lay reader would experience an actual intellectual pleasure in examining these "confessions."'

5. McNeill (1986b), p. 5.

6. Unfortunately, Bryson's account does not include human history.

7. This is not at all an original point of view. Many scholars, including William McNeill (1986a&b) and David Christian (2004), have argued along these lines.

8. This is, unfortunately, not an accurate statement. No one can probe back in time, because the past is gone forever. Astronomers also sometimes use other confusing phrases, such as 'this galaxy is at a distance of 1.5 billion light years away from us.' The only thing we can be fairly sure of is that it is not there today and certainly not in the way we observe it. Alexander von Humboldt was already acutely aware of this. As he formulated it (1845), p. 153: 'These events in the universe belong, however, with reference to their historical reality, to other periods of time than those in which the phenomena of light are first revealed to the inhabitants of the Earth: they reach us like the voices of the past.'

9. From a very detached point of view, one may argue that, in principle, there is no reason why scientific principles ought to be applied to analyzing data in the present to reconstruct an account of events that may once have happened. One may, for example, decide to accept literally what sacred texts have to say regarding the past. This may not be scientific in the current meaning of the term, but I cannot see any reason why this would be an issue as long as one does not care about science.

10. In Hinduism, there are, in fact, no origins but only endless recycling. Some scientists suggest the same for big bang cosmology, namely that before the big bang there would have been a big crunch, which was preceded by another big bang with subsequent expansion, etc. Unfortunately, we do not have any scientific evidence at our disposal that would support or refute such ideas. I, therefore, prefer to begin big history with the big bang.

11. 'CE' means 'Common Era.' It is equivalent to the term 'AD,' *Anno Domini* (the Year of the Lord). The use of 'Common Era' represents an effort to define time without directly referring to religious events. The term 'BCE' equals 'BC' (Before Christ).

12. Cf. Moore (1997).

13. It is, therefore, no coincidence that the United Nations has been producing human histories while world history emerged at US secondary schools as a result of immigration from around the globe. This led to a fierce discussion about establishing national standards for world history, focusing, among other things, on the question of whether such global studies would produce 'good' US citizens. Cf. Crabtree & Nash (1994), Ravitch & Schlesinger Jr. (1996), Thomas (1996) and Woo (1996).

14. Especially cultural anthropologists are often uncomfortable with the emphasis on literacy defining what constitutes history. This is perhaps best expressed in the influential book written by the late US cultural anthropologist Eric Wolf: *Europe and the People without History* (1982).

15. See Smail (2005 & 2007). Bishop Ussher published his calculation of the moment of creation in *The Annals of the World*, which is, in fact, a human history from the beginning of time to 70 AD. One wonders whether the time span of biblical history was in fact inspired by some historical knowledge of the length of the period during which the surrounding state societies of Egypt and Mesopotamia had already existed. Clearly, with the exception of the first five days, the entire biblical account offers a history focused on humanity, with special emphasis on one supposedly privileged group. This is a rather common approach in pre-scientific origin stories.

16. Leopold von Ranke: 'A Fragment from the 1860's,' in Stern (1956). Original German version: Leopold von Ranke: 'Vorwort' in *Weltgeschichte, Neunter Theil, zweite Abtheilung*, pp. XV–XVI. David Christian made me aware of this quotation.

17. In Hume's *The Natural History of Religion*, the great philosopher sought to trace the origins of religion in the form of polytheism. Yet Hume was unclear about the time span in which these developments would have taken place ('more than 1700 years'). This book was deemed too controversial during his lifetime and was only published posthumously in 1757.

18. Barraclough (1955), p. 17ff. For instance, in 2008 British economic historian Patrick O'Brien described the situation in the 1970s as follows: 'Just four decades ago departments of history in Britain really did consist mainly of scholars who worked on their own countries, complemented by a somewhat isolated minority for undergraduate teaching and postgraduate supervision on an alien world – which in those days included the mainland of Europe as well as the kingdom's decolonized empire' (2008, p. 1).

19. Von Humboldt (1997), p. 340.

20. See von Humboldt (1995) and *Kosmos: Entwurf einer physischen Weltbeschreibung* (published between 1845 and 1862), translated into English as *Cosmos* (1997). See also Helferich (2004). The quotations are from *Cosmos* (1997), pp. 55–6 and pp. 79–80.

21. Chambers, Einstein and Lovelock had not been so lucky to live off an inheritance but they made their money in other ways while doing their scientific work.

22. Von Humboldt (1995), p. IX. His views had also been shaped by the French Revolution, including its intellectual and emotional aspects.

23. According to von Humboldt (1995), p. 18: 'I was authorized to freely use my physical and geodesical instruments, that in all the Spanish possessions I could make astronomical observations, measure the height of mountains, collect whatever grew on the ground, and carry out any task that might advance the Sciences.'

24. Surprisingly, even though the first wave of the Industrial Revolution coincided with von Humboldt's life, this does not appear to have influenced him directly as a young man, when he formulated and executed his scientific ambitions. For instance, in his *Personal Narrative*, von Humboldt's account of his travels in the Spanish Americas, he did not mention any steam engines or their effects, yet he did pay a great deal of attention to contemporary science. This was probably related to the fact that the Industrial Revolution had not yet taken off in that part of the world,

while in 1799, when he left on his tour, such effects were perhaps not yet clearly visible in French-dominated continental Europe.

25. At the time, there was no separation between biologists and geologists. While, for instance, Darwin and Lyell called themselves naturalists, today we would call them a geologist and a biologist. For Darwin and Lyell, however, these two aspects of nature were very much intertwined. Interestingly, Lyell later became a major culture hero for geologists, while his biological interests were downplayed. The opposite happened to Darwin. In other words, the formation of academic disciplines led to far more limited images of these scholars than they actually were. Today, we would call them interdisciplinary thinkers. Such a term would not have made any sense to them, because these disciplines had not yet been demarcated as clearly as they are today.

26. According to www.monticello.org, Jefferson acquired Baron d'Holbach's book *Système de la nature* in France between 1784 and 1789. This does not prove, of course, that Jefferson knew this book in 1776, when he drafted the Declaration of Independence, which was proclaimed about 13 miles to the south from where I wrote this paragraph.

27. See Descartes (1977) and Kant (1755 & 1963). I have used these documents as they are published on various web sites in both their original languages and English.

28. For Hegel's *Enzyklopädie der philosophischen Wissenschaften,* see www.zeno.org.

29. Chambers (1994), pp. 306–10. In *Cosmos* (1845), pp. 71–2, von Humboldt argued that the description of all things always entails describing their history. In his words: 'Their form is their history.'

30. Secord (2000) *Victorian Sensation.* See also Secord's *Introduction* in Chambers' *Vestiges.* This is my summary of a whole range of motivations mentioned by Secord.

31. Charles Darwin was well aware of the works by von Humboldt, Lyell, Chambers and others, most of which he greatly admired.

32. Wells (1930), p. VI.

33. There were attempts to produce all-embracing overviews, such as Dutch school teacher Kees Boeke's pioneering picture book *Cosmic View: The Universe in 40 Jumps* (1957). It became the basis of the far better known book and movie by Philip and Phylis Morrison, *Powers of Ten: About the Relative Size of Things in the Universe,* produced during the late 1960s and 1970s. Although these productions – there are many variations on this theme now – should not be considered big histories (because they do not deal with history), their authors probably had a very similar goal in mind.

34. Thomas Kuhn (1970) explained his concept of scientific paradigms in his famous book *The Structure of Scientific Revolutions.* The central idea is that the natural sciences are kept together by general theories to which most practitioners subscribe. Today these include big bang cosmology, plate tectonics and Darwinian evolution. Most of the research is done within these paradigms. When too many anomalies are discovered, a new competing theory may gain ground, which may produce a scientific revolution. Within the social sciences, by contrast, all-embracing paradigms do not yet exist.

35. For the chronometric revolution, see Christian (2009a&b).
36. See Belgium: Verburgh (2007); Canada: Reeves (1991); Colombia: Vélez (1998); France: Morin and Kern (1993), Reeves, Rosnay, Coppens & Simonnet (1996 & 1998) and Nottale, Chaline & Grou (2000); Germany: Lesch & Zaun (2008); The Netherlands: Drees (1996 & 2002), Spier (1996, 1998 & 1999a&b) and Lange (1997); Russia: Neprimerov (1992) and Nazaretyan (2004); United Kingdom: May, Moore & Lintott (2006), Aunger (2007a&b) and Lloyd (2008); United States: Chaisson (1977, 1981, 1987, 1998a&b, 2001, 2003, 2004, 2005, 2008 & 2009), Asimov (1987), Kutter (1987), Swimme & Berry (1992), Adams & Laughlin (1999), Morowitz (2002), Gonzalez & Richards (2004) [this book is an attempt to link big history to intelligent design], Primack & Abrams (2006), Brown (2007), Gehrels (2007), Genet (2007), Genet, Genet, Swimme, Palmer & Gibler (2009) and Potter (2009).
37. See W. H. McNeill (1992, 1998a & 2001). In 1996, when McNeill was awarded the Erasmus Prize in Amsterdam, he most generously donated half of the prize money to our big history project.
38. See Mears (1986 & 2009). All of us who are teaching big history have experienced a huge interest among students. Every year, a good many students tell me that our big history course has been the best university course they have taken and that it has changed their world views profoundly. For a short history of the University of Amsterdam big history course, see Spier (2005b).

Notes for Chapter Two

1. Monod (1971).
2. I am aware of the fact that within quantum mechanics everything is regarded as the result of chance effects. Yet I have never understood why the interactions between particles, which to some extent influence these chance effects and thus modify them to some extent, should not be considered part of the picture.
3. The reluctance among social scientists to use the term 'system' may well be a reaction to the rather static social systems approach developed by US sociologist Talcott Parsons, which was dominant in the 1950s and 1960s.
4. In *The Structure of Big History*, a regime was defined as 'a more or less regular but ultimately unstable pattern that has a certain temporal permanence,' Spier (1996), p. 14. In his book *The Self-organizing Universe* (1983), Erich Jantsch advanced the term 'process-structure,' which, in my opinion, conveys a meaning that is very similar to regime. While writing *The Structure of Big History*, I was not aware of Jantsch's book.
5. Chaisson (2001), p. 234.
6. Energy is often defined as the ability to do work or the capacity to exert a force over a distance (see Trefil & Hazen (1995), section G-8) or the ability to do work or to produce change (see Chaisson (2001), p. 232). This leads to the question of what work is. In my view, both work and the effects of forces are simply changes in matter.

7. Smil (2006), p. 1.
8. The perhaps most widely accepted definition of 'complexity,' developed for so-called complex adaptive systems (basically all forms of complexity based on life), is in terms of its information content, namely its shortest possible description; see Gell-Mann (1994), p. 23ff. This definition does not appear to be very useful for describing all forms of complexity, most of which are lifeless complex nonadaptive systems. If one tried to describe any type of complexity in all of its aspects in terms of information, one would soon discover that there is virtually no end to it. For how far would one go? All the way down to describing all the quantum states of all the tiniest building blocks, all their positions, their movements, etc.? In other words, any description of any larger-scale form of complexity in terms of information would have an extremely fractal character.
9. Cf. Gell-Mann (1994), Chaisson (2001), pp. 12–13. For classic overviews of the emerging science of complexity studies, see Waldrop (1993), Lewin (1993), Gell-Mann (1994) and Kauffman (1993 & 1995).
10. The term 'relative autonomy' was elaborated by sociologist Norbert Elias (1978a), p. 32ff. In his series of books *Cours de philosophie positive*, Auguste Comte used the argument of what later became known as 'relative autonomy' to justify sociology as the new science of societies, which could not be reduced to physics or biology.
11. During the Santa Fe Institute (SFI) conference on complexity in history in Hawaii in March of 2008, I presented these ideas on how to define different levels of complexity. In response, SFI president Geoffrey West said that the SFI did not have a shared approach on how to define different levels of complexity. West expressed their current approach to complexity studies as follows: 'We just do it, like sex.' The discussion stimulated him to put this question on their agenda.
12. This is why the meme approach as advanced by Richard Dawkins in 1976 is, in my opinion, a fruitless exercise in futility.
13. Cf. Adams & Laughlin (1999).
14. Smil (1999), p. X.
15. For power density, see Chaisson (2001), p. 134, (2008 & 2009).
16. A few years ago, Vaclav Smil pointed out to me that this was not an entirely new insight. Following Engelbert Broda's book *The Evolution of Bioenergetic Processes* of 1975, Smil mentioned in his book *General Energetics* of 1991 that (what he called) the power intensities of living organisms, including schoolchildren and certain bacteria, are much greater than the sun's power intensity; see Broda (1978), p. 41, and Smil (1991), p. 63. Smil's power intensity was defined in the same way as Chaisson's power density, while Broda called it 'energy production per unit weight.' Yet unlike Chaisson, these authors did not construct a general table of power intensities or energy production per unit weight for big history/cosmic evolution as a whole or elaborate these insights in the novel ways that Chaisson did. Eric Chaisson wrote to me that he had not been aware of these works, and that he had first published his calculations in his book *The Life Era* (1987), p. 253ff. This is clearly a case of several scholars independently following a similar track, which strengthens the idea that this approach is viable.

17. Chaisson (2001), p. 139. In his table, Chaisson provided his power densities in erg $s^{-1}g^{-1}$, which is the same as 10^{-4} watt/kg. In this book, I use the SI system of units (Système International d'Unités.).

18. Chaisson (2001), pp. 136–9.

19. Chaisson (2001), p. 186.

20. Chaisson (2001), p. 138, used an 'average male body mass of 70 kg,' while he assumed that humans 'consume typically 2,800 kcal per day (or 130 watts in the form of food) to drive our metabolism.'

21. One order of magnitude equals one factor of 10.

22. Chaisson's numbers for human history include a power density of 4 watt/kg for fire-controlling *Homo habilis*; see (2001), pp. 202–3. He did not provide any numbers for fire-controlling *Homo sapiens*. For Reijnders' critique, see Reijnders (2006a). Scholars such as Stephen Pyne (1982 & 2001), Johan Goudsblom (1992) and Frank Niele (2005) have pointed out that human fire use was a very important energy source for early humans. More recently, Chaisson has recognized the importance of fire use for agricultural societies, yet in my opinion he still underestimates the potential energy effects of early fire use. In an email in 2008, Chaisson wrote that, in his opinion, Reijnders' numbers were far too large. Clearly it will take some time before reliable numbers can be established.

23. Chaisson (2001), p. 201.

24. In addition to our vacuum cleaner, my 8-year-old son, Louis, and I weighed a number of human-made (usually man-made) contraptions and then calculated their power densities using the energy consumption provided by the manufacturers. This led to some surprising results. A 40-watt incandescent light bulb, for instance, has a power density of 1,600 watt/kg (8 million times the sun's value), while a more modern energy-saving lamp only reaches 170 watt/kg. We also found that my laptop computer, by contrast, has a power density of a mere 24 watt/kg (yet still more than our brains). An HO (1:87) scale model steam engine (type: American, manufactured by Bachmann) running on electricity proved to have a very similar power density of 23 watt/kg, while one of the largest steam locomotives ever built, the US Big Boy operated by the Union Pacific Railroad (540 tons, 6,200 horsepower, 1 horsepower = 746 watt, and assuming 25 per cent energy efficiency) reaches only 35 watt/kg. A modern Dutch Railways (N.S.) Series 1,700 electric locomotive (86 tons, 44,540 kw) does a little better, namely 52.8 watt/kg, while its HO scale model equivalent (Lima) reaches about 23 watt/kg.

25. Gell-Mann (1994), p. XIV. If critics were to point out that by doing so, the approach becomes invalid, one would wonder whether they know of any scientific approaches without such problems. The scientific community may be aiming for perfection, yet we may never be able to achieve it. All scientists, including historians, are in the business of building models of reality, which should never be confused with reality itself, whatever that is.

26. Chaisson (2001), pp. 143–4.

27. For a modern version of the Goldilocks story, see Marshall (1998).

28. The idea of calling this the Goldilocks Principle was first suggested to me by David Christian in March of 2003, while commenting on the first draft of my article 'How Big History Works.' He wrote: 'Yes, I like this, and the idea is missing from my text. Here's a sort of 'Goldilocks' principle applied to complexity: the energy flows must be just right. But are excessive energy flows the only explanations for absence of complexity? Is not time vital too, in the sense that some complex things are simply statistically rare, so you would expect it to take time for them to appear, on the principle of the random walk?' I responded by saying that he was completely right, but that I was reluctant to use the term 'Goldilocks Principle' because I was not sure whether this Anglo-Saxon term would be understood by a global audience. I did not employ this term therefore in my article, which was published in Russia.

    After having done more research into the degree of globalization of the Gold-ilocks story, and after having found that my audience invariably liked it when I explained my theory this way – including Russia – I decided to use this term systematically. In the meantime, the term 'Goldilocks Principle' has become more popular. Scientists including Vaclav Smil (2006) and Paul Davies (2006) had begun using it. For Davies, it is a way of restating the anthropic principle first formulated by Brandon Carter in 1973 and elaborated by John Barrow and Frank Tipler (1986). In his book of 2007 *Humanity: The Chimpanzees Who Would be Ants*, US astronomer Russell Genet mentioned the term 'Goldilocks Principle' as 'one of the general laws of the Universe' (p. 24). He used it in his description of cosmic history but, strangely, not for human history, which is the main thrust of his book.

29. Although the process of cold fusion has become discredited, it has not yet been completely ruled out.

30. I coined the term 'Goldilocks gradients' on January 25, 2007, while contemplating how to deal with the emergence of complexity at the end of chapter three. For almost four years, I had been aware of a deficiency in my theory, namely an answer to the question of why the edges of matter regimes appear to be especially good places for greater complexity to emerge. On that snowy day in North Hills, Pennsylvania, I realized that this concept might solve many of these problems.

31. See Spier (2008). For instance, in 2004 two astronomers, Eric Chaisson and Tom Gehrels, took part in a big history panel during the Annual Conference of the Historical Society in Boothbay Harbor, Maine. In Russia, interdisciplinary conferences on big history were organized at Belgorod Sate University in 2004 (Conference: Processes of Self-Organization in Big History) and at the International University Dubna in 2005 (International Conference on Self-Organization and Big History). In March of 2008, the Santa Fe Institute organized a conference on complex adaptive systems thinking in history in Hawaii, while a similar panel was organized in Moscow in 2009 (Panel Macroevolution: Hierarchy, Structure, Laws, and Self-Organization within the Fifth International Conference 'Hierarchy and Power in the History of Civilizations.'). I took part in all these conferences. In Amsterdam, we organized a one-day conference on this theme in 2004 with contributions from scholars ranging from an astronomer to a sociologist. These are among the liveliest scientific meetings I have attended.

Notes for Chapter Three

1. Our current account of cosmic evolution is based on centuries of astronomical observations and interpretations with the aid of scientific concepts which, in their turn, evolved out of a great many scientific studies of nature on our home planet. All of this has provided powerful tools for a better understanding of cosmic history. A great many books explain the early history of the universe. My rendering of this story is mostly based on Steven Weinberg's *The First Three Minutes* (1977), Erich Jantsch's *The Self-organizing Universe* (1983), Eric Chaisson's *Cosmic Evolution* (2001) and *Epic of Evolution* (2005), Eric Chaisson & Steve McMillan's *Astronomy Today* (2008), David Levy's *The Scientific American Book of the Cosmos* (2000) and Armand Delsemme's *Our Cosmic Origins* (1998). Also Eric Chaisson's web site Cosmic Evolution www.tufts.edu/as/wright_center/cosmic_evolution/index.html on the Wright Center for Science Education web site has been very helpful. In addition, a number of other books were consulted, which are mentioned in the literature list.

2. The problem of how to define a year is also related to the difference between the tropical year and the sidereal year. The tropical year is usually defined as the time it takes for the sun to move from one spring equinox to the next. Mostly as a result of the precession of the Earth's axis, the tropical year is about 20 minutes shorter than the sidereal year, which is the time it takes for Earth to return to its apparent position in the sky (which more or less coincides with one orbit around the sun). For calendars, the tropical year is used to define the year.

3. According to the brochure published by the Bureau International des Poids et Mesures, *The International System of Units (SI)* (2006), p. 113, the second is defined as the duration of 9,192,631,770 periods of the radiation corresponding to the transition between the two hyperfine levels of the ground state of the caesium 133 atom at 0 K. It is assumed that the frequency of these oscillations has not changed over the course of time. The second may be among the oldest intuitive units of time people have used, because it almost exactly corresponds with the normal male heartbeat at rest.

4. To be sure, all heavy chemical elements produced since the big bang came as a result of fusion processes within stars. Yet even today, these amounts are marginal compared to the quantities of hydrogen and helium that originated right after the big bang.

5. Until today, no one has been able to find any dark matter on Earth. Yet according to the interpretation of the movements of other galaxies, dark matter appears to cluster with ordinary matter. The currently small number of observed little satellite galaxies accompanying our galaxy may constitute another problem for the theory of dark matter; see Chown (2009). The best-known alternative theory of gravity is known as Modified Newtonian Dynamics (MOND). See, for instance, Shiga (2006) and Chown (2007).

6. For an overview of issues related to dark energy, see Shiga (2007). Regarding the problem of whether the extinction of light emitted by Type 1a supernovae during

its travel through the universe might cause errors of interpretation regarding dark energy, US astronomer Neil Gehrels wrote me: 'Indeed SN Ia are extincted. Careful correction must be made for the extinction in order to use them as standard candles.' This makes me wonder how astronomers would know for sure how much light would have been absorbed by matter along the way after having travelled over such large distances. Clearly, as a nonspecialist, I cannot possibly be required to resolve these issues. In actual fact, there are a good many more problems with the current big bang scenario. All of this makes me, as well as many others, suspect that there still is a great deal of theoretical work to be done and that some of the cherished scientific theories may have to be reformulated somewhere in the future.

As a result, the views presented here can only be regarded as preliminary. Yet, as Eric Chaisson has argued, while it may turn out to be that the age of the universe will be calculated differently as a result of future insights, the sequence of events would perhaps not change a great deal. See Chaisson (2001), pp. 98–9. For overviews of problems concerning big bang cosmology, see Chown (2005) and Lerner (2004).

7. The term 'Radiation Era' was borrowed from Eric Chaisson. It is unknown to me who was the first to underline the importance of the transition from an early radiation-dominated universe into a matter-dominated cosmos. In his book *The First Three Minutes*, Steven Weinberg suggested this already without any further reference (1993), p. 80. Although the formula $E = mc^2$ is usually attributed exclusively to Einstein's genius, according to Indian Physicist Ajay Sharma (2004): 'Before Einstein, among other physicists, Isaac Newton, English S. T. Preston in 1875, French Poincaré in 1900, Italian De Pretto in 1903, German F. Hasenöhrl made significant contributions in speculations and derivations of $E = D \, mc^2$. After Einstein Planck has also derived $E = mc^2$ independently. J J Thomson in 1888 is also believed to have anticipated $E = D \, mc^2$ from Maxwell's equations.'

In my account of early cosmic history, the idea of cosmic inflation originally developed by US physicist Alan Guth is not discussed. This very short and rapid expansion of the very early universe would have happened at around 10^{-36} seconds after the big bang, just before the elementary particles began to form. It accounts for the fact that space in the observable universe appears to be flat and homogeneous. Other than that, however, cosmic inflation does not appear to have influenced the rise and demise of complexity in the universe.

8. The best-known book dealing with this period is probably Steven Weinberg's *The First Three Minutes* (1993). Weinberg admits that a more accurate title would have been *The First Three and Three-quarter Minutes* (p. 110). For decades, the astronomical community has wondered why these three forces and their natural constants have the values we measure today. This is an important question, for had they been different, more complex matter regimes might not have been able to form. Today, no one is able to explain why these forces, including their constants, emerged in the specific ways they did. This has led to the idea of the anthropic principle formulated by British astrophysicist Brandon Carter in 1973. Subse-

quently, British astronomers John Barrow and Frank Tipler (1986) formulated two variants: the so-called weak and strong anthropic principles. The weak version implies that had these natural constants been different, we would not have been around to observe them. The strong principle entails the idea that there were certain initial conditions that constrained our universe, including the constants, to become what it is now. As yet no one knows, though, what these conditions would be. If the natural constants had evolved by pure chance, one might expect other universes to exist in which these constants are different.

This has led to the as yet speculative idea that our universe may be part of a set of universes, jointly called a 'multiverse,' which are all developing in their own ways. Currently, British astronomer royal Sir Martin Rees is a leading advocate of this idea (1997). Unfortunately, we do not have any direct evidence at our disposal of other universes, and in my opinion, we never will, because by definition everything that we can observe forms part of our universe.

There is another twist to this discussion. Already decades ago, Indian astronomer Subrahmanyan Chandrasekhar noted that like light, matter appears to be quantized. This means that both energy and matter regimes do not consist of a continuum but rather of a number of discrete steps. For matter, we now recognize the nuclear levels, the atomic and molecular levels, the level of daily objects (varying from viruses to rocks to ourselves), the solar and planetary levels, the galactic levels, clusters of galaxies and the 'observable' universe as a whole. All these different levels are separated by huge gaps. Very recently, US astronomer Tom Gehrels suggested that there may be a clear mathematical pattern in these regimes of mass quantization. If his argument turns out to be correct, by extrapolating this trend to the next level, namely to a collection of universes, one might indirectly infer data about such a possible multiverse (2007 & 2009). Because by definition all direct observations deal with things that belong to our own universe, it will be impossible to observe other universes directly. As a result, any evidence for a multiverse must by definition be indirect. However interesting these speculations are, in my big history account the multiverse will not play any further role.

9. Baryons consist of subatomic building blocks called 'quarks,' which cannot exist all by themselves. During the period of baryon formation, the quarks first emerged. They merged subsequently into protons and neutrons and are held together by the strong (nuclear) force.

10. Chaisson (2001), p. 110ff.

11. Jantsch (1983), pp. 82–9. It seems to me that the term 'cosmic co-evolution' may be preferable to distinguish it from other types of co-evolution, most notably biological co-evolution.

12. Astrophysicists calculate the energy content of radiation with the aid of Max Planck's famous formula $E = hv$, while the energy content of matter is assessed by using the formula $E = mc^2$.

13. Chaisson & McMillan (2008), p. 735.

14. A black-body curve is the radiation emitted by a perfect black body at different temperatures. Instead of the term 'neutralization,' the word 'recombination' is

often used for the period during which positively and negatively charged particles combined. However, the term 'recombination' suggests that such particles had combined earlier also, which is thought not to have been the case. I therefore prefer to avoid using this word.

15. One exception might be laser rays.
16. The lower limit for the size of black holes is perhaps as low as three times the sun's mass; see Chaisson & McMillan (2008), pp. 592–3. Yet it seems to me that matter concentrations up to 200 times the sun's mass would form stars, and not black holes, unless they were pushed together so quickly that star formation could not take place.
17. Chaisson Cosmic Evolution web site, page First stars.
18. There is still a great deal of controversy about quasars, much more than I can discuss here. See, for instance, Chaisson & McMillan (2008), p. 670ff.
19. Chaisson (2001), p. 126.
20. All known galaxies are thought to have existed for many billions of years. Yet the period during which humans have been recording celestial observations amounts to only about 5,000 years. This pales into insignificance compared to galactic life spans. Humans have therefore not been able to observe the unfolding history of any single galaxy. As a consequence, all historical accounts of galaxies are reconstructions based on a large number of galactic images, with their supposed ages ranging from about 13 billion years to almost the present (our own galaxy). All images are interpreted as galaxies in different stages of evolution. The same approach is followed for stars, most of which are also much older than human beings. Within our own galaxy, for instance, astronomers study the light emitted by stars of supposedly different ages.
21. Hammer, Puech, Chemin, Flores & Lehnert (2007).
22. Jantsch (1983), p. 89.
23. See Getman, Feigelson, Luhman, Sicilia-Aguilar, Wang & Garmire (2009).
24. The process of nuclear fusion inside stars is, in fact, more complicated. See, for instance, Chaisson & McMillan (2008), p. 439ff.
25. Jantsch (1983), p. 91.
26. Currently accepted approximate values for the sun are mass: 2×10^{30} kg, luminosity: 4×10^{26} watt and radius: 7×10^8 m.
27. Chaisson (2001), p. 148ff.
28. Chaisson (2001), p. 150 and p. 240.
29. The discovery in September 2006 of the unusually bright supernova SN 2006gy, calculated to have been about 150 times as massive as the sun, in galaxy NGC 1260, situated about 240 million light years away from Earth, may be a late example of such explosions; see Ofek, Cameron, Kasliwal et al. (2007) and Smith, Li, Foley et al. (2007). This has led astrophysicists to reconsider their models of similar explosions in the early universe. 'The SN 2006gy data suggest that spectacular supernovas from the first stars – rather than complete collapse to a black hole – may be more common than previously believed. "In terms of the effect on the early Universe, there's a huge difference between these two possibilities," said [Nathan]

Smith. "One pollutes the galaxy with large quantities of newly made elements and the other locks them up forever in a black hole."' www.newswise.com, 7 May 2007: NASA's Chandra Sees Brightest Supernova Ever.

Notes for Chapter Four

1. The analysis of the composition of planetary atmospheres in search of clues for life was an approach invented by James Lovelock, which put him on the track of his later Gaia hypothesis, explained in chapter five (1987 & 2000).

2. The scientific data for this chapter are manifold and include many centuries of astronomical observations, the data returned by space probes and manned space flights, the dating of rocks and the long-established studies of geology and biology, including biochemistry.

3. For a speculative overview of possible life forms elsewhere in the universe, see Fox (2007).

4. We should refrain from stating that the emergence of life and culture within our own cosmic neighborhood are stages characteristic of the entire universe, cf. Aunger (2007a&b). We simply cannot attribute important phases such as the emergence of life and culture that we observe here on Earth to all of big history. Such an approach would amount to new forms of terra- and anthropocentrism.

5. The chapters four and five are based on a great many sources that, more often than not, are not explicitly mentioned in the main text, because that would have led to a lengthy note after almost every sentence. My most important general sources are in alphabetic order: Chaisson (2001 & 2005), Christian (2004), Cloud (1988), Drury (1999), Jantsch (1983), Lovelock (1987 & 2000), Lunine (1999), Priem (1993 & 1997), Smil (1999 & 2002), Ward & Brownlee (2004) and Westbroek (1992).

6. Lineweaver, Fenner & Gibson (2004), pp. 59–62.

7. Most of these Goldilocks requirements may need no further explanation, but the concept of a corotation circle may not be familiar. The orbital velocity of objects around their centers can be expressed in terms of angular velocity, which is the time within which a certain section of the orbit is completed. One entire orbit has, of course, a total angle of 360 degrees. As in our solar system, where the outer planets take much longer to orbit the sun than the inner planets as a result of the laws of gravity, the outer stars of our galaxy take much longer to circle the central core than stellar objects that are situated more toward the center. In other words, the farther out objects are, the smaller their angular velocities. The corotation circle of a galaxy is defined as the area in which the angular velocity of an object around the galactic center equals the average of the angular velocities of all the objects that orbit the galactic center. In our galaxy, the radius of that area, called the 'corotation circle,' would be about 23,500 light years (with a margin of error of about 4,200 light years), while the distance between the sun and the center of the Milky Way would be about 24,500 light years. In other words, our cosmic neighborhood would be located very close to the corotation circle. According to cosmologists, this is

where one would expect the fewest collisions between objects orbiting the galactic center, which would be the most favorable position for life to flourish. See Mishurov, Zenina, Dambis, Mel'Nik & Rastorguev (1997), pp.775–80. The authors mention the galaxy's corotation radius as 7.2 ± 1.3 kpc (kiloparsec) and the distance of the sun from the center of the Milky Way as 7.5 kpc (1 kiloparsec equals 3,260 light years).

8. In 2007, European astronomers announced the discovery of an Earth-like planet, called Gliese 581, close to such a small star. This discovery was described on the CNN web site (25 April 2007) as follows: 'The "sun" wouldn't burn brightly. It would hang close, large and red in the sky, glowing faintly like a charcoal ember. And it probably would never set if you lived on the sunny side of the planet. You could have a birthday party every 13 days because that's how fast this new planet circles its sun-like star. But watch the cake – you'd weigh a whole lot more than you do on Earth. You might be able to keep your current wardrobe. The temperature in this alien setting will likely be a lot like Earth's – not too hot, not too cold. And that "just right" temperature is one key reason astronomers think this planet could conceivably house life outside our solar system. It's also as close to Earth-sized as telescopes have ever spotted. Both elements make it the first potentially habitable planet besides Earth or Mars. ... The new planet's star system is a mere 20.5 light years away, making Gliese 581 one of the 100 closest stars to Earth.'

9. See, for instance, Chown (2008).

10. Kant (1755).

11. See, for instance, Cloud (1988), pp. 10–15. This account introduces a problem. During its first few billion years, the galactic habitable zone would have been characterized by a low level of supernovae events. Yet ever since the cataclysmic event that produced our solar system, no other supernovae would have gone off so close as to destroy it or at least extinguish life on Earth. This makes one wonder what the chances are that a supernova explosion would have happened about 4.6 billion years ago and since that time never again anywhere close to us.

Whatever the case may be, there may well have been other supernovae events a little farther away from our cosmic neighborhood that did actually influence our history, the effects of which may be unknown. It may be that about 2.5 million years ago a supernova exploded somewhere between 60 and 300 light years away from Earth. According to US astronomer Brian Fields (*New Scientist*, 3 November 2007, p. 19): 'It didn't hit us, or we wouldn't be here.' This coincided with an extinction peak, but, according to Fields, there is no direct evidence of a link. See also Ellis, Fields & Schramm (1996); Knie, Korschinek, Faestermann, Wallner, Scholten & Hillebrandt (1999); Knie, Korschinek, Faestermann, Dorfi, Rugel & Wallner (2004) and Fields & Ellis (1999). In 2007, there was a discussion about the possibly imminent huge supernova explosion of the most luminous star known in our Galaxy, Eta Carinae, about 7,500 light years away from Earth, following the supernova explosion of SN 2006gy; see Ofek, Cameron, Kasliwal et al. (2007) and Smith, Li, Foley et al. (2007). '"We don't know for sure if Eta Carinae will explode soon, but we had better keep a close eye on it just in case," said Mario Livio of the

Space Telescope Science Institute in Baltimore. "Eta Carinae's explosion could be the best star-show in the history of modern civilization."'

12. For my calculation, I used the following data: according to an average of various estimates, there is currently about 1.3×10^{21} liter of water on our planet; 1 joule = 0.239 calories, while one calorie is defined as the amount of heat needed to raise the temperature of one gram of water from 15.5 to 16.5 degrees Celsius.

13. The values for the accretion and differentiation heat come from Priem (1997), p. 40. Other terms used are 'separation heat' and 'core segregation heat.' It is unclear to me whether the heat added by the collision with a Mars-sized object that would have created the moon (see below) is included in the accretion heat. It is thought that this violent encounter caused the early Earth to melt at least partially, which means that it added a considerable amount of energy.

14. See, for instance, Ward & Brownlee (2004), p. 49.

15. Morrison, Morrison & The Office of Charles and Ray Eames (1994), p. 7.

16. See, for instance, Gleick (1988) and Peterson (1995). In *Opticks* (1979), p. 402, Newton defended the notion that God's influence was behind the regular planetary orbits by saying: 'For while Comets move in very eccentrick Orbs in all manner of positions, blind Fate could never make all the Planets move one and the same way in Orbs concentrick, some inconsiderable irregularities excepted, which may have risen from the mutual Actions of Comets and Planets upon one another, and which will be apt to increase, till this System wants a Reformation.' One wonders whether Newton also implicitly pointed at supposed similarities between the history of the solar system and of the Roman Catholic Church. In other words, Newton may have suggested that there was some cosmic support for the Protestant Reformation, during which the role of the church and its theology were redefined.

17. Kasting, Whitmire & Reynolds (1993), p. 108. In fact, the concept of a solar system habitable zone appears to have emerged first, while this idea was later used to identify the galactic habitable zone.

18. Ward & Brownlee (2004), p. 15ff.

19. See, for instance, Westbroek (1992 & 2009).

20. See, for instance, McSween (1997), p. 119, and May, Moore & Lintott (2006), p. 108.

21. See, for instance, Budyko (1986) and Smil (2006), p. 22ff.

22. See Cloud (1988), p. 123.

23. Cf. Strangway (1970).

24. See, for instance, van Andel (1994), p. 90–4. In fact, the changes in Earth's orbit as a result of celestial influences are more complicated, among other things because the axis of Earth's elliptic orbit moves around the sun, while it also wobbles.

25. Van Andel (1994), p. 126.

26. This view is not entirely uncontested. In 2005, US scientist Feng Tian and coworkers suggested that the early atmosphere would have consisted of up to 40 per cent hydrogen, which slowly but surely would have disappeared into space. This hydrogen would have been helpful in forming the chemicals that were needed for life.

27. For an overview, see White (1959), p. 34ff. For example, Austrian energy specialist E. Broda (1975) and US biologist Ronald Fox (1988) have written excellent books dealing with life as an energy-driven process. More recent books include Vaclav Smil's also excellent writings on the biosphere and life.

28. For an overview, see Hamilton (2008).

29. My definition of life is very close to the description of it by the evolutionary biologist Konrad Lorentz: 'Life is an eminently active enterprise aimed at acquiring both a fund of energy and a stock of knowledge, the possession of one being instrumental to the acquisition of the other. The immense effectiveness of these two feedback cycles, coupled in multiplying interaction, is the pre-condition, indeed the explanation, for the fact that life had the power to assert itself against the superior strength of the pitiless inorganic world' quoted in Chaisson (2001), p. 176. See also Lehninger (1975), pp. 3–4. In my definition of life, viruses are not life, yet together with the cells that they use for their own ends, they form living entities.

30. Jantsch (1983), pp. 102–3.

31. See, for instance, Smil (2006), p. 24.

32. According to the online *Encyclopedia of Science* (www.daviddarling.info/encyclopedia/D/DarwinC.html), 'Darwin speculated, in a letter to the botanist Joseph Hooker (1871), on the possibility of a chemical origin for life: "It is often said that all the conditions for the first production of a living organism are present, which could ever have been present. But if (and Oh! what a big if!) we could conceive in some warm little pond, with all sorts of ammonia and phosphoric salts, light, heat, electricity, etc., present, that a protein compound was chemically formed ready to undergo still more complex changes, at the present day such matter would be instantly devoured or absorbed, which would not have been the case before living creatures were formed." Recognizing, however, that the science of his time was not yet ready for such a concept, he added: "It is mere rubbish thinking at present of the origin of life; one might as well think of the origin of matter."'

33. See, for instance, Pleij (1995), Whitfield (2004) and Koonin & Martin (2005). In 2005, I formulated a few options that might help recover the earliest possible genome in an unpublished paper. This includes investigating ribosomal RNA as a direct survival of what may have been the earliest genetic code. In all modern cells, ribosomal RNA is very important for making proteins. It may have evolved out of an autocatalytic RNA set that was able to both make proteins and replicate itself. As a result, modern ribosomal RNA can perhaps shed some light on the RNA World scenario that helps to explain the emergence of life.

34. Chaisson (2001), pp. 169–70.

35. Niele (2005), p. 8.

36. Cf. Cairns-Smith (1995).

37. It is tempting to speculate on the emergence of possible biochemical mechanisms that provided life's in-built drive for survival. The spontaneously emerging autocatalysis within cells may have been part of this process. Its action must have led

to a need for certain chemicals, and thus to a matter and energy gradient within cells that stimulated the emergence of a mechanism that actively absorbed these chemicals from outside.

38. See Belderok (2008). The formation of oil and especially natural gas (methane) is contested. Some scientists claim that they have abiotic origins; see Glasby (2006). For methane this may be plausible, because considerable amounts of this gas exist also on other planets, such as Jupiter, and moons, such as Titan. It is very unlikely that this methane has been produced by life.

Notes for Chapter Five

1. The data used for reconstructing the developments discussed in this chapter are manifold and have been generated by many centuries of geological and biological studies, including biochemistry.

2. Austrian scientist Engelbert Broda (1975) and US scientist Ronald Fox (1988) wrote insightful books summarizing many of these aspects decades ago. More recently, Vaclav Smil has been a leading author on such matters, while in 2005, Dutch scientist Frank Niele summarized the history of life and culture in terms of energy regimes.

3. In 2007, Russian paleontologist Alexander Markow showed that the number of marine genera has increased hyperbolically ever since 550 million years BP; see Markow & Korotayev (2007).

4. For a definition of 'complex adaptive systems,' see Gell-Mann (1994), p. 16ff. In October of 1996, I was very fortunate to spend two weeks at the Santa Fe Institute near Santa Fe, New Mexico, where I presented my book *The Structure of Big History*. This led to fascinating discussions with most notably Murray Gell-Mann and Stuart Kauffman. In retrospect, many of my ideas about the rise and decline of complexity in big history then began to take shape.

5. Erich Jantsch (1983), p. 100, formulated this slightly differently: 'Dissipative structures [structures that keep themselves going thanks to a continuous energy flow] imply an extraordinary intensification and acceleration of processes which otherwise might not lead anywhere. Simple catalysis leads to linear growth, autocatalysis to exponential growth. If in cosmic evolution the "task" was sometimes to delay the processes of energy liberation in order to ensure a fuller unfolding of evolution, it is now primarily the acceleration of processes.'

6. David Christian (2003), personal communication. In 2004 during a one-day conference in Amsterdam devoted to the themes discussed in this book, Belgian biologist Koen Martens posed the fascinating question of whether there would be a relationship between the power densities and the longevities of individuals and of species. This question has been addressed by British scientist Geoffrey West, president of the Santa Fe Institute, who claims that greater body size, lower metabolic rates (power densities) and longer individual life spans are directly related.

7. Broda (1975), p. 41.
8. See Westerhoff, Hellingwerf & van Dam (1983) and Rutgers, van der Gulden & van Dam (1989). These authors were inspired by the work of Swiss pharmacologist Jörg Stucki (1980), who performed calculations on theoretical models of thermodynamical optimalization strategies by bacteria.
9. Makarieva, Gorshkov, Li, Chown, Reich & Gavrilov (2008).
10. There may also be examples of achieving greater efficiency without paying the price of greater complexity. The change from radio tubes to transistors, for example, may represent such a transition. It is unknown to me whether in the realm of living organisms similar transitions ever occurred.
11. Tainter, Allen, Little & Hoekstra (2003). See also Allen, Tainter & Hoekstra (2003).
12. Alexander von Humboldt's Goldilocks circumstances included isotherms (the first isotherm map containing lines of equal average temperatures); isogones (magnetic equal deviation); isoclines (equal magnetic declination); isogeothermal, isothermal and isobarometric lines; and isotheral and isochimenal lines (lines connecting places that have the same mean summer or winter temperature).
13. Cf. Chaisson (2001), p. 32.
14. Graedel & Crutzen (1993), pp. 32–3.
15. Ward & Brownlee (2004), p. 201.
16. Cf. Vernadsky (1998), Carroll (2000) and Priem (1993).
17. I cannot resist telling a small anecdote. Ever since 1995, Dutch geophysiologist Peter Westbroek has graphically lectured in the annual Amsterdam big history course on the major influence life exerts on geology, which never fails to surprise the students. While lecturing in Cusco, Peru, in 1997, I explained such things to students of the local university UNSAAC, to which I received very similar reactions. Yet when I subsequently discussed these things, such as moss eating rocks, with some of my Andean compadres from Zurite near Cusco while working on the land, I received reactions like: 'Sure, compadre, that is what they are doing there.' In other words, they knew it. Apparently, these things are new to people who grew up in urban environments, while it may well turn out to be that people who are making a living from the land in more traditional ways are very aware of these things. This made me wonder how much valuable knowledge is getting lost (collective forgetting) as part of the current global processes of urbanization and industrialization of the countryside.
18. The degree to which inorganic processes and life would have influenced the level of carbon dioxide in the atmosphere and thus contributed to keeping the planetary temperature relatively stable over the aeons is still a matter of discussion (see, for instance, Allègre & Scheider (2000), p. 222). The same is the case for the retention of water during this period. Lovelock thinks that life has been responsible for this phenomenon (2000, p. 128), while Kasting, Whitmire & Reynolds (1993, pp. 118–19) agree that a planet without an oxygen-rich atmosphere would indeed lose its water quicker. But this would have been a slow process, and the current Earth would as yet not have been completely dry.
19. See Lovelock (1987 & 2000), p. 96, and Raup (1993).

20. See Lovelock (2000 & 2006).
21. It is exactly because stromatolites clung together so tenaciously that we are now able to find their remnants. Many contemporary single cells, by contrast, may well have perished without leaving any traces.
22. Niele (2005), p. 11.
23. De Vos (2004).
24. University of California Museum of Paleontology web site: www.ucmp.berkeley.edu/bacteria/cyanofr.html.
25. According to a review article by Nick Lane (2009), sex may already have emerged among the first eukaryotic cells.
26. In 2009, it was suggested that animal life may have evolved as early as 850 million years ago, but that it remained marginal until ice ages changed their environment; see Fox (2009).
27. See, for instance, Gould & Eldredge (1989), Conway Morris (1998) and O'Donoghue (2007a).
28. See, for instance, Walker (2003).
29. Graedel & Crutzen (1993), p. 194.
30. See Perkins (2009).
31. See Pavlov, Toon, Pavlov, Bally & Pollard (2005) and Reich (2005).
32. The 'unbeatable head start' would be the exact opposite of the 'law of the retarding lead' formulated by Dutch historian Jan Romein in 1937.
33. The best overview of the evolution of brains known to me is Allman (1999).
34. Karel van Dam (2007), personal communication.
35. Koshland (1980), p. 2 and p. 144.
36. In his book of 1980, Koshland came very close to the model proposed by Karel van Dam, especially on p. 145ff., yet he did not pursue these ideas.
37. A great many biology textbooks exist outlining these developments in greater or smaller detail. My favorite textbooks are Wicander & Monroe (1993) and Gould & Keeton (1996).
38. In 2008, Sarah Adamowicz, Andy Purvis and Matthew Wills found that during their evolution, crustaceans tend to become more complex rather than less complex. Apparently there is a path dependency pushing these organisms toward greater complexity. This may well be a more general pattern.
39. Tuzo Wilson, quoted in Wicander & Monroe (1993), p. 194.
40. Rodinia is named after the Russian word *rodina*, 'motherland.' 'Pannotia' means 'All Southern,' because this landmass was mostly situated in the Southern hemisphere, while Pangea means 'the entire Earth' in Greek.
41. Gould & Keeton (1996), p. 612.
42. Pyne (2001), p. 7.
43. Cf. Potts (1996), p. 21. For a short history of terrestrial plants, see O'Donoghue (2007b).
44. Osborne & Tarling (1995), p. 104.
45. Von Humboldt (1997), p. 346ff., and Darwin (1985), p. 135.
46. Wicander & Monroe (1993), p. 449.

47. Curt Wiederhielm suggested a causal connection between the asteroid impact near Yucatán and the volcanic activities that created the Deccan traps already in 1992. In his unpublished paper Theory for the origin of the Deccan traps (2008), David Weber argues that at the time of the impact, India was situated almost exactly on the opposite side of the world, which makes such a causal effect more likely, because that is where the seismic waves would have been concentrated.

Notes for Chapter Six

1. The scientific data used in this chapter came from geological, climate, palaeo-anthropological and archeological studies of many different kinds.
2. Cf. Trefil (1997). Many observations about brains mentioned in this chapter can be found in Allman (1999).
3. Chaisson (2001), p. 139.
4. Magistretti, Pellerin & Martin (2000).
5. Christian (2004). This is not an entirely new point of view. Already Alexander von Humboldt had fostered very similar thoughts (1995, p. 80), while in 1960, US scientist Lyon Sprague de Camp explained the speed of inventions in very much the same way (1993, p. 17).
6. See, for instance, Potts (1996), p. 181ff.
7. For niche construction, see, for instance, Odling-Smee, Laland & Feldman (2003). The scientific approach to niche construction may have started with Charles Darwin's study of 1881 on the effects of worms on the landscape.
8. See, for instance, White (1943 & 1959), Harris (1975, 1980 & 1997), Elias (1978a), McNeill (1963 & 1992), pp. vii–xiii, Smil (1994), McNeill & McNeill (2003), Christian (2004) and Crosby (2006).
9. Quoted in Cook (1976), p. xii.
10. For an insightful cultural anthropological study of how people balance costs and benefits, see Smith (2000).
11. Simmons (1994), p. 30.
12. Cook (1971), p. 136. These data were provided in kcal/day/capita. To convert them into watt/kg, I assume for the sake of simplicity that the average body weight throughout human history has been about 40 kilograms (adults and children combined). As a result, Cook's data would be exactly the same in watt/kg. All these numbers are, of course, preliminary estimates and should be viewed with due caution.
13. Such a view was already held by Charles Darwin in 1871; see Darwin (2004), pp. 72–3. For more recent literature, see, for instance, van Andel (1994), pp. 90–4; Gamble (1995), pp. 79–84; Tudge (1993 & 1996); Vrba (1993) and Vrba, Denton, Partridge & Burckle (1995). Thorpe, Holder & Crompton (2007) suggest that bipedalism may have evolved from earlier attempts to walk upright on tree branches by ape-like ancestors to reach other branches that were otherwise not accessible.
14. See, for instance, Potts (1996), p. 50ff.

15. Kortlandt (1972); see also Coppens (1994) and Kortlandt vs. Coppens (1994).
16. See Potts (1996).
17. Kortlandt (1980).
18. Cf. Goudsblom (1990 & 1992) and Gamble (1995), pp. 66–70.
19. Dutch astronomer Anton Pannekoek (1953) may have been the first to discuss the feedback mechanism between tool making and brain growth. The earliest version of his argument in Dutch can be found in Pannekoek (1909).
20. Potts (1996), pp. 11–12.
21. Potts (1996), p. 121.
22. In 1918, Dutch anatomist Louis Bolk suggested the idea of neoteny during a speech at the University of Amsterdam. Bolk subsequently published his ideas first in Dutch and later in German (1918 & 1926). See also Gould & Eldredge (1977), pp. 63–9, (1993) and Vélez (1998).
23. Aiello & Wheeler (1995), pp. 199–221. See also Roebroeks (2007).
24. Aiello and Wheeler used the term 'mass-specific metabolic rate,' which is the same as power density. Their brain value is slightly less than the power density of 15 watt/kg reported by Chaisson, yet within the same order of magnitude.
25. There is no reason to think that the process of co-evolution between brains and guts has now come to an end. Indeed, with the currently rich diets in wealthy countries, it may well be that another round of co-evolution between guts and brains is underway without most of us noticing it. Today, there appears to be a rapid rise in the number of autistic children, many of whom have severe digestive problems. Such children cannot tolerate foodstuffs usually considered harmless, including milk proteins and gluten, while they do much better on rather restrictive diets. This is now recognized within some established medical circles in the United States, Great Britain and Australia. See, for instance, Neimark (2007). At the same time, quite a few of these kids are intellectually gifted. In fact, it is thought today that some people who have made important contributions to science, including Sir Isaac Newton, Madame Curie and Albert Einstein, may have been autistic to some degree. Perhaps in early human history, every time there was a spurt in the co-evolution between guts and brains, similarly talented people invented the first tools and later controlled the first fires, cf. Fitzgerald (2004). One wonders whether today, there would be an unusually high percentage of autistic kids among children born with a caesarean section, because for them the restriction on head size had been removed. This means that such babies are not eliminated anymore. As a result, their brains can become larger again, which may be genetically linked to smaller intestines.
26. Darwin (2004), p. 68.
27. Alperson-Afil (2008) for early fire control in Africa and Israel; see also Goudsblom (1992), p. 16ff., and Simmons (1994), pp. 38–9.
28. Pyne (2001), p. 30.
29. Niele (2005), p. 29ff.
30. See, for instance, Gamble (1995), pp. 66–70, Goudsblom (1992) and Pyne (2001).
31. Goudsblom (1992), p. 20ff.

32. Reijnders (2006a).
33. Pyne (2001), p. 24ff.
34. See, for instance, Gamble (1995); Simmons (1994), pp. 38–42; and Williams, Dunkerley, DeDeckker, Kershaw & Stokes (1993), pp. 190–221.
35. Cf., for instance, McNeill (1963) and Harris (1975), p. 164ff.
36. Reed, Smith, Hammond, Rogers & Clayton (2004). Body lice would have evolved from head lice.
37. See, for instance, Smith (2007).
38. In 1988, during my stay as an anthropologist in the Peruvian Andean village of Zurite, Peruvian anthropologist Dr. Jorge Villafuerte R., in whose house I stayed, proudly showed me his new little grass porch there, adorned with a few trees. He told me that it was Kikuyu grass (*Pennisetum clandestinum*, a native plant from the highlands of Central Africa, as I later found out), because that was the only type of grass that would actually survive the often harsh Andean circumstances. Still, to survive during the dry season it needed to be watered almost every day.
39. Trefil (1994), p. 11, and Barrow (1995), p. 91ff.
40. McNeill (1976), pp.15–33.
41. Sherratt (1996 & 1997).
42. Sherratt (1996), p. 133.
43. See, for instance, Potts (1996) and McBrearty & Brooks (2000).
44. De Vos (2004).
45. Cavalli-Sforza (2000), p. 93ff.
46. For summaries of the theories of how modern humans would have migrated, including the importance of climate change, see, for instance, Mellars (2006), Burroughs (2006), p. 109ff., and Jones (2007).
47. Zeilinga de Boer & Sanders (2002), pp. 155–6.
48. Two pioneering scholars emphasizing coastal migration into the Americas are Fladmark (1979) and Gruhn (1988). See also Pringle (2007b) and Dillehay (1997) for early Chilean settlement.
49. The fate of the Neanderthals and of other, similar, early humans is the subject of an ever-continuing academic discussion. For diverging points of view, see Stringer & Gamble (1993) and Wolpoff & Caspari (1997). After these books were published, the discussion has swung back and forth several times between replacement and some intermixing. The discovery of Neanderthal genes now makes scientists think that they had white skins and red hair; see Lalueza-Fox, Römpler, Caramelli et al. (2007) and Culotta (2007). According to Reed, Smith, Hammond, Rogers & Clayton (2004), their studies on the evolution of body lice made them think that close interaction between archaic and modern humans must have taken place. Yet this does not necessarily imply sexual interaction. The *Homo floresiensis* (better known as the Hobbit, because it was so little) might have been a *Homo erectus* that lived until about 18,000 years ago (perhaps even as recently as 12,000 years ago) on the island of Flores in the Indonesian archipelago; see Brown, Sutikna, Morwood et al. (2004).
50. Simmons (1994), p. 43.

51. Simmons (1994), p. 44.
52. Cf. Pyne (2001).
53. See, for instance, Simmons (1994), p. 37 and pp.74–5. The idea of a Pleistocene overkill is not undisputed.
54. See, for instance, Zeilinga de Boer & Sanders (2002 & 2005) and Fagan (2004).
55. Pringle (2007a) and Firestone, West, Kennett et al. (2007). See also van der Hammen & van Geel (2008).
56. Wenke & Olszewski (2007), p. 172.
57. Spier (1994).
58. In my sociological approach of religion, I do not seek to address the question of whether certain world views or religions are true and others false. In my understanding of science, such things are not for academics to decide, because scientific method does not allow us to obtain definite proof of either the existence or the absence of supernatural forces. What academics can do, however, is observe what people express about their religious world views as well as what types of religious practices they engage in. For an analysis of religion and politics in Peru during its entire known history in terms of religious needs and constraints, see Spier (1994). For a similar overview in Dutch of religion and politics in human history, see Spier (1990). Unfortunately, until today I have not found sufficient time to translate this article into English. In Spier (1996), I mentioned a few of these ideas in English.

Notes for Chapter Seven

1. The scientific data used in this chapter vary from archeological studies to a wide variety of historical studies.
2. One of the great pioneers who traced human genetic change is Italian-born US geneticist Luigi Luca Cavalli-Sforza (1994 & 2000). Both his work and the studies performed by his student, US geneticist Spencer Wells, have greatly contributed to the current view of worldwide human migration during the past 50,000 years. More likely than not, the current efforts at further elucidating the workings of the human genome will contribute a great deal to a better understanding of the interplay between culture and human genetics during the past 10,000 years. The only study known to me in which a thorough effort is made to provide an all-round view of human beings in terms of their genetic and cultural makeup was written by Colombian engineer Antonio Vélez (2007). While finalizing the manuscript in 2009, I became aware of two controversial books dealing with human genetic change over the past 10,000 years, namely Wills (1999) and Cochran & Harpending (2009). Both claim that human culture has accelerated human biological evolution.
3. To my knowledge, Alexander von Humboldt was the first scholar to use such an approach. See also Chambers (1994), White (1943, 1959 & 1975), McNeill (1976), Darlington (1969), Tainter (1988), Smil (1994), Lapperre (1997), Diamond (1997), Spier (1992, 1996 & 2005a), Allen, Tainter & Hoekstra (2003), McNeill & McNeill (2003), Christian (2004), Crosby (2006) and Burroughs (2006).

4. The idea that human history is an unplanned process has often been emphasized by, among others, Norbert Elias and, in his wake, Johan Goudsblom.

5. For an English translation of the original account, see Caesar (1984). I am aware of the possibility that not all of the things reported by Caesar might reflect his honest views of what really happened. Perhaps he did not even write the text himself. It is also possible that the text was altered after he wrote it. These are problems characteristic of all historical documents. But even if things went differently than described, Caesar's story can at least be interpreted as an attempt to convey a plausible account of how things had happened.

6. I found this (in my view excellent) summary on 12 April 2007 on the following web site: http://sights.seindal.dk/sight/766_Julius_Caesar-3.html. The text was probably written by Danish interdisciplinary scientist René Seindal.

7. William McNeill, personal letter dated 30 November 2007.

8. To be sure, some animals were domesticated for purposes other than converting bio-energy. Dogs, for instance, were domesticated as hunting companions, thus helping to improve the concentration of prey animals. Within the agrarian regime, they became useful for safeguarding people and their possessions, thus replacing humans for these jobs. It is only very recently that dogs began to be kept for affective purposes, again replacing humans to at least some extent. Cats were domesticated for catching rodents, which would prey on the stored food supplies. Much more recently, cats also began to serve affective needs. A considerable variety of plants has served purposes other than providing food. These functions include dyes and many types of decoration.

9. Niele (2005), p. 51ff.

10. Interestingly, in his book *On the Origin of Species*, Darwin first outlined the process of domestication and then used it to explain natural selection.

11. Budiansky (1992).

12. See, for instance, Cohen (1977), Reed (1977), Redman (1978), Heiser (1990), Renfrew & Bahn (1991), Budiansky (1992), Fiedel (1992), Cunliffe (1994), Simmons (1994), Sanderson (1995), Smith (1995), Bellwood (2005) and Burroughs (2006).

13. See, for instance, Lewis (1972), Cohen (1977), pp. 21–7, Fiedel (1992), p. 168, Harris (1990), Reed (1977) and Smith (1995), pp. 16–18.

14. In 1992, Australian scientists Spriggs, Wickler and Loy discovered traces of domesticated taro strains on ancient tools dating back some 28,000 years in the Solomon Islands, while British archaeologist Gordon Hillman would have found grinding stones and tubers at Wadi Kubbaniya, a site in Egypt, which is between 17,000 and 18,000 years old; see Dayton (1992), p. 14, Loy, Spriggs & Wickler (1992) and Harris & Hillman (1989). In 2009, Kuijt and Finlayson published results of their long-term research into the transition from hunters and gatherers into farmers in the Jordan village of Dhra'. It is well known that agriculture has not been an exclusive human invention. Ants, for instance, cultivate fungus inside their holes; see, for instance, Mueller, Gerardo, Aanen, Six & Schultz (2005).

15. Kennett, Kennett, West et al. (2009).

16. Cf. Gamble in Cunliffe (1994), p. 18, and Wright Jr. in Reed (1977), pp. 281–318.

17. Smith (1995), p. 211.

18. Harris (1990).

19. Burroughs (2006), p. 191 & p. 193. See also Hillman, Hedges, Moore, Colledge & Pettitt (2001).

20. British archaeologist Andrew Sherratt elaborated the importance of animal use for other purposes than eating. He called it the 'secondary products revolution' (1981).

21. Crosby (1972, 1993 & 2006). In 1998, these arguments were presented very eloquently by US scientist Jared Diamond in his book *Guns, Germs and Steel.* These insights are, however, much older. British geneticist Cyril Darlington mentioned them in his book *The Evolution of Man and Society* (1969), pp. 70–1 and pp. 578–82 (which served as a source of inspiration to Jared Diamond), while already Alexander von Humboldt wrote in *Cosmos* (1845), p. 294: 'How totally different would be the condition of the temperature of the earth, and consequently, of the state of vegetation, husbandry, and human society, if the major axis of the New Continent had the same direction as that of the Old Continent; if, for instance, the Cordilleras, instead of having a southern direction, inclined from east to west; if there had been no radiating tropical continent, like Africa, to the south of Europe; and if the Mediterranean, which was once connected with the Caspian and Red Seas, and which has become so powerful a means of furthering the intercommunication of nations, had never existed, or if it had been elevated like the plains of Lombardy and Cyrene?' On p. 327 he added that: 'these circumstances have at all times exercised a powerful influence on the character and cultivation of natural products, and on the manners and institutions of neighboring nations, and even on the feelings with which they regard one another. This character of geographical individuality attains its maximum, if we may be allowed so to speak, in countries where the differences in the configuration of the soil are the greatest possible, either in a vertical or horizontal direction, both in relief and in the articulation of the continent.' In *Cosmos*, p. 48, von Humboldt mentioned Carl Ritter's *Erdkunde Im Verhältniss zur Natur und zur Geschichte* as an important contribution to the discussion of how geography had influenced both biological and human history.

22. Roberts (1998), p. 136.

23. Population numbers: US Census Bureau, March 2009, www.census.gov/ipc/www/worldhis.html. These numbers are, of course, rough estimates.

24. Wolf (1982), p. 88ff.

25. Mann (1987), p. 39ff.

26. Smith (1995), pp. 211–12.

27. For an account of the dynamics of competitive feasting in the Peruvian Andes, see Spier (1995). For a more general account, see Wolf (1966).

28. These ideas come from Allen, Tainter & Hoekstra (2003), p. 61ff.

29. Norbert Elias's analysis of the emergence of time as a cultural concept in his book *Time: An Essay* (1992b), first published in Dutch in 1982, is by far the best academic analysis of this subject that I have read.

30. For the balance between self-constraint and external constraint, see Elias (1982), pp. 229–333.

31. For the emergence of agrarian religions, see, for instance, Goudsblom, Jones & Mennell (1996), pp. 70–8; McNeill (1963), pp. 18–22 and pp. 33–40; Elias (1992b) and Spier (1994 & 1996).
32. Cf. Spier (1994).
33. For an example of how this works in Andean Peru, see Spier (1995).
34. Anthropologists may argue that gatherer-hunter societies, although small, had perhaps more multifunctional, and therefore more complex, connections than agriculturists. Yet all things considered, agricultural societies appear to be more complex to me.
35. For a summary of the discussion about the migration of farmers throughout Europe vs. the adoption of farming in Europe by gatherer-hunters, see Burroughs (2006), pp. 204–7.
36. I observed such a situation during my study of Peruvian Andean agriculturists; see Spier (1994 & 1995).
37. See, for instance, Rathje & Murphy (1992), pp. 32–3.
38. See, for instance, Simmons (1994), pp. 14–27.
39. See, for instance, White (1959), pp. 45–57; Cohen (1977); Redman (1978); Heiser (1990); Budiansky (1992); Fiedel (1992); Simmons (1994); Sanderson (1995); Smith (1995); Mears (2001); Christian (2004) and Bellwood (2005).
40. See McNeill (1976) and Swabe (1998). Infectious diseases may also have jumped from humans to animals. Tuberculosis may be such a case (Hershkovitz, Donoghue, Minnikin et al. (2008)).
41. Cook (1971), p. 136. Cook expressed his data in kcal/24 hours. I recalculated them by assuming that 1 cal = 4.19 joules. As a result 1,000 kcal/24 hours = 48.5 watt. Assuming an average body weight for gatherer-hunters of 40 kg, Cook's data yield a power density for gatherer-hunters of 3 watt/kg. This is fairly close to Chaisson's estimate of 2 watt/kg, which was based on an average body weight of 70 kg (which, I think, is a little too high). Yet if we use that average weight, the correspondence between Cook's and Chaisson's data becomes virtually perfect. See also Simmons (1994), p. 24, and Bennett (1976), pp. 42–3.
42. See Weber (1997), p. 154, and Elias (1978b & 1982).
43. Cf. McNeill (1976 & 1984) and Crone (1989), pp. 39–40.
44. Carneiro (1970). As mentioned in chapter one, such ideas are in fact much older. Already in 1844, Robert Chambers had suggested that the rise of 'civilizations' could only have taken place under rather confined conditions (1994), pp. 300–4.
45. See Kennett & Kennett (2006).
46. For sociological discussions of the importance of religion during early state formation, see, for instance, Goudsblom in Goudsblom, Jones & Mennell (1996), p. 70ff, and Mann (1987), pp. 45–9.
47. Fagan (1999, 2000, 2004 & 2008).
48. See, for instance, Fagan (1999, 2000, 2004 & 2008) and Geel, Bokovenko, Burova et al. (2004).
49. For trade, see, for instance, Philip Curtin's pioneering study of 1984; see Curtin (1994).

50. Anderson (1991).
51. A claim to be able to solve hopeless problems by religious means for a certain price, namely a leaflet dropped into our mailbox in Amsterdam on 22 January 2008, contained the following message in both Dutch and English: 'Mr. Khadim: payment after result. May I intorduce [sic] myself: I am a real african, International, very quick medium. I can help you with: return of your beloved people or your lover, your carrier [sic], examen, chance of happiness, sexual impotence, infertility or bad spirits, even when your problem is hopeless. I guarantee you a quick result.'
52. McNeill & McNeill (2003), p. 7.
53. McNeill (1976), p. 6ff.
54. Sprague de Camp (1993), p. 372 and p. 13.
55. For Lyon Sprague de Camp (1993), p. 372, the term 'civilization' was not necessarily a positive one: 'Civilization is a matter of power over the world of nature and skill in exploiting this world. It has nothing to do with kindness, honesty, or peacefulness. These virtues are found scattered – rather thinly, alas – through the entire human species, although they occur in some people more than in others and are encouraged in some cultures more than in others.'
56. Mumford (1961), p. 75.
57. Rathje & Murphy (1992), pp. 34–5.
58. Rathje & Murphy (1992), p. 35; Blegen (1963) and Gunnerson (1973).
59. Cf. McNeill (1998b).
60. Sprague de Camp (1993), p. 147.
61. Niele (2005), p. 65ff.
62. See, for instance, McNeill (1963 & 1984).
63. Christian (2004), p. 389ff.
64. For an excellent book on the importance of printing, see Eisenstein (1993).
65. See, for instance, Sanderson (1995), p. 175.
66. See, for instance, Crosby (1972 & 1993) and Flynn & Giráldez (1995, 2002 & 2008). It is sometimes argued that the volumes transported by these early globalists were actually tiny compared to the amounts of freight transported today; see, for instance, Emmer (2003). As a result, their impact would actually have been very small. Yet many of these products, such as plants, seeds and animals, were what can be called 'multipliers,' because they multiplied either guided by human hands or through escape into the wild far beyond any numbers that were actually carried on board of these ships.
67. For such arguments, see, for instance, Weber (1927), p. 337; Wallerstein (1974) and Allen, Tainter & Hoekstra (2003), p. 140ff.
68. Allen, Tainter & Hoekstra (2003), p. 148.
69. Crosby (1997).
70. See, for instance, Snow (1988) and Menzies (2002).
71. There are a great many books about the scientific revolution. The best one, in my opinion, was written in Dutch by Dutch historian of science Floris Cohen (2007). An English version is planned to be published by Johns Hopkins Press.

72. Von Humboldt (1995), pp. 74–5. For a nice overview of the many uses of oil in Central Asia before engines, see Bilkadi (1995).
73. The account of early industrialization given here cannot possibly cover the enormous and sophisticated scholarly literature that has been devoted to this subject in recent decades, much of it directed to the question why industrialization did not occur in other places or at other times. It may be observed, however, that just as my argument shows how Goldilocks circumstances were necessary to the development that actually took place, and points to some of the main circumstances that brought them about, it could readily be demonstrated, conversely, that Goldilocks circumstances did not exist at other times and places, or that obstacles to their creation were not overcome.
74. See, for instance, De Vries (2008), Fieldhouse (1973), Hobsbawm (1968), Landes (1969 & 1998), Pollard (1992), Pomeranz (2000), Smil (1994), Stearns (1993) and Wallerstein (1989).
75. Livi-Bacci (1992), pp. 100–1.
76. This technology produces much more complexity while using far less matter and energy. Clearly, an impressive drive has taken place toward reaching ever higher levels of efficiency.
77. Interestingly, while a great deal of information has become accessible as a result of the digitization of data on the Internet, it may also be causing the destruction of information. For instance, while seeking to trace the issue of *Time Magazine* of January 1969 that had carried the Earthrise picture, I found that all the libraries accessible through the Internet appear to have discarded their hard copies of this magazine, while www.Time.com only contains the articles of all the past issues but not photos or advertisements. This silent massive destruction of data may be part of a more general process of cultural forgetting. I succeeded in tracing this issue by searching for second-hand bookstores on the Internet that might sell it.
78. The globalization of the traditional Andean religion is first of all the result of efforts by Peruvian anthropologist Juan Víctor Núñez del Prado. See, for instance, Jenkins (1997).
79. In 1948, British astronomer Fred Hoyle predicted the effects of a whole Earth picture as follows: 'Once a photograph of the Earth, taken from outside, is available, we shall, in an emotional sense, acquire an additional dimension. ... Once let the sheer isolation of the earth become plain to every man, whatever his nationality, or creed, and a new idea as powerful as any in history will be let loose,' quoted in Goldberg (1991), p. 52. To be sure, by now humans may have sent terrestrial microorganisms all across the solar system as unintended travelers on unmanned space probes.
80. International Energy Agency (2007), downloaded from www.iea.org. To facilitate a comparison with numbers that were mentioned earlier, they were converted into watt per capita. This was done also with data provided in the other tables. Interestingly, in these statistics a few poor countries such as Burundi are entirely lacking. According to the International Energy Agency, a tonne of oil equivalent (toe) is the energy contained in a metric ton (1,000 kg) of crude oil and equals

10^7 kilocalories, 41.868 gigajoule, or 11,628 kilowatt-hour (kwh). As a result, 1 toe/second $= 1.33 \times 10^3$ watt.

81. I calculated the power density of a Dutch windmill by using the total weight, about 60,000 kg, of the windmill that was shipped a decade ago to the United States where it was rebuilt in the year 2000 in Fulton, Mississippi. According to several Dutch web sites, such windmills have an average output of about 10,000 watt. The power density of the space shuttle engine was calculated using data from the NASA web site, while I calculated the value for a modern German windmill with the aid of data from a German web site that I am now unable to trace.

82. An excellent analysis of urban life in terms of energy use is Trefil (1994).

83. Committee on the Societal and Economic Impacts of Severe Space Weather Events (2008).

84. See Trivedi (2007). For excellent general overviews of human influence on the planetary ecology, see, for instance, Ponting (1992) and McNeill (2000).

85. See, for instance, Diamond (1987), Leakey & Lewin (1995) and Vitousek, Mooney, Lubchenco & Melillo (1997).

Notes for Chapter Eight

1. Between 2 and 5 billion years from now, our galaxy and the Andromeda nebula will meet. This will have unpredictable consequences for any life that may then still exist in our solar system.

2. Cf. Raup (1993).

3. Broda (1975 & 1978), Cook (1971 & 1976), Debeir, Deléage & Hémery (1991), Fox (1988) and Odum (1971). See also *Scientific American* Special Issue: 'Energy and Power.' (1971). Recent important energy studies include MacKay (2008), Niele (2005) and Smil (1991, 1994, 1999, 2002, 2003 & 2006).

4. Hubbert (1971), p. 61. In 1956 in a (now classic) conference paper, M. King Hubbert predicted peak oil in the United States to take place between 1965 and 1970 (1956), p. 24. Peak oil is the maximum attainable level of oil production, after which an inevitable decrease will set in resulting from its exhaustion. Peak oil in the United States actually took place in 1971. In the same paper, Hubbert predicted world peak oil (excluding oil from tar sands) to take place around 2000; see Hubbert (1956), p. 22. In 2007, a reliable source from within the oil industry told me that his company thought that world peak oil (of easily recoverable oil) had happened in 2004.

5. Odum (1971), p. 18.

6. It is remarkable that the variables chosen by the MIT researchers almost exactly coincide with the theoretical approach advocated in this book. This makes me wonder why it has taken so long before these principles were applied to the study of history, as well as why it has taken me so long to do so. As I see it, very few social scientists and historians are currently willing to think systematically along such lines, because they feel that their field of study deals with more elevated cultural

issues and not with such mundane considerations. Future events may well prove them wrong.

7. For the Brundtland report, see World Commission on Environment and Development (1987).

8. Cortright (1975).

9. Turner (2008).

10. See Allen, Tainter & Hoekstra (2003). In an unpublished paper in Dutch (1984) titled *Een natuurkundige beschouwing van ekologische problemen* (A physical approach to ecological problems), I analyzed the emerging ecological issues with the aid of thermodynamics.

11. Population growth outstripping natural resources was the basis of the argument outlined by British scholar Thomas Robert Malthus (1798) in *An Essay on the Principle of Population*.

12. In most generalized pension systems, the younger generations still pay substantial amounts of money to maintain the elderly. Yet urban children are expensive, while they are not directly needed for one's own pension later in life. As a result, many people do not feel an economic need to have children, which contributes considerably to the current decrease of fertility. In this paragraph, I do not claim to provide an exhaustive overview of all the determinants of population growth. For a general overview, see Livi-Bacci (1992).

13. Strahan (2008). The estimate of 'several decades' for uranium is based on the assumption that its consumption will increase very substantially when other fuel reserves begin to run out. The reserves of methane clathrates on cold sea beds appear to be very large, perhaps as large as all the other fossil fuels combined. Their extraction may well be problematic, not least because methane is a very powerful greenhouse gas. While exploiting these reserves, it may be very difficult to prevent uncontrolled large 'burbs' into the atmosphere leading to further global warming, cf. Pearce (2009).

14. Many people emphasize that we will need to return to a lifestyle based on renewable energy. Excellent books on future energy include Smil (2003) and Niele (2005).

15. Daviss (2007).

16. McKenna (2008).

17. The idea that people will have to live more moderately as a result of environmental constraints was eloquently formulated by British economist E. F. Schumacher (1989) in his (often maligned) book *Small Is Beautiful: Economics as if People Mattered*.

18. For phosphate reserves, see, for instance Zapata & Roy (2004) and EcoSanRes (2008).

19. See, for instance, Christian (2004).

20. This information was available in May 2009 at http://science.nasa.gov/headlines/y2009/27may_phantomtorso.htm.

21. The (possibly genetically based) human characteristic of harvesting more matter and energy than is needed for survival and reproduction is, in my opinion, the major root cause of the global economic downturn that began in 2008.

BIBLIOGRAPHY

Adamowicz, Sarah J., Purvis, Andy & Wills, Matthew A. 2008. 'Increasing morphological complexity in multiple parallel lineages of the Crustacea.' *Proceedings of the National Academy of Science 105*, 12 (4789–91).

Adams, Fred & Laughlin, Greg. 1999. *The Five Ages of the Universe: Inside the Physics of Eternity*. New York, The Free Press.

Aiello, Leslie C. & Wheeler, Peter. 1995. 'The Expensive-Tissue Hypothesis: The Brain and the Digestive System in Human and Primate Evolution.' *Current Anthropology 36*, 2 (199–221).

Allègre, Claude & Scheider, Stephen H. 2000. 'The Evolution of the Earth.' In: Levy, David H. (ed.) *The Scientific American Book of the Cosmos*. New York, St. Martin Press & London, MacMillan (219–26).

Allen, Timothy F. H., Tainter, Joseph A. & Hoekstra, Thomas W. 2003. *Supply-Side Sustainability*. New York, Columbia University Press.

Allman, John Morgan. 1999. *Evolving Brains*. New York, W.H. Freeman & Co., Scientific American Library Series, No. 68.

Alperson-Afil, Nira. 2008. 'Continual fire-making by Hominins at Gesher Benot Ya'aqov, Israel.' *Quaternary Science Reviews 27*, 17–18, September (1733–9).

'Ancient blast too close for comfort.' *New Scientist*, issue 2628, 3 November 2007 (19).

Andel, Tjeerd H. van. 1994. *New Views on an Old Planet: A History of Global Change*. Cambridge, Cambridge University Press (1985).

Anderson, Benedict. 1991. *Imagined Communities: Reflections on the Origin and Spread of Nationalism*. London & New York, Verso (1983).

Asimov, Isaac. 1987. *Beginnings: The Story of Origins of Mankind, Life, the Earth, the Universe*. New York, Berkeley Books.

Aunger, Robert. 2007a. 'Major transitions in "big" history.' *Technological Forecasting and Social Change 74*, 8 (1137–63).

Aunger, Robert. 2007b. 'A rigorous periodization of "big" history.' *Technological Forecasting and Social Change 74*, 8 (1164–78).

'The Awesome Views from Apollo 8.' *Time Magazine* (Atlantic edition), 10 January 1969 (29).

Baron d'Holbach, Paul Henri Thiry. 1770. *Système de la nature. Ou des loix du monde physique & du monde moral* [published under the pseudonym of Jean Baptiste de Mirabaud]. London [= Amsterdam]: no publisher or printer mentioned.

Baron d'Holbach, Paul Henri Thiry. 2001. *The System of Nature or Laws of the Moral and Physical World*. Kitchener, Ontario, Canada, Batoche Books (1868).

Barraclough, Geoffrey. 1955. *History in a Changing World*. Oxford, Basil Blackwell.

Barrow, John D. 1995. *The Artful Universe*. Oxford, Clarendon Press.

Barrow, John D. & Tipler, Frank J. 1986. *The Anthropic Cosmological Principle*. Oxford, Oxford University Press.

Beatty, J. Kelly, Collins Petersen, Carolyn & Chaikin, Andrew (eds.). 1999. *The New Solar System, Fourth Edition*. Cambridge, Mass., Sky Publishing.

Belderok, Stein. 2008. 'Goldilocks in Petroleum Geology.' In: Keestra, Machiel (ed.) *Van denkrichting veranderen*. Amsterdam, Institute for Interdisciplinary Studies, University of Amsterdam (15–16).

Bellwood, Peter. 2005. *The Origins of Agricultural Societies*. Oxford, Blackwell.

Bennett, John W. 1976. *The Ecological Transition: Cultural Anthropology and Human Adaptation*. New York, Pergamom Press.

Bilkadi, Zayn. 1995. 'Land of the Naphtha Fountain.' *Saudi Aramco World* September/October (26–33). www.saudiaramcoworld.com/issue/199505/land.of.the.naphtha.fountain.htm.

Blegen, Carl W. 1963. *Troy and the Troyans*. New York, Frederick A. Praeger.

Bloch, Marc. 1984. *The historian's craft*. Manchester, Manchester University Press (1954, originally in French: 1949).

Boeke, Kees. 1957. *Cosmic View: The Universe in 40 Jumps*. New York, John Day Company.

Bolk, Louis. 1918. *Hersenen en cultuur [Brains and Culture]*. Amsterdam, Scheltema & Holkema.

Bolk, Louis. 1926. *Das Problem der Menschwerdung [The Problem of Becoming Human]*. Jena, Gustav Fisher.

Bradley, Raymond S. 1991. *Global Changes of the Past*. Boulder, Co., UCAR/Office for Interdisciplinary Earth Studies.

Broda, E. 1975. *The Evolution of Bioenergetic Processes*. Oxford & New York, Pergamon Press.

Broda, E. 1978. *The Evolution of Bioenergetic Processes: Revised Reprint*. Oxford & New York, Pergamon Press.

Brown, Cynthia Stokes. 2007. *Big History: From the Big Bang to the Present*. New York, The New Press.

Brown, P., Sutikna, T., Morwood, M. J. et al. 2004. 'A new small-bodied hominin from the Late Pleistocene of Flores, Indonesia.' *Nature 431*, 28 October (1055–61).

Brown, James H., Gillooly, James F., Allen, Andrew P., Savage, Van M. & West, Geoffrey B. 2004. 'Toward a Metabolic Theory of Ecology.' *Ecology 85*, 7, July (1771–89).

Bryson, Bill. 2003. *A Short History of Nearly Everything*. London, Random House.

Budiansky, Stephen. 1992. *The Covenant of the Wild: Why Animals Chose Domestication*. New York, William Morrow.

Budyko, M. I. 1986. *The Evolution of the Biosphere*. Dordrecht, Netherlands & Boston, D. Reidel Publishing Company.

Bureau International des Poids et Mesures. 2006. *The International System of Units (SI)*. Organisation Intergouvermentale de la Convention du Métre. www.bipm.fr/en/home.

Burger, Richard L. 1992. *Chavín and the Origins of Andean Civilization*. London, Thames and Hudson.

Burroughs, William J. 2006. *Climate Change in Prehistory: The End of the Reign of Chaos*. Cambridge, Cambridge University Press (2005).

Caesar, Gaius Julius. 1984. *The Conquest of Gaul (De bello Gallico)*. Harmondsworth, Penguin Books.

Cairns-Smith, A. G. 1995. *Seven Clues to the Origin of Life*. Cambridge, Cambridge University Press, Canto (1985).

Carneiro, Robert L. 1970. 'A theory of the origin of the state.' *Science 169*, 3947 (733–8).

Carr, E. H. 1968. *What is History?* Harmondsworth, Penguin Books. (1961).

Carroll, Robert. 2000. 'Towards a new evolutionary synthesis.' *TREE 15*, 1 (27–32).

Caspari, Rachel & Wolpoff, Milford. 1998. *Race, Culture and Human Evolution*. Boulder, Co., Westview Press.

Cavalli-Sforza, Luigi Luca. 2000. *Genes, Peoples, and Languages*. New York, North Point Press.

Cavalli-Sforza, Luigi Luca & Cavalli-Sforza, Francesco. 1994. *The Great Human Diasporas: The History of Diversity and Evolution*. Reading, Mass., Addison-Wesley.

Chaikin, Andrew & Kohl, Victoria. 2009. *Voices From the Moon: Apollo astronauts describe their lunar experiences*. New York, Viking Studio.

Chaisson, Eric J. 1977. 'The Scenario of Cosmic Evolution.' *Harvard Magazine*, November–December (21–33).

Chaisson, Eric J. 1981. *Cosmic Dawn: The Origins of Matter and Life*. New York, W.W. Norton & Co.

Chaisson, Eric J. 1982. 'The broadest view of the biggest picture: An essay on radiation, matter, life.' *Harvard Magazine*, January–February (21–5).

Chaisson, Eric J. 1987. *The Life Era: Cosmic selection and conscious evolution*. New York, Atlantic Monthly Press.

Chaisson, Eric J. 1998a. *Universe: An Evolutionary Approach to Astronomy*. Englewood Cliffs, N.J., Prentice Hall.

Chaisson, Eric J. 1998b. 'The cosmic environment for the growth of complexity.' *Biosystems 46* (13–19).

Chaisson, Eric J. 2001. *Cosmic Evolution: The Rise of Complexity in Nature*. Cambridge, Mass., Harvard University Press.

Chaisson, Eric J. 2003. 'A unifying concept for astrobiology.' *International Journal of Astrobiology 2*, 2 (91–101).

Chaisson, Eric J. 2004. 'Complexity: An Energetics Agenda.' *Complexity 9*, 3 (14–21).

Chaisson, Eric J. 2005. *Epic of Evolution: Seven Ages of the Cosmos*. New York, Columbia University Press.

Chaisson, Eric J. 2008. 'Long-term global heating from energy usage.' *EOS, Transactions of the American Geophysical Union 89*, 28 (253–4).

Chaisson, Eric J. 2009. 'The heat to come …' *New Scientist* issue 2702, 6 April (24–5).

Chaisson, Eric J. & McMillan, Steve. 2008. *Astronomy Today, Sixth Edition*. San Francisco, Pearson Addison Wesley.

Chambers, Robert. 1994. 'Vestiges of the Natural History of Creation.' In: Secord, James A. (ed.) *Vestiges of the Natural History of Creation and Other Evolutionary Writings*. Chicago & London, University of Chicago Press (i–390) (1844).

Chandler, David L. 2006. 'New World Order.' *New Scientist* issue 2579, 28 November (40–3).

Chown, Marcus. 2005. 'Did the big bang really happen?' *New Scientist* issue 2506, 2 July (30).

Chown, Marcus. 2007. 'Rival theory fights back against dark matter.' *New Scientist* issue 2623, 27 September (12–13).

Chown, Marcus. 2008. 'Land of the rising suns.' *New Scientist* issue 2670, 23 August (40–3).

Chown, Marcus. 2009. 'O others, where art thou?' *New Scientist* issue 2722, 22 August (37–9).

Christian, David. 1991. 'The Case for "Big History."' *Journal of World History 2*, 2 (223–8).

Christian, David. 2004. *Maps of Time: An Introduction to Big History*. Berkeley & Los Angeles, University of California Press.

Christian, David. 2009a. 'The Evolutionary Epic and the Chronometric Revolution.' In: Genet, Cheryl, Genet, Russell, Swimme, Brian, Palmer, Linda & Gibler, Linda (eds.) *The Evolutionary Epic: Science's story and humanity's response*. Santa Margarita, Ca., Collins Foundation Press (91–9).

Christian, David. 2009b. 'History and Science after the Chronometric Revolution.' In: Dick, Steven J. & Lupisella, Mark L. (eds.) *Cosmos & Culture: Cultural Evolution in a Cosmic Context* (441–62).

Cloud, Preston. 1978. *Cosmos, Earth and Man: A Short History of the Universe*. New Haven & London, Yale University Press.

Cloud, Preston. 1988. *Oasis in Space: Earth History from the Beginning*. New York, W.W. Norton & Co.

Cochran, Gregory & Harpending, Henry. 2009. *The 10,000 Year Explosion: How Civilization Accelerated Human Evolution*. New York, Basic Books.

Cohen, Marc Nathan. 1977. *The Food Crisis in Prehistory: Overpopulation and the Origins of Agriculture*. New Haven & London, Yale University Press.

Cohen, H. Floris. 1994. *The Scientific Revolution: A Historiographical Inquiry*. Chicago & London, University of Chicago Press.

Cohen, H. Floris. 2007. *De herschepping van de wereld: Het ontstaan van de moderne natuurwetenschap verklaard*. Amsterdam, Bert Bakker.

Collingwood, R. G. 1993. *The Idea of History*. Oxford, Clarendon Press (1946).

Committee on the Societal and Economic Impacts of Severe Space Weather Events. 2008. *Severe Space Weather Events – Understanding Societal and Economic Impacts Workshop Report*. Washington D.C., National Academies Press. www.nap.edu/catalog/12507.html.

Conway Morris, Simon. 1998. *The Crucible of Creation: The Burgess Shale and the Rise of Animals*. Oxford, Oxford University Press.

Cook, Earl. 1971. 'The Flow of Energy in an Industrial Society.' *Scientific American 225*, 3, September (134–47).

Cook, Earl. 1976. *Man, Energy, Society*. San Francisco, W.H. Freeman & Co.

Coppens, Yves. 1994. 'East Side Story: The Origin of Humankind.' *Scientific American 270*, 11, May (62–9).

Cortright, Edgar M. (ed.). 1975. *Apollo Expeditions to the Moon*. Washington, D.C., NASA SP-350.

Crabtree, Charlotte & Nash, Gary B. (Project Co-directors). 1994. *National Standards for World History: Exploring Paths to the Present: Grades 5–12 Expanded Edition*. Los Angeles, National Center for History in the Schools.

Crone, Patricia. 1989. *Pre-industrial Societies: New perspectives on the past*. Oxford, Basil Blackwell.

Crosby, Alfred W. 1972. *The Columbian Exchange: Biological and Cultural Consequences of 1492*. Westport, Conn., Greenwood Press.

Crosby, Alfred W. 1993. *Ecological Imperialism: The Biological Expansion of Europe, 900–1900*. Cambridge, Cambridge University Press (1986).

Crosby, Alfred W. 1997. *The Measure of Reality: Quantification and Western Society, 1250–1600*. Cambridge, Cambridge University Press.

Crosby, Alfred W. 2006. *Children of the Sun: A History of Humanity's Unappeasable Appetite for Energy*. New York, W.W. Norton & Co.

Culotta, Elizabeth. 2007. 'Ancient DNA Reveals Neandertals With Red Hair, Fair Complexions.' *Science 318*, 5850, 26 October (546–7).

Cunliffe, Barry (ed.). 1994. *The Oxford Illustrated Prehistory of Europe*. Oxford & New York, Oxford University Press.

Curtin, Philip D. 1994. *Cross-cultural Trade in World History*. Cambridge, Cambridge University Press (1984).

Darlington, C. D. 1969. *The Evolution of Man and Society*. London, George Allen & Unwin.

Darwin, Charles. 1881. *The formation of vegetable mould, through the action of worms*. London, John Murray.

Darwin, Charles. 1985. *The Origin of Species by Means of Natural Selection, or the Preservation of Favoured Races in the Struggle for Life*. Harmondsworth, Penguin Books (1859, original title: *On the Origin of Species ... etc.*).

Darwin, Charles. 1989. *Voyage of the Beagle: Charles Darwin's Journal of Researches* (Edited and Abridged with an Introduction by Janet Browne and Michael Neve). London, Penguin Books (1839).

Darwin, Charles. 2004. *The Descent of Man: Selection in Relation to Sex* (James Moore & Adrian Desmond Editors & Introduction). Harmondsworth, Penguin Books (1871).

Davies, Paul. 1994. *The Last Three Minutes: Conjectures about the Ultimate Fate of the Universe*. London, Weidenfeld & Nicolson.

Davies, Paul. 2006. *The Goldilocks Enigma*. London, Allen Lane.

Daviss, Bennett. 2007. 'Our Solar Future.' *New Scientist* issue 2633, 8 December (32–7).

Dawkins, Richard. 1989. *The Selfish Gene*. Oxford, Oxford University Press (1976).

Dayton, Leigh. 1992. 'Pacific islanders were world's first farmers.' *New Scientist* issue 1851, 12 December (14).

Debeir, Jean-Claude, Deléage, Jean-Paul & Hémery, Daniel. 1991. *In the Servitude of Power: Energy and Civilization through the Ages*. London & Atlantic Highlands, N.J., Zed Books (1986).

De Camp, L. Sprague. 1993. *The Ancient Engineers: Technology and Invention from the Earliest Times to the Renaissance*. New York, Barnes & Noble Publishing (1960).

Delsemme, Armand. 1998. *Our Cosmic Origins: From the Big Bang to the emergence of life and intelligence*. Cambridge, Cambridge University Press.

Descartes, René. 1977. *Le Monde, ou, Traité de la lumière*. New York, Abaris Books (1664).

Diamond, Jared. 1997. *Guns, Germs and Steel: The Fates of Human Societies*. London, Jonathan Cape.

Diamond, Jared. 1987. 'Human Use of World Resources.' *Nature 328*, 6 (479–80).

Diderot & d'Alembert. 1751. *l'Encyclopédie, ou Dictionnaire Raisonné des Sciences, des Arts et des Métiers, par un société de gens de lettres*. Paris, Briasson, David, Le Breton, Durand. 17 volumes (1751–72).

Dillehay, Tom. 1997. *Monte Verde: A Late Pleistocene Settlement in Chile, Volume 2: The Archaeological Context and Interpretation*. Washington, D.C., Smithsonian Institution Press.

Drees, Willem B. 1996. *Van Niets tot Nu: Een wetenschappelijk scheppingsverhaal*. Kampen, Uitgeverij Kok.

Drees, Willem B. 2002. *Creation: From nothing until now*. London, Routlegde.

Drury, Stephen. 1999. *Stepping Stones: The making of our home world*. Oxford, Oxford University Press.

EcoSanRes. 2008. *Closing the Loop on Phosphorus*. Stockholm Environment Institute. www.ecosanres.org/pdf_files/ESR-factsheet-04.pdf.

Eisenstein, Elizabeth L. 1993. *The Printing Revolution in Early Modern Europe*. Cambridge, Cambridge University Press (1983).

Elias, Norbert. 1978a. *What is Sociology?* London, Hutchinson.

Elias, Norbert. 1978b. *The History of Manners. The Civilizing Process: Volume I*. New York, Pantheon Books.

Elias, Norbert. 1982. *Power and Civility. The Civilizing Process: Volume II*. New York, Pantheon Books.

Elias, Norbert. 1987a. 'The Retreat of Sociologists into the Present.' *Theory, Culture & Society 4*, 2–3 (213–22).

Elias, Norbert. 1987b. *Involvement and Detachment*. Oxford, Basil Blackwell.

Elias, Norbert. 1992a. *The Symbol Theory* (edited with an introduction by Richard Kilminster). London, Sage Publications.

Elias, Norbert. 1992b. *Time: An Essay*. Oxford, Basil Blackwell.

Ellis, J., Fields, B. D. & Schramm, D. N. 1996. 'Geological Isotope Anomalies as Signatures of Nearby Supernovae.' *Astrophysical Journal 470* (1227–36).

Emmer, P. C. 2003. 'The myth of early globalization: the Atlantic economy, 1500–1800.' *European Review 11*, 1 (37–47).

'Energy and Power.' *Scientific American Special Issue 225*, 3 (September 1971).

Fagan, Brian. 1999. *Floods, Famines, and Emperors: El Niño and the Fate of Civilizations.* New York, Basic Books.

Fagan, Brian. 2000. *The Little Ice Age: How Climate Made History, 1300–1850.* New York, Basic Books.

Fagan, Brian. 2004. *The Long Summer: How Climate Changed Civilization.* New York, Basic Books.

Fagan, Brian. 2008. *The Great Warming: Climate Change and the Rise and Fall of Civilizations.* London, Bloomsbury Publishing.

Feng Tian, Toon, Owen B., Pavlov, Alexander A. & De Sterck, H. 2005. 'A Hydrogen-Rich Early Earth Atmosphere.' *Science 308*, issue 5724 (1014–17).

Fiedel, Stuart J. 1992. *Prehistory of the Americas, second edition.* Cambridge, Cambridge University Press (1987).

Fieldhouse, D. K. 1973. *Economics and Empire, 1830–1914.* London, Weidenfeld & Nicolson.

Fields, Brian. 2007. *When Stars Attack! Live Undersea Radioactivities as Signatures of Nearby Supernova Explosions.* Geological Society of America Denver Annual Meeting (28–31 October 2007), Paper No. 218-10.

Fields, Brian D. & Ellis, John. 1999. 'On deep-ocean ^{60}Fe as a fossil of a near-earth supernova.' *New Astronomy 4*, 6 (419–30).

'50 years in space: My favourite photo.' *New Scientist*, issue 2620, 8 September 2007 (40).

Firestone, R. B., West, A., Kennett, J. P. et al. 2007. 'Evidence for an extraterrestrial impact 12,900 years ago that contributed to the megafaunal extinctions and the Younger Dryas cooling.' *Proceedings of the National Academy of Sciences 104*, 41 (16016–21).

Fitzgerald, Michael. 2004. *Autism and creativity: is there a link between autism in men and exceptional ability?* Hove, Brunner-Routledge.

Fladmark, Knut R. 1979. 'Routes: Alternative Migration Corridors for Early Man in North America.' *American Antiquity 44*, 1 (55–69).

Flynn, Dennis O. & Giráldez, Arturo. 1995. 'Born with a "Silver Spoon": The Origin of World Trade in 1571.' *Journal of World History 6*, 2 (201–22).

Flynn, Dennis O. & Giráldez, Arturo. 2002. 'Cycles of Silver: Global Economic Unity through the Mid-Eighteenth Century.' *Journal of World History 13*, 2 (391–428).

Flynn, Dennis O. & Giráldez, Arturo. 2008. 'Born Again: Globalization's Sixteenth Century Origins (Asian/Global Versus European Dynamics).' *Pacific Economic Review 13*, 3 (359–87).

Fox, Douglas. 2007. 'Life but not as we know it.' *New Scientist* issue 2607, 5–15 June (35–9).

Fox, Douglas. 2009. 'Dawn of the animals.' *New Scientist* issue 2716, 11 July (39–41).

Fox, Ronald F. 1988. *Energy and the Evolution of Life.* New York, W.H. Freeman & Co.

Gamble, Clive. 1995. *Timewalkers: The Prehistory of Global Colonization*. Harmondsworth, Penguin Books (1993).

Garraty, John A. & Gay, Peter (eds.). 1972. *The Columbia History of The World*. New York, Harper & Row Publishers.

Geel, B. van, Bokovenko, N. A., Burova, N. D. et al. 2004. 'Climate change and the expansion of the Scythian culture after 850 BC: a hypothesis.' *Journal of Archaeological Science 31* (1735–41).

Gehrels, Tom. 2007. *Survival through Evolution: from Multiverse to Modern Society*. Charleston, S.C., BookSurge Publishing.

Gehrels, Tom. 2009. *The Cosmological Foundation of Our World, seen in a Revised History of our Universe*. University of Arizona at Tucson. www.lpl.arizona.edu/~tgehrels/Foundation2.pdf.

Gell-Mann, Murray. 1994. *The Quark and the Jaguar: Adventures in the Simple and the Complex*. New York, W.H. Freeman & Co.

Genet, Cheryl, Genet, Russell, Swimme, Brian, Palmer, Linda & Gibler, Linda. 2009. *The Evolutionary Epic: Science's story and humanity's response*. Santa Margarita, Ca., Collins Foundation Press.

Genet, Russell Merle. 2007. *Humanity: The Chimpanzees Who Would be Ants*. Santa Margarita, Ca., Collins Foundation Press.

Getman, Konstantin V., Feigelson, Eric D., Luhman, Kevin L., Sicilia-Aguilar, Aurora, Wang, Junfeng & Garmire, Gordon P. 2009. 'Protoplanetary Disk Evolution Around the Triggered Star-Forming Region Cepheus B.' *The Astrophysical Journal 699* (1454–72).

Glasby, Geoffrey P. 2006. 'Abiotic Origin of Hydrocarbons: An Historical Overview.' *Resource Geology 56*, 1 (85–98).

Gleick, James. 1988. *Chaos: Making a New Science*. Harmondsworth, Penguin Books (1987).

Goldberg, Vicky. 1991. *The Power of Photography: How photographs changed our lives*. New York, Abbeville Publishing Group.

Gonzalez, Guillermo & Richards, Jay Wesley. 2004. *The Privileged Planet: How our place in the cosmos is designed for discovery*. Washington, D.C., Regnery Publishing, Inc.

Goudsblom, Johan. 1990. 'The Impact of the Domestication of Fire Upon the Balance of Power Between Human Groups and Other Animals.' *Focaal 13* (55–65).

Goudsblom, Johan. 1992. *Fire and Civilization*. London, Allen Lane.

Goudsblom, Johan, Jones, Eric & Mennell, Stephen. 1996. *The Course of Human History: Economic Growth, Social Process, and Civilization*. New York, Armond & London, M.E. Sharpe.

Gould, James L & Keeton, William T. 1996. *Biological Science (Sixth Edition)*. New York & London: W.W. Norton & Co.

Gould, Stephen J. & Eldredge, N. 1977. 'Punctuated Equilibria: The tempo and mode of evolution reconsidered.' *Paleobiology 7* (115–51).

Gould, Stephen J. & Eldredge, N. 1989. *Wonderful Life: The Burgess Shale and the Nature of History*. New York & London, W.W. Norton & Co.

Gould, Stephen J. & Eldredge, N. 1993. 'Punctuated Equilibrium Comes of Age.' *Nature* 366 (223–7).

Graedel, T. E. & Crutzen, Paul J. 1993. *Atmospheric Change: An Earth System Perspective*. New York, W.H. Freeman & Co.

Gruhn, Ruth. 1988. 'Linguistic Evidence in Support of the Coastal Route of Earliest Entry into the New World.' *Man* (New Series) 23 (77–100).

Gunnerson, Charles G. 1973. 'Debris Accumulation in Ancient and Modern Cities.' *Journal of the Environmental Engineering Division 99*, 3, May/June (229–43).

Hacker, Jörg & Carniel, Elisabeth. 2001. 'Ecological fitness, genomic islands and bacterial pathogenicity: A Darwinian view of the evolution of microbes.' *EMBO Reports* 2, no.5 (376–81).

Hamilton, Garry   2008. 'Welcome to the Virosphere.' *New Scientist* issue 2671, 30 August (38–41).

Hammen, T. van der & Geel, B. van. 2008. 'Charcoal in soils of the Allerød-Younger Dryas transition were the result of natural fires and not necessarily the effect of an extra-terrestrial impact.' *Netherlands Journal of Geosciences – Geologie en Mijnbouw* 87, 4 (359–61).

Hammer, F., Puech, M., Chemin, L., Flores, H. & Lehnert, M. D. 2007. 'The Milky Way, an Exceptionally Quiet Galaxy: Implications for the Formation of Spiral Galaxies.' *The Astrophysical Journal 662*, 1 (322–34).

Harris, Marvin. 1975. *Culture, People, Nature: An Introduction to General Anthropology*. New York, Harper & Row.

Harris, Marvin. 1980. *Cultural Materialism: The Struggle for a Science of Culture*. New York, Vintage Books.

Harris, Marvin 1997. *Culture, People, Nature: An Introduction to General Anthropology*. New York, Longman.

Harris, David R. (ed.). 1990. *Settling Down and Breaking Ground: Rethinking the Neolithic Revolution*. Amsterdam, Stichting Nederlands Museum voor Anthropologie en Praehistorie, Twaalfde Kroon-Voordracht.

Harris, David R. (ed.). 1996. *The Origins and Spread of Agriculture and Pastoralism in Eurasia*. London, UCL Press.

Harris, D. R. & Hillman, G. C. (eds.). 1989. *Foraging and farming: the evolution of plant exploitation*. London, Allen & Unwin.

Hecht, Jeff. 2007. 'Prehistoric mammals: Big, bad and furry.' *New Scientist* issue 2589, 3 February (32–5).

Hegel, Georg Wilhelm Friedrich. 2000. *Enzyklopädie der philosophischen Wissenschaften im Grundrisse*. Hamburg, Felix Meiner Verlag (1817).

Heiser, Charles B., Jr. 1990. *Seed to Civilization: The Story of Food*. Cambridge, Mass., Harvard University Press.

Helferich, Gerard. 2004. *Humboldt's Cosmos: Alexander von Humboldt and the Latin American Journey That Changed the Way We See the World*. New York, Gotham Books.

Hershkovitz, I., Donoghue, Helen D., Minnikin, David E. et al. 2008. 'Detection and Molecular Characterization of 9000-Year Old *Mycobacterium tuberculosis* from a

Neolithic settlement in the Eastern Mediterranean,' *PLoS ONE 3*, 10, e3426, 15 October, doi:10.1371/journal.pone.0003426.

Hillman, G., Hedges, Robert, Moore, Andrew, Colledge, Susan & Pettitt, Paul. 2001. 'New evidence of Lateglacial cereal cultivation at Abu Hureyra on the Euphrates.' *The Holocene 11*, 4 (383–93).

Hobsbawm, E. J. 1968. *Industry and Empire*. Harmondsworth, Penguin.

Holmes, Bob. 2008. 'Beastly Tales.' *New Scientist* issue 2639, 19 January (30–3).

Hoyle, Fred & Wickramasinghe, Chandra. 1996. *Our Place in the Cosmos: The Unfinished Revolution*. London, Phoenix (1993).

Hubbert, M. King. 1956. *Nuclear Energy and the Fossil Fuels*. Houston, Tex., Shell Development Company, Publication No. 95.

Hubbert, M. King. 1971. 'The Energy Resources of the Earth.' *Scientific American 225*, 3, September (60–84).

Huizinga, Johan. 1995. *De taak der cultuurgeschiedenis. Samengesteld, verzorgd en van een nawoord voorzien door W.E. Krul*. Groningen, Historische Uitgeverij.

Humboldt, Alexander von. 1845. *Kosmos: Entwurf einer physischen Weltbeschreibung*. Stuttgart and Tübingen, J. G. Cotta'scher Verlag (1845–62).

Humboldt, Alexander von 1995. *Personal Narrative of a Journey to the Equinoctial Regions of the New Continent* (Abridged and Translated with an Introduction by Jason Wilson and a Historical Introduction by Malcolm Nicolson). London, Penguin Books (1814–25).

Humboldt, Alexander von. 1997. *Cosmos, Volume 1 (Foundations of Natural History)*. Baltimore, Johns Hopkins University Press (1845).

Hume, David. 1757. *The Natural History of Religion*. London, A. and H. Bradlaugh Bonner.

Hurwitz, Ellen & Ostrowski, Donald. 1983. 'The Many Varieties of Historical Writing: Caterpillars and Butterflies Reexamined.' *Harvard Ukrainian Studies* Vol. 7 (296–308).

International Energy Agency. 2007. *Key World Energy Statistics 2007*. Paris, International Energy Agency.

Jantsch, Erich. 1983. *The Self-organizing Universe: Scientific and Human Implications of the Emerging Paradigm of Evolution*. Oxford & New York, Pergamon Press (1980).

Jenkins, Elizabeth B. 1997. *Initiation: A Woman's Spiritual Adventure in the Heart of the Andes*. E. Rutherford, N.J., Putnam Pub. Group.

Jones, Dan. 2007. 'Going global: How humans conquered the world.' *New Scientist* issue 2627, 27 October (36–41).

Joyce, Gerald F. 2002. 'The antiquity of RNA-based evolution.' *Nature 418* (214–21).

Kant, Immanuel. 1755. *Allgemeine Naturgeschichte und Theorie Des Himmels oder Versuch von der Verfassung und dem mechanischen Ursprunge des ganzen Weltgebäudes, nach Newtonischen Grundsätzen abgehandelt*. Königsberg: Petersen (anonymously published).

Kant, Immanuel. 1963. *On History* (edited with an Introduction by Lewis White Beck). Indianapolis: Bobbs-Merrill Company, Inc. (Original title: *Idee zu einer allgemeinen Geschichte in weltbürgerlicher Absicht*, 1784).

Kasting, James F., Whitmire, Daniel P. & Reynolds, Ray T. 1993. 'Habitable Zones around Main Sequence Stars.' *Icarus 101* (108–28).

Kauffman, Stuart A. 1993. *The Origins of Order: Self-Organization and Selection in Evolution.* New York & Oxford, Oxford University Press.

Kauffman, Stuart A. 1995. *At Home in the Universe: The Search for Laws of Complexity.* London, Viking / The Penguin Press.

Kennett, Douglas J. & Kennett, James P. 2006. 'Early State Formation in Southern Mesopotamia, Sea Levels, Shorelines, and Climate Change.' *The Journal of Island and Coastal Archaeology 1*, 1 (67–99).

Kennett, D. J., Kennett, J. P., West, A., et al. 2009. 'Nanodiamonds in the Younger Dryas Boundary Sediment Layer.' *Science 323*, no. 5910, 2 January (94).

Kitson Clark, G. 1967. *The Critical Historian.* New York, Basic Books.

Knie, K., Korschinek, G., Faestermann, T., Wallner, C., Scholten, J. & Hillebrandt, W. 1999. 'Indication for Supernova Produced ^{60}Fe Activity on Earth.' *Physical Review Letters 83*, 1 (18–21).

Knie, K., Korschinek, G., Faestermann, T., Dorfi, E. A., Rugel, G. & Wallner, A. 2004. '^{60}Fe Anomaly in a Deep-Sea Manganese Crust and Implications for a Nearby Supernova Source.' *Physical Review Letters 93*, 17 (171103-1–171103-4).

Koonin, Eugene V. & Martin, William. 2005. 'On the origin of genomes and cells within inorganic compounds.' *Trends in Genetics 21*, 2 (647–54).

Kortlandt, Adriaan. 1972. *New Perspectives on Ape and Human Evolution.* Amsterdam, Stichting voor Psychobiologie.

Kortlandt, Adriaan. 1980. 'How might early hominids have defended themselves against large predators and food competitors?' *Journal of Human Evolution 9*, 2 (79–112).

Kortlandt, Adriaan vs. Coppens, Yves. 1994. 'Rift over Origins.' *Scientific American 271*, 4 October (5).

Koshland, Daniel E., Jr. 1980. *Bacterial chemotaxis as a model behavioral system.* New York, Raven Press.

Kuhn, Thomas S. 1970. *The Structure of Scientific Revolutions. Second Edition, Enlarged.* Chicago, University of Chicago Press (1962).

Kuijt, Ian & Finlayson, Bill. 2009. 'Evidence for food storage and predomestication granaries 11,000 years ago in the Jordan Valley.' *Proceedings of the National Academy of Science 106*, 27 (10966–70).

Kutter, G. Siegfried. 1987. *The Universe and Life: Origins and Evolution.* Boston, Jones & Bartlett Publishers.

Lalueza-Fox, Carles, Römpler, Holger, Caramelli, David et al. 2007. 'A Melanocortin 1 Receptor Allele Suggests Varying Pigmentation Among Neanderthals.' *Science 318*, no. 5855, 30 November (1453–5).

Landes, D. S. 1969. *The Unbound Prometheus: Technological change and industrial development in Western Europe from 1730 to the present.* Cambridge, Cambridge University Press.

Landes, D. S. 1998. *The Wealth and Poverty of Nations: Why Some Are So Rich and Some So Poor.* New York, W.W. Norton & Co

Lane, Nick. 2009. 'Why sex is worth losing your head for.' *New Scientist* issue 2712, 13 June (40–3).

Lange, Frits de. 1997. *Gevoel voor verhoudingen: God, evolutie en ethiek*. Kampen, Uitgeverij Kok.

Lapperre, P. E. 1997. *Sociologie en Techniek: Lange termijn wisselwerkingen tussen technologie en maatschappij [Sociology and Technology: Long-term interactions between technology and society]*. Eindhoven, the Netherlands, Eindhoven University of Technology, Department of Technology Management.

Leakey, Richard E. & Lewin, Roger. 1995. *The Sixth Extinction: Patterns of Life and the Future of Humankind*. New York, Doubleday.

Ledeboer, A. M., Kroll, A. J. M., Dons, J. J. M. et al. 1976. 'On the isolation of TI-plasmid from Agrobacterium tumefaciens.' *Nucleic Acid Research 3*, 2 (449–63).

Lehninger, Albert L. 1975. *Biochemistry: The Molecular Basis of Cell Structure and Function, Second Edition*. New York, Worth Publishers.

Lerner, Eric. 2004. 'Bucking the Big Bang.' *New Scientist* issue 2448, 22 May (20).

Lesch, Harald & Zaun, Harald. 2008. *Die kürzeste Geschichte allen Lebens: Eine Reportage über 13,7 Milliarden Jahre Werden und Vergehen*. München, Piper Verlag.

Levy, David H. (ed.). 2000. *The Scientific American Book of the Cosmos*. New York, St. Martin Press & London, MacMillan.

Lewin, Roger. 1993. *Complexity: Life at the edge of chaos*. London, J.M. Dent Ltd.

Lewis, Henry T. 1972. 'The Role of Fire in the Domestication of Plants and Animals in Southwest Asia: A Hypothesis.' *Man 7*, 2 (195–222).

'Life in the Universe.' *Scientific American 271*, 4 (October 1994). Published in 1995 as *Life in The Universe: Scientific American Special Issue*. New York, W.H. Freeman & Co.

Lineweaver, Charles H., Fenner, Yeshe & Gibson, Brad K. 2004. 'The Galactic Habitable Zone and the Age Distribution of Complex Life in the Milky Way.' *Science 303*, 2, January (59–62).

Livi-Bacci, Massimo. 1992. *A Concise History of World Population*. Cambridge, Mass. & Oxford, Blackwell Publishers (1989).

Lloyd, Christopher. 2008. *What on Earth Happened? The Complete Story of the Planet, Life and People from the Big Bang to the Present Day*. London, Bloomsbury.

Lovelock, James E. 1987. *Gaia: A New Look at Life on Earth*. Oxford & New York, Oxford University Press.

Lovelock, James E. 2000. *Gaia: The Practical Science of Planetary Medicine*. Oxford & New York, Oxford University Press (1991).

Lovelock, James E. 2006. *The Revenge of Gaia: Earth's Climate Crisis and the Fate of Humanity*. New York, Basic Books.

Loy, T., Spriggs M. & Wickler, S. 1992. 'Direct Evidence for Human Use of Plants 28,000 years ago: Starch Residues on Stone Artifacts from the Northern Solomons.' *Antiquity 66* (898–912).

Lunine, Jonathan I. 1999. *Earth: Evolution of a Habitable World*. Cambridge, Cambridge University Press.

MacKay, David J. C. 2008. *Sustainable Energy – without the hot air*. Cambridge, UIT Cambridge. www.withouthotair.com.

MacLeish, Archibald. 1968. 'A Reflection: Riders on Earth Together, Brothers in Eternal Cold.' *New York Times*, 25 December (1).

Magistretti, Pierre J., Pellerin, Luc & Martin, Jean-Luc 2000. *Brain Energy Metabolism: An Integrated Cellular Perspective*. American College of Neuropsychopharmacology. www.acnp.org/G4/GN401000064/.

'Magnificent Cosmos: Exploring the Universe, from our solar neighborhood to beyond distant galaxies.' *Scientific American 9*, 1 (Spring 1998).

Makarieva, A. M. & Gorshkov, V. G. 2006. 'Biotic pump of atmospheric moisture as driver of the hydrological cycle on land.' *Hydrology and Earth System Sciences Discussion 3* (2621–73).

Makarieva, Anastassia M., Gorshkov, Victor G., Li, Bai-Lian, Chown, Steven L., Reich, Peter B. & Gavrilov, Valery M. 2008. 'Mean mass-specific metabolic rates are strikingly similar across life's major domains: Evidence for life's metabolic optimum.' *Proceedings of the National Academy of Science 105*, 44 (16994–9).

Malthus, T. R. 1992. *An Essay on the Principle of Population (Cambridge Texts in the History of Political Thought)*. Cambridge, Cambridge University Press (1798).

Mann, Michael. 1987. *The Sources of Social Power. Volume I: A history of power from the beginning to A.D. 1760*. Cambridge, Cambridge University Press (1986).

Mann, Michael. 1993. *The Sources of Social Power. Volume II: The rise of classes and nation-states, 1760–1914*. Cambridge, Cambridge University Press.

Margulis, Lynn & Olendzendski, Lorraine. 1992. *Environmental Evolution: Effects of the Origin and Evolution of Life on Planet Earth*. Cambridge, Mass., MIT Press.

Margulis, Lynn & Sagan, Dorion. 1995. *What is Life?* London, Weidenfeld & Nicolson.

Margulis, Lynn & Sagan, Dorion. 1997. *Microcosmos: Four Billion Years of Microbial Evolution*. Berkeley, University of California Press.

Markow, Alexander V. 2009. 'Alpha diversity of Phanerozoic marine communities positively correlates with longevity of genera.' *Paleobiology 35*, 2 (231–50).

Markow, Alexander V. & Korotayev, Andrey V. 2007. 'Phanerozoic marine biodiversity follows a hyperbolic trend.' *Palaeoworld 16* (311–18).

Marshall, James. 1998. *Goldilocks and the Three Bears: Retold and Illustrated by James Marshall*. New York, Puffin Books.

May, Brian, Moore, Patrick & Lintott, Chris. 2006. *Bang! The Complete History of the Universe*. Bristol, Carlton Books.

McBrearty, Sally & Brooks, Alison S. 2000. 'The revolution that wasn't: a new interpretation of the origin of modern human behavior.' *Journal of Human Evolution 39* (453–563).

McKenna, Phil. 2008. 'Plumbing the oceans could bring limitless clean energy.' *New Scientist* issue 2683, 19 November (28–9).

McNeill, J. R. 2000. *Something New Under the Sun: An Environmental History of the Twentieth Century World*. London, Penguin Books.

McNeill, J. R. & McNeill, W. H. 2003. *The Human Web: A Bird's-Eye View of World History*. New York, W.W. Norton & Co.

McNeill, William H. 1963. *The Rise of the West: A History of the Human Community*. Chicago & London, University of Chicago Press.

McNeill, William H. 1976. *Plagues and Peoples*. Garden City, New York, Anchor Press / Doubleday.

McNeill, William H. 1984. *The Pursuit of Power: Technology, Armed Force and Society since AD 1000*. Chicago, University of Chicago Press (1982).

McNeill, William H. 1986a. 'Organizing Concepts for World History.' *Review: Fernand Braudel Center 10*, 2 (211–29).

McNeill, William H. 1986b. *Mythistory and Other Essays*. Chicago & London, University of Chicago Press.

McNeill, William H. 1991. *The Rise of the West: A History of the Human Community; with a retrospective essay*. Chicago & London, University of Chicago Press.

McNeill, William H. 1992. *The Global Condition: Conquerors, Catastrophes and Community*. Princeton, Princeton University Press.

McNeill, William H. 1995. *Keeping Together in Time: Dance and Drill in Human History*. Cambridge, Harvard University Press.

McNeill, William H. 1998a. 'History and the Scientific Worldview.' *History & Theory 37*, 1 (1–13).

McNeill, William H. 1998b. *The disruption of traditional forms of nurture: Essay and discussion*. Amsterdam, Het Spinhuis.

McNeill, William H. 2001. 'Passing Strange: The Convergence of Evolutionary Science with Scientific History.' *History & Theory 40*, 1 (1–15).

McNeill, William H. 2005. *The Pursuit of Truth: A Historian's Memoir*. Lexington, Ky., The University of Kentucky Press.

McSween, Harry Y. Jr. 1997. *Fanfare for Earth: The Origin of Our Planet and Life*. New York, St. Martin's Press.

Meadows, Donella H., Meadows, Dennis L., Randers, Jørgen & Behrens III, William W. 1972. *The Limits to Growth: A Report for the Club of Rome Project on the Predicament of Mankind*. New York, Potomac Associates (authorized reprint from Universe Books).

Meadows, Dennis L. 1972. *Rapport van de Club van Rome: De grenzen aan de groei*. Utrecht/Antwerpen, Het Spectrum, Aula 500.

Mears, John A. 1986. 'Evolutionary Process: An organizing principle for general education.' *The Journal of General Education 37*, 4 (315–25).

Mears, John A. 2001. 'Agricultural Origins in Global Perspective.' In: Adas, M. (ed.) *Agricultural and Pastoral Societies in Ancient and Classical History*. Philadelphia, Temple University Press (36–70).

Mears, John A. 2009. 'Implications of the Evolutionary Epic for the Study of Human History.' In: Genet, Cheryl, Genet, Russell, Swimme, Brian, Palmer, Linda & Gibler, Linda. (eds.) *The Evolutionary Epic: Science's story and humanity's response*. Santa Margarita, Ca., Collins Foundation Press (135–46).

Mellars, Paul. 2006. 'Why did modern human populations disperse from Africa ca. 60,000 years ago? A new model.' *Proceedings of the National Academy of Sciences* *103*, 25, 20 June (9381–6).

Menzies, Gavin. 2002. *1421: The Year China Discovered America.* London, Bantam Press.

Mishurov, Yu. N., Zenina, I. A., Dambis, A. K., Mel'Nik, A. M. & Rastorguev, A. S. 1997. 'Is the Sun located near the corotation circle?' *Astronomy and Astrophysics* *323* (775–80).

Monod, Jacques. 1971. *Chance and Necessity.* New York, Alfred Knopf.

Moore, R. I. 1997. 'World History.' In: Bentley, Michael (ed.) *Companion to Historiography.* London, Routledge (941–59).

Morin, Edgar & Kern, Anne Brigitte. 1993. *Terre-Patrie.* Paris, Editions du Seuil.

Morowitz, Harold J. 2002. *The Emergence of Everything: How the World Became Complex.* Oxford, Oxford University Press.

Morrison, Philip, Morrison, Phylis & The Office of Charles and Ray Eames. 1994. *Powers of Ten: About the Relative Size of Things in the Universe.* New York, W.H. Freeman & Co., Scientific American Library.

Mueller, Ulrich G., Gerardo, Nicole M., Aanen, Duur K., Six, Diana L. & Schultz, Ted R. 2005. 'The Evolution of Agriculture in Insects.' *Annual Review of Ecology, Evolution, and Systematics 36* (563–95).

Muir, Hazel. 2005. 'Milky Way: There is no place like home.' *New Scientist* issue 2499, 14 May (30).

Muir, Hazel. 2006. 'Half-life heresy: Accelerating radioactive decay.' *New Scientist* issue 2574, 21 October (36–9).

Mumford, Lewis. 1961. *The City in History: Its Origins, Its Transformations, and Its Prospects.* New York, Harcourt, Brace, and World Inc.

National Geographic. 2009. *Energy For Tomorrow: Repowering the Planet.* Special Spring Issue.

Nazaretyan, Akop P. 2004. *Civilization Crises within the context of Big (Universal) History: Self-Organization, Psychology, and Futorology* (in Russian). Moscow, Mir-Publishers.

Neimark, Jill. 2007. 'Autism: It's Not Just in the Head.' *Discover Magazine,* April 2007 (p. 33ff.). http://discovermagazine.com/2007/apr/autism-it2019s-not-just-in-the-head.

Neprimerov, N. N. 1992. *Mirozdanie [The Universe].* Kazan, Kazan State University.

Newton, Sir Isaac. 1979. *Opticks.* New York, Dover Publications (1730).

Niele, Frank. 2005. *Energy: Engine of Evolution.* Amsterdam, Elsevier, Shell Global Solutions.

Nottale, Laurent, Chaline, Jean & Grou, Pierre. 2000. *Les arbres de l'evolution: Universe, vie, sociétés.* Paris, Hachette.

O'Brien, Patrick. 2008. *Global History for Global Citizenship.* London School of Economics: Global History and Maritime Asia Working and Discussion Paper Series, Working Paper No. 7.

O'Donoghue, James. 2007a. 'Ediacarans: the "long fuse" of the Cambrian explosion?' *New Scientist* issue 2599, 14 April (34–8).

O'Donoghue, James. 2007b. 'A forest is born.' *New Scientist* issue 2631, 24 November (38–41).

Odling-Smee, F. John, Laland, Kevin N. & Feldman, Marcus W. 2003. *Niche construction: the neglected process in evolution.* Princeton, Princeton University Press.

Odum, Howard T. 1971. *Environment, Power and Society.* New York, John Wiley & Sons.

Ofek, E. O., Cameron, P. B., Kasliwal, M. M. et al. 2007. 'SN 2006gy: An Extremely Luminous Supernova in the Galaxy NGC 1260.' *The Astrophysical Journal 659*, 1, Part 2, L13–L16.

Osborne, Roger & Tarling, Don. 1995. *The Viking Historical Atlas of the Earth.* Harmondsworth, Penguin Books.

Ostrowski, Donald. 1989. 'The Historian and the Virtual Past.' *The Historian* Vol. LI, No.2 (201–20).

Ostrowski, Donald. 2003. *Three criteria of historical study.* http://hudce7.harvard.edu/~ostrowski/dawnciv/history.pdf.

Pannekoek, Anton. 1909. *Darwinisme en marxisme.* Beverwijk 1980 Brochure 1, Herdrukken 1/3, Groep Radenkommunisme.

Pannekoek, Anton. 1953. *Anthropogenesis: A Study of the Origins of Man.* Amsterdam, North-Holland Publishing Co.

Pavlov, Alexander A., Toon, Owen B., Pavlov, Anatoli K., Bally, John & Pollard, David. 2005. 'Passing through a giant molecular cloud: "Snowball" glaciations produced by interstellar dust.' *Geophysical Research Letters 32*, 3 (3705).

Pearce, Fred. 2009. 'Ice on Fire.' *New Scientist* issue 2714, 24 June (30–3).

Perkins, Sid. 2009. 'The iron record of Earth's oxygen: Scientists are decoding the geological secrets of banded iron formations.' *Science News 175*, 13 (24–8).

Peterson, Ivars. 1995. *Newton's Clock. Chaos in the Solar System.* New York, W.H. Freeman & Co. (1993).

Pleij, C. W. A. 1995. *Een wandeling in de 'RNA-Wereld.' [A Walk through RNA World].* Oratio, Leiden, Rijskuniversiteit Leiden.

Pollard, Sidney. 1992. *Peaceful Conquest: The Industrialization of Europe 1760–1970.* Oxford & New York, Oxford University Press (1981).

Pomeranz, Kenneth. 2000. *The Great Divergence: Europe, China, and the Making of the Modern World Economy.* Princeton, Princeton University Press.

Ponting, Clive. 1992. *A Green History of the World.* Harmondsworth, Penguin Books.

Poole, Robert. 2008. *Earthrise: How Man First Saw the Earth.* New Haven & London, Yale University Press.

Potter, Christopher. 2009. *You Are Here: A Portable History of the Universe.* New York, HarperCollins

Potts, Rick. 1996. *Humanity's Descent: The consequences of ecological instability.* New York, William Morrow & Co.

Priem, Harry N. A. 1993. *Aarde en Leven: Het Leven in relatie tot zijn planetaire omgeving – Earth and Life: Life in Relation to its Planetary Environment.* Dordrecht, Boston & London, Wolters Kluwer Academic Publishers.

Priem, Harry N. A. 1997. *Aarde: Een planetaire visie*. Assen, Van Gorcum.

Prigogine, Ilya & Stengers, Isabelle. 1984. *Order Out of Chaos: Man's New Dialogue with Nature*. London, Heinemann.

Primack, Joel R. & Abrams, Nancy Ellen. 2006. *The View from the Center of the Universe: Discovering Our Extraordinary Place in the Cosmos*. New York, Riverhead Books.

Pringle, Heather. 2007a. 'Firestorm from space wiped out prehistoric Americans.' *New Scientist* issue 2605, 8–9 May (26).

Pringle, Heather. 2007b. 'Follow that kelp.' *New Scientist* issue 2616, 11 August (40–3).

Pyne, Stephen J. 1982. *Fire in America: A Cultural History of Wildland and Rural Fire*. Princeton, Princeton University Press.

Pyne, Stephen J. 2001. *Fire: A Brief History*. London, The British Museum Press.

Ranke, Leopold von. 1888. 'Vorwort.' *Weltgeschichte, Neunter Theil, zweite Abtheilung*. Leipzig, Verlag von Dunder & Humblot.

Rathje, William & Murphy, Cullen. 1992. *Rubbish! The Archaeology of Garbage: What our garbage tells us about ourselves*. New York, HarperCollins Publishers.

Raup, David M. 1993. *Extinction: Bad Genes or Bad Luck?* Oxford & New York, Oxford University Press.

Ravitch, Diane & Schlesinger Jr., Arthur. 1996. 'The New, Improved History Standards.' *The Wall Street Journal*, 3 April (A14).

Raymond, Sean N., Mandell, Avi M. & Sigurdsson, Steinn. 2006. 'Exotic Earths: Forming Habitable Worlds with Giant Planet Migration.' *Science 313* (1413–16).

Redman, Ch. L. 1978. *The Rise of Civilization: From Early Farmers to Urban Society in the Ancient Near East*. San Francisco, W.H. Freeman & Co.

Reed, David L., Smith, Vincent S., Hammond, Shaless L., Rogers, Alan R. & Clayton, Dale H. 2004. 'Genetic Analysis of Lice Supports Direct Contact between Modern and Archaic Humans.' *Public Library of Science Biology 2*,11, e340.

Reed, Charles A. (ed.). 1977. *Origins of Agriculture*. Den Haag & Paris, Mouton Publishers.

Rees, Martin. 1997. *Before the Beginning: Our Universe and Others*. London, Simon & Schuster.

Reeves, Hubert. 1991. *Hour of Our Delight: Cosmic Evolution, Order, and Complexity*. New York, W.H. Freeman & Co.

Reeves, Hubert, Rosnay, Joël de, Coppens, Yves & Simonnet, Dominique. 1996. *La Plus Belle Histoire du Monde: Les secrets de nos origins*. Paris, Editions du Seuil.

Reeves, Hubert, Rosnay, Joël de, Coppens, Yves & Simonnet, Dominique. 1998. *Origins: Cosmos, Earth and Mankind*. New York, Arcade Publishing.

Reich, Eugenie Samuel. 2005. 'Interstellar gas cloud linked to Snowball Earth.' *New Scientist* issue 2487, 19 February (9).

Reijnders, Lucas. 2006a. 'Is increased energy utilization linked to greater cultural complexity? Energy utilization by Australian Aboriginals and traditional swidden agriculturalists.' *Environmental Sciences 3*, 3 (207–20).

Reijnders, Lucas. 2006b. *Energie: Van brandhout tot zonnecel*. Amsterdam, Uitgeverij Van Gennep.

Renfrew, Colin & Bahn, Paul. 1991. *Archaeology: Theory, Methods and Practice*. London, Thames & Hudson.

Roberts, John M. 1976. *History of the World*. New York, Alfred M. Knopf.

Roberts, Neil. 1998. *The Holocene: An Environmental History (Second Edition)*. Oxford, Basil Blackwell.

Roebroeks, Wil (ed.). 2007. *Guts and Brains: An Integrative Approach to the Hominin Record*. Amsterdam, Amsterdam University Press.

Romein, Jan Marius. 1937. 'De dialectiek van de vooruitgang. Bijdrage tot het ontwikkelingsbegrip in de geschiedenis' In: *Het onvoltooid verleden: .kultuurhistorische studies*. Amsterdam, Querido (9–64).

Rutgers, Michiel, Gulden, Hanneke M. L. van der & Dam, Karel van. 1989. 'Thermodynamical efficiency of bacterial growth calculated from growth yield of *Pseudomonas oxalaticus* OX1 in the chemostat.' *Biochim. Biophys. Acta 973* (302–7).

Sanderson, Stephen K. 1995. *Social Transformations: A General Theory of Historical Development*. Oxford, Basil Blackwell.

Schumacher, E. F. 1989. *Small Is Beautiful: Economics as if People Mattered*. New York, Harper Perennial (1973).

Secord, James A. 2000. *Victorian Sensation: The Extraordinary Publication, Reception, and Secret Authorship of Vestiges of the Natural History of Creation*. Chicago, University of Chicago Press.

Semeniuk, Ivan. 2007. 'Blasts from the past.' *New Scientist* issue 2602, 5–11 May (46–9).

Sharma, Ajay. 2004. 'Origin and Escalation of the Mass-Energy Equation $\Delta E = \Delta mc^2$, *General Science Journal*. www.wbabin.net/ajay/sharma3.pdf.

Sherratt, A. 1981. 'Plough and pastoralism: aspects of the secondary products revolution.' In: Hodder, Ian, Isaac, Glynn & Hammond, Norman (eds.) *Pattern of the Past. Studies in honour of David Clarke*. Cambridge, Cambridge University Press (261–305).

Sherratt, A. 1996. 'Plate tectonics and imaginary prehistories: structure and contingency in agricultural origins.' In: Harris, David R. (ed.) *The Origins and Spread of Agriculture and Pastoralism in Eurasia*. London, UCL Press (130–40).

Sherratt, A. 1997. 'Climatic cycles and behavioural revolutions: the emergence of modern humans and the beginning of farming.' *Antiquity 71*, 272 (271–87).

Shiga, David. 2006. 'Gravity: Were Newton and Einstein wrong?' *New Scientist* issue 2549, 29 April (52).

Shiga, David. 2007. 'Supernova shift may distort dark-energy readings.' *New Scientist* issue 2625, 13 October (14).

Shipp, Thomas. 2007. 'Clash of World Views.' *New Scientist* issue 2608, 16 June (26).

Simmons, I. G. 1994. *Changing the Face of the Earth: Culture, Environment, History*. Oxford, Basil Blackwell (1989).

Slicher van Bath, Bernard. 1978. *Geschiedenis: theorie en praktijk*. Utrecht/Antwerpen, Het Spectrum.

Smail, Daniel Lord. 2005. 'In the Grip of Sacred History.' *The American Historical Review 110*, 5 (1337–61).

Smail, Daniel Lord. 2007. *On Deep History and the Brain*. Berkeley, University of California Press.

Smil, Vaclav. 1991. *General Energetics: Energy in the Biosphere and Civilization*. New York, John Wiley & Sons.

Smil, Vaclav. 1994. *Energy in World History*. Boulder, Co., Westview Press.

Smil, Vaclav. 1999. *Energies: An Illustrated Guide to the Biosphere and Civilization*. Cambridge, Mass., The MIT Press.

Smil, Vaclav. 2002. *The Earth's Biosphere: Evolution, Dynamics, and Change*. Cambridge, Mass., The MIT Press.

Smil, Vaclav. 2003. *Energy at the Crossroads: Global perspectives and uncertainties*. Cambridge, Mass., The MIT Press.

Smil, Vaclav. 2006. *Energy: A Beginner's Guide*. Oxford, OneWorld Publications.

Smith, Bruce D. 1995. *The Emergence of Agriculture*. New York, W.H. Freeman & Co., Scientific American Library.

Smith, M. Estellie. 2000. *Trade and Trade-offs: Using Resources, Making Choices, and Taking Risks*. Prospect Heights, Ill., Waveland Press.

Smith, Virginia. 2007. *Clean: A history of personal hygiene and purity*. Oxford, Oxford University Press.

Smith, Nathan, Li, Weidong, Foley, Ryan J. et al. 2007. 'SN 2006gy: Discovery of the Most Luminous Supernova Ever Recorded, Powered by the Death of an Extremely Massive Star like η Carinae.' *The Astrophysical Journal 666*, 2 (1116–28).

Snow, Philip. 1988. *Star Raft: China's Encounter with Africa*. Ithaca, N.Y., Cornell University Press.

Snow, Charles Percy. 1959. *The Two Cultures and the Scientific Revolution*. Cambridge, Cambridge University Press

Spier, Fred. 1990. 'Religie in de mensheidsgeschiedenis: Naar een model van de ontwikkeling van religieuze regimes in een lange-termijnperspectief.' (Religion in the History of Humankind: Toward a model of the development of religious regimes in a long-term perspective) *Amsterdams Sociologisch Tijdschrift 16*, 4 (88–122).

Spier, Fred. 1992. 'Een oud probleem: de relaties tussen mensen en het natuurlijk milieu in een lange termijnperspectief.' (An Old Problem: The relations between humans and the natural environment seen from a long-term perspective) *De Gids 150*, 2 (96–108).

Spier, Fred. 1994. *Religious Regimes in Peru: Religion and state development in a long-term perspective and the effects in the Andean village of Zurite*. Amsterdam, Amsterdam University Press.

Spier, Fred. 1995. *San Nicolás de Zurite: Religion and Daily Life of an Andean Village in a Changing World*. Amsterdam, VU University Press.

Spier, Fred. 1996. *The Structure of Big History: From the Big Bang until Today*. Amsterdam, Amsterdam University Press.

Spier, Fred. 1998. *Big History: Was die Geschichte im Innersten zusammenhält*. Darmstadt, Primus Verlag.

Spier, Fred. 1999a. *Geschiedenis in het Groot: Een alomvattende visie*. Amsterdam, Amsterdam University Press.

Spier, Fred. 1999b. 'СТПУКТУПА БОДЬШОЙ ИСТОПИИ' (The Structure of Big History). *ОБЩЕСТВЕННЫЕ НАУКИ И СОВПЕМЕННОСТЬ* (Social Sciences Today) 5. Moscow, Russian Academy of Sciences (152–63).

Spier, Fred. 2002. *The Apollo 8 Earthrise Photo*. Amsterdam, Institute for Interdisciplinary Studies.

Spier, Fred. 2005a. 'How Big History Works: Energy Flows and the Rise and Demise of Complexity.' *Social Evolution & History 4*, 1 (87–135), Moscow, 'Uchitel' Publishing House.

Spier, Fred. 2005b. 'The Small History of the Big History Course at the University of Amsterdam,' *World History Connected 2*, 2. http://worldhistoryconnected.press.uiuc.edu/2.2/spier.html.

Spier, Fred. 2008. 'Big history: The emergence of a novel interdisciplinary approach.' *Interdisciplinary Science Reviews 33*, 2 (141–52).

Stavrianos, Leften S. 1989. *Lifelines from our Past: A new World History*. New York, Pantheon Books.

Stavrianos, Leften S. 1995. *A Global History: From Prehistory to the Present*. Englewood Cliffs, N.J., Prentice-Hall (1971).

Stearns, Peter N. 1993. *The Industrial Revolution in World History*. Boulder, Co., Westview Press.

Steinlin, Uli W. 1977. 'Kugelsternhaufen.' *Neue Zürcher Zeitung*, 26 April.

Stern, Fritz (ed.). 1956. *The Varieties of History: From Voltaire to the Present*. Cleveland & New York, Meridian Books.

Strahan, David. 2008. 'The great coal hole.' *New Scientist* issue 2639, 19 January (38–41).

Strangway, David W. 1970. *History of the earth's magnetic field*. New York, McGraw-Hill Book Company.

Stringer, Chris & Gamble, Clive. 1993. *In Search of the Neanderthals*. London, Thames & Hudson.

Stucki, Jörg W. 1980. 'The Optimal Efficiency and the Economic Degrees of Coupling of Oxidative Phosphorylation.' *European Journal of Biochemistry 109*, 1 (269–83).

Swabe, Joanna. 1998. *Animals, Disease and Human Society: Human-animal Relations and the Rise of Veterinary Medicine*. London, Routledge.

Swimme, Brian & Berry, Thomas. 1992. *The Universe Story: From the Primordial Flaring Forth to the Ecozoic Era: A Celebration of the Unfolding of the Cosmos*. San Francisco, HarperCollins Publishers.

Tainter, Joseph A., Allen, T. F. H., Little, Amanda & Hoekstra, Thomas W. 2003. 'Resource Transitions and Energy Gain: Contexts of Organization.' *Conservation Biology 7*, 3 (4). www.consecol.org/vol7/iss3/art4.

Tainter, Joseph A. 1988. *The Collapse of Complex Societies*. Cambridge, Cambridge University Press.

Thomas, Jo. 1996. 'Revised History Standards Defuse Explosive Issues.' *New York Times*, 3 April.

Thorpe, S. K. S., Holder, R. L. & Crompton, R. H. 2007. 'Origin of Human Bipedalism As an Adaptation for Locomotion on Flexible Branches.' *Science 316*, 5829 (1328–31).

Tosh, John. 1992. *The Pursuit of History: Aims, Methods & New Directions in the Study of Modern History, 2nd Edition.* London & New York, Longman.

Trefil, James S. 1989. *Reading the Mind of God: In Search of the Principle of Universality.* New York, Charles Scribner's Sons.

Trefil, James S. 1994. *A Scientist in the City.* New York, Doubleday.

Trefil, James S. 1997. *Are We Unique? A scientist explores the unparalleled intelligence of the human mind.* New York, John Wiley & Sons.

Trefil, James & Hazen, Robert M. 1995. *The Sciences: An Integrated Approach.* New York, John Wiley & Sons.

Trivedi, Bijal. 2007. 'Toxic cocktail.' *New Scientist* issue 2619, 1 September (44–7).

Tsiganis, K., Gomes, R., Morbidelli, A. & Levison, H. F. 2005. 'Origin of the orbital architecture of the giant planets of the Solar System.' *Nature 435*, 26 May (459–61).

Tudge, Colin. 1993. 'Taking the pulse of evolution: Do we owe our existence to short periods of change in the world's climate?' *New Scientist*, issue 1883, 24 July (32–6).

Tudge, Colin. 1996. *The Day Before Yesterday: Five Million Years of Human History.* London, Random House (1995).

Turner, Graham M. 2008. 'A comparison of The Limits to Growth with 30 years of reality.' *Global Environmental Change 18*, 3 (397–411).

Vélez, Antonio. 1998. *Del big bang al Homo sapiens.* Medellín, Colombia, Editorial Universidad de Antioquia.

Vélez, Antonio. 2007. *Homo Sapiens.* Bogotá, Colombia, Villegas Editores S.A.

Verburgh, Kris. 2007. *FANTASTISCH! Over het universum in ons hoofd.* Antwerp, Houtekiet.

Vernadsky, Vladimir I. 1998. *The Biosphere.* New York, Copernicus Springer-Verlag.

Vitousek, Peter M., Mooney, Harold A., Lubchenco, Jane & Melillo, Jerry M. 1997. 'Human Domination of Earth's Ecosystems.' *Science 25* July (494–9).

Vos, John de. 2004. 'Evolution of man: the adaptive radiation model.' In: Rubio Jara, Susana & Baquedano Pérez, Enrique (eds.) *Miscelanea en homenaje a Emiliano Aguirre, Vol. 3, Paleoantropología* (406–13).

Vrba, Elizabeth S. 1993. 'Mammal Evolution in the African Neogene and a New Look at the Great American Interchange.' In: Goldblatt, Peter (ed.) *Biological Relationships between Africa and South America.* New Haven & London, Yale University Press (393–432).

Vrba, E. S., Denton, G. H., Partridge T. C. & Burckle, L. H. (eds.). 1995. *Paleoclimate and Evolution, with Emphasis on Human Origins.* New Haven & London, Yale University Press.

Vries, Jan de. 2008. *The Industrious Revolution: Consumer Behavior and the Household Economy, 1650 to the Present.* Cambridge, Cambridge University Press.

Waldrop, M. Mitchell. 1993. *Complexity: The emerging science at the edge of order and chaos.* London, Viking (1992).

Walker, G. 2003. *Snowball Earth: The Story of the Great Global Catastrophe That Spawned Life as We Know It.* New York, Random House.

Wallerstein, Immanuel M. 1974. *The Modern World-System: Capitalist Agriculture and the Origins of the European World-Economy in the Sixteenth Century*. San Diego, Academic Press.

Wallerstein, Immanuel M. 1980. *Modern World System II: Mercantilism and the Consolidation of the European World Economy, 1600–1750*. San Diego, Academic Press.

Wallerstein, Immanuel M. 1983. *Historical Capitalism*. London, Verso.

Wallerstein, Immanuel M. 1989. *The Modern World-System III: The Second Era of Great Expansion of the Capitalist World-Economy, 1730–1840s*. New York, Academic Press.

Walsh, William Henry. 1951. *An Introduction to Philosophy of History*. London, Hutchinson.

Ward, Peter D. & Brownlee, Donald. 2004. *Rare Earth: Why Complex Life is Uncommon in the Universe*. New York, Copernicus Books (2000).

Weber, Max. 1927. *General economic history* (translated by Frank H. Knight). London, George Allen & Unwin Ltd.

Weber, Max. 1978. *Economy and Society: An outline of interpretive sociology (two volumes)*. Berkeley, Los Angeles & London, University of California Press.

Weber, Max. 1997. *The Theory of Social and Economic Organization*. New York, The Free Press.

Weinberg, Steven. 1993. *The First Three Minutes: A Modern View of the Origin of the Universe*. London, Flamingo (1977).

Wells, H. G. 1930. *The Outline of History: Being a Plain History of Life and Mankind*. New York, Garden City Publishing Company (1920).

Wenke, Robert J. & Olszewski, Deborah I. 2007. *Patterns in Prehistory: Humankind's First Three Million Years (Casebooks in Criticism)*. New York & Oxford, Oxford University Press.

Wesseling, H. L. 1995. *Onder historici: Opstellen over geschiedenis en geschiedschrijving*. Amsterdam, Uitgeverij Bert Bakker.

Westbroek, Peter. 1992. *Life as a Geological Force: Dynamics of the Earth*. New York & London, W.W. Norton & Co.

Westbroek, Peter. 2009. *Terre! Menaces et espoir*. Paris, Editions du Seuil.

Westerhoff, Hans V., Hellingwerf, Klaas J. & Dam, Karel van. 1983. 'Thermodynamic Efficiency of Microbial Growth is Low but Optimal for Maximal Growth Rate.' *Proceedings of the National Academy of Sciences 80*, 1 (305–9).

White, L. A. 1943. 'Energy and the Evolution of Culture.' *American Anthropologist 45* (335–56).

White, L. A. 1959. *The Evolution of Culture: The Development of Civilization to the Fall of Rome*. New York, McGraw-Hill.

White, L. A. 1975. *The Concept of Cultural Systems: A Key to Understanding Tribes and Nations*. New York & London, Columbia University Press.

Whitfield, John. 2004. 'Born in a watery commune.' *Nature 247*, 19 February (674–6).

Wicander, Reed & Monroe, James S. 1993. *Historical Geology: Evolution of the Earth and Life through Time*. Minneapolis/St. Paul, West Publishing Company.

Wiederhielm, Curt A. 1992. 'Impact scenarios.' *Science News 141*, 14, 4 April (211).

Wildeman, Diederick. 2006. *De Wereld in het klein: Globes in Nederland*. Zutphen, De Walburg Pers.

Williams, M. A. J., Dunkerley, D. L., De Deckker, P., Kershaw, A. P. & Stokes, T. 1993. *Quaternary Environments*. London, Edward Arnold.

Wills, Christopher. 1999. *Children of Prometheus: The accelerating pace of human evolution*. New York, Basic Books.

Wolf, Eric R. 1966. *Peasants*. Englewood Cliffs, N.J., Prentice-Hall.

Wolf, Eric R. 1982. *Europe and the People without History*. Berkeley, University of California Press.

Wolpoff, Milford & Caspari, Rachel. 1997. *Race and Human Evolution: A Fatal Attraction*. New York, Simon & Schuster.

Woo, Elaine. 1996. 'Standards for Teaching History Unveiled – Again.' *Los Angeles Times*, 3 April (A-1).

World Commission on Environment and Development. 1987. *Our Common Future*. Oxford / New York (Brundtland report).

Zapata, F. & Roy, R. N. 2004. *Use of Phosphate Rocks for Sustainable Agriculture* (Fertilizer and Plant Nutrition Bulletin 13). Rome: FAO Land and Water Development Division and the International Atomic Energy Agency. www.fao.org/docrep/007/y5053e/y5053e00.htm#Contents

Zeilinga de Boer, Jelle & Sanders, Donald Theodore. 2002. *Volcanoes in Human History: The Far-Reaching Effects of Major Eruptions*. Princeton & Oxford, Princeton University Press.

Zeilinga de Boer, Jelle & Sanders, Donald Theodore. 2005. *Earthquakes in Human History: The Far Reaching Effects of Seismic Disruptions*. Princeton & Oxford, Princeton University Press.

INDEX